Re-Visioning Psychology

BOOKS BY JAMES HILLMAN

The Dream and the Underworld

Interviews

Freud's Own Cookbook (with Charles Boer)

Anima: An Anatomy of a Personified Notion

Healing Fiction

A Blue Fire (edited by Thomas Moore)

Re-Visioning Psychology

Emotion: A Comprehensive Phenomenology of Theories and Their Meanings for Therapy

Suicide and the Soul

Insearch: Psychology and Religion

The Myth of Analysis: Three Essays in Archetypal Psychology

The Feeling Function

An Essay on Pan

"Psychological Commentary" to Gopi Krishna's Kundalini

Loose Ends: Primary Papers in Archetypal Psychology

Re-Visioning

Psychology
James Hillman

Harper Perennial
A Division of HarperCollins*Publishers*

A hardcover edition of this book was published in 1976 by Harper & Row, Publishers.

RE-VISIONING PSYCHOLOGY. Copyright © 1975 by James Hillman. All rights reserved. Printed in the United States of America. No part of this book may be used or reproduced in any manner whatsoever without written permission except in the case of brief quotations embodied in critical articles and reviews. For information address HarperCollins Publishers, 10 East 53rd Street, New York, NY 10022.

Designed by Dorothy Schmiderer

First Harper Colophon edition published 1977. First HarperPerennial edition published 1992.

LIBRARY OF CONGRESS CATALOG CARD NUMBER 91-50502

ISBN 0-06-090563-8

04 05 RRD-H   26 27 28 29 30

To the Reader, without whom all is Vanity

Contents

One / Personifying or Imagining Things

Two / Pathologizing or Falling Apart

Three / Psychologizing or Seeing Through

Four / Dehumanizing or Soul-making

. . . man is but a paltry thing,
A tattered coat upon a stick, unless
Soul clap its hands and sing, and louder sing
For every tatter in its mortal dress,
Nor is there singing school but studying
Monuments of its own magnificence . . .

YEATS, "Sailing to Byzantium"

Preface: A Memoir from the Author for the 1992 Edition

The following pages are so crammed with ideas, arguments, quotes, and references that the most diverting move I can make upon reissuing this book might simply be to reconstruct the occasions of its writing; that is, to complement its content with a personal memoir. For the personal has been deliberately omitted in conformity with the style of a book that intends to dehumanize psychology. This dehumanizing (the very title of the last chapter) aims to free psychology from personalistic confines and to revert its vision to poetic principles and polymorphic Gods. Call it a program of animism, of ensouling the nonhuman, a program that would relieve the human of its self-importance. That self-importance appears in all psychologies that find the personal self important, considering their task to be the study of the human person and assigning to human persons the focus of psychological therapy and the source of psychological theory.

Yet, the personal, so deliberately omitted, permeates every page of the book, its themes, its moods, its structure, and in the selection of references, those significant others with whom it wants to keep company. How can one truly repress the personal, since psychology is always and inescapably confession? Every text reveals the weaver's predilections. You may look at a carpet and see only an impersonal pattern of floral ornamentation and repetitiously obsessive borders, but woven throughout is the singular voice that chanted out the little colored woolen knots which compose the particular perfection and errors of that unique carpet. Like the carpet, the book is a highly idiosyncratic product.

Nothing is repressed; in fact, nothing can be repressed. The idea of repression belongs to the nineteenth-century's era of colonialism, predatory industrialism, and white male supremacy, when repression was the law of life. The word belongs to politics, not to writing, where anything and everything comes flowing onto a page. Of course Freud considered repression to be his essential discovery on which rested even his ideas of the unconscious and the sexual theory of the libido. Goodness! He was a Jewish man in Bohemia and Vienna during the Hapsburg Empire—how could he not have come up with the idea of *Verdrängung* or not have recognized repression as a fundamental of existence. But now, after existentialism and phenomenology, after recent physics and deconstruction, a postmodern mind can't take repression with the same literalism as did Freud and his followers.

The literal absence of the personal does not mean that the personal is absent; instead it is even more present in the book by shining through its phrases than if it were set out as an autobiographical appendix or cased in self-effusive sentences in which the author reminds the reader about his "experiences." The absence of autobiography, the diffidence toward biographical blurbs and photos, and the resistance to the first person singular do not indicate repression of the personal.

If an author's personal presence is able to be discerned only when declared in literalized statements about "himself," then we have divided the personal and the impersonal in the old Cartesian way. Here a subject, there an object. Author as subjective personal agent, book as materialized impersonal object. The exposition of the author's subjectivity objectifies the book into his product, repressing its personality in favor of his. It's not, after all, Descartes's life we go on fighting, for Descartes is dead, although not his *Method*, nor his *Meditations*. That's where he lives. To find the author go to the book. If the author is anywhere, he's in the book, *is* the book; the book is his person wrapped in a dust jacket; that is his true likeness, not the photographed face on the back flap.

Therefore, the four chapters—delivered rather chaotically and intensively as sixty- to ninety-minute harangues to some three to four hundred attentive and sympathetic listeners and critical discussants; by the author wearing a European suit and a pretentious puer beard when he was forty-five years old at Becton Hall, Davies Auditorium, Yale University, on February 29, March 3, 7, and 14, 1972, as the Terry Lectures (see note 2, page 231, below), a series that goes back to the early years of the twentieth century and had been given previously by many *illustri* and *luminosi* including John Dewey, C. G. Jung, and Paul Ricoeur—reveal at every turn the intimate history and personal inclinations of the author. This statement of the personal facts that you are now reading is merely another genre of revelation and one no more revelatory of the personal than the book itself, for all its repression, its rhetorical disguises, and its "hidden" agenda.

That agenda is clear enough: To restore the mythical perspective to depth psychology by recognizing the soul's intrinsic affinity with, nay, love for, the Gods. Or, as the Greeks may have said, to reaffirm the tragic connection between the mortal and the immortal, that natural plight of the soul that lies at the base of any psychology claiming to speak of psyche. To this intrinsic connection we must attribute, as did the Ancients, the Renaissance Humanists, and the Romantics, the founding sources of human pathologies (Chapter 2). That's the agenda—hardly hidden; so, how more personal, more confessional can an author be than to expose the depths of his religious passion?

This kind of religious passion seems so impersonal in a culture where personalism confines passion to "my" emotions inside my private developmental history and my own body, and religion to "my" beliefs in a personal lord and savior whose focus is my salvation. Because religious passion so defined becomes so personalized, the feeling that pervades the rhetoric in this book seems dissociated, if not repressed. There then arises in the culture's mind the idea of repression of the personal: "Author, you're not telling us enough about yourself, what you believe, what you went through personally to get where you are. How did your feelings and experiences lead you to your thinking and ideas? Show us your self. Give us the true story"—by which is meant the personal story, by which is meant unidimensional literal report by and about a fiction called "me."

Since the culture's personalized criteria of confession are not met, the author must be repressing; whereas the truth is rather that the whole book bears witness to the joyful agony of exhibitionism, an affronting parade of pleasurable display to shock and fascinate the public, as well as propitiate the very Gods who are invoked by the offerings to them of the book's ideas, arguments, and references as earthly allies to their powers and as mortal sustenance for their limited capacities.

Immortals, maybe, but limited nonetheless. Isn't that what Dike and Themis (Moira, Aisa, and Ananke, too) really mean? A bounding perimeter, a binding inhibition that confines the powers so they cannot escape their own laws. They frown upon hubris, grandiosity, and inflation, because to them too it is not permitted to exceed their constraints. And the greatest constraint must be placed on the greatest of all tendencies, that enemy of mortals and immortals both, Titanism, which longs toward the boundless and indefinable, represented in current psychologies as the boundless notion of Self.

And so this book is not about Self. It fails as a volume of self-help, self-analysis, or self-improvement. For to be about the Self is not to be about the Gods. I would not encourage Titanism, a menace far greater than Narcissism, which presents only a pensive pretty-boy compared with the titanic grandiosity of Self.

If language has been cut loose from the signified object of its discourse (as contemporary philosophy asserts), and if the use of a term does not refer to a thing, there are no clear references to fixed identities. Then, the term "Self" doesn't refer either. Nor is there even the comfort of self-identity. The "me" is anchored elsewhere, floatingly, and that's what keeps the ship from foundering. Consequently, if there be no literal self, there can be no *self*-improvement or *self*-knowledge (only improvement and knowledge as such), and all self-revelation merely adds to the culture's delusions of psychological grandeur rather than to the culture itself.

Yet simply by pronouncing the term we are seized by the inflating belief that there is such a thing, a Self, which transcends any limitation that might be imposed upon it. And so it can never be really "wrong." Self can be defined only from within itself by its own representations. Principal among these are the irrefutable truth of personal experience and the inflating feelings of personal significance. Utterly self-referent, it knows no God greater than itself. Now, most psychology takes all this quite literally, so that behind psychology's devotion to the personal stands neither humanism nor individualism, but rather a literalism of Self like an invisible nonexistent God absolutely believed in. Absolute belief is either fundamentalism, delusion, or literalism—or all of the Above. Perhaps, it's then right to say there is no greater literalism in psychology than its idea of Self, a literalism that converts our supposedly investigative field into a branch of mystic fundamentalism. This leads me further to think that our culture's omnipotent and omniscient Godhead who supposedly replaced the mutually limiting pagan beings of myth is none other than a Titan returned from Tartaros to a too high place, and, worse, all alone.

Inasmuch as our selves are cast in the image of that all-powerful and all-knowing Creator, our culture's Godhead demands an account from the creative self, literal, historical, from the beginning, how the book actually happened, to which personal account one tends to give almighty importance. Tell us a Genesis story, how you got to give the lectures and write the book. But, good Reader, a personal memoir by which an author supposedly confirms his creative identity—this memoir you are now reading—serves no further purpose than inflating the personal, thereby abetting the culture's Titanism, its monomania or monotheism of Self, and defeating the most passionate purpose of this book.

That I had in the late summer of 1971 given the Eranos Lecture "Abandoning the Child" and felt it not received, neither by my peers nor by the audience; that the larger opus I was engaged in seemed to be in a pit; that the marriage I was committed to was steeply declining in favor of what was to become a different wife; that out of the blue William Sloan Coffin phoned Zurich from New Haven inviting me to come to Yale (his having just read my book *Insearch*); that I responded by saying I preferred the set piece and formal audience to smaller workshops; that he then arranged the Terry opportunity; that I could not free myself until the next year owing to my immersion in a book on the Puer (a prolonged and still incomplete defense of my traits and behaviors); that I went to Casa Gabriella near Moscia in the Tessin and began the lecture "Pathologizing," and was still writing that particular lecture in Florida, where for a few days prior to Yale I had gone with Patricia Berry to store strength for the Terrys; that the exhilarating strain of these talks had me confusedly on campus so I arrived lost and late for the fourth lecture unable to again locate the hall; that the first version of the book was rejected, requiring complete rewriting and editorial help; that Clayton Carlson of Harper's imagined its final typographical format and concluded the contract; that all sorts of offshoots emerged from the writing during 1973–74, including the later book *Anima*; that I suffered my first dismembering encounter with radical feminists and my first paralyzing encounter with Freudian interrogation in seminars at Yale, yet made new long-lasting friends like Edward S. Casey then teaching philosophy there—all this supposedly is the story, the personal experience, of the author of the book.

But who did write the book? That's the right question because that is the very subject of the book—subject as topic and subject as person. Who is the subject?

Now the answer, which will be derived from Chapter 3, pages 138 and following, will hardly refer to a biographical person. Instead, that discussion will lead us to conclude that the book was written by means of personifications—and is read by personifications, too; i.e., Reader, you are not quite "who" you may believe yourself to be. The primary personification in this case will be Author as scribe, as authenticator only of his scrivening. Thus, the book becomes an example of personifying (Chapter 1). By this I mean not only book as written by what lies beyond (not behind or within) "me" in sentences that do not begin with "I" as agent, but even more, book as a personified power that goes forth with its life, its death, an archetypal animation issuing into the world apart from its ascribed author, his life, and his death.

The very word "author" also raises questions such as what gives the book enough authority to carry it into yet another printing twenty years after the lectures? And, what authenticates that which its pages assert? If this autonomous power is theoretically traced to the personal self (self = *auto*), the repressed and hidden "me" with my personal story, then the theory that requires a biographical memoir in order to grasp the book more personally vanishes into thin air. For my "journey" to Yale and the circumstances of delivery and writing give not one jot of authentication to the book in your hands or to the now twenty years' authority of its ideas. Whatever power it had at first and has since accrued derives from powers other than what can be accounted for by my witness.

The question of authorship cannot be answered except by imagining psychology as religion (the last theme of the book, page 228) and the book, like a totem object, a fetish statue kept alive by its readers, who, by picking it up and turning its pages with quiet attention and emotional participation, polish the statue called a "book." Like that statue, a book gives physical form to invisible presences, gives to the angels in words a local habitation and a name. May both the readers and the angels be pleased to linger a while longer.

J.H.
Thompson, Connecticut
July 27, 1991

Introduction:
To Begin With...

This book is about soul-making. It is an attempt at a psychology of soul, an essay in re-visioning psychology from the point of view of soul. This book is therefore old-fashioned and radically novel because it harks back to the classical notions of soul and yet advances ideas that current psychology has not even begun to consider. Because the soul cannot be understood through psychology alone, our vision even leaves the field of psychology as it is usually thought of, and moves widely through history, philosophy, and religion. Although this book reaches toward a new kind of psychological thinking and feeling, it stays rooted in the main ground of our psychological culture; it is nourished by accumulated insights of the Western tradition, extending from the Greeks through the Renaissance and Romantics to Freud and Jung.

The term *soul-making* comes from the Romantic poets. We find the idea in William Blake's *Vala,* but it was John Keats who clarified the phrase in a letter to his brother: "Call the world if you please, 'The vale of Soul-making.' Then you will find out the use of the world. . . ."[1] From this perspective the human adventure is a wandering through the vale of the world for the sake of making soul. Our life is psychological, and the purpose of life is to make psyche of it, to find connections between life and soul.

The notion of soul-making demands more precision, however, when it is used by a therapeutic psychologist rather than a Romantic poet, for it is not enough to evoke soul and sing its praises. The job of psychology is to offer a way and find a place for soul within its own field. For this we need basic psychological ideas. The four chapters that follow attempt to lay out four such ideas necessary for the soul-making process.

While working on the first draft of these chapters—which were delivered as the 1972 Dwight Harrington Terry Lectures at Yale University[2]—I had on the wall in front of my writing table this sentence from the Spanish philosopher and psychological essayist Ortega y Gasset: "Why write, if this too easy activity of pushing a pen across paper is not given a certain bull-fighting risk and we do not approach danger-ous, agile, and two-horned topics?"[3]

The first of these two-horned topics is the soul itself; how to define it, how describe it, how write of it at all? Psychology books generally save themselves a great deal of risk by avoiding this challenge al-together. But since "soul" is the dominant theme of my entire work, let us set down a few fence-poles to begin with.

By *soul* I mean, first of all, a perspective rather than a substance, a viewpoint toward things rather than a thing itself. This perspective is reflective; it mediates events and makes differences between ourselves and everything that happens. Between us and events, between the doer and the deed, there is a reflective moment—and soul-making means differentiating this middle ground.

It is as if consciousness rests upon a self-sustaining and imagining substrate—an inner place or deeper person or ongoing presence—that is simply there even when all our subjectivity, ego, and consciousness go into eclipse. Soul appears as a factor independent of the events in which we are immersed. Though I cannot identify soul with anything else, I also can never grasp it by itself apart from other things, perhaps because it is like a reflection in a flowing mirror, or like the moon which mediates only borrowed light. But just this peculiar and paradoxical intervening variable gives one the sense of having or being a soul.[3a] However intangible and indefinable it is, soul carries highest impor-tance in hierarchies of human values, frequently being identified with the principle of life and even of divinity.

In another attempt upon the idea of soul I suggested that the word refers to that unknown component which makes meaning possible, turns events into experiences, is communicated in love, and has a religious concern. These four qualifications I had already put forth some years ago;[4] I had begun to use the term freely, usually interchange-ably with psyche (from Greek) and anima (from Latin). Now I am adding three necessary modifications. First, "soul" refers to the *deepen-ing* of events into experiences; second, the significance soul makes possible, whether in love or in religious concern, derives from its special *relation with death*. And third, by "soul" I mean the imaginative possi-bility in our natures, the experiencing through reflective speculation, dream, image, and *fantasy*—that mode which recognizes all realities as primarily symbolic or metaphorical.

More particular implications of soul will become evident in the chap-ters below, which may perhaps be read as a prolonged encounter with the notion and an attempt to discover and vivify soul through my writing and your reading.

This first two-horned topic invites a second and equally difficult one. What is fantasy? Here I follow C. G. Jung very closely. He considered the fantasy images that run through our daydreams and night dreams, and which are present unconsciously in all our consciousness, to be the primary data of the psyche. Everything we know and feel and every statement we make are all fantasy-based, that is, they derive from psychic images. These are not merely the flotsam of memory, the reproduction of perceptions, rearranged leftovers from the input of our lives.

Rather, following Jung I use the word fantasy-image in the poetic sense,[5] considering images to be the basic givens of psychic life, self-originating, inventive, spontaneous, complete, and organized in archetypal patterns. Fantasy-images are both the raw materials and finished products of psyche, and they are the privileged mode of access to knowledge of soul. Nothing is more primary. Every notion in our minds, each perception of the world and sensation in ourselves must go through a psychic organization in order to "happen" at all. Every single feeling or observation occurs as a psychic event by first forming a fantasy-image.

Here I am working toward a psychology of soul that is based in a psychology of image. Here I am suggesting both a *poetic basis of mind* and a psychology that starts neither in the physiology of the brain, the structure of language, the organization of society, nor the analysis of behavior, but in the processes of imagination.

By calling upon Jung to begin with, I am partly acknowledging the fundamental debt that archetypal psychology owes him. He is the immediate ancestor in a long line that stretches back through Freud, Dilthey, Coleridge, Schelling, Vico, Ficino, Plotinus, and Plato to Heraclitus—and with even more branches which have yet to be traced. Heraclitus lies near the roots of this ancestral tree of thought, since he was the earliest to take psyche as his archetypal first principle, to imagine soul in terms of flux and to speak of its depth without measure.

"Depth psychology," the modern field whose interest is in the unconscious levels of the psyche—that is, the deeper meanings of the soul—is itself no modern term. "Depth" reverberates with a significance, echoing one of the first philosophers of antiquity. All depth psychology has already been summed up by this fragment of Heraclitus: "You could not discover the limits of the soul *(psyche)*, even if you traveled every road to do so; such is the depth *(bathun)* of its meaning *(logos)*."[6] Ever since Heraclitus brought soul and depth together in one formulation, the dimension of soul is depth (not breadth or height) and the dimension of our soul travel is downward.

Jung's work, as well as his life, belongs to this great tradition of imaginative psychology. As Jung offers a way into that line of psychology, this book offers a way into Jung—and a way out of Jung, especially his theology. For to stay wholly with this one thinker is to remain a Jungian, which as Jung himself said is possible only for Jung. Essential to soul-making is psychology-making, shaping concepts and images that express the needs of the soul as they emerge in each of us.

Since my soul, my psychological constitution, differs from Freud's and from Jung's, so my psychology will be different from theirs. Each psychology is a confession, and the worth of a psychology for another person lies not in the places where he can identify with it because it satisfies his psychic needs, but where it provokes him to work out his own psychology in response. Freud and Jung are psychological masters, not that we may follow them in becoming Freudian and Jungian, but that we may follow them in becoming psychological. Here psychology is conceived as a necessary activity of the psyche, which constructs vessels and breaks them in order to deepen and intensify experience.

This emphasis upon depth and intensity implies another basic perspective in this book. I see all psychology as depth psychology. Usually depth or therapeutic psychology occupies only a marginal area of the academic field. The bottom land is claimed by others—social psychologists, behaviorists, developmentalists. But beginning with soul means that psychology immediately goes into depths and has a therapeutic implication. The leading question is: What does this observation, this study imply for soul? Where there is a connection to soul, there is psychology; where not, what is taking place is better called statistics, physical anthropology, cultural journalism, or animal breeding.

Therapy is a heavy word, bringing to mind the suffering of illness and what we go through to cure it. This book takes therapy right into each individual's symptomatic peculiarities, the awareness of his or her complexes, and also, right through them. Therapy, or analysis, is not only something that analysts do to patients; it is a process that goes on intermittently in our individual soul-searching, our attempts at understanding our complexities, the critical attacks, prescriptions, and encouragements that we give ourselves. We are all in therapy all the time insofar as we are involved with soul-making. The idea here is that if we are each and every one a psychological patient, we are also each and every one a psychotherapist. Analysis goes on in the soul's imagination and not only in the clinic. And it is this internal sense of therapy that I ask you to bear in mind as we proceed.

One more word we need to introduce is *archetype*. The curious difficulty of explaining just what archetypes are suggests something specific to them. That is, they tend to be metaphors rather than things. We find ourselves less able to say what an archetype is literally and more inclined to describe them in images. We can't seem to touch one or point to one, and rather speak of what they are like. Archetypes throw us into an imaginative style of discourse. In fact, it is precisely as metaphors that Jung—who reintroduced the ancient idea of archetype into modern psychology—writes of them, insisting upon their indefinability.[7] To take an archetypal perspective in psychology leads us, therefore, to envision the basic nature and structure of the soul in an imaginative way and to approach the basic questions of psychology first of all by means of the imagination.

Let us then imagine archetypes as the *deepest patterns of psychic functioning*, the roots of the soul governing the perspectives we have of ourselves and the world. They are the axiomatic, self-evident images to which psychic life and our theories about it ever return. They are similar to other axiomatic first principles, the models or paradigms, that we find in other fields. For "matter," "God," "energy," "life," "health," "society," "art" are also fundamental metaphors, archetypes perhaps themselves, which hold whole worlds together and yet can never be pointed to, accounted for, or even adequately circumscribed.

All ways of speaking of archetypes are translations from one metaphor to another. Even sober operational definitions in the language of science or logic are no less metaphorical than an image which presents the archetypes as root ideas, psychic organs, figures of myth, typical styles of existence, or dominant fantasies that govern consciousness. There are many other metaphors for describing them: immaterial potentials of structure, like invisible crystals in solution or form in plants that suddenly show forth under certain conditions; patterns of instinctual behavior like those in animals that direct actions along unswerving paths; the *genres* and *topoi* in literature; the recurring typicalities in history; the basic syndromes in psychiatry; the paradigmatic thought models in science; the world-wide figures, rituals, and relationships in anthropology.

But one thing is absolutely essential to the notion of archetypes: their emotional possessive effect, their bedazzlement of consciousness so that it becomes blind to its own stance. By setting up a universe which tends to hold everything we do, see, and say in the sway of its cosmos, an archetype is best comparable with a God. And Gods, religions sometimes say, are less accessible to the senses and to the intellect than they are to the imaginative vision and emotion of the soul.

The archetypal perspective offers the advantage of organizing into clusters or constellations a host of events from different areas of life. The archetype of the hero, for example, appears first in *behavior*, the drive to activity, outward exploration, response to challenge, seizing and grasping and extending. It appears second in the *images* of Hercules, Achilles, Samson (or their cinema counterparts) doing their specific tasks; and third, in a style of *consciousness*, in feelings of independence, strength, and achievement, in ideas of decisive action, coping, planning, virtue, conquest (over animality), and in psychopathologies of battle, overpowering masculinity, and single-mindedness.

This example limps, of course, because the hero archetype appears not so much in a list of contents as it does in maintaining the heroic *attitude* toward all events, an attitude now so habitual that we have come to call it the "ego," forgetting that it is but another archetypal style. We shall have a good deal more to say about, and against, the heroic ego in the following pages. But our aim throughout this book is to circumvent him and his ego psychology altogether. So this is a psychology book without mention of conative striving, motivation or learning, free-will or choice.

The hero example does, however, serve to show the *collective* aspect of any archetype. First, by means of it we can collect together disparate personal events and discover a sense and depth in them beyond our individual habits and quirks. Second, the archetypal perspective provides a common connection between what goes on in any individual soul and what goes on in all people in all places in all times. It allows psychological understanding at a collective level. Archetypal, in other words, means fundamentally human.

You will have noticed that we have been speaking of archetypes in the plural. We are working from the premise that there are many valid points of view toward any psychological event, and that these points of view have an archetypal basis. Our psychology is, to begin with, polytheistic, less out of religious confession than out of psychological necessity. The many-sidedness of human nature, the variety of viewpoints even within a single individual, requires the broadest possible spectrum of basic structures. If a psychology wants to represent faithfully the soul's actual diversity, then it may not beg the question from the beginning by insisting, with monotheistic prejudgment, upon unity of personality. The idea of unity is, after all, only one of many archetypal perspectives.

This book moves away from the monotheistic bias that has ruled our habitual psychological thinking; we are in search of further structures and wider myths. Our internal confusions are a latent richness. They require a differentiated background if they are to be appraised adequately. Often we condemn images and experiences as wrong, weak, sick, or mad simply because we have not discovered their archetypal sense. Because our minds have been monotheistically prejudiced we forget to see things through other colors of the pluralistic spectrum. Polytheism, which many call a heresy, implies radical relativism; it is another two-horned topic which will be breathing down our necks throughout the book.

Further, the structure of the book needs explanation. The four divisions represent the four original lectures, reproducing their titles, their themes, and their main movement. Each works within a traditional area: mythology, psychiatry, philosophy, and the humanities. (Religion and psychology are involved all the way through, as they must be in a book on soul.)

But this division is not strictly maintained, for the psychological approach to these fields does not recognize the old borders. For example: there are frequent references to history—of psychiatry, of ideas, and of specific periods of our culture. History runs all through the book as it runs all through our lives. While respecting the work of the historians, we do not read their reports in the same way as they do. History has a psychological function of providing a kind of genealogy myth, telling us how it all started and then happened. The figures of history taken psychologically are the progenitors, the cultural ancestors, of the ideas in our minds. In part, we turn to history, this depository of cultural memory, as a therapeutic exercise. We search for the myths within the facts, the archetypal patterns that can broaden and deepen connections in ourselves, offering our painfully raw experiences a bed of culture. Unlike historians, we use books and make footnotes without sticking to "primary sources"—psychological method as presented in Chapter 3 obliges us to take all materials as primary sources.

A second example of our breaking through traditional boundaries is psychiatry. For psychopathology does not belong to a field of specialists. It is something we suffer in our experience and a perspective we take toward certain kinds of experiences, so that it too can be opened to new psychological insight. This is the main work of Chapter 2.

The movement of the book is episodic and circular; it has no rigid beginning or ending. It doesn't move in a straight line from start to finish, because it is not written as an argument toward a conclusion.

Polytheistic psychology has more than one thing to say and more than one way of saying it, and its many different angles are better perceived if they are not made to fit rigidly together.

The object of these chapters is to open anew the questions of the soul and to open the soul to new questions. I want to shed light on obscure issues, but not the kind of light that brings an end to searching. As they lay out the groundwork of an archetypal psychology, these chapters also demonstrate how this new field is to be worked. When I stress that the book is not the development of a single theme in a unified manner toward final point, I am in keeping with basic psychological experience—that the soul is ceaselessly talking about itself in ever-recurring motifs in ever-new variations, like music; that this soul is immeasureably deep and can only be illumined by insights, flashes in a vast cavern of incomprehension; and that in the realm of soul the ego is a paltry thing.

And so we shall be exploring widely and with polemical contention. Strife (*polemos*), as Heraclitus also said, is the father of all. Of course I hope these pages evoke the soul's longing for a depth psychology of understanding, yet I believe that for such light we must strike steel on flint and provoke irritating sparks.

Why it is necessary to sally so far forth and take on so many comers will, I hope, become evident in the course of reading. Psychology has no limits when it is true to the limitless soul that Heraclitus envisioned. But although to re-vision psychology means that one must range widely, I have not gone East, gone primitive, gone animal, or gone off into the future or on my own private inner voyage. This book has the geographical, historical, and religious limits of our Western tradition, which issues forth here and now into the amazing soul questions of today. To these contemporary Western soul questions I am attempting to speak with whatever passion and imagination the *daimones* grant my command. *Serio ludere.*

*

It is more than a debt that I owe to Cynthia Owen Philip. She re-visioned the book itself, thought it through with me in broad lines and precise details, and made possible this final version of my helter-skelter lectures. James Fitzsimmons generously found space in the pages of his *Art International* (Lugano) during 1973 for Chapters 2 and 3 in an earlier form. Edward Casey at Yale and David Miller at Syracuse gave encouragement when it was needed; Adam Diment made helpful suggestions; and Annabel Learned fine-combed a last typescript still crawling with my tenacious errors. Lyn Cowan and Cornelia Schroeder prepared the index, condensing as many entries as possible into the space allowed.

J. H.

Casa Gabriella
Moscia, Switzerland.
May 29, 1974

One / Personifying
or Imagining Things

many are the forms of daemonia . . .
EURIPIDES

A Preview of This Chapter

In this book I shall frequently use *psyche* or *soul* as the subject of the sentence, making statements such as "the psyche claims, hungers, needs," "the soul sees," "the psyche reflects upon itself." This way of speaking has wider than rhetorical implications. For to give subjectivity and intentionality to a noun means more than moving into a special kind of language game; it means that we actually enter into another psychological dimension. The noun takes on consciousness, it becomes personified.

Personifying has always been fundamental to the religious and poetic imagination, and it is today fundamental to the experience—and to thinking about the experience—of archetypal psychology. But we cannot begin to understand why *personifying* is crucial to religious and psychological experience, or even freely employ the term, until we have cleared up some of the shadow cast upon it by our modern world view.

This view confines the idea of subjectivity to human persons. Only they are permitted to be subjects, to be agents and doers, to have consciousness and soul. The Christian idea of person as the true focus of the divine and the only carrier of soul is basic to this world view. The Christian concentrated focus upon actual living persons has also come to mean that the psyche is too narrowly identified with the ego personality. Also basic to this modern view of persons is the psychology of Descartes; it imagines a universe divided into living subjects and dead objects. There is no space for anything intermediate, ambiguous, and metaphorical.

This is a restrictive perspective and it has led us to believe that entities, other than human beings, taking on interior subjective qualities are merely "anthropomorphized" or "personified" objects, not really persons in the accepted meaning of that word. If we find persons elsewhere than in living human bodies, we conclude that these persons have been transferred from "in here" to "out there." We believe we have unconsciously put our experiences into them; they are merely fictional or imaginary. We have made them up just as the persons in our dreams are supposedly made up out of the experiences of our ego. We do not believe that imaginary persons could possibly *be as they present themselves*, as valid psychological subjects with wills and feelings like ours but not reducible to ours. Such thinking we say is legitimate only for animistic primitive people, or children, or the insane.

This view moreover believes that each individual body can contain no more than one psychic person: as we have one body so we are one soul. To find other persons within oneself, to be divided into several souls, a field of multiple personalities—although this notion has often been maintained even in our Western culture—is an "aberration" called personified thinking. Persons appearing either in the world or in myself other than my ego-subjectivity are called personifications, their livingness is said to be resultant of mine, their animation derived from my breath.

Psychotherapy busies itself with returning these so-called displaced persons from the world out there or the unconscious in here, back to where psychotherapists assume they belong, in the conscious ego-centered human being. Thus, diversification of personality, and its differentiation and vivification have been suppressed. "Integration of personality" has become the moral task of psychotherapeutics. Like the Christian tradition and Cartesian philosophy, psychotherapy too is at war with personifications. In fact, psychologists in general denigrate personifying, labelling it a defensive mode of perception, a projection, a "pathetic fallacy," a regression to delusional, hallucinatory or illusory modes of adaptation. At best, psychologists regard personifying as a fanciful figure of speech, as a game, or as a therapeutic tool by means of which the ego may learn about its fears and desires.

Psychology, whose very name and title derives from soul, *(psyché)*, has stopped soul from appearing in any place but where it is sanctioned by this modern world view. Just as modern science and metaphysics have banned the subjectivity of souls from the outer world of material events, psychology has denied the autonomy and diversity of souls to the inner world of psychological events. Intentions, behavior, voices, feelings that I do not control with my will or cannot connect to with my reason are alien, negative, psychopathological. All my subjectivity and all my interiority must literally be *mine*, in ownership of my conscious ego-personality. At best we *have* souls; but no one says we *are* souls. Psychology does not even use the word soul: a person is referred to as a self or an ego. Both the world out there and in here have gone through the same process of depersonification. We have all been de-souled.

We shall of course depart from this well-worn track. Exploring the animistic jungle in keeping with its own ideas, listening to the many autonomous voices for what they tell, unarmed with the interpretative kit of modern psychology, we shall probably lose touch with the main party altogether. But on this expedition we shall penetrate the interior realm of animism. For we are in search of *anima,* or soul. From the outset we are assuming that the close connection between the personified world of animism and anima—soul—is more than verbal, and that personifying is a way of soul-making. That is, we are assuming that soul-making depends upon the ability to personify, which in turn depends upon anima. Anima as a term, a function, and a figure, will receive fuller explication as we enter more deeply into her precincts.

By refusing to go along with the usual arguments against personifying, we expect to find a new way or refine an old way: (a) of revivifying our relations with the world around us, (b) of meeting our individual fragmentation, our many rooms and many voices, and (c) of furthering the imagination to show all its bright forms. Our desire is *to save the phenomena of the imaginal psyche.* And so we must free the vision of the psyche from the narrow biases of modern psychology, enabling the psyche to perceive itself—its relations, its realities, its pathologies— altogether apart from psychology's modern perspective.

The modern vision of ourselves and the world has stultified our imaginations. It has fixed our view of personality (psychology), of insanity (psychopathology), of matter and objects (science), of the cosmos (metaphysics), and of the nature of the divine (theology). Moreover it has fixed the methods in all these fields so that they present a unified front against soul. Some people in desperation have turned to witchcraft, magic and occultism, to drugs and madness, anything to rekindle imagination and find a world ensouled. But these reactions are not enough. What is needed is a revisioning, a fundamental shift of perspective out of that soulless predicament we call modern consciousness.

So let us begin. First we must go backward into the history of the view against personification in order to appreciate fully the strength of its hold upon our minds.

A Little History of Depersonifying

The Christian and Cartesian views against personifying coalesce in Marin Mersenne (8 September 1588—1 September 1648). Correspondent, friend, or enemy of Descartes, Galileo, Pascal, Fludd, Torricelli, Richelieu, Hobbes, Grotius, Huygens, and other major contemporaries, he was a central figure of his age.[1] Mersenne vigorously combated an animistic, personified view of nature. Baptized on the day of his birth, educated by the Jesuits at La Flèche (eight years ahead of Descartes), member of the Minimes Order derived from the Franciscans, vegetarian who took neither meat, milk, nor eggs, Mersenne joined the holy war that had simmered since the age of Constantine: the battle to maintain Christian psychology against that of polytheistic antiquity. He personifies a style of consciousness present in any of us when we turn against imaginary persons in the name of reason, science, or belief.

The wider background against which Mersenne's work must be viewed is fifteenth-century Renaissance thought, which had flourished partly by means of revived images of personified powers.[2] Astrology, alchemy, and medicine; the allegories of painting and poetry, Latin literature and Greek hermeticism; Orphism and Neoplatonism—all displayed a personified world in nature and psyche. Whereas earlier centuries had confined their crowd of personified images generally to the Scriptures, the Saints, and the Virtues and Vices, Renaissance imagery returned to the tradition called "classical" which also implies pagan and polytheistic. Renaissance animism led to pluralism, which threatened Christian universal harmony. For when inner soul and outer world reflect each other as enlivened souls and substances, and when the images of these souls and substances are pagan, then the familiar figures of Christianity diminish to only one relative set among many alternatives.

Between 1619 and 1648 with feverish activity and personal torment Mersenne carried on a thirty-years' war of his own against the threatening recrudescence of the hosts of paganism. Robed in black to his ankles and ensconced in his monkish Parisian cell near the Place Royale, but traveling too for talks and meetings, he became the arachnoid center of the European learned world, always attacking the "magical" early Renaissance—especially alchemy—in order to further the "mechanical" later Renaissance.[3] His writings, except in the areas of music and mathematics, did not contribute much that was new; his great value lay rather in the keenness with which he sensed the intellectual danger of animism for Christianity and the ardor with which he supported all scientific work that could meet that danger rationally.[4]

It is precisely the *literal* mode of his mind that makes Mersenne crucial to both religion and science. He stands unyieldingly for concrete knowledge of facts. Like Bacon, he preferred contemporary empirical experience to the opinions of the ancients. Since he believed that facts alone could dispel both skepticism in religion and magic in science, he took metaphorical statements at their literal level, asking "scientifically," for instance, "How high is Jacob's ladder?" He also transposed the mystical question of the Unity and Trinity of God into a scientific problem to be worked out by means of a parabolic mirror that could reduce multiple visible images to a single point. He even committed himself personally to the scientific viewpoint, leaving instructions that his corpse be dissected to ascertain the cause of his death.[5]

The seventeenth-century world had no place for an imaginal population. That population was damned into demonism which then reached its richest flourishing as a contemporary counterpart to the new science of Mersenne. Soul was confined to the persons of Christ and those baptized in his name, all else burnt out of Being or moving mechanically around a clockwork orbit. Animals were bereft of psyche,[6] and children, even when baptized, did not have the full reality of souls.[7] Both modern science as it was then being formed and modern Christianity as it was then being reformed, required that subjectivities be purged from everywhere and everything except the authorized place of persons: the rational Christian adult. To experience otherwise was heresy and witchcraft.

Mersenne is himself a personification of that figure both in our Western collective history and in each of us who upholds reason at the cost of imagination. It is Mersenne's voice we hear when we ask for the facts, when souls must be located in literal bodies, and when we would reduce the images and metaphors of the psyche to dogmas on the one hand or to scientific measurement on the other. His is the position that allows no third place between theology and science, no place for psyche.

If Mersenne represents the attack upon the reality of the image, another intellectual force has been attacking the reality of the word. This is nominalism which too has been instrumental in de-personifying our existence. Nominalism empties out big words; nominalists consider universal laws and general types to be only names *(nomina)*. Words have no inherent substance of their own. From the fourteenth century (or the eleventh if one begins with Roscellinus) to Wittgenstein and his contemporary heirs, there has been an accelerating decay of large, abstract, polyvalent ideas in favor of small, concrete, particular, single-meaning names. The word has moved from being a power of its own to an implement in the hand of specialists called philosophers. We have suffered "a tidal wave of nominalism," as C.S. Pierce says. Descartes, Locke, Berkeley, Hume, Leibniz, Kant, and Hegel—"all modern philosophy of every sect has been nominalistic."[8]

This great wave, which is our major Western tradition of thought, devastated the psyche by insisting that big words were labels given by the mind, with only subjective reality. Words which were not particular with referents that could be pointed at could be fashioned by their users to mean anything at all. Invisibles, principles, generals, and universal powers—such as Truth, Terror, Time—were merely names, defined according to the operations we put them through, making sense only within mental word-games. They had no substance, said nominalism; they were not real. Thus, the soul came to distrust its speech of spiritual and imaginal realities. Such realities were, according to nominalism, only secondary, abstracted or inferred from particular instances of the concrete perceptible world. A counter-position, deriving mainly from Plato, held to the reality in and of these grand words and was called realism. But in the course of time nominalism even renamed realism, so that a "realist" today is one who points his finger at facts independent of ideas about them and looks with suspicion upon universal words with capital letters.

By not according these invisibles and universal powers a reality equal to that of concrete particulars—equal even to the experience of them (for Truth, Terror, and Time can have as much impact on the soul as can table, tooth, or tea)—nominalism deprived big words of their sanity. The plain man of common sense with his fists full of facts is a nominalist and his view of reality has obtained. Consequently, only madmen are supposed to see the figments of the mind as real, and the content of madness has become defined in part by the subjects nominalism has rejected.

Although the Renaissance had liberated madness from its medieval constraints, the seventeenth century, the century of Descartes and Mersenne, of nominalistic science and theology, imprisoned madness again in immense new houses of confinement. Psychiatry, its history written mainly by progressive positivists, has lauded this development as an enlightened and charitable awareness about insanity. But if we make a parallel between developments in the realm of reason (science, philosophy, and theology) and the development of facilities for incarcerating unreason,[9] we would see that the battle between nominalism and realism, between fact and fiction or *reason and imagination,* was being enacted from the seventeenth century onward as a struggle between nominalistic professions (law, medicine, theology) and realistic patients. One of these patients, John Perceval (who has now been lifted from the anonymity of insanity through the work of Gregory Bateson[10]) while incarcerated in 1831–32, conversed with, or named the persons in his surroundings, such substantial spirits as Contrition, Joy, Gladness, Joviality, Mirth, Mockery, Honesty, Sincerity, Simplicity.

An Excursion on Allegorizing

There was one other place where personified and capital-letter words were allowed, and this was in poetry. But even here personified thinking verged on sick thinking. When the literary critic Joseph Addison in the early eighteenth century examined imagination, he discovered that personifying tended to occur with vehement feelings, as products of dream or trance, with irregularity and wildness of imagery, in states of heightened unreason.[11] Personifications were the result of a special state of the psyche, when it was not its usual rational mechanical self. Addison's psychology was based on those sober thinkers, Hobbes and Locke. However Addison did, when he was young, recognize the imaginative importance of personification in creating a second, fairy world. As he grew older, he considered the use of pagan personifications "unpardonable in a Poet that is past Sixteen."[12]

When eighteenth-century poetry personified, as it was inordinately fond of doing, it confined its persons to the rational realm of allegory. The goal of such enlightened personifying was ultimately instruction: by means of personification "fictions of mind" became "objects of sight," so that the reader could also become a spectator.[13] Personified images with capital letters were employed to reinforce abstract universal ideas: Justice, Harmony, Nature. But this allegorical use of such images vitiates even as it seems to reinforce. Like any system that explains mythological imagery, its mythic persons were depotentiated by the allegorism that was brought forward to account for them.

There are two reasons for this. First, allegory keeps the autonomy and reality of the Gods at bay. By being "used" for moral examples or educational homilies,[14] they are no longer powers but rather technical tricks, categories, conceits. They become instruments of reason rather than the very forms that organize reason. This we shall explore in detail in Chapter 3, and we shall see that the Gods govern our thinking so that our thoughts become an allegory of their styles, rather than their becoming allegories of our thought. That the Gods cannot be held by reason, by the allegorical attempt to make them emblems of concepts, is amply demonstrated by eighteenth-century poetry: it became Romanticism, Blake, Keats, Shelley, the Gods rampant again, Prometheus Unbound, allegories no longer.[15]

Second, we treat mythic persons as allegories whenever we wish to forget or deny their peculiar pathological natures. Then we poeticize them. They become delightful, curious, charming—and they lose their effect. Mythology, without its pathological side of animal monsters, cruel slayings, perverse arrangements, wanton rapes, ruinous penances, no longer touches the passions or speaks of and to the individual soul in its distress. This thesis we shall elaborate in Chapter 2. But we can suggest now that *allegory is a defensive reaction of the rational mind against the full power of the soul's irrational personifying propensity.* Gods and demons become mere poetic allusions.

The use of allegory as a defense continues today in the interpretations of dreams and fantasies. When images no longer surprise us, when we can expect what they mean and know what they intend, it is because we have our "symbologies" of established meanings. Dreams have been yoked to the systems which interpret them; they belong to schools—there are "Freudian dreams," "Jungian dreams," etc. If long things are penises for Freudians, dark things are shadows for Jungians. Images are turned into pre-defined concepts such as passivity, power, sexuality, anxiety, femininity, much like the conventions of allegorical poetry. Like such poetry, and using similar allegorical techniques, psychology too can become a defense against the psychic power of personified images.

If the mother in our dream, or the beloved, or the wise old counselor, says and does what one would expect, or if the analyst interprets these figures conventionally, they have been deprived of their authority as mythic images and persons and reduced to mere allegorical conventions and moralistic stereotypes. They have become the personified conceits of an allegory, a simple means of persuasion that forces the dream or fantasy into doctrinal compliance. The image allegorized is now the image in service of a teaching.

In contrast, archetypal psychology holds that the true iconoclast is the image itself which explodes its allegorical meanings, releasing startling new insights. Thus the most distressing images in dreams and fantasies, those we shy from for their disgusting distortion and perversion, are precisely the ones that break the allegorical frame of what we think we know about this person or that, this trait of ourselves or that. The "worst" images are thus the best, for they are the ones that restore a figure to its pristine power as a numinous person at work in the soul.

The Soul of Words

A more general result of nominalism is "logophobia," a dread of words, especially of big words which might harbor irrealities. Our difficulty with the word archetype and with envisioning the reality of archetypal images and ideas is one of the effects of nominalism. We are in a peculiar double bind with words; they fascinate and at the same time repel. For because of nominalism words have become both bloated in importance and dried in content. In the modern language-games of

Wittgenstein, words are the very fundamentals of conscious existence, yet they are also severed from things and from truth. They exist in a world of their own. In modern structural linguistics, words have no inherent sense, for they can be reduced, every single one of them, to basic quasi-mathematical units. The fantasy of a basic number of irreducible elements out of which all speech can be constituted is a dissecting technique of the analytic mind which applies logical atomism to *Logos* itself—a suicide of the word.

Of course there is a credibility gap, since we no longer trust words of any sort as true carriers of meaning. Of course, in psychiatry, words have become schizogenic, themselves a cause and source of mental disease. Of course we live in a world of slogan, jargon, and press releases, approximating the "Newspeak" of Orwell's *1984*.

As one art and academic field after another falls into the paralyzing coils of obsession with language and communication, speech succumbs to a new semantic anxiety. Even psychotherapy, which began as a "talking cure"—the rediscovery of the oral tradition of telling one's story—is abandoning language for touch, cry, and gesture. We dare not be eloquent. To be passionate, psychotherapy now says we must be physical or primitive. Such psychotherapy promotes a new barbarism. Our semantic anxiety has made us forget that words, too, burn and become flesh as we speak.

A new angelology of words is needed so that we may once again have faith in them. Without the inherence of the angel in the word—and angel means originally "emissary," "message-bearer"—how can we utter anything but personal opinions, things made up in our subjective minds? How can anything of worth and soul be conveyed from one psyche to another, as in a conversation, a letter, or a book, if archetypal significances are not carried in the depths of our words?

We need to recall the angel aspect of the word, recognizing words as independent carriers of soul between people. We need to recall that we do not just make words up or learn them in school, or ever have them fully under control. Words, like angels, are powers which have invisible power over us. They are personal presences which have whole mythologies: genders, genealogies (etymologies concerning origins and creations), histories, and vogues; and their own guarding, blaspheming, creating, and annihilating effects. For words are persons. This aspect of the word transcends their nominalistic definitions and contexts and evokes in our souls a universal resonance. Without the inherence of soul in words, speech would not move us, words would not provide forms for carrying our lives and giving sense to our deaths. "Death" itself, and "soul," "Gods," "persons," would become, as Antiphon the Sophist said thousands of years ago, mere conventions and artifacts.[16] Personifying would be simply a manner of nominalistic speech.

It is this *person in the word*, its angelic power, that nominalism dreads. Nominalism is not simply a philosophical position which would disembowel words, emptying them into windbags, *flatus voci*. It is a psychological defense against the psychic component of the word. The bigness it fears and would reduce refers to the complex nature of words, which act upon us as complexes and release complexes in us. Philosophy works wholly with words, so it must bring their complexities into rational order. This is the job of rational speech whether in logic, theology, or science. In fact, rational use of words was what the word "sanity" originally meant in Latin. Therefore, nominalism refuses to recognize the person in the word or to personify them; to do so implies insanity.

I admit that the personifying path we are on is, indeed, deviant if not mad. But it is from this psychological perspective that we must look at all judgments against personifying. For these judgments come from a tradition that has progressively depotentiated both images and words in order to maintain a particular vision of man, reason, and reality. This vision divides the world into objects and egos, giving to the soul no more place than the pea-sized pineal gland, to which island in the middle of the brain Descartes banished the psyche at the beginning of our modern period.

Where We Are Now

The push of progress has left corpses in its wake. Totems, idols, and the personages of myth were the first to be mocked and scorned. Then followed images of every sort—Gods, demons, saints, the forces of nature, the qualities of character, the substantives of metaphysics. In the middle of the sixteenth century the Council of Trent, which established Catholic doctrine for the modern period, removed substance and virtue from all holy images. In the middle of the seventeenth century, Cromwell's pious Protestants tore down and smashed the images of Christ, Mary, and the Saints in the English cathedrals because, to their Puritan minds, images were not Christian. Because subjectivities can be made visible in images, these were especially damnable; smashing them furthered the destruction of the visible carriers of personifying. Personifying was driven out of churches and into the madhouse.

Roundhead minds were more concrete than the stones they smashed.

Cromwell's men acted out the new literalism that was losing touch with metaphorical imagination. Their abstract monotheism and one-sided view of doctrine had psychological concretism at its back. But they had lost imagination, for intolerance of images is also an intolerance of the imagination and results from a lost imagination.

It is difficult for us today to remember—especially at a time when we are inundated by images (commercial, cinematographic, electronic, etc.) and have incorporated *image* into usual speech as a replacement for idea, notion, style—the long historical fear of the image and of fantasy in our tradition.[17] The degradation of the image in monotheistic Hebrewism and of *phantasia* in Hellenistic philosophy, reappear in the Protestant Reformation and Catholic Counter-Reformation, which are only two particularly forceful expressions of an image-phobia in Western theological and philosophical writing. Systems which did work in and through images, such as Gnosticism, Neoplatonism, alchemy, Rosicrucianism, and Swedenborg, could not enter the main current of our tradition and were forced instead into the occult or even the heretical.

On the one hand the destruction of the personified image led finally to the twentieth century's contempt for representational painting: no recognizable images, no persons—anything, everything for the eye, nothing for the soul. On the other hand, it brought on the destruction of the personified word: lower-case letters replace capitals in a full democracy of the word, all equal, none more noble, more privileged, none with divine right. Today we have lost both the eighteenth century's poetic capitals and the nineteenth-century's oratorical ones, used to imbue with power and substance such jingoes as Liberty, Progress, and Empire. Our "gods" have become small, save one, and with the exception of a few last conventions of proper names, titles, and places, and the nonsense capitals of corporate abbreviations (nominalism is capitalism, letters as units of exchange), the one magnification persisting as a capital refers to the one person still remaining in a depersonified world: I. Only I and God, one to one, and some say God is dead.

"Personification," "Anthropomorphism," "Animism"

The reforming imagination-smashers and the nominalist word-emptiers found one way of quietly making place for personifying within their rational terms. Personifying received acceptable descriptions—personification, anthropomorphism, animism—even if the practice itself was unacceptable for civilized man and to be found legitimately only among fetishists, mystics, and poets; among "the masses whose wits are not potent enough to receive things clearly and distinctly" (Spinoza);[18] among those who had been caught by language, concretizing the masculine and feminine genders and subjects doing things through verbs; among children as their childish kind of reasoning (Piaget),[19] and especially among "primitives."

Anthropomorphism, "the attribution of human form or character . . . ascription of a human attribute of personality to anything impersonal or irrational"[20] enters the English language in 1753 via the French. Animism, "the attribution of a living soul to inanimate objects and natural phenomena"[21] occurs a century later in the present sense made familiar by the anthropologist Tylor's *Primitive Culture* (1871). The first is an emissary into English of the French Enlightenment with its acute sensitiveness to the irrationality of religion and its investment in the Cartesian world of dead and impersonal objects. The second is a product of Victorian progressive scientism. Both are heritages of nominalism. Both deprive that mode of experience to which they purportedly refer of its native validity. So we shall not use the terms *anthropomorphism* and *animism* but rather the term *personifying* to signify the basic psychological activity—*the spontaneous experiencing, envisioning and speaking of the configurations of existence as psychic presences*—and hopefully thereby save this authentic activity from being condemned as personification.

Personification is a psychologism. It implies a human being who creates Gods in human likeness much as an author creates characters out of his own personality.[22] These Gods depict his own needs; they are his projections. Personification cannot imagine that these psychic presences (Gods, daemons, and other persons of the mythical realm) have autonomous substantial reality. It cannot imagine that an author, say, is driven to bear the messages of "his" characters, that it is *their* will that is done, that he is *their* scribe, and that they are creating him even while he creates them. An author's fictions are often more significant than his own reality, containing more psychic substance, which lasts long after their "creator" has gone. An author creates only by their authority. The notion that literary fictions have an inherent autonomy is itself visioned by means of a personified Muse, without whose aid the entire writing venture becomes precarious.

All three terms—anthropomorphism, animism, personification—contain one basic idea:[23] there exists a "mode of thought" which takes an inside event and puts it outside, at the same time making this content alive, personal, and even divine. These three terms, by saying that human beings tend to imagine things into souls, are actually describing a manner of soul-making. But by calling this activity a "mode of thought" it becomes an act we perform—conscious or unconscious—rather than something we immediately *experience*. Where these three terms assume thought makes soul, personifying recognizes soul as existent prior to reflection. Personifying is a way of being in the world and *experiencing the world as a psychological field*, where persons are given with events, so that events are experiences that touch us, move us, appeal to us.

But as van der Leeuw has said we waste breath trying to disprove the theory of animism. It can, however, be seen through as a psychological statement saying less about the soul of primitives than about the primitive soul of those writing about them. Animism is an anthropological report about the soul of anthropology. "In its entire structure and tendency," says van der Leeuw, "this theory suits the second half of the nineteenth century far better than it does the primitive world."[24]

The theory of animism represents a condition of soul (anima) which cannot find soul except as projected into infantile behavior, psychopathology of fetishism, the common people of the collective mind, or the dark places and peculiar behaviors of exotic peoples in distant islands or insane asylums. Through these concepts—personification, anthropomorphism, animism—reason could indeed make stones live again and even create souls and Gods. The rational tradition, having lost its base in the psyche, was trying to rediscover it through the anthropology of animism.

The Case for Personifying

But there was another tradition, which continued to regard personifying as a necessary mode of understanding the world and of being in it. It began with the Greeks and Romans, who personified such psychic powers as Fame, Insolence, Night, Ugliness, Timing, Hope, to name but a few. These were regarded as "real daemons to be worshipped and propitiated and no mere figments of the imagination. And, as is well known, they were actually worshipped in every Greek city. To mention Athens alone, we find altars and sanctuaries of Victory, Fortune, Friendship, Forgetfulness, Modesty, Mercy, Peace, and many more. . . ."[25]

Many consider this practice as merely animistic, but it was really an act of ensouling; for there is no question that the personifying of the ancient Greeks and Romans provided altars for configurations of the soul. When these are not provided for, when these Gods and daemons are not given their proper place and recognition, they become diseases —a point Jung made often enough.

The need to provide containers for the many configurations of the soul was formulated in the third century A.D. by the greatest of all Platonist philosophers, Plotinus. In a section of his *Enneads* called appropriately "The Problems of the Soul" we find this passage:

> I think, therefore, that those ancient sages, who sought to secure the presence of divine beings by the erection of shrines and statues, showed insight into the nature of the All; they perceived that, though this soul is everywhere tractable, its presence will be secured all the more readily when an appropriate receptacle is elaborated, a place especially capable of receiving some portion or phase of it, something reproducing it, or representing it and serving like a mirror to catch an image of it.[26]

When in the next passage (IV, 3, 12) he speaks of "the souls of men, seeing their images in the mirror of Dionysus," he seems again to be referring to the ability of the soul to divide into many parts, and that its portions and phases reflect the various images of divine persons.

Personifying not only aids discrimination; it also offers another avenue of loving, of imagining things in a personal form so that we can find access to them with our hearts. Words with capital letters are charged with affect, they jump out of their sentences and become images. The tradition of depersonifying recognized full well that personified words tend to become cherished and sacred, affecting the reason of the heart. Hence nominalists disparage the personified style of expression, calling it rhetoric with emotive meaning only. But this very recognition, that personifying emotionalizes, shifts the discussion from nominalism to imagination, from head to heart.

The image of the heart— *"l'immagine del cuor"*[27]—was an important idea in the work of Michelangelo who was strongly influenced by the Platonist tradition. Imagining with the heart refers to a mode of perception that penetrates through names and physical appearances to a personified interior image, from the heart to the heart. When Michelangelo portrayed Lorenzo and Giuliano Medici in the Sacristy of San Lorenzo, the features which he depicted were unnatural, not as they appeared in life but rather transfigured to conform with the true image of their persons in the heart. While the scientific Renaissance (Bacon and Galileo) insisted on the primacy of sense perception, Michelangelo's *"imagine del cuor"* implied that *perception is secondary to imagination.* By imagining through and beyond what the eye sees, the imagination envisions primordial images. And these present themselves in personified forms.

Nearer our own times another Mediterranean, the Spaniard Miguel de Unamuno (b. 1864), returned to the relationship of heart and personified images and explained the necessary interdependence between love and personifying:

> In order to love everything, in order to pity everything, human and extra-human, living and non-living, you must feel everything within yourself, you must personalize everything. For everything that it loves, everything that it pities, love personalizes . . . we only love—that which is like ourselves . . . it is love itself . . . that reveals these resemblances to us. . . . Love personalizes all that it loves. Only by personalizing it can we fall in love with an idea.[28]

He sums up, saying: "Our feeling of the world, upon which is based our understanding of it, is necessarily anthropomorphic and mythopeic." Loving is a way of knowing, and for loving to know, it must personify. Personifying is thus a way of knowing, especially knowing what is invisible, hidden in the heart.

In this perspective personifying is not a lesser, primitive mode of apprehending but a finer one. It presents in psychological theory the attempt to integrate heart into method and to return abstract thoughts and dead matter to their human shapes. Because personifying is an epistemology of the heart, a thought mode of feeling, we do wrong to judge it as inferior, archaic thinking appropriate only to those allowed emotive speech and affective logic—children, madmen, poets, and primitives. Method in psychology must not hinder love from working, and we are foolish to decry as inferior the very means by which love understands. If we have not understood personifying, it is because the main tradition has always tried to explain it rather than understand it.

This distinction between knowing through understanding and knowing through explaining begins importantly with Wilhelm Dilthey (1833–1911) of Berlin.[29] He noted that as religious personified imagination declined, scientific objectivity grew in its place and at its expense. He saw that we have moved from methods which helped us understand to those which help us to explain. Dilthey attempted to refound psychology on the basis of understanding: psychology must base itself outside the laboratory and inside subjective understanding. Despite their estrangement,[30] Dilthey shared with Nietzsche a root psychological idea: the fundamental place of subjectivity in all human thought.

My soul is not the result of objective facts that require explanation;

rather it reflects subjective experiences that require understanding. To understand anything at all, we must envision it as having an independent subjective interior existence, capable of experience, obliged to a history, motivated by purposes and intentions. We must always think anthropomorphically, even personally. "The secret of the 'person,'" wrote Dilthey, "attracts for its own sake to ever newer and deeper efforts to understand."[31] Even the intentions, purposes, and other subprocesses that enter into experience cannot be reduced to explanations; they too are open only to an anthropomorphic understanding. So studies of human being, all human studies, in order to know their subject must necessarily be anthropomorphic. In his coagulated Germanic style Dilthey cumbersomely recapitulated the personified vision of psychology he had gained from research into the Greeks, the Renaissance, and Giambattista Vico.

Vico, the Neapolitan philosopher (1668–1744)—a lone voice against the powerful Parisian influences that had been spread by the work of Mersenne—was the first modern to perceive the connection between personified thinking and "mythopeic" understanding, as Unamuno called it.[32] Wherever this tradition emerges, in Vico's Naples or Dilthey's Berlin, and whenever it blooms, in the Neoplatonic thought of Michelangelo, the romantic thought of Blake, or the critical thought of Cassirer, it is *the necessity of personifying for the mythic perspective* that this tradition particularly stresses. To enter myth we must personify; to personify carries us into myth.

To the mythic perspective the world appears personified, implying a passionate engagement with it. We do not ask: "Are things alive or dead?" or "Are Gods real or are they symbolic projections?" Questions of this sort "may be thought illegitimate," says the most psychological of all classicists, E. R. Dodds, "so long as myth-making is a living mode of thought to confront it with this sort of brutal 'either-or' is to force upon it a choice which destroys its being."[33] Mythic consciousness answers with Cassirer: "There is nowhere an 'it' as a dead object, a mere thing."[34] Subject and object, man and Gods, I and Thou, are not apart and isolated each with a different sort of being, one living or real, the other dead or imaginary. The world and the Gods are dead or alive according to the condition of our souls. A world view that perceives a dead world or declares the Gods to be symbolic projections derives from a perceiving subject who no longer experiences in a personified way, who has lost his *immagine del cuor*. To rekindle this life we start with soul, reimagining its internal processes anthropomorphically.

This leads to the ultimate conclusion that *we* do not actually personify at all. Mythical consciousness is a mode of being in the world that brings with it imaginal persons. They are given with the imagination and are its data. Where imagination reigns, personifying happens. We experience it nightly, spontaneously, in dreams. Just as we do not create our dreams, but they *happen* to us, so we do not invent the persons of myth and religion; they, too, happen to us. The persons present themselves as existing prior to any effort of ours to personify. *To mythic consciousness, the persons of the imagination are real.*

The late German classical scholar who had the deepest insight into the nature of mythical persons, Walter F. Otto, made this same point in an attack against his rationalist and reductive colleagues:

> There is no such thing as personification, only a depersonification—just as there is no mythologizing (in the authentic sense) only a demythologizing. Schelling said that the question how did man ever come to God is senseless; there is only the question, how did man ever come away from God. So-called abstract concepts and words would never have been raised into the personal had they not been from the very beginning personal, that is, divine forms.[35]

Personifying in Freud and Jung

However, personifying was not restored as a valid idea through classics or philosophy, any more than it was through studies of primitives, Renaissance humanism, or Romantic poetry. It forced passage for itself in our times through psychopathology, through the work of Freud and Jung. It was rediscovered as a fundamental psychological idea, not in the halls of learning but in the consulting room and the insane asylum. Although we shall devote the entire next chapter to the overwhelming significance of psychopathology for our vision of the psyche and its psychology, the thoughts presented there are foreshadowed here in the evidence concerning personifying. For it was psychopathology—multiple personalities, hysterical dissociations, hallucinations—that forced the attention of Freud and Jung, and through them of our epoch, upon the psyche's propensity to personify.

The personifications of psychoanalysis are familiar, though disguised: the Censor, the Superego, the Primal Horde and the Primal Scene, free-floating Anxiety, the polymorphous perverse Child. Others enter more subtly. For example, memories from childhood are not quite the reminiscences of actual persons that they seem to be. This Freud discovered at a quite early date. A child's memories are always inextricably mixed with and further fabricated by fantasy images. Thus the scenes and persons we "remember" from childhood are personified complexes, personified wishes and dreads which we place back then, calling them Mother and Sister, Father and Brother. These persons are less historical humans from a historical past than soul fantasies returning in human guise. We would like to take them literally, believing that they "really happened" and that the mother in my reminiscent image is my actual mother, because then the discomfort of psychic reality can be avoided. It is easier to bear the truth of facts than the truth of fantasies; we prefer to literalize memories. For to realize that the psyche fabricates memories means to accept the reality that experiences themselves are being made by the soul out of itself and independently of the ego's engagement in its so-called real world. It means, in short, that *personifying is going on all the time;* persons in scenes are continually being "invented" by the soul and presented to us in the guise of memories.

Memory not only records, it also confabulates, that is, it makes up imaginary happenings, wholly psychic events. Memory is a form imagination can borrow in order to make its personified images feel utterly real. Because we experience these events in the "past," we believe they really happened as facts. By recognizing this imaginative inventiveness of memory, Freud rediscovered psychic reality. Instrumental to this rediscovery were psychic persons. Freud saw that though they did not have literal, factual reality, they presented the truth and validity of psychic reality.

As memory itself wrestles with fact and fancy, so Freud wrestled with the two great modes of thinking—conceptual and mythic—that stood opposed, especially at the beginning of this century. He tried to construct a scientific conceptual psychology, but like Plato he used mythical modes to present his psychological insights. For example, Freud believed that the persons in dreams were disguises for instinctual processes. He tried to reduce the dream's natural personifying to conceptual terms: libido, wish-fulfillment, sleep-protection. But he expressed the conceptual terms themselves by means of anthropomorphic animisms. The Oedipus complex is the most famous. His science turned, willy-nilly, into a mythology. Psychoanalysis is a comprehensive fiction of the human soul, of its genealogy, its prehistoric cataclysms, its transpersonal realms and the powers that govern its fate. It succeeds not as a science but as a cosmological fiction. The Italian writer Giovanni Papini in an apocryphal interview with the Viennese Master records this "confession" from Freud:

A man of letters by instinct, though a doctor by necessity, I conceived the idea of changing over a branch of medicine—psychiatry—into literature. Though I have the appearance of a scientist I was and am a poet and novelist. Psychoanalysis is no more than an interpretation of a literary vocation in terms of psychology and pathology.[36]

Freud, it should be remembered, did not win the Nobel prize for medicine, but rather the Goethe prize for literature.

Freud's struggle between the conceptual and mythic modes of formulating psychology appears, personified, in the struggle between him and Lou Andreas-Salomé, who was his closest woman pupil for a brief period during his late middle years and a deep friend into his old age. Anthropomorphism became the focus of her influence upon Freud's mind.[37] During their crucial first year (1912) she brought him the ideas of Nietzsche and Dilthey,[38] emphasizing the essential methodological dependency of psychoanalysis upon anthropomorphic thinking. She insisted upon a psychology that understood, and not only explained (as was Freud's habit) by means of abstract, quantitative, and topographical constructs in "objective" language.

Like Diotima with Plato,[39] Lou Salomé taught Freud that love requires personifying. She believed that we can be in an emotional relationship "only with whatever we experience anthropomorphically and only such can we include in our love. If by contrast we explore nature objectively and scientifically, we alienate the objects from us" and defeat the very purpose of psychoanalysis.[40] She performed a psychologizing upon Freud's psychology, seeing through its conceptual explanations, attempting to keep it anthropomorphic, loving, and alive.

Freud's concepts, such as the libido[41]—and especially his Eros, Thanatos, and Oedipus—are indeed ancient images explicitly drawn from a long history of mythological personification. (The Greek world always fascinated Freud; he even kept a boyhood notebook in Greek.[42]) Others of his terms—projection, sublimation, condensation—once belonged to the poetics of alchemy. Freud himself wrote: "The theory of instincts is, as it were, our mythology. The instincts are mythical beings, superb in their indefiniteness."[43] And Freud's id, "under the domination of the mute but powerful death instincts,"[44] may be compared, as I have done elsewhere in some detail, with the underworld of invisible Hades.[45]

Wittgenstein's evaluation of Freud's work points accurately to its mythical basis; Freud "has not given a scientific explanation of the ancient myth. What he has done is to propound a new myth."[46] His translation of personified images into conceptual processes and functions does not truly separate us from the mythic roots of psychoanalysis. The concepts are myths in other terms. Castration Anxiety, Penis Envy, the Repetition Compulsion—all these work upon us as once did invisible *daimones*. We fall into their power and are held in their grip. Now the dynamisms are depersonified and located inside our own skins or skull or at our body's apertures (erogenous zones). And as old demons once were exorcised, the new ones may be abreacted. One main difference is in their visualization as personifications: once we saw winged creatures and long serpents emerging from orifices, or tiny soul persons, whereas now we have geometric diagrams or algebraic formulae for describing the dynamisms of the psyche. Our point here is not to reduce demons to complexes or complexes back to an old demonology, but to insist that *psychology so needs mythology that it creates one as it proceeds.* A mythic manner of speaking is fundamental to the soul's way of formulating itself. Indeed, Papini and Wittgenstein are right in this sense: depth psychology is today's form of traditional mythology, the great carrier of the oral tradition, the telling of tall tales.

Jung's namings are even more radically animistic: Shadow, Old Wise Man, Great Mother, Anima and Animus, are indeed persons. "The fact that the unconscious spontaneously personifies . . . is the reason why I have taken over these personifications in my terminology and formulated them as names."[47]

Some have considered Jung's most important discovery to be the psychological complex, others the archetype, but perhaps his main contribution lies not so much in these ideas as in his radical, personified formulation of them. Certainly a field of dim representations and unknown motives in the back of the mind had been part of philosophical thought since Leibniz and Kant. But whereas philosophers had conceived such forces as mental events, Jung described them as persons. Jung harked back to Renaissance, Hellenic, and archaic thought forms. His discovery was rather a rediscovery: personifying refound.

Jung's early work with word associations did not rest with quantifying results; he personified them. He discovered complexes which were invested with feeling, intention, autonomy, and fragments of consciousness. They were independent entities because they behaved as such. The same complex can alter the association of words, show itself as unwanted symptoms, and appear as a person in a dream.[48] Dream persons are complexes walking around; symptoms are the irruption of these persons into our normal lives. Our personal complexities are indeed the persons of our complexes.

Where other psychologists might have used a so-called objective and neutral language of numbers, structures, or functions to account for the same disturbances, Jung reverted courageously to the direct mode of personifying which in his day was still considered a primitive formulation.[49] He stood firmly by his method of naming, explicitly comparing it with the spontaneous speech of the insane and the noncivilized. What was radically courageous then we now take for granted, so easily imagining ourselves to play roles, enter into games, and be composed of different characters.

Perhaps Jung's animism is more radical than Freud's because of their different clinical backgrounds. Jung reflected his ideas against the extremities of psychosis in an asylum, while Freud reflected his insights through neurotics in a consulting room. Jung's subjects were more estranged, more possessed; as psychosis may be differentiated from neurosis partly in terms of the degree of conviction in delusions and hallucinations, so the differences in value Freud and Jung give to personification exemplifies the difference between their starting milieus.

Jung's predilection for animism in contrast with Freud's search for a scientific psychology may be taken also as the particular expression of the archetypal psychology of each: Freud governed more by the monotheistic paternal and the masculine, Jung by the polytheistic feminine and the *anima* (soul-image).[50] In Freudian fantasy the heroic ego, like Oedipus, develops through slaying the father; in Jungian fantasy the heroic ego battles for deliverance from the mother. Freud invented the Primal Father of the Primal Horde, the stern superego, the fear of castration, and the protective censor. In old age Freud wrote on Moses; Jung's late work lauds Mary and Sophia. Freud's early and main pupils were men. Jung invented the Great Mother; wrote only one minor paper on the father, but major ones—and repeatedly—on the mother and the anima. His early and chief pupils were women.

Jung's animism is tightly tied to his notion of anima,[51] which is the word he uses for one's personal and personified soul-image. The Anima is a person and anima is a conceptual notion and *anima* means soul. Jung calls her "she," and she it is who creates conflicting confusions and attractions, who brings moods and desires and neurovegetative symptoms, who kindles the peculiar fascinations of fantasy that turn one's head, and yet also conveys a vague sense of interiority, a sense of soul.

A person may converse with her, as for example, when a poet talks with his muse, a philosopher with his daimon, a mystic with his tutelary angel, or a madman with his hallucination. We find her in mythology in countless forms, and expressly as the maiden Psyche. Jung has defined anima as "a personification of the unconscious in general, so that she is the particular archetypal figure involved with the activity of personifying and the psychological confusions about it.[52] We shall examine the implications of this when we discuss the experiencing of imagination.

Jung's Archetypal Persons: "The Little People"

In Jungian practice the words Shadow, Self, Ego, Anima, and the like refer to the structural components of the personality. These basic structures are *always imagined to be partial personalities,* and the interplay between them is imagined more as in fiction than in physics. Rather than a field of forces, we are each a field of internal personal relationships, an interior commune, a body politic. Psychodynamics becomes psychodramatics; our life is less the resultant of pressures and forces than the enactment of mythical scenarios. Moreover, these components of personality, playing through *their* archetypal scenes, which we call *our* life problems, receive personal pronouns. We speak familiarly of them: "She (the mother complex) paralyzes me." "He (the father complex) never stops driving me; he wants me perfect." And we wrestle with a concealed counterpersonality whom Jung named Shadow because we keep him in the dark; he must shadow our life with his surreptitious intentions. Jung called all these figures "the little people." Yet even in spite of this tongue-in-cheek kind of naming, he recognized that they are more important in steering fate than is our usual "I."[53]

As Jung refined his insight into these complex persons, the persons of our complexes, he discovered that their autonomy and intentionality derives from deeper figures of far wider significance. These are the archetypes, the persons to whom we ultimately owe our personality. In speaking of them, he says that "we are obliged to reverse our rationalistic causal sequence, and instead of deriving these figures from our psychic conditions, must derive our psychic conditions from these figures. . . . It is not we who personify them; they have a personal nature from the very beginning."[54] By the founding of the psyche upon personified structures—rather than upon concepts borrowed from the sciences or philosophy—even Jung's metapsychology remains psychology. He never deserts the psyche in search of explanatory principles outside its own imaginal world. *We are always talking about persons even at the most abstract level of discussion,* for these foundations, too, are archetypal persons.

Jung's position here states that the fundamental facts of existence are the "fantasy-images" of the psyche. All consciousness depends on these images. Everything else—ideas of the mind, sensations of the body, perceptions of the world around us, beliefs, feelings, hungers—must present themselves as images in order to become experienced. " 'Experience' is, in its most simple form, an exceedingly complicated structure of mental images."[55] Should we ask: just what *is* psyche? What do you mean by psychic experience and psychic reality? The answer is: fantasy-images. "Image *is* psyche," says Jung.[55a] "The psyche consists essentially of images . . . a 'picturing' of vital activities."[55b]

In the beginning is the image; first imagination then perception; first fantasy then reality. Or as Jung puts it: "The psyche creates reality every day. The only expression I can use for this activity is fantasy."[56] Man is primarily an imagemaker and our psychic substance consists of images; our being is imaginal being, an existence in imagination. We are indeed such stuff as dreams are made on.

Since we can know only fantasy-images directly and immediately, and from these images create our worlds and call them realities, we live in a world that is neither "inner" nor "outer." Rather the psychic world is an imaginal world, just as image is psyche. Paradoxically, at the same time these images are in us and we live in the midst of them. The psychic world is experienced empirically as inside us and yet it encompasses us with images. I dream and experience my dreams as inside me and yet at the same time I walk around in my dreams and am inside them.

Because our psychic stuff is images, image-making is a *via regia*, a royal road to soul-making. The making of soul-stuff calls for dreaming, fantasying, imagining. To live psychologically means to imagine things; to be in touch with soul means to live in sensuous connection with fantasy. To be in soul is to experience the fantasy in all realities and the basic reality of fantasy.

Fantasy images that are the stuff and values of soul are structured by archetypes. They "direct all fantasy activity into its appointed paths," says Jung.[57] These paths are mythological; or rather, we see that fantasy flows into particular motifs (mythologems) and constellations of persons in actions (mythemes). These patternings appear in myths the world over, and in literature, art, scientific theories, and theological doctrines; also in dreams, even the dreams of children, and in the delusional systems of the insane—wherever imagination manifests itself in the products of the mind. Within these fantasy-images are the archetypal persons of myths. Their interrelations are the structural principles of psychic life. This interrelation between myths and soul will be examined further in Chapter 3, which centers on the activity of psychologizing or "seeing-through" events into their myths.

It is to Jung's credit that when he experienced personifying in the pathological context of schizoid multiplicity, he continued to account for it within that same context. He did not desert the pathology from which his insight had come—neither his own, nor his patient's, nor the field itself. I refer to his early cases and to his first great book, *Symbols of Transformation* (1912), which is subtitled "An Analysis of the Prelude to a Case of Schizophrenia." I refer equally to Jung's own descent into the underworld (described so graphically in his autobiography), where he met a host of figures—first a dwarf; then the old man Elijah, who soon turned into the pagan Philemon with "an Egypto-Hellenistic atmosphere"; and the blind girl Salomé[58]—all of whom he took as seriously as the figures experienced by his patients; he painted their shapes in his notebooks, spoke to the voices that spoke to him, and wrote down what they said. Although personifying occurred in what was then considered a pathological context, Jung did not prejudge it from a psychiatric standpoint. He experienced it imaginally, thereby opening it to insight.

Jung's lead into this imaginal territory has opened a view of personality that is no longer single-centered but polycentric. Owing to the depth psychologies of Freud and Jung we have a more complete model of ourselves. We conceive our psychological nature to be naturally divided into portions and phases, a composition of earlier and later historical levels, various zones and developmental strata, many complexes and archetypal persons. We are no longer single beings in the image of a single God, but are always constituted of multiple parts: impish child, hero or heroine, supervising authority, asocial psychopath, and so on. Because we have come to realize that each of us is normally a flux of figures, we no longer need be menaced by the notion of multiple personality. I may see visions and hear voices; I may talk with them and they with each other without at all being insane.

The Empire of the Roman Ego: Decline and Falling Apart

In the early years of this century, cases of multiple personality caused a stir. But not because they were something new. Possession by devils, speaking with several tongues, automatic writing, the experience of the *Doppelgänger* and *déjà vu,* and other modes of "personality dissociation" were long familiar phenomena. The idea of a divided soul, even of dismemberment, is older than Greek myth, yet only in the early years of this century was "schizophrenia" named and given a careful description. Only at this extreme level of psychic distress could personifying again force itself upon our monocentric consciousness.

Multiple personality was ending the rule of reason and so of course this phenomenon became the focus of the defenders of reason: psychiatrists. They have often to deal with a culture's critical concern presented *in extremis,* symptomatically. During the thirties and forties we lived through what was called The Age of Anxiety. Recently, "hallucinations" (LSD) have put into question our materialist theory of perception and the world-view built upon it; "depression" has made us aware of our culture's addiction to a manic superficiality in growth and movement; and "autism" is reminding us of the possibility of the psyche's refusal to enter the world at all, full retreat to the interior castle.

"Schizophrenia" was officially coined in the period just before the First World War, a period which saw a corresponding fragmentation in painting, music and literature and a corresponding relativization of the ego position in natural science. Cases of multiple personality were important because they confirmed the multiplicty of the individual at a time when the same phenomenon was beginning to appear in the culture in general. Through this multiple schizoid perspective we saw a world no longer held together by reason, *no longer held and centered at all.* Instead: disordering spontaneity, relativity, discontinuities, a-harmonies, an overpopulation of spirits and living soul images—the return of archetypal persons.

The phenomena of dissociation—breaking away, splitting off, personification, multiplication, ambivalence—will always seem an illness to the ego as it has come to be defined. But if we take the context of the psychic field as a whole, these fragmenting phenomena may be understood as reassertions against central authority by the individuality of the parts. We sense an obdurate "willfullness"[59] to do and say things that are alien to the ego, buying what we do not want, eating more than we intend, taking on the habits of mother or father or a sudden new friend. New partial personalities spring up with feelings, opinions, needs. A sociologist might speak of subcultures; a political scientist of states' rights and grass-roots government. Whatever the category, central command is losing control.

If it is common today to fantasy our culture against that of old Rome, it is partly because our psyche has undergone a long Pax Romana. The gradual extension and civilization of outlying barbarous hinterlands is nothing else than ego-development. The classical description of this romanizing process in the psyche is that of Freud: "To strengthen the ego, to make it more independent of the super ego, to widen the field of perception and enlarge its organization so that it can appropriate fresh portions of the id, where id was there ego shall be. It is a work of culture."[60]

He concludes this paragraph with a simile of draining the sea-marshes to reclaim land, also a preoccupation of the old Romans. Freud's brilliant follower Otto Fenichel, whose authoritative textbook organizes the psychoanalytic theory of neurosis into a compendium, confirms this imperialistic fantasy: "The common denominator of all neurotic phenomena is an insufficiency of the normal control apparatus."[61] The weak ego is the neurotic ego; neurosis is an ego fault; cure is control from headquarters. From the bastion of Rome, reactions (that I have not ordered) by other persons in my psyche are alien, and they will be chronicled by the case historian as peculiar personifications of my primitive hinterlands, strange behavior honoring strange Gods.

Furthermore, the fantasy of "Roman decline," including the disintegration and paganization of society, describes what happens to the psyche when its old ego weakens and consciousness is no longer slave to the ego center. Then consciousness is released from its Roman identification, from centered rule by will and reason. This identification does the psyche a disservice; it sets up a counter-position—the unconscious as fragmentation and disintegration. Both of these positions are stereotypes and need to be revisioned as *different styles of consciousness.* The center and the periphery, Rome and the hinterlands, present differing value systems, patterns of fantasy, and degrees of strength. But the Roman central ego is no more "conscious" than are the outlandish styles of other complexes. Consciousness may be reapportioned without thereby being diminished; it may return to the bush and fields, to its polycentric roots in the complexes and their personified cores, that is, to a consciousness based upon a polytheistic psychology.

Polytheistic psychology refers to the inherent dissociability of the psyche and the location of consciousness in multiple figures and centers.[62] A psychological polytheism provides archetypal containers for differentiating our fragmentation and, what is of utmost significance, offers another perspective to pathology. The interconnection between the "splinter psyches" of our multiple persons and the many Gods and Goddesses of polytheism is brought out in this passage from Jung:

If tendencies towards dissociation were not inherent in the human psyche, fragmentary psychic systems would never have been split off; in other words, neither spirits nor gods would have ever come into existence. That is also the reason why our time has become so utterly godless and profane: we lack all knowledge of the unconscious psyche and pursue the cult of consciousness to the exclusion of all else. *Our true religion is a monotheism of consciousness, a possession by it,* coupled with a fanatical denial of the existence of fragmentary autonomous systems.[63]

When the monotheism of consciousness is no longer able to deny the existence of fragmentary autonomous systems and no longer able to deal with our actual psychic state, then there arises the fantasy of returning to Greek polytheism. For the "return to Greece" offers a way of coping when our centers cannot hold and things fall apart. The polytheistic alternative does not set up conflicting opposites between beast and Bethlehem, between chaos and unity; it permits the coexistence of all the psychic fragments and gives them patterns in the imagination of Greek mythology. A "return to Greece" was experienced in ancient Rome itself, and in the Italian Renaissance, and in the Romantic psyche during the times of revolution. In recent years it has been an intrinsic part of the lives of such artists and thinkers as Stravinsky, Picasso, Heidegger, Joyce, and Freud. The "return to Greece" is a psychological response to the challenge of breakdown; it offers a model of disintegrated integration.

An Excursion on the Return to Greece

Enough has been written to justify the "return to Greece" from aesthetic, philosophical, and cultural points of view. We have all tended to look to Greece for past glory, for perfection, grace, and clarity of mind, and also when in search of "origins", for Greece is where our culture began. But our aim here is to look to Greece for psychological insight. We are trying to understand both what is this "Greece" that so draws the psyche and what the psyche finds there.

When the dominant vision that holds a period of culture together cracks, consciousness regresses into earlier containers, seeking sources for survival which also offer sources of revival. Critics are right when they see the "return to Greece" as a regressive death wish, an escape from contemporary conflicts into mythologies and speculations of a fantasy world. But looking backward makes it possible to move forward, for looking backward revives the fantasy of the child archetype, *fons et origo,* who is both the moment of helpless weakness and the future unfolding. "Renaissance" (rebirth) would be a senseless word without the implied dissolution, the very death out of which that rebirth comes. Critics miss the validity and necessity of regression. Critics also miss the necessity of a regression that is particularly "Greek."

Our culture shows two alternative paths for regression. These paths have been called Hellenism and Hebrewism, and they represent the psychological alternatives of multiplicity and unity. We see the alternatives at critical junctures of Western history, for instance at the time of the decline of Rome which accompanied Constantine into Christianity (as Hebrewism had then been renamed). We see them again at the time of the Renaissance and Reformation, when south Europe returned to Hellenism and northern Europe returned to Hebrewism.

Hebrewism reconfirms the monotheism of ego-consciousness. This path suits when the consciousness of an era or of an individual senses that its survival is best served by an archetypal pattern of heroism and unity. The early image of Christ was compounded with the military Mithra and the muscular Hercules, and Constantine's conversion, which finally turned the tide against classical polytheism, was heralded by a martial vision which came to him before he set forth into battle. Similarly the Hebrewism of the Reformation, despite its tolerance for protest, variety, and splittings, is archetypally inspired by the fantasy of unified heroic strength; the individual is conceived as an undivided unit of arms-bearing responsibility who stands before God, one to one, the primal encounter. Today, the monocentric path is followed whenever we try to resolve a crisis in the soul by means of ego psychology, whenever we try to "reform."

The psyche in crisis has, of course, other fantasies. Hellenism's many and Hebrewism's one are not the only ways out of the psyche's pathological dilemma. There is flight into futurism and its technologies, turning East and inward, going primitive and natural, moving upward and out altogether in transcendence. But these alternatives are less authentic. They are simplistic; they neglect our history and the claims of its images upon us; and they urge escaping from the plight rather than deepening it by providing it with cultural background and differentiated structure.

Science fictions and the fictions of science, instruction from American Indians or Oriental counselors—brilliant and wise as they all may be—fail to remind us of our Western imaginal history, of the actual images at work in our souls. By circumventing our imaginal tradition, they cut us off even further from it. Then the alternative paths to Hebrewism and Hellenism work as repressions, actually adding to the soullessness which their messages would help repair. Hebrewism fails to meet the present dilemma simply because it is too well established, too identical with our world view: there is a Bible in every wanderer's bedroom, where there might better be the *Odyssey*. We can find no renewal in our ego's conscious tradition, only reinforcement for drying habits of a monocentric mind that would hold its universe together with guiltmaking sermons. Hellenism, however, brings the tradition of the unconscious imagination; Greek polytheistic complexity bespeaks our complicated and unknown psychic situations. Hellenism furthers revival by offering wider space and another sort of blessing to the full range of images, feelings, and peculiar moralities that are our actual psychic natures. They need no deliverance from evil if they are not imagined to be evil in the first place.

If in our disintegration we cannot put all our bits into one monotheistic ego psychology, or cannot delude ourselves with the progressive futurism or the natural primitivism that once worked so well, and if we need a complexity to match our sophistication, then we turn to Greece. "No other mythology known to us—developed or primitive, ancient or modern—is marked by quite the same complexity and systematic quality as the Greek."[64] Greece provides a polycentric pattern of the most richly elaborated polytheism of all cultures,[65] and so is able to hold the chaos of the secondary personalities and autonomous impulses of a field, a time, or an individual. This fantastic variety offers the psyche manifold fantasies for reflecting its many possibilities.

Behind and within all Greek culture—in art, thought, and action—is its mythical polycentric background. This was the psychic imaginal world from which came the "glory that was Greece." This mythical background was perhaps less bound to ritual and actual religious cults than were the mythologies of other high cultures. In other words, Greek myth serves less specifically as a religion and more generally as a psychology, working in the soul as both the stimulus and the differentiated container for the extraordinary psychic richness of ancient Greece.

But the "Greece" to which we turn is not literal; it includes all periods from Minoan to Hellenistic, all localities from Asia Minor to Sicily. This "Greece" refers to a historical and geographical *psychic* region, a fantasy or mythic Greece, an inner Greece of the mind which is only indirectly connected with actual geography and actual history—so that these then become devalued. " . . . until the age of Romanticism, Greece was no more than a museum inhabited by people beyond contempt."[66]

Petrarch, who in the fourteenth century did more than anyone to revive the literature of antiquity, could not read Greek. Winckelmann in the eighteenth century, who did more than anyone to revive classicism and who invented the modern worship of Greece, never set foot there and may never have seen an original major piece of Greek sculpture. Nor did Racine go there, nor Goethe, Hölderlin, Hegel, Heine, Keats, or even Nietzsche. Yet they all reconstituted "Greece" in their works. Byron is the absurd—and fatal—exception. Of course, Greek language and literature was known during those centuries, Socrates was worshipped, statuary, architecture and metrics copied, but few went to the empirical Greece and rarely did anyone even go to the original Greek texts. It was the "emotion charged image of Greece" that held sway.[67] And this image has maintained its charge of emotion by means of *a continuing body of myths* (the "Greek myths" and the metaphor "Greece"), persisting in consciousness from post-Hellenic times until today.

"Greece" persists as an inscape rather than a landscape, a metaphor for the imaginal realm in which the archetypes as Gods have been placed. We may therefore read all the documents and fragments of myth left from antiquity also as accounts or witnesses of the imaginal. Archeology becomes archetypology, pointing less to a literal history than to eternal actualities of the imagination, speaking to us of what is going on now in psychic reality.

The return to Greece is neither to a historical time in the past nor to an imaginary time, a utopian Golden Age that was or may come again. Instead "Greece" offers us a chance to revision our souls and psychology by means of imaginal places and persons rather than historical dates and people, a precision of space rather than time. We move out of temporal thinking and historicity altogether, to an imaginal region, a differentiated archipelago of locations, *where* the Gods *are* and not *when* they were or will be.

Quarrels may arise between Greece as fact and as fancy, since historical and literary scholarship traditionally views its Greece literally, each generation of scholars delighting in seeing through the fanciful interpretation of the facts perpetrated by the generation preceding. Indeed, it may be said that the inner Greece of the imagination affects the perspectives of classical scholarship—a field so engrossed in the buried, the broken, the remnant, in unknown roots and origins, in myths and Gods, that it is especially subject to the influence of the archetypes in the arrangement and intepretation of its "facts." The Gods seem to do battle in this very field, and owing to that archetypal passion the dead languages, which have a hard time to prove rationally their relevance for today, are kept vital by the psyche itself because of their importance for the imagination.

We return to Greece in order to rediscover the archetypes of our mind and of our culture.[68] Fantasy returns there to become archetypal. By stepping back into the mythic, into what is nonfactual and nonhistorical, the psyche can reimagine its factual, historical predicaments from another vantage point. Greece becomes the multiple magnifying mirror in which the psyche can recognize its persons and processes in configurations which are larger than life but which bear on the life of our secondary personalities.

Personifying and the Polytheistic Psyche

Now having reviewed personifying and the contentions it has prompted, in the history of Western consciousness, we can examine it more psychologically, asking such questions as: What is personifying's deepest service to the soul? As an activity so closely associated with psychopathology, what special twist of vision does it give the soul about itself? And if personifying is so spontaneous, so basic to understanding and loving, why have we abandoned it? Where can we find it now in our lives?

The starting point for some of our answers lies in psychopathology, in the phenomenon of psychic multiplicity where personifying appears spontaneously. Multiplication of persons occurs in two kinds of clinical conditions. First, it may happen when the importance of any single individual becomes so overwhelming to a patient that he must split the individual's image, multiplying it into more manageable parts. The patient then has two doctors, or more, with the same name (or several names for the same doctor), two or more beloveds or dead spouses, or even two or more selves. In this way personifying is protective; it prevents an unbearable concentration of numinous power in any single figure.[69]

Second, multiplication of persons may be used as a therapeutic tool in order to bring home the realization that "the ego complex is not the only complex in the psyche."[70] By actively imagining the psyche into multiple persons, we prevent the ego from identifying with each and every figure in a dream and fantasy, each and every impulse and voice. For the ego is not the whole psyche, only one member of a commune. Therapy works through the paradox of admitting that all figures and feelings of the psyche are wholly "mine," while at the same time recognizing that these figures and feelings are free of my control and identity, not "mine" at all.

Personifying helps place subjective experiences "out there"; thereby we can devise protections against them and relations with them. Through multiplicity we become internally more separated; we become aware of distinct parts. Even should unity of personality be an aim, "only separated things can unite,"[71] as we learn from the old alchemical psychologists. Separation comes first. It is a way of gaining distance. This *separatio* (in the language of alchemy) offers internal detachment, as if there were now more interior space for movement and for placing events, where before there was a conglomerate adhesion of parts or a monolithic identification with each and all, a sense of being stuck in one's problem.

Essential to this internal separation is naming the personalities;[72] as if only by naming the animals in Eden could Adam become who he was. Through naming, they became *they,* and Adam could now recognize and be separate from each of their characters. His leonine, wolfish, and apelike aspects were no longer him, or his, but "out there" sharing the same garden. By objectifying in this personified manner, we can be spared other objective methods which psychology employs for similar purposes. Naming with images and metaphors has an advantage over naming with concepts, for personified namings never become mere dead tools. Images and metaphors present themselves always as living psychic subjects with which I am obliged to be in relation. They keep me aware of the power of the words I work with, whereas concepts tend to delude me into nominalism.

Whether personifying occurs in a patient as a protection or in a therapist as a means of making separations, its purpose is the same: *to save the diversity and autonomy of the psyche from domination by any single power,* whether this domination be by a figure of archetypal awe in one's surroundings or by one's own egomania. Personifying is the soul's answer to egocentricity.

Besides its clinical appearance, personifying happens with each of us, every night, in dreams. The dream is the best model of the actual psyche, because it shows various styles of consciousness co-present in one scene. These styles are embodied in persons who are embroiled with each other. So psychologists say: dreams show you your conflicts. But conflicts presuppose wishes, viewpoints, whole styles of personality different from the ego-complex. These we see in the dream's drama, which is also a critique of the ego-complex from the viewpoints of the other members of the troupe. The secondary personalities in waking life usually find their way to criticize the ego's rule only through symptomatic interferences (psychopathologies), but in dreams they turn the tables and show the ego its limitations.

Each of these dream persons influences the habitual personality which we too, as did Jung, call "personality Number One."[73] Number One usually rules the day world. Number One is rather responsible, continuous, and socially recognized; when he looks in the mirror, he sees the same familiar body. The secondary personalities are apt to be fragmentary, intermittent, inconsistent, usually without social sanction. The dream is the mirror where they show themselves, and their bodies have many surprising levels of reality. As Number One, we have one name, one vote, one social security number, even though our complete psychic reality is multiple and may be fragmented. We sense these other persons and call them "roles"—mother, mistress, daughter, witch, crone, nurse, wife, child, nymph, innkeeper, slave, queen, whore, dancer, sibyl, muse. But can there be roles without persons to play them? To call them roles and games is itself a game by which Number One may deny the autonomy of these persons and keep them all under his control.

The many personalities of the night world infuse themselves into the attitudes that dominate our daily lives. We can perceive a preview of this infusing process when a specific figure appears frequently in dreams. A fantasy figure, by becoming a nightly companion, begins to affect my consciousness as would a companion with whom I lived during the day. As Jung says: "The activity of such figures very often has an anticipatory character; something that the dreamer himself will do later is now being done in advance."[74]

To define my person by my waking state neglects these figures and their influences. I then become tyrannical, reflecting the jealous monotheism of Number One, who will not recognize the existence of independent partial personalities, and through this denial places them outside in the world, where the internal influences of complexes now become paranoid fears of invasions by enemies. On the one hand, we have individual insanity; on the other, insane collective projections upon other people, whole races and nations.

If I let myself be defined as well by the little people of dreams, I am free of self-tyranny. For this reason dreams are crucial in any therapy of depth, any therapy that would make soul and not only build ego. Dreams are important to the soul—not for the messages the ego takes from them, not for the recovered memories or the revelations; what does seem to matter to the soul is the nightly encounter with a plurality of shades in an underworld, as if dreams prepared for death, the freeing of the soul from its identity with the ego and the waking state. It has often been said that in dreams the soul "wanders," which means not literal walking through the world, but leaving the confines of the ego's concerns. In dreams the fragmentation into parts is held together by scenes and woven into stories. What we learn from dreams is what psychic nature really is—the nature of psychic reality: not I, but we; not one, but many. Not monotheistic consciousness looking down from its mountain, but polytheistic consciousness wandering all over the place, in the vales and along rivers, in the woods, the sky, and under the earth.

By employing the dream as model of psychic actuality, and by conceiving a theory of personality based upon the dream, we are imagining the psyche's basic structure to be *an inscape of personified images*. The full consequences of this structure imply that the psyche presents its own imaginal dimensions, operates freely without words, and is constituted of multiple personalities. We can describe the psyche as a polycentric realm of nonverbal, nonspatial images.

Myth offers the same kind of world. It too is polycentric, with innumerable personifications in imaginal space. Just as dream images are

not mere words in disguise—how rarely we dream in words or texts,
hear or read in our dreams—so the ancient personifications of myths
are not concepts in disguise. The healing dream is an Asklepian ritual
of cure through sleeping within the temple precinct. It required in
ancient times being touched by the God in person, or in his snake or
dog form.[75] The cure was the God's presence in person, and healing did
not require translation of images into concepts, dog into "instinct." Or,
as another example, the God Pan aroused panic when he appeared at
midday or in one of his nightmare forms.[76] Pan was not the concept
"panic" personified, for he was seen to be in headlong panic himself.
The person of Pan was witnessed in the state of panic before the concept
"panic" was born. Pan and his panic, Asklepios and his healing appear
simultaneously; the God is not a later conceptualization or allegory of
the affect. So the figures appearing on Greek vases and named Fate,
Death, Old Age, for instance, are not words depicted as persons, anthropomorphic acts of personification. These figures are imaginal statements recognizing the personal nature of the word, and the captions
stress that in the mythic perspective words too are persons. These
persons continue to appear in our dreams. Nymphs and sirens, heroes
and demons, priapic satyrs, monsters, talking animals, are not only on
the Grecian urn; they riot through our dreams in contemporary dress.
So do the strident clashes of opposing Gods and Goddesses, and the
tragedies they create, appear in the complexes of our dreams.

When a complex is imagined as a distinctly separated entity, a full
"person," equal to my notion of ego in intentions, mood, and willfulness, then my relations to my complexes will be as in a dream where
they are no more or less real than the dream "I." When the complex
is fully personified, I can perceive its specific qualities and yield to it
the specific respect it requires. In Lou Salomé's sense, I am now able
to love it. What was once an affect, a symptom, an obsession, is now
a figure with whom I can talk. In Jung's sense we are reversing history
in our souls, for by personifying I restore to the disease its God and give
the God its due. "To serve a mania is detestable and undignified, but
to serve a God is full of meaning."[77]

According to Jung, this God must be experienced as a personification, which is an "essential precondition" for the idea of a God.[78]
Through personifying, the alien God in an intrusive complex can find
understanding in Dilthey's sense. This understanding can change the
very being of a complex, enabling it to move into psychological reality.
The hallucinated animisms of insanity may now be seen as attempts at
reconstructing, in Unamuno's sense, a loving and pitying cosmos, at-

tempts at reestablishing a feeling connection with the immutable personifications who govern all life, always.

But I must insist again that *this movement of consciousness into
psychological reality is experienced at first as pathological;* things fall
apart as the one becomes many. Recognition of the multiple persons of
the psyche is akin to the experience of multiple personality. Personifying means polycentricity, implicating us in a revolution of consciousness—from monotheistic to polytheistic. It will feel like breakdown and
regression. We are now in the place of old Kronos who swallowed all
his children, or the old Fathers of the Church who "took prisoner every
thought for Christ."[79] The rock crumbles; there is rebellion from within
and below.

Clinically, this polycentricity would be condemned as schizoid fragmentation, demonstrating the ambivalence of a center that cannot hold.
But mythically we might look for a God in the disease, perhaps
Hermes-Mercury or the Trickster. For schizoid polycentricity is a style
of consciousness and not only a disease; and this style thrives in plural
meanings, in cryptic double-talk, in escaping definitions, in not taking
heroic committed stances, in ambisexuality, in psychically detached
and separated body parts.

Or this style of consciousness could be given another clinical name:
hysteria.[80] Then we might look for Dionysus and his community, where
self-division, dismemberment, and a flowing multiplicity belong to a
mythical pattern. Again, consciousness is not heroic and fixed to one
point, but seeps as if through mystical participation in a processional
of personifications, interfused, enthusiastic, suggestible, labile. Whether
schizoid and Mercurial, whether hysterical and Dionysian, there are
archetypal patterns at work, Gods affecting our styles of consciousness.

Archetypes or Gods?

By considering the personified archetypes as Gods, they become more
than constitutional propensities and instinctual patterns of behavior,
more than ordering structures of the psyche, the ground of its images
and vital organs of its functions. They become now recognizable as
persons, each with styles of consciousness, or in Jung's language, "typical modes of apprehension."[81] They present themselves each as a guiding spirit *(spiritus rector)* with ethical positions, instinctual reactions,
modes of thought and speech, and claims upon feeling. These persons,
by governing my complexes, govern my life. My life is a diversity of
relationships with them. As *persons* they do not differ from the Gods,

heroes, and daemons; only as *concepts* in the abstractions of a science can we distinguish them from the figures of myth and cult. Man invents concepts, his tools for grasping, sorting and taking apart. But he does not invent Gods and daemons, from whom too, in the last instance, as structures of consciousness, concepts can be derived. We can replace concepts, even dispense with them altogether, but the archetypal persons are vital organs, and "there is no 'rational' substitute for the archetype any more than there is for the cerebellum or the kidneys."[82] They are indispensable to the life of the psyche just as the Gods sustain the universe. "All ages before us have believed in gods of some form or other. Only an unparalleled impoverishment of symbolism could enable us to rediscover gods as psychic factors, that is, as archetypes of the unconscious."[83]

But today that is precisely where we do discover the Gods—in the unconscious psyche—and because of this unconsciousness we are unable to distinguish Gods from archetypes, or archetypes from heroes and daemons.[84] Therefore, our descriptions of the archetypes and the classical descriptions of the Gods, heroes, and daemons have to be analogous. In both descriptions we run into the same style of question: Where are they located? Are they knowable—if so by what means, and how can we "prove" their existence? What is their origin? How many are there, and do they form hierarchies and subclasses? Do they change or age or go through history? What sort of "body" do they have? How soon a psychology of archetypes begins to sound like a mythology of Gods! How necessary it is to speak of both in metaphorical language—[85]

Whenever we try to define conceptually either a God or an archetype we find that neither can be grasped adequately by conceptual means. As metaphysical principles they elude our knowledge. The Greeks learned about their Gods through unwritten mythology. We learn about our archetypes through lived psychology. Both can be grasped best as persons.

Today we are so unconscious of these persons that we call their realm the unconscious. Once they were the people of the imagination, as the unconscious was once the imaginal realm of *memoria*. But now we cannot distinguish between fancy and fantasy, between imaginary, imaginative, and imaginal.[86] And we struggle in vain with the conceptual semantics of allegory, metaphor, model, paradigm, and symbol. Wavering between delusion and prophecy, between visions and illusions, we cannot discriminate among the apparitions themselves. Although these aspects of the imaginal are defined in the textbooks of rhetoric and psychiatry, the definitions have not affected the tissue of experience in which these imaginal events remain webbed together. What was once better known by Neoplatonists, Gnostics, Kabbalists, and by alchemists—and perhaps too by the ordinary believer in his circle of imagery and calendar of saints—all of whom had intricate means of distinguishing the persons of the imaginal and discerning the spirits, is known to us no longer. Of course the Gods of mythology become "psychic factors," and of course the archetypes of psychology become mythological Gods.

Our situation is that we cannot perceive differences between kinds of imaginary voyages. We are at a loss in sorting the fish hauled in by contemporary adventurers. How do we classify the denizens of the deep soul? And the adventurers themselves—are they visionary poets of the new Aquarian age or junkies? Are they exploring or drowning in the deeps of an uncharted imagination—or only drowning when human voices wake them and they drown? Is this how stout Cortez and Captain Cook would appear today, mapping an undiscovered world of interior geography, an Atlantis below the surface? Why are reports of these contemporary voyagers always in the language of "likeness"; not reports of the marine biologist, Linnaean in systems of names, measurements, behaviors. They come back from their trips having suffered a sea-change in language; they now speak analogically, metaphorically, telling us what it is "like." Have they been with mermaids, hallucinating, because what was seen is private, seen by no one else, not predictable, repeatable at will, only I alone? Yet what is this notion of "I alone"; why must the idea of reality be correlated with public repeatability, controlled by an ego of will power; and what are hallucinations? Is it a question of giving images too much belief and reality, or rather not enough, so that they must force their reality upon us? If we do not give faith to them, then the spontaneous image, the unique vision and still small voice—those wicks to which the flame of each individual life clings—will always seem unreliable fantasies. We need an imaginal ego that is at home in the imaginal realm, an ego that can undertake *the major task now confronting psychology:* the differentiation of the imaginal, discovering its laws, its configurations and moods of discourse, its psychological necessities. Until we know these laws and necessities we are caught in calling its activities "pathology," thereby condemning the imagination to sickness and the persons of it to making their appearances mainly through pathological manifestations. But this major psychological task of differentiating the imaginal begins only when we allow it to speak as it appears, as personified. Personifying is thus both a way of psychological experience and a method for grasping and ordering that experience.

Modern Disciplines of the Imagination

The struggle to differentiate the imaginal in modern times begins in 1916 with Jung's "active imagination," his method of engaging the persons of the psyche in direct dialogue. Since then there have been others in psychotherapy pursuing this path: for example, the techniques initiated by Desoille, Leuner, Assagioli, and Gerard,[87] and the approach of Gestalt psychology to the dream. The virtue of these disciplines is that they encourage exploration of the interior and give recognition to our many parts.

However, the difficulty in all methods of actively engaging the imagination is, Who is doing the activity? When it is the ego personality in its usual stance, then the autonomy of the field it enters becomes disturbed by this intrusion. The figures of the imaginal psyche have to react in accordance with the ego's needs and patterns. Their responses become ego-linked; they lose their autonomy, or they can show it only by disappearing. When Hercules went into the underworld, he forced the God Hades to flee from his throne after having wounded him in the shoulder. Hercules entered the realm of the shades in order to take something, and while he was there he wrestled, he drew his sword, he slaughtered, and was confused about the reality of images. Each of us tends to be Hercules in ego when we begin to engage imaginal figures.

Gestalt psychology seems to circumvent this obstacle by approaching all figures through empathy. One feels oneself into each of the persons and scenes in a dream or fantasy, acknowledging that yes, this too is mine. By my identifying with their feelings they become my feelings, thereby assigning the autonomous images *that are not mine* straight to the ego. Although this approach helps overcome fear of images and estrangement from them, its ultimate aim is their depotentiation and the strengthening of the feeling-ego.

Other approaches usually suggest a plan for exploring the "inner world." There are descents to caverns or returns to childhood scenes, an internal guide with prearranged stops on a tour, ways of overcoming blocks and shocks, and the quiet counsel of the therapist who has been there before. This way confines us again in the authoritarianism—albeit gentle and sophisticated—of a spiritual discipline. We are again locked into an ego of will and reason which manages a program for the psyche from a superior viewpoint, governing and guiding imaginal experience.

The aim is less the realization of the images (as in an art, say) than it is the realization of the personality performing the exercise, i.e., the ego.

The therapeutic emphasis upon training the personality through confrontation with its images prejudges the imaginal from the start. The very idea that the imagination is a wild, fearsome jungle or madhouse which needs a practiced hand to keep it in order confines us in a heroic fantasy, just as the idea that the imagination is a deep irrational mystery requiring sagacious counsel confines us in a wise-old-sage fantasy. Our approach to imagining is predetermined by our idea of it. Disciplines of the imagination turn into a disciplining of the images. Insidiously we become biased against the world we wish to enter. And active imagination becomes subverted into mind control, gaining knowledge, strength, and wisdom at the expense of the images of the soul.

I cannot raise my voice strongly enough against these methods. In them lies the abuse of the soul's first freedom—the freedom to imagine. This is the source of our peculiar individualness and of our art, science, and culture. The autonomy of fantasy is the soul's last refuge of dignity, its guarantor against all oppressions; it alone we can take with us into the barracks behind the barbed wire. If we are willing to accept internal controls upon the imagination, we will have succumbed already in soul to the same authoritarianism that would dominate the body politic. The connection between submission to technical manipulation of imagination and submission to external controls is subtle, but it is real. Transcendental meditation systems, Skinnerian ideas of control, and Siberia are closer to one another than we may realize, and they come closer to each of us when we neglect the importance of the freedom and dignity of fantasy.

We sin against the imagination whenever we ask an image for its meaning, requiring that images be translated into concepts. The coiled snake in the corner cannot be translated into my fear, my sexuality, or my mother-complex without killing the snake. We do not hear music, touch sculpture, or read stories with meaning in mind, but for the sake of the imagination. Though art may hide a multitude of psychological ignorances, at least it does not ask images what they mean. Interpretations and even amplifications of images, including the whole analytical kit of symbolic dictionaries and ethnological parallels, too often become instruments of allegory. Rather than vivifying the imagination by connecting our conceptual intellects with the images of dreams and fantasies, they exchange the image for a commentary on it or digest of it. And these interpretations forget too that they are themselves fantasies induced by the image, no more meaningful than the image itself.

Discipline of the imagination does not have to become a program for the imagination. The alchemical psychologists worked with intense discipline, with ethical devotion to their work, careful formulae, and high purposes. Yet the entire alchemical operation is marked by freedom and diversity, with full place for the bizarre and heretical. Each alchemist worked with his images in his own way and none would think that repeatability and conformity of an operation was the main mark of its success. We learn from the alchemical psychologists to let the images work upon the experimenter; we learn to become the object of the work—even an object, or objectified image, of the imagination.

It is therefore less a matter of program than of attitude, of giving over to the images and cultivating them for their sake. The imaginal realm has its own paths of exploration which start with whatever comes to mind—any fantasy or image—much like alchemy, which begins with a primary material called by at least sixty different names. Since it starts anywhere, it can break off anywhere. Fantasy does not need to achieve a goal. It steps around the instructions of spiritual disciplines which require intense focus, choices toward prescribed goals, moral commitments, and strengthening exercises. For the soul this kind of approach can be called a spiritual fallacy, using religious or meditative disciplines as models for working with images. Fantasy work is closer to the arts, to writing and painting and making music, than it is to contemplation and yoga. Imaginative activity is both play and work, entering and being entered, and as the images gain in substance and independence the ego's strength and autocracy tends to dissolve. But ego dissolution does not mean disorder, since all fantasy is carried by a deeper, archetypal order. Even the order of the ego comes from its base in archetypal principles of the hero myth. These principles of the imagination that lay out its laws according to mythical persons, themes and patterns, basic elements, spatial qualities and directions, have been described by Jung, by Gaston Bachelard, and more recently by Gilbert Durand and his school, in their work on thematics of the imagination.[88] They have begun charting the natural archetypology of the imaginal.

Exploring the internal psychic world encourages us to become naturalists of the image or portraitists of angels and animals, discriminating the complexes, their features and behaviors, discerning among the little people. But we are not charting the heavens or mapping the wilds for later colonizing, since the differentiations that stand out sharply one day may recede into the underbrush or behind a cloud the next. The extraordinary fact of the imagination is just that it is truly extraordinary; no matter how known, it is always able to surprise, shock, horrify, or break into ravishing beauty. The distinctions we make when exploring it can never be from known vantage points; rather the experience of imagination shatters these vantage points. The best test of authenticity concerning our disciplines of exploring the imaginal is that the habitual ego senses itself at a loss and is unable to identify with the images. They must be alien even while familiar, strangers even if lovers, uncanny although we rely on them. They must have full autonomy, and the ego enters their realm at first as a stalker, then as their pupil, finally as their maintenance man, performing small adjustments, keeping the building in repair, the fires stoked, warming.

This relation with images means giving them full credit; it means restoring fallen idols and cracked icons which have been reformed and counterreformed into pale likenesses of once holy numens. The restoration of the image, however, does not mean literal reinstitution of idolatry but rather restoring the image in our sight—not so much in *what* we see but in the *way* we see it.[88a] It means bringing the imaginal perspective, bringing fantasy, to all that we see. Thus everything is transformed into images of significance, and with that change in view we view ourselves differently; we see that we too are ultimately a composition of images, our person the personification of their life in the soul.

If we set off in this direction, the first hurdle to be taken is psychological. We can do little exploration of the imaginal until we have surmounted our own egocentricity, that capital *I* appearing in the monotheism of consciousness (Jung), in monotheistic science and metaphysics,[89] and in the root of all: the monotheism of Christian humanism with its tolerance for but one historical, unique divine personification. The egocentric psyche with its one eye fixed on wholes and unities may grudgingly admit personifying as a figure of speech, but never that the imaginal realm and its persons are actual presences and true powers.

We are driven, therefore, to learn something from psychopathology, taking imaginal persons as seriously (if not as literalistically) as does someone with his delusions or hallucination. Then our idea of personifying would include its full "pathological" implications. This means nothing less than dethroning the dominant fantasy ruling our view of the world as ultimately a unity—that real meaning, real beauty and truth require a unified vision. It also means that we would abandon a notion of our personality as ultimately a unity of self. Instead of trying to cure pathological fragmentation wherever it appears, we would let the content of this fantasy cure consciousness of its obsession with unity. By absorbing the plural viewpoint of "splinter psyches" into our consciousness, there would be a new connection with multiplicity and we would no longer need to call it disconnected schizoid fragmentation. Consciousness, and our notion of consciousness, would reflect a world view that is diverse and unsettled.

Not merely would our psychological ideas about self, consciousness, and even God change shape; not merely would precise differentiation of qualities replace the measurement of quantities as the method of psychological knowing; but we would find ourselves no longer alone in our subjectivity. Our possessive notion of ownness, our privative notion of privacy—the private self—indeed the very notion of the unit as basis for the fantasy of ourselves, would no longer provide the model on which our house of splinters is built. All would depart together: unity and uniqueness, identity, integration and integrity as simplicity, and individuality as undividedness. And with the departing dominant unitary fantasy would go as well its dominant emotion: loneliness.

For the house the psyche actually inhabits is a compound of connecting corridors, multi-leveled, with windows everywhere and with large ongoing extensions "under construction," and sudden dead ends and holes in the floorboards; and this house is filled already with occupants, other voices in other rooms, reflecting nature alive, echoing again the Great God Pan alive, a pantheism rekindled by the psyche's belief in its personified images. Here is space to receive the mass immigration, the resurrection of the repressed, as the Angels and Archons, Daemons and Nymphs, Powers and Substances, Virtues and Vices, released from the mental reservations that restrain such primitivenesses and from the conceptual prisons of small-letter descriptions, now return to enter again into the commerce of our daily lives.

Anima

This vision cannot be enacted unless archetypal persons strike us as utterly real. To experience imaginal reality, a psychic function—the specific function of the imaginative soul—must be active. This soul person is the person of our moods, self-reflections, and reveries, of our sensuous longing beyond the sensately concrete, the spinner of fantasy who is the personification of all unknown psychic capacities that lie waiting, drawing us seductively, uncannily inward to the dark of the uncut forest and the deeps below the waves. Anima means both psyche and soul, and we meet her in her numerous embodiments as soul of waters without whom we dry, as soul of vegetation who greens our hope or blights with symptoms, as Lady of the Beasts riding our passions.

She is father's daughter and mother's daughter, and my sister, my soul. She is also a worrying succubus drawing off our life's juice, a harpy with talons, a cold white wraith with mad addictions—but a nurse as well, and a serving maid, a Cinderella nymphet, vague with no history, a *tabula rasa* waiting for the word. And she is also the Sophia of wisdom, the Maria of compassion, the Persephone of destruction, compelling Necessity and Fate, and the Muse.

The multiplicity of her forms in fictions and lives, and the intensely personified and intensely subjectified reality of her nature, bespeak a world into which she calls and over which she rules. Vico, Cassirer, and Otto have connected personifying and the mythical mode; Dilthey and Unamuno have connected personifying with understanding and love. Lou Salomé personified these ideas to Freud, and Jung specified anima as the personification of the unconscious.

As the latter, anima has a series of meanings.[90] First, (a) she is the personification of our unconsciousness—our stupidities, follies, intractable problems. Then (b) she is a particular personification appearing in a particular moment—call girl, shopgirl, schoolgirl—who presents a precise image of the current emotions of the soul. She is also (c) the feeling of personal interiority. She brings the sense of having an interior life, changing events into experience that means "me." She makes possible the inner ground of faith in myself as a person, giving the conviction that what happens matters to the soul and that one's existence is personal and important.[91] She thus (d) personalizes existence. Anima, moreover, is (e) that person by means of whom we are initiated into imaginal understanding, who makes possible experiencing through images, for she embodies the reflective, reactive, mirroring activity of consciousness. Functionally anima works as that complex which connects our usual consciousness with imagination by provoking desire or clouding us with fantasies and reveries, or deepening our reflection. She is both bridge to the imaginal and also the other side, personifying the imagination of the soul. Anima is psyche personified, as Psyche in the ancient story of her by Apuleius personified the soul.

So the movement into psychological existence proceeds through her in one form or another. The movement through the constructed world of concepts and dead things into an animistic, subjective, mythical consciousness, where fantasy is alive in a world alive and means "me," follows anima. She teaches personifying, and the very first lesson of her teaching is the reality of her independent personality over and against the habitual modes of experiencing with which we are so identified that they are called ego, I. The second lesson is love; she comes to life through love and insists on it, just as Psyche in the old tale is paired forever with Eros.[92]

Perhaps the loving comes first. Perhaps only through love is it possible to recognize the *person* of the soul. And this connection between love and psyche means a love for everything psychological, every symptom or habit, finding place for it within the heart of imagination, finding a mythical person who is its supportive ground. The connection between love and psyche means as well bringing a psychological eye to all of love's manifestations—that all its mad and deviate cravings seek ultimately the connection with psyche.

Whether we conceive of this interior person as Anima or as an Angel, a Daemon, a Genius, or a Paredros, or one of the personified souls in the traditions of ancient China and Egypt, this figure is indispensable to the notion of human personality. Some traditions, in fact, have asserted that an individual without his soul figure is not a human being. Such a one has lost soul.

Depersonalization

Clinically, loss of soul is spoken of as "depersonalization,"[93] a condition in which the "personal coefficient" standing behind the ego and its relation with self and world is suddenly absent. All particular functions of ego-consciousness operate as before; associating, remembering, perceiving, feeling, and thinking are unimpaired. But one's conviction in oneself as a person and the sense of reality of the world have departed. Everything and oneself become automatic, unreal, emptied out. The sense of "me-ness," of emotional importance, has vanished, and now the world is as if behind glass; depth perspective no longer seems to function as near and far merge into flatland.

Depersonalization is not limited to any psychiatric condition. It appears in organic brain diseases and toxic states, in epilepsy, melancholia, and hysteria; in schizophrenic and manic-depressive psychoses, in the neuroses; and it happens to normal human beings. It may occur for but a moment or two, or last as a chronic complaint; it can happen in puberty or in old age. Depersonalization belongs not to a syndrome but to a person—or to the absence of the sense of person.

As we might expect, this same word "depersonalization" refers to a "philosophy of the universe, which no longer regards natural forces as manifestations of supernatural agents or Gods."[94] As the same word applies to both worlds, "in here" and "out there," so the same factor, anima, animates the world (animism) and gives the sense of personality, turning events into experiences that mean "me." For clinical depersonalization demonstrates that another factor than ego, a "personal coefficient" as it has been termed, must come into play for us to experience the reality of self and world. As Jung describes it,

> Anima is a factor in the proper sense of the word. Man cannot make it; on the contrary, it is always the *a priori* element in his moods, reactions, impulses, and whatever else is spontaneous in psychic life. It is something that lives of itself, that makes us live; it is the life behind consciousness that cannot be completely integrated with it, but from which, on the contrary, consciousness arises.[95]

Anima here is not a projection but the projector. Our consciousness is the result of her prior psychic life. Anima thus becomes the primordial carrier of psyche, the archetype of psyche itself, and the crucial factor in the psychological calling and in any psychology that would base itself upon the psyche as it is actually experienced.

The essence of her work as "factor" is her person-making. The soul makes images in personified form; the personal coefficient works spontaneously through personal feelings and personified images. This has long been recognized—in reverse—by our anti-imaginal, antipersonifying tradition which attempted to keep control over the spontaneity and natural polytheism of soul by controlling the use of images. The Fathers of the Church, for instance, assembled in 787 at the second council of Nicaea, declared that "the composition of religious imagery is not left to the initiative of artists, but is formed upon principles laid down by the Catholic Church and by religious tradition."[96] Painters were to be mere technicians following the instructions of Church officials regarding subject, selection, and arrangement of the images. This method obtained in principle and in general for centuries.

But as the art historian E. H. Gombrich has observed, this devious lady soul slipped through the grasp of her captors. Personified images continued to appear.

> . . . We tend to take it for granted rather than to ask questions about this extraordinary predominately feminine population which greets us from the porches of cathedrals, crowds around our public monuments, marks our coins and our banknotes, and turns up in our cartoons and our posters; these females variously attired, of course, came to life on the mediaeval stage; they greeted the Prince on his entry into a city, they were invoked in innumerable speeches, they quarrelled or embraced in endless epics where they struggled for the soul of the hero or set the action going. . . .[97]

And she went on making public appearances in those marvellous fictional characters of novels, in paintings of the nude and in society portraits, and on the stage; there is still a glamorous flicker of her in the films. But now our novels have become depopulated, our monuments and canvases are abstractions and our buildings stripped clean of carvings. Even pornography has replaced the exciting personified image with clippings of depersonalized organs.

Personalizing and Personalism

If personifying is so basic to our loving and understanding, so closely involved with the soul and our experiencing of the vitality and reality of ourselves and the world, where can we discover it happening today in our lives? Where are the angels and demons and archetypal configurations, now that these persons have been refused admittance to the theological, natural, and psychological worlds?

Of course we find the missing persons in psychopathology. There they are at least recognized as authentic even if they are identified with sickness. But personifying appears mainly today in personalizing—the magnification of personal life—which is perhaps a sickness disguised as health. Personifying, having been dismissed from consciousness, returns surreptitiously as personalizing.

An axiom of depth psychology asserts that what is not admitted into awareness irrupts in ungainly, obsessive, literalistic ways, affecting consciousness with precisely the qualities it strives to exclude. Personifying not allowed as a metaphorical vision returns in concrete form: we seize upon people, we cling to other persons. They become invested with repressed images so that they grow in importance, become idealized, idolized, while the psyche finds itself more fascinated, more glued and stuck to these concrete individuals than it would have been to the metaphorical persons that are at the root of the projection onto people. Without metaphorical persons, we are forced into desperate clutching literalisms.

Thus we are more obsessive and enslaved by the sublimated forms of culture than by the original metaphors. We are more pornographically sexualized than our sexuality, more aggressively power-driven than our ambition, more hungry and dependent than our needs, more masochistically victimized than our suffering requires. The literalisms into which we constrict our drives hold us faster than do the drives themselves. The obsessive literalism of our belief in other people holds us tighter than any personified totem or fetish. How quick others are to become angels or demons, nymphs or heroes; how we expect—how they disappoint! Others carry our souls and become our soul figures, to the final consequence that without these idols we fall into the despair of loneliness and turn to suicide.

By our use of them to keep ourselves alive, other persons begin to assume the place of fetishes and totems, becoming keepers of our lives. Through this worship of the personal, personal relationships have become the place where the divine is to be found, so the new theology asserts. The very condition that modern rational consciousness would dissuade us from—personifying—returns in our relationships, creating an animistic world of personified idols. Of course these archetypally loaded relationships break down, of course they require constant propitiatory attention, of course we must turn to priests of this cult (therapists and counselors) for instruction concerning the right ritual for relation to persons. For persons are no longer just human beings; they have been dehumanized by being divinized. Our weekends of encounter, our group sessions and sensitivity workshops, are religious phenomena: they attest to where the divine persons now reside—in human beings.

While unquestioningly accepting the convention that personifying is pathological, we spoil our actual friendships, marriages, loves, and families by looking to people for redemption. We seek salvation in personal encounters, personal relations, personal solutions. Human persons are the contemporary shrines and statues where personifying is lodged. The neighbor's nod is the numen. Our cult worships or propitiates actual people—the family, the beloved, the circle of encounters—while ignoring the persons of the psyche who compose the soul and upon whom the soul depends.

The worship of the personal appears even in philosophy, where it is called "personalism." This emerged as an intellectual force with the decline of personifying. It became basic to philosophers who held the person to be the ultimate ground of being, and it reached its fullest flower as a philosophical fantasy in the post-Kantian Protestant consciousness of Germany, Britain, and the United States, with a vigorous offshoot nourished by Christian thought in France. Emmanuel Mounier, the French personalist (1905–1950), said quite simply: "The personal is the mode of existence proper to man."[98] His American contemporary E. S. Brightman raised the personal principle even higher, saying: "Personalism is the view that personality of self is the first right principle which unites and explains all other first principles."[99]

Personalism speaks in protest against the new social, biological, and mechanical models of man; it is an appeal of the psyche for help against the crushing impersonalization of the universe. But the alienations from which we suffer cannot be resolved by recharging the individual personality meta-physically. The world out there, just as my inner life, remains depersonified until the personified mode of mythical consciousness revivifies it. The personal may be the first principle and the mode most proper to man, because it bespeaks the personified soul; however, the conviction that this is so depends not on a metaphysical position but on a psychological factor, anima, the state of the soul itself.

The present cult of person in psychology in every one of its manifestations—personality development, personality inventory, personal psychodynamics, research into personal differences and opinions, their fascination as subjects for research—is based upon an ideological literalism: personalism. Psychology has taken the metaphor of personifying and literalized it into an ontology of persons. We have *personalized the soul,* pressing it all into the human being.

Psychology itself is a part of this steady withdrawal of soul into the narrow confines of the human skin. The last stage of this process is shrinking soul to its single and narrowest space, the ego, and thereby swelling this "I" into the inflation called "ego psychology." For ego psychology is what our souls today are left with; whether body-ego, feeling-ego, or individuating-ego, psychology is engaged in ego-making and not soul-making. The field dedicated by its very name to psyche expends its resources in strengthening and developing a phantom which may at any moment fall prey to depersonalization. By identifying the soul and psychological work with the subjective ego and its aims, psychology becomes satanic. For precisely this identification of soul or of personality with the experiencing subject is, according to the visionary psychologist William Blake, the way of Satan.[100]

The "I" has its function, which is expressed by its capitalization. The "I" is legitimately written with a large letter, not because it is the capital person of the psyche, but because it too has a particular mythic part to play in the dramatics of the psyche—as the one personification whose necessary perspective is to take itself as literally real. An ego's specific characteristic, and its specific function, is to represent the literal view: it takes itself and its view for real. Literalism is an ego viewpoint; it means being locked into an ego. Ego psychology results from being trapped by the ego into its perspective: the other characters on the stage are merely characteristics, projections of mine. Only I am literally real.

Our symptoms, however, can save us from this literalism. For this we owe them a great debt, and we shall pay them special respect in the next chapter. Symptoms tell us that we can never take back into our ownership the events caused by the little people of the psyche. Symptoms remind us of the autonomy of the complexes; they refuse to submit to the ego's view of a unified person. Moreover, nothing makes me more certain of my own metaphorical existence—that I too am a personification whose reality depends on something other than my own will and reason—than depersonalization, the symptom which gives me the sense of being an automation, or—in Plato's words[101]—in the hands of the Gods. The mythic perspective toward myself and my existence can begin right in psychopathology: my own person with all its personal passions and experiences can evaporate. It does not depend on "me."

This "me," even most deeply experienced as if from the ground of being, seemingly so unique, so truly my own, is utterly collective. For psyche is not mine, and the statements that express my deepest person, such as: "I love you," "I am afraid," "I promise," are collective universals whose value lies just in their impersonality, that they are said by everyone, everywhere. As collective universals, these statements are archetypally personal, but not literally so.

To speak of *my* anima and *my* soul expresses the personalistic fallacy. Although these archetypal experiences of the personal give salt and substance to my personal individuality, making me feel that there is indeed a soul, this "me-ness" is not mine. To take such experiences literally as mine puts the anima inside me and makes her mine. The more profoundly archetypal my experiences of soul, the more I recognize how they are beyond me, presented to me, a present, a gift, even while they feel my most personal possession. Under the dominion of anima our soulfulness makes us feel unique, special, meant—yet paradoxically this is when we are least individual and most collective. For such experiences derive from the archetype of the personal, making us feel both archetypal and personal at the same instant.

We can sum up with Jung who says: "Man derives his human personality . . . his consciousness of himself as a personality . . . from the influence of quasi-personal archetypes."[102] The anima represents "the personal nature"[103] of these autonomous systems; she is their soul and ours.

Even the size of the "I"—that it can shrink and swell into clinical proportions which we name depression and inflation—is her gift; she gives that grandeur to personality when it is infused with soul. Anima amplifies with beauty, nature, and the alien archaic past—and the pandemonium of the fantastic. This is part of her archetypal role. In her absence we shrivel—no beauty, no nature, no fantasy. Depersonalized, the flavor's gone, the scent, and the salt that keeps things lastingly. But through her imaginal presence in which I play a part, "there is established a psychology of capital letters."[104] Importance mounts. So we gain in grandeur when voices speak to us. This is megalomania, *la folie de grandeur,* only when we take it literally rather than "as-if" mine. These voices sometimes shriek and chatter; their silence is worse. Mocking, scorning, warning, still it is to me they turn, me they mean. They come to live in my house—or do I live in their house, my home with them? Without these visitations of the little people, who is there to back me up? There is nobody home but "I." By means of personifications my sense of person becomes more vivid for I carry with me at all times the protection of my *daimones:* the images of dead people who mattered to me, of ancestral figures of my stock, cultural and historical persons of renown and people of fable who provide exemplary images —a wealth of guardians. They guard my fate, guide it, probably *are* it. "Perhaps—who knows," writes Jung, "these eternal images are what men mean by fate."[105] We need this help, for who can carry his fate alone?

The prime factor—and factor means maker—introducing me to these images is the anima. On her depends my faith in the reality of the external world and my faith in myself as a person. Reality of world and self depends upon the faith of this soul in me. No longer is it a question of whether I believe in soul, but whether soul believes in me, grants me the capacity to have faith in it, in psychic reality.

Psychological Faith

The work of soul-making is concerned essentially with the evocation of psychological faith, the faith arising from the psyche which shows as faith in the reality of the soul. Since psyche is primarily image and image always psyche, this faith manifests itself in the belief in images: it is "idolatrous," heretical to the imageless monotheisms of metaphysics and theology. Psychological faith begins in the *love of images,* and it flows mainly through the shapes of persons in reveries, fantasies, reflections, and imaginations. Their increasing vivification gives one an increasing conviction of having, and then of being, an interior reality of deep significance transcending one's personal life.

Psychological faith is reflected in an ego that gives credit to images and turns to them in its darkness. Its trust is in the imagination as the only uncontrovertible reality, directly presented, immediately felt.

Trust in the imaginal and trust in soul go hand in hand, as depth psychologists have recognized.[106] The reverse is also true: when imagination is not evoked, there is a deep-seated lack of confidence to imagine fantasies in regard to one's problems and to be free of the ego's literalizations, its sense of being trapped in "reality." Lack of psychological faith is compensated by exaggerated personalizing, a fantastic need for people (and a need for fantastic people), of which transference on the analyst is only one manifestation.

Soul-making, as work on anima through images, offers a way of resolving the dependencies of transference. For it is not the therapist or any actual person whatever who is the keeper of my soul beyond all betrayals, but the archetypal persons of the Gods to whom the anima acts as bridge. The shaping of her amorphous moods, sulphuric passions, bitter resentments, and bubbles of distraction into distinct personalities is the main work of therapeutic analysis or soul-making. Therefore it works in imagination, with imagination, and for imagination. It discovers and forms a personality by disclosing and shaping the multiple soul personalities out of the primary *massa confusa* of arguing voices and pushing demands.

Before we turn to this *massa confusa* in the soul—what we nowadays call its psychopathology—let us recall the main insight of this chapter. Psychology always has the opportunity to see through its main convictions and assumptions. It can bring psychological reflection to itself. It may thus dissolve the literal belief in persons by repersonifying them into metaphors. Then personality may be imagined in a new way: that I am an impersonal person, a metaphor enacting multiple personifications, mimetic to images in the heart that are my fate, and that this soul which projects me has archetypal depths that are alien, inhuman, and impersonal. My so-called personality is a persona through which soul speaks. It is subject to depersonalization and is not mine, but depends altogether upon the gift of belief in myself, a faith given through anima in my worth as carrier of soul. Not I personify, but the anima personifies me, or soul-makes herself through me, giving my life her sense —her intense daydream is my "me-ness"; and "I," a psychic vessel whose existence is a psychic metaphor, an "as-if being," in which every single belief is a literalism except the belief of soul whose faith posits me and makes me possible as a personification of psyche.

Two/Pathologizing or Falling Apart

Ladies and Gentlemen—I am sure you all recognize in your dealings, whether with persons or things, the importance of your starting point. It was the same with psychoanalysis: the course of development through which it passed, and the reception which it has met with, have not been unaffected by the fact that what it began working upon was the symptom, a thing that is more foreign to the ego than anything else in the mind.

FREUD

We shall now be working within an area—psychopathology—that is central to the experience of soul. In this chapter we shall attempt to understand why pathologized events must necessarily be central to soul and therefore must be essential to any psychology that bases itself upon soul. By coming to grips with the perplexities of psychic disorder, symptoms, and suffering, our hope is to gain a new purchase upon the psyche's pathologizing tendency so as to comprehend it from another angle. We shall be attempting to envision pathologizing psychologically.

Our starting point is in the main tradition of depth psychology, for like Freud in the motto above,[1] we begin in the odd, ununderstandable, and alien symptom rather than in the familiar ego, and as in all depth psychology we draw our insights about the familiar from the alien, or as Erik Erikson has put it: "Pathography remains the traditional source of psychoanalytic insight."[2]

The insights of depth psychology derive from souls *in extremis,* the sick, suffering, abnormal, and fantastic conditions of psyche. Our souls in private to ourselves, in close communion with another, and even in public exhibit psychopathologies. Each soul at some time or another demonstrates illusions and depressions, overvalued ideas, manic flights and rages, anxieties, compulsions, and perversions. Perhaps our psychopathology has an intimate connection with our individuality, so that our fear of being what we really are is partly because we fear the psychopathological aspect of individuality. For we are each peculiar; we have symptoms; we fail, and cannot see why we go wrong or even where, despite high hopes and good intentions. We are unable to set matters right, to understand what is taking place or be understood by those who would try. Our minds, feelings, wills, and behaviors deviate from normal ways. Our insights are impotent, or none come at all. Our feelings disappear in apathy; we worry and also don't care. Destruction seeps out of us autonomously and we cannot redeem the broken trusts, hopes, loves.

The study of lives and the care of souls means above all a prolonged encounter with what destroys and is destroyed, with what is broken and hurts—that is, with psychopathology. Between the lines of each biography and in the lines of each face we may read a struggle with alcohol, with suicidal despair, with dreadful anxiety, with lascivious sexual obsessions, cruelties at close quarters, secret hallucinations, or paranoid spiritualisms. Ageing brings loneliness of soul, moments of acute psychic pain, and haunting remembrances as memory disintegrates. The night world in which we dream shows the soul split into antagonisms; night after night we are fearful, aggressive, guilty, and failed.

These are the actualities—the concrete mess of psychological existence as it is phenomenologically, subjectively, and individually—in which I want to set these chapters. Through them, I hope to find some psychological necessity in the pathologizing activity of the soul.

Psychopathology in Medicine and Religion

The very word *pathology* which we use for these troubling experiences demonstrates the role medicine plays in psychology's viewpoint toward the psyche. By far the majority of the specific terms of psychopathology, such as *paranoid, schizoid, psychopathic,* have entered our speech via psychiatric medicine, so that when we think of psychopathology we think immediately of illness.

However, in recent years there have been doubts about the validity of the medical model for depth psychology. It has been said that the peculiar conditions of the soul and the complaints it presents may not be sickness in the medical sense. Nor do these conditions and complaints respond to treatments based on the medical model. Ever since Freud, we have come to recognize that the treatment of psychopathology has required psychological methods to the exclusion of usual medical procedures (physical examination, pharmaceutical prescription, physiological etiologies). In fact, thinking in terms of causes and material substrates as well as prescriptions of any sort about what to do is generally contraindicated in depth psychology. Slowly we have been led to conclude that perhaps these conditions that we have been calling psychopathologies are not true pathologies in the medical sense.

Further, because the psyche has not responded to the medical notion of treatment, psychotherapy has begun to cast out the medical model altogether, including its fundamental idea, pathology. Today psychotherapy seeks to understand the soul's disorders as snarled communication, or as a disrupted social nexus, or as frustrated spiritual fulfillment, and is shifting away from the medical toward other models—linguistic, sociological, and especially religious.

The religious model has an even longer history than the medical model in our attempts to comprehend psychic trouble and usually the two are coupled together or presented as alternatives. We suffer, it has been customary to say, because we are either sick or sinful, and the cure of our suffering calls for either science or faith. But in both cases pathologizing has had negative implications. For both sickness and sin imply that pathologizing is wrong.

In order to approach the psychology of pathology afresh, I am introducing the term *pathologizing* to mean the psyche's autonomous ability to create illness, morbidity, disorder, abnormality, and suffering in any aspect of its behavior and to experience and imagine life through this deformed and afflicted perspective.

We need a fresh start. We have been confined so long by medical and religious analogies that psychology has been unable to approach what are essentially psychological phenomena from a perspective of its own. Possibly pathologized events would not be so wrong were they viewed less from positions borrowed from material medicine and spiritual religion. Here our intention is not to replace either the idea of illness or the idea of sin, nor to question the authenticity of medical and religious perceptions of the psyche. Our aim is to see them, and see through them, as perspectives, while maintaining another view that differs from theirs and is psychological. Were we able to discover its psychological necessity, pathologizing would no longer be wrong or right, but merely necessary, involving purposes which we have misperceived and values which must present themselves necessarily in a distorted form. These are the sorts of questions that lie before us.

Our attempt to envision pathologizing psychologically is to find a place for it, a way of accepting it, in general and as a whole. We want to know what it might be saying about the soul and what the soul might be saying by means of it. And this attitude must come before making moves to treat it, condemn it, justify it, or do anything else for or against it. We must begin with psychopathology as it is, which means not discarding the term pathology or any of its diagnostic labels and categories, from *autism* to *zoophilia*. For these coinages represent a long psychological investment which bears more and more interest as time goes on. To throw them away because they have usually begun in medicine or often have a religious implication—to start all over minting a new vocabulary—would be to neglect the main importance of these terms and of *pathology* in particular; that word aims point-blank at sickness and suffering, and just this we do not wish to elude.

The terms of the field—*neurosis, complex, repression,* again to mention but a few—refer to a highly differentiated awareness of the soul's conditions, accumulated through the last two centuries of psychological observation and reflection. They provide tools of discrimination and reflect certain realities of the soul. We need only hold in abeyance the medical model from which they come and in which there are still echoes of medical thinking. And during this chapter we can keep our sicknesses and our sins in mind without at the same time placing our pathologies against the background of either medicine or religion. Let us stand for the pathological psyche by standing in it long enough to advance our claim that pathologizing is valid, authentic, and necessary.

For to deny or omit pathologizing from the study of the soul denies the soul this area of its phenomenology, refusing this mode of its life, this language of its expression, this means of reflecting itself. A psychology book or a psychological system that does not fully validate psychopathology, or lays it to one side as a separate field called "abnormal psychology," is insufficient—even dangerous. It divides in theory what is not divided in actuality. To treat pathologizing as secondary and extraneous rather than as primary and inherent, neglects the reality that pathologizing is not a field but a fundament, a strand in all our being, woven into every complex. It is a belonging of each thought and feeling, and a face of each person of the psyche. To neglect the primary validity of the soul's sickness-imagery and sickness-experience distorts our notion of soul and our work with it. Erikson's statement that "pathography remains the traditional source of psychoanalytic insight" and Freud's that the "starting point" is the "symptom" are not merely methodological, i.e., about the soul's analysis. These are *ontological* statements, statements about the soul's very *being,* a source of whose native insight is its native pathology.

But before we pursue our claim we shall have to encounter the main oppositions to the idea of the substantial importance of pathologizing. These oppositions are also the main ways in which psychopathology is today denied.

Three Styles of Denial: 1. Nominalism

The first of these we may call the *nominalistic denial* for its focus is on words, on the naming and classifying of psychic complaints.

All through the eighteenth and nineteenth centuries it was high psychiatric vogue to isolate specific disorders by inventing new names.

Almost all the words now so familiar were made up then—*alcoholism, autism, catatonia, claustrophobia, exhibitionism, homosexuality, masochism, schizophrenia,* and also *psychiatry, psychopathology,* and *psychotherapy.* It was a fond dream of the Enlightenment, as it is of the rational person in any period, to classify the world of the mind, like the world of plants and animals, into categories, with subclasses, genera, and species. Soon disputes broke out between regional schools, as French, British, and German medical psychology used different terms. A typical and famous dispute lasting into Freud's time was between the French and Germans in regard to hysteria, the Germans insisting that it could only appear in women because the word *hystera* meant uterus, and that if French psychiatry found hysteria also in men this told more about Frenchmen than about hysteria.

The classifying approach reached its monumental culmination, as did so much else in the human effort to force rational control upon nature, at the time of the First World War. Then Emil Kraepelin of Munich presented a new edition of his comprehensive four-volume textbook of psychiatry in which the seams joining his observations with his prejudices showed so little and held so tightly that his system of classifying every known form of psychopathology has permeated, if not dominated, psychiatric nomenclatures the world over into our own day.

But curiously enough at the same time Karl Jaspers, also a German and then a psychiatrist, brought out his massive philosophical critique of psychopathology, casting fundamental doubt upon categories and classifications.[3] What value have they really? To what do they truly refer? How subjective are they? Practitioners know, for instance, that the same patient presenting the same clinical picture may receive a different diagnosis and prognosis according to the practitioner, the system he uses, the city he lives in, and the language he speaks. Moreover, two practitioners using the same strict textbook definitions may give them differing connotations, with radical effect upon the patient. A diagnostic label is a peculiar concatenation of at least four sets of circumstance: a nomenclature, a milieu, a doctor, and a patient. The permutations are subtle, and exactly what is being named remains uncertain.

Besides these specific disputes over nomenclature, other critics, using semantic, political, and sociological arguments, have been tearing away at the organized system of psychiatric namings, its words, its effects on people, and the very idea of classification itself.[4] Today these questions of naming and ordering (nosology and taxonomy) the diseases and sufferings of the soul remain as troubled as ever.[5]

The main attack upon the nosology and taxonomy of psychic pathology has been directed at the relation between the words used and the events they are supposed to signify. These words, strictly speaking, are empty nomina such as we saw in the first chapter. They have no intrinsic connection with the conditions, or any underlying reasons for them, which the labels so carefully describe.

But there is a historical background for eschewing explanations and underlying reasons and sticking to accurate descriptive terms instead. Modern medical psychology derives from the Enlightenment, which had had enough explanations and "deeper causes" such as witches and curses and humors and stars, and enough therapies based on these "underlying principles." Thomas Sydenham and John Locke (who was a physician as well as philosopher and political theorist) contended that the physician's job is therapy, and that therapy is an empirical practice in which larger ideas only interfere.[6] Therapy does not need to know causes in order to produce cures; even less so if the "causes" are fanciful speculations that lead one away from the picture of the case in hand.

Whether cynical or not, as some have thought, this approach is the main attitude behind psychiatric nomenclatures. The technical terms—which are now also often popular insults—stress accurate clinical sketches of symptoms, their onset and course, and their statistically expected outcome. Nothing further about the nature of the person exhibiting the syndrome or about the nature of the syndrome itself is necessary for applying one of these psychopathological labels. Schizophrenic behavior can be precisely described and attributed to a person independent of whatever might be its underlying reasons: genetic, toxic, psychodynamic, biochemical, social, familial, semantic. The empirical nominalistic view calls for nothing more, nothing deeper than mastering a technical vocabulary.

So we discover that the classificatory approach denies with its left hand what its right hand is doing. While obsessively busy with psychopathological terms, the nominalistic denial is not fundamentally concerned with psychopathology—with the nature, reasons, or meaning of the afflictions it so carefully catalogues. Its terms are without inherent psychic necessity, for they refer neither to what a person has or what a person is. The words refer to nothing beyond descriptions and the descriptions describe nothing real. There may be no underlying pathology, no actual illness at all. A logic of descriptions is appropriate for inanimate, depersonified things, for the world of science, but psychopathology refers to the world of soul. Words used for describing its afflictions require a *subjectivity* which expresses and contains the

painful and bizarre complaints of the soul if they are truly to conform
to what they claim to describe. For this we need an archetypal psychopathology. Until one can discover the archetypal person in these words,
giving them psychological significance by connecting syndromes to
archetypes,[7] nominalism will fill its empty terms by personalizing them
with actual people.

And indeed this is the case. For the terms, so arbitrary and so empty,
are attached to persons who, by so becoming "alcoholics," "suicidals,"
"schizophrenics," "homosexuals," seem thereby to substantiate the
words, giving through their visible persons an empirical psychic reality
to the terms. The terms acquire substance from the bodies they name;
they live parasitically from their instances. These instances, these cases
of "paranoid depression," of "acute psychotic episodes," of "hysterical
personality" empirically confirm and justify the terminological system.
Labels like "psychopath" or "manic-depressive," while bringing intellectual clarity also seal off in closed jars the content of what is named,
and the person so named is relegated to a shelf marked "abnormal
psychology."

2. Nihilism

Eventually the invention of ever-new empty names leads to a second
style of denial, anarchic nihilism. The *anarchic denial* goes like this:
classifications are linguistic conventions deriving their authority wholly
from a consensus of experts, from tradition and textbooks. These words
become power words, political words, words of a psychiatric priest-
hood. They are ways of wrapping prejudices in a white coat so that
certain political, medical, and cultural styles can be guiltlessly condemned. They help the namers and hurt the named; their importance
is only for those who win at the language game called psychopathology.

Furthermore, since the true causes, conditions, and meanings of the
soul's distempers are unknown, and probably unknowable, and since all
our systems are but names we can pick up and put down at will—names
used generally, but which under scrutiny refer only to particulars, each
case being different—then why, declare these nihilists, have any "abnormal psychology"? Let's apply the famous philosophical razor of
Occam and slice off this intractable field. Let's do away with psychopathology altogether.

This denial finds shelter in existentialism. Let us treat the other
person as fundamentally, respectfully other, in his or her concrete
existence. Diagnoses must be done away with, for they merely draw a

person into the doctor's existential situation of sickness and his fantasy of the future called prognosis. There are no neuroses, only cases; no cases, only persons in situations; so throw it all out, start with nothing *(nihil)*, simply be present in simple authenticity, communicating, encountering. Be open, use intuition—but foremost, allow the other to exist in whatever style of life, "mad" or "sane," he or she chooses. The border between madness and sanity, which created the field of psychopathology by placing some events here and others there, is a positivistic fiction and not an existential reality—so say the existential nihilists.

The anarchic denial's most immediate source is in the existential philosopher Karl Jaspers. His masterly critique exposed the profound questions about man raised by psychopathology and cast doubt upon the possibility of the field as such, so that lesser thinkers who followed him, rather than sort it through, threw it all out. Other sources lie in those philosophers who have refused as valid for human fields the objective method of science. Objective observation and objective explanation of oneself or of another, they believe, is in principle the wrong method in psychology. This we have already heard from Dilthey (and Lou Salomé). And we hear it again in Nietzsche, who wrote: "Never observe for the sake of observing! Such things lead to a false point of view, to a squint, something forced and exaggerated. . . . A born psychologist instinctively avoids seeing for the sake of seeing."[8] In place of categories based upon keen clinical observations there must be subjective experience and intuitive empathy, which leads to each person elaborating his own psychopathology in anarchic freedom.

Today the desperadoes of nihilism, anarchism, and existentialism abound in many quarters. In France there is Michel Foucault, who regards psychopathology as mainly the result of society's system of power interlocked with its idea of reason.[9] In the United States there is Thomas Szasz, who has courageously labored to expose the political and social damage of diagnostic classifications: "To classify human behavior is to constrain it."[10] This has implied to some that to free human behavior is to do away with psychiatric terms, even psychiatry. In Switzerland the studies of the brilliant and disciplined medical historian Erwin Ackerknecht have demonstrated the ethnological relativism of psychiatric judgments—what is sick is sick only in this society and in this period, the normals of one age and culture being the abnormals of another time and place.[11] To take this relativism to its final consequences can suggest that if there are no kinds of psychic sickness to be found universally, then the universals of psychopathology disappear and we are left with an empty bag called "psychopathology," into which each society dumps some of its people for exhibiting certain disapproved classes of psychic events. But the bag itself means nothing beyond the occasions it serves to contain.

The most extreme of these men is Ronald Laing of Scotland, who turns the whole matter upside down, suggesting that madness may be in many ways better than sanity, or is an attempt at sanity, or the true path to full sanity, or is sanity itself in a world insane, thus reversing the significance of psychopathology.[12] By affirming it so strongly, even recommending the schizophrenic style as a therapy, the value of psychopathology is radically transposed and loses its sense as such. Laing shifts the burden of schizophrenic madness from the individual to the society, saying for instance: "If the formation itself is off course, then the man who is really 'on course' must leave the formation."[13]

But the problem of psychopathology remains; it has merely found a new home. At first there is indeed relief in being able to say: I am sane in a mad world rather than I am mad in a sane world. But have the fundamentals of the question been touched? Something is still sick, still insane, even if that something is now "out there" and called society. Moreover, by giving such virtue to schizophrenic insanity, the very ugliness, misery, and madness of psychopathology disappears. And it is this we must come to terms with, just as it is, whitewashing none of its despair. Laing's approach can be regarded as a classical denial mechanism, a projection of blame from man onto society, a form of repression in the psychoanalytic sense.

Surprisingly, there is a deep foundation for Laing's affirmation of insanity in the philosophy Hegel, who considered insanity as a necessarily occurring form or stage in the development of the soul,"[14] a stage in which "the soul is divided against itself, on the one hand already master of itself, and on the other hand not yet master of itself. . . ."[15] Here, Laing's "divided self" and Gregory Bateson's "double bind" (on which Laing often relies[16]) are already prefigured. The internal contradiction which characterizes schizophrenia (and Laing, by the way, particularizes all insanity into schizophrenia, as Szasz uses hysteria for his model) finds in Hegel a necessity more profound than the sociopolitical rebellion of Laing. For Hegel insanity is inherent in the soul's nature; it is not a result or a strategem. "In insanity the soul strives to restore itself to the perfect inner harmony out of existing contradiction."[17] Where both see psychological necessity in insanity, Hegel, unlike Laing, qualifies his recommendation that the soul go through it by explaining that his affirmation is general—not for particulars, "as if we were asserting that *every* mind, every soul, must go through this stage of extreme derangement."[18] Hegel's vision of madness is that it is a kind of soul experience that cannot be gained in another manner. This must be fundamentally recognized. Then the pathologizing of "extreme derangement" finds its authentic ground in the soul's very being. Laing's politicizing of insanity becomes irrelevant, and in its place there is a philosophy in which madness belongs.

Before turning to the third style of denial, we must ask ourselves whether these existential, political, and cultural critics have not missed something rather important. Yes, they have seen the misuses of psychopathology—a subject to which we too shall return. And yes, they have given validity to the full freedom, the anarchic freedom, of the individual to choose his mode of existence. They point as well to the interdependence of what we do in psychology with what takes place in the social and political world. But does this necessitate abandoning the entire psychopathological enterprise? What else have we for meeting the psyche's pathologizing. For here we must keep a distinction between pathologizing as a universal and necessary characteristic and psychopathology as a mode of grappling with it, a distinction the critics have blurred. They regard the sickness as resulting from the system that deals with it: it is the straitjacket that makes the patient mad; pathologizing is made by psychopathology. In this subtle if often noisy way, these critics all deny pathologizing and would get rid of it by getting rid of psychopathology. Their different sorts of attacks upon psychiatry are all concealed ways of denying pathologizing itself.

3. Transcendence

A third way to refuse psychopathology is to stand above it. This is the transcendental denial. It comes in several varieties, one of which is humanistic psychology, which will have more attention in the fourth of these chapters. We must open the topic here, however, because of its way of handling psychopathology.

For all the value of humanistic psychology in standing against the denigrations of most experimental, analytical, and behavioristic psychologies, it has swung to another extreme. In attempting to restore his dignity to man, this psychology idealizes him, sweeping his pathologies under the carpet. By brushing pathologies aside or keeping them out of its sight, this kind of humanism promotes an ennobled one-sidedness, a sentimentalism which William James would have recognized as tender-mindedness.

It shows immediately in the words favored by contemporary psychological humanism.[19] Unlike the terms of professional psychopathology, these resonate with a positive glow: health, hope, courage, love, maturity, warmth, wholeness; it speaks of the upward-growing forces of human nature which appear in tenderness and openness and sharing and which yield creativity, joy, meaningful relationships, play, and peaks. We find the same one-sidedness in its goals, such as freedom, faith, fairness, responsibility, commitment. Besides the fact that its notion of growth is simplistic, of nature romantic, and love, innocent —for it presents growth without decay, nature without catastrophes or inert stupidity, and love without possession—besides all this, its idea of the psyche is naïve if not delusional. For where is sin, and where are viciousness, failure, and the crippling vicissitudes that fate brings through pathologizing? When we turn to its literature we find scarce mention of such saturnine and sobering ideas as necessity, limitation, ancestry, or fundamental lacks or wants—the basic lacunae of each personality. It is out of touch with the stoic, tragic view of existential, irrational, pathological man.

Whereas tender-minded humanism uses the baby and growing toddler for its developmental model of man,[20] the tradition of depth psychology sees that same child with a more perverse, tough-minded eye. Depth psychology builds upon the darker perceptions of Freud and Jung, their well-tempered pessimism and eye for shadow. By insisting on the brighter side of human nature, where even death becomes "sweet,"[21] humanistic psychology is shadowless, a psychology without depths, whose deep words remain shallow because transcendence is its aim. To transcend, it leaves the lower, baser, and darker behind as "regression-values."

The method that this humanism uses for denying the soul the depths of its afflictions goes as follows: Yes, there is pathology, it would agree. But psychopathology indicates an existence hindered and a consciousness focused upon its hindrances. As human nature is basically a consciousness-developing organism of increasing information, a negentropic or positive energy field, the larger wholeness of each personality can integrate the smaller disturbances of its functions. In actualizing and realizing higher needs, lower ones become integrated. Order can always encompass disorder, because positive energies are synthetic and create as they move up. We can each move up and out of our pathological conditions. These disturbances need mainly to be felt, expressed, and shared, or cried forth in primordial exorcism. When no longer frustrated but given sympathetic acceptance, they transform into good green, growing energies, returning chastened and matured to the garden of our wholeness. The model for the positive transcendence of our pathologies is called the "peak experience."

"Peak" evokes the work of Abraham Maslow, who fathered and still epitomizes the main attitudes of contemporary psychological humanism, whether in therapy groups, in church pulpits, or in the ways private persons would transcend their conflicts. What some critics, notably William Blanchard, have recognized in Maslow's peak experiences is the underlying hedonistic philosophy, which offers a morality of heightened pleasure. Highs and peaks say nothing about the worth of person undergoing them, for they can occur also in psychopaths and criminals, having nothing to do either with creativity or maturity, Maslow's goals. Any textbook of abnormal psychology bears witness to the fact that pathologizing itself can produce peaks: kleptomanic stealing, pyromanic barn-burning, sadism, grave desecrations—all can provide ecstatic joys. So can bombing and bayoneting, and so can watching them on television. Whenever the importance of experience is determined only by intensity, by absoluteness, by ecstatic Godlikeness or God-nearness and is self-validating,[23] there is risk of possession by an archetypal person and a manic inflation. Transcendence by means of a "high," an idea so widespread throughout the different forms of humanistic practice (body-highs, weekend-highs, LSD-highs), easily turns into a manic way of denying depression. Rather than a new means for meeting psychopathology, it is itself a psychopathological state in disguise.

Another form of transcendental denial occurs in (Westernized) Oriental solutions to psychopathology. Again, it is admitted as existentially there, but is seen from another, finer perspective. Our pathologizings are but part of the ten thousand illusions to be encountered on the path of life, a piece of appearance that may be a goad, or even a load of karma to which one pays duty. But fundamentally, pathological events are evidence of the lower, unactualized rungs of the ladder. Our way shall be around them. Meditate, contemplate, exercise through them and away from them, but do not dwell there for insight. Analysis of them leads downward into fragmentation, into the bits and functions and complexes of partial man and away from wholeness and unity.

This denial sees in psychopathological events misplaced energies by which one may be scourged but which ultimately shall be transformed to work for one and toward the One. Psychopathology in and for itself is not an authentic expression of the soul's divinity. Divinity is up at the peaks, not in the swamps of our funk, not in the sludge of depression and anxiety, the depths to which actual life regularly returns. This the alchemical soul-makers knew, as do painters and writers and anyone dependent upon the movements of the imagination.

If divinity is in our freedom from hindrances and not in our inhibitions, complaints, and grotesqueries, then Oriental transendence will hardly look to pathology for what might be entering us through it, asking what door is opened into soul through our wounds. Instead it urges: rise above psychological hassles and tangles, be wise—not snared, court bliss—not affliction.

My characterization of the Oriental denial of pathologizing is Western, reflecting the way it is used by Westerners. For what we do with Oriental transcendent methods derives as much from the Western psyche as it does from the Eastern spirit. In the East this spirit is rooted in the thick yellow loam of richly pathologized imagery—demons, monsters, grotesque Goddesses, tortures, and obscenities. It rises within a pathologized world of want and despair, chained by obligations, agonized. But once uprooted and imported to the West it arrives debrided of its imaginal ground, dirt-free and smelling of sandalwood, another upward vision that offers a way to bypass our Western psychopathologies. The archetypal content of Eastern doctrines as experienced through the archetypal structures of the Western psyche becomes a major and systematic denial of pathologizing.

If I have disparaged the transcendental approaches of humanistic and Oriental psychology, it is because they disparage the actual soul. By turning away from its pathologizings they turn away from its full richness. By going upward towards spiritual betterment they leave its afflictions, giving them less validity and less reality than spiritual goals. In the name of the higher spirit, the soul is betrayed.

An Excursion on Differences Between Soul and Spirit

Here we need to remember that the ways of the soul and those of the spirit only sometimes coincide and that they diverge most in regard to psychopathology. A main reason for my stress upon pathologizing is just to bring out the differences between soul and spirit, so that we end the widespread confusions between psychotherapy and spiritual disciplines. There is a difference between Yoga, transcendental meditation, religious contemplation and retreat, and even Zen, on the one hand, and the psychologizing of psychotherapy on the other. This difference is based upon a distinction between spirit and soul.

Today we have rather lost this difference that most cultures, even tribal ones, know and live in terms of. Our distinctions are Cartesian: between outer tangible reality and inner states of mind, or between body and a fuzzy conglomerate of mind, psyche, and spirit. We have lost the third, middle position which earlier in our tradition, and in others too, was the place of soul: a world of imagination, passion, fantasy, reflection, that is neither physical and material on the one hand, nor spiritual and abstract on the other, yet bound to them both. By having its own realm psyche has its own logic—psychology—which is neither a science of physical things nor a metaphysics of spiritual things. Psychological pathologies also belong to this realm. Approaching them from either side, in terms of medical sickness or religion's suffering, sin, and salvation, misses the target of soul.

But the threefold division has collapsed into two, because soul has become identified with spirit. This happens because we are materialists, so that everything that is not physical and bodily is one undifferentiated cloud; or it happens because we are Christians. Already in the early vocabulary used by Paul, *pneuma* or spirit had begun to replace *psyché* or soul.[24] The New Testament scarcely mentions soul phenomena such as dreams, but stresses spirit phenomena such as miracles, speaking in tongues, prophecy, and visions.

Philosophers have tried to keep the line between spirit and soul by keeping soul altogether out of their works or assigning it a lower place. Descartes confined soul to the pineal gland, a little enclave between the opposing powers of internal mind and external space. More recently, Santayana has put soul down in the realm of matter and considered it an antimetaphysical principle.[25] Collingwood equated soul with feeling and considered that psychology had no business invading the realm of thought and ideas.[26] The spiritual point of view always posits itself as superior, and operates particularly well in a fantasy of transcendence among ultimates and absolutes.

Philosophy is therefore less helpful in showing the differences than is the language of the imagination. Images of the soul show first of all more feminine connotations. *Psyché,* in the Greek language, besides being soul denoted a night-moth or butterfly and a particularly beautiful girl in the legend of Eros and Psyche. Our discussion in the previous chapter of the anima as a personified feminine idea continues this line of thinking. There we saw many of her attributes and effects, particularly the relationship of psyche with dream, fantasy, and image. This relationship has also been put mythologically as the soul's connection with the night world, the realm of the dead, and the moon. We still catch our soul's most essential nature in death experiences, in dreams of the night, and in the images of "lunacy."

The world of spirit is different indeed. Its images blaze with light, there is fire, wind, sperm. Spirit is fast, and it quickens what it touches. Its direction is vertical and ascending; it is arrow-straight, knife-sharp, powder-dry, and phallic. It is masculine, the active principle, making forms, order, and clear distinctions. Although there are many spirits, and many kinds of spirit, more and more the notion of "spirit" has come to be carried by the Apollonic archetype, the sublimations of higher and abstract disciplines, the intellectual mind, refinements, and purifications.

We can experience soul and spirit interacting. At moments of intellectual concentration or transcendental meditation, soul invades with natural urges, memories, fantasies, and fears. At times of new psychological insights or experiences, spirit would quickly extract a meaning, put them into action, conceptualize them into rules. Soul sticks to the realm of experience and to reflections within experience. It moves indirectly in circular reasonings, where retreats are as important as advances, preferring labyrinths and corners, giving a metaphorical sense to life through such words as *close, near, slow,* and *deep.* Soul involves us in the pack and welter of phenomena and the flow of impressions. It is the "patient" part of us. Soul is vulnerable and suffers; it is passive and remembers. It is water to the spirit's fire, like a mermaid who beckons the heroic spirit into the depths of passions to extinguish its certainty. *Soul is imagination,* a cavernous treasury—to use an image from St. Augustine—a confusion and richness, both. Whereas spirit chooses the better part and seeks to make all One. Look up, says spirit, gain distance; there is something beyond and above, and what is above is always, and always superior.

They differ in another way: spirit is after ultimates and it travels by means of a *via negativa.* "Neti, neti," it says, "not this, not that." Strait is the gate and only first or last things will do. Soul replies by saying, "Yes, this too has place, may find its archetypal significance, belongs in a myth." The cooking vessel of the soul takes in everything, everything can become soul; and by taking into its imagination any and all events, psychic space grows.

I have drawn apart soul and spirit in order to make us feel the differences, and especially to feel what happens to soul when its phenomena are viewed from the perspective of spirit. Then, it seems, the soul must be disciplined, its desires harnessed, imagination emptied, dreams forgotten, involvements dried.[27] For soul, says spirit, cannot *know,* neither truth, nor law, nor cause. The soul is fantasy, all fantasy. The thousand pathologizings that soul is heir to by its natural attachments to the ten thousand things of life in the world shall be cured by making soul into an imitation of spirit. The *imitatio Christi* was the classical way; now there are other models, gurus from the Far East or Far West, who, if followed to the letter, put one's soul on a spiritual path which supposedly leads to freedom from pathologies. Pathologizing, so says spirit, is by its very nature confined only to soul; only the psyche can be pathological, as the word psychopathology attests. There is no "pneumopathology," and as one German tradition has insisted, there can be no such thing as *mental* illness ("Geisteskrankheit"), for the spirit cannot pathologize. So there must be spiritual disciplines for the soul, ways in which soul shall conform with models enunciated for it by spirit.

But from the viewpoint of the psyche the humanistic and Oriental movement upward looks like repression. There may well be more psychopathology actually going on while transcending than while being immersed in pathologizing. For any attempt at self-realization without full recognition of the psychopathology that resides, as Hegel said, inherently in the soul is in itself pathological, an exercise in self-deception. Such self-realization turns out to be a paranoid delusional system, or even a kind of charlatanism, the psychopathic behavior of an emptied soul.

Rejoining Soul and Symptom

Many modern methods of psychotherapy want to retain the spirit of analysis but not its soul. They want to retain the methods and forms without the pathologizings. Then the doctor can become a master, and the patient is metamorphosed into a pupil, client, partner, disciple—anything but a patient. Analysis itself is called a dialogue or a transaction, for "therapy" smacks of pathology. The focus upon inwardness and the goal of integration of the interior person may remain, but disintegration tends to be excluded, without which such integration has no significance. In their view, falling apart is never for the sake of the parts, the multiple persons who are the richness of psychic life; falling apart is but a phase preliminary to reconstituting a stronger ego.

These approaches that would synthesize rather than analyse, integrate rather than differentiate, and keep the therapeutic rituals without the pathological contents, neglect one of the deepest insights resulting from the last century of psychotherapy. *The psyche does not exist without pathologizing.* Since the unconscious was discovered as an operative factor in every soul, pathologizing has been recognized as an inherent aspect of the interior personality. Freud declared this succinctly: "We can catch the unconscious only in pathological material."[28] And after her last visit to Freud in 1913 Lou Salomé wrote: ". . . he put exceptionally strong emphasis on the necessity of maintaining the closest and most persistent contact with the pathological material. . . ."[29]

Pathologizing is present not only at moments of special crisis but in the everyday lives of all of us. It is present most profoundly in the individual's sense of death, which he carries wherever he goes. It is present also in each person's inward feeling of his peculiar "differentness," which includes, and may be even based upon, his sense of individual "craziness." For we each have a private fantasy of mental illness; "crazy," "mad," "insane"—all their substitutes, colloquialisms, and synonyms—form a regular part of our daily speech. As we cast our internal deviance from us with these exclamations about others, we are at the same time acknowledging that we each have a deviant, odd second (or third) personality that provides another perspective to our regular life. Indeed, pathologizing supplies material out of which we build our regular lives. Their styles, their concerns, their loves, reflect patterns that have pathologized strands woven all through them. The deeper we know ourselves and the other persons of our complexes, the more we recognize how well we, too, fit into the textbook sketches of abnormal psychology. Those case histories are also our own biographies. To put it in sociological language: nearly every individual in the United States of America has been, now is, or will have been in the hands of professional soul care of one kind or another, for a shorter or longer period, for one reason or another.

Discovery of the unconscious has meant the widespread and overwhelming recognition of the psyche's autonomous activity of pathologizing. That discovery and that recognition have led to one even more significant: the rediscovery of soul. But unfortunately and mistakenly we have confused these three interrelated discoveries: the unconscious, pathologizing, and soul. We confusedly believe that everyone needs professional *therapy* as if that is where soul could be refound. But this is not so. For then we are confusing the rediscovery of soul during the twentieth century with the place where it happened—therapeutic analysis. But therapy or analysis was not the carrier of that discovery. Psychopathology was. Symptoms, not therapists, led this century to soul. The persistent pathologizings in Freud and in Jung and in their patients—pathologizings that refused to be repressed, transformed, or cured, or even understood—led this century's main explorers of the psyche ever deeper. Their movement through pathology into soul is an experience repeated in each of us. We owe them much, but we owe our pathologizing more. We owe our symptoms an immense debt. The soul can exist without its therapists but not without its afflictions.

Analysis has merely given psychopathology a hearing outside the asylums, prisons, and church institutions where it had been kept; the new therapy provided the only place given secular sanction for a prolonged and intense involvement with pathologizing. Symptoms were the very point and focus of its attention. So analysis offered the vessel into which our unconscious pathologizing could be poured and then cooked long enough for its significance to emerge, for it to make soul. Out of *psyché-pathos-logos* came the meaning of suffering of the soul, or the soul's suffering of meaning.

Again a confusion beset this experience: a special state of being—"being-in-therapy"—seemed required for this discovery of soul through pathologizing, and so for many people therapy became a religious ritual, even replacing religious ritual. One was "in" analysis, and analysis was "in." There were the initiates: those who had been analysed. And there were the others: those who had never even been in therapy or had not been "properly" or "thoroughly" analysed. To refind the sense of soul one had to "go through" analysis with its regular appointments, its techniques, and its stages of "beginning an analysis," "working through," and "terminating." Inevitably and without knowing it, the ritual of analysis had produced a new cult of soul. Finally, some have taken this religious direction literally, declaring that actually this is what therapy is all about, an expression of the religious activity of the soul: the psychotherapeutic movement is correctly a religious movement; therapists are indeed a new kind of ministers to soul—gurus or priests.

In this movement toward religion pathology now tends to be left behind. By shifting its ground from pathology to self-development, recent analysis no longer recognizes the primacy of affliction. One goes to therapy to grow, not because one is afflicted—as if growth and affliction excluded each other. A gulf has developed between soul and symptom.

On the one hand analysis regards itself as a professional contract for solving problems, a variety of medical science without soul, ritual, or mystery. On the other, it imitates the transcendental disciplines, fostering ritual, community, and teachings. Pathologizing again foundered upon its old division, illness or sin, and a further division emerged. Now, to be in soul therapy for growth and realization of personality, symptoms are left out; to be in medical or behavioral therapy for relief of symptomatic afflictions, soul is left out. Soul and symptom have broken in two.

This chapter and this book want to mend that division. By retaining psychopathology as a descriptive language of the psyche which indeed speaks to and of the soul, I would keep psyche and pathology close together. If I seem to be making the soul sick again by such stress on pathologizing, I am at the same time giving sickness soul again. By returning symptoms to the soul, I am attempting to return soul to symptoms, restoring them to the central value in life that soul itself has.

Remnants of the Medical Model

Ideas left from the days of medical thinking about the psyche still stand as barriers between our symptoms and our souls. Especially stubborn is the idea of treatment. We still tend to think that pathologizing calls for treatment; if not directly a medical treatment then at least psychological. Treatment, of course, assumes that something is wrong—that when the psyche is pathologizing in a fantasy, an emotion, or a symptom this is to be corrected or alleviated by practical measures. Since one tends to find a great deal psychologically "wrong" with oneself and with others, we are engaged in a treatment fantasy during a considerable part of each day. If a friend cannot sleep, and I respond by asking —"What are you doing about it, what are you taking for it?"—I am in the treatment fantasy. So, too, when I give myself directions to overcome psychological habits, subdue emotions, or prevent recurring fantasies. One part of myself is treating the other part as a patient. By doctoring my sick self, I have plunged head over heels into the medical fantasy.

The psychological perspective is altogether different. From this viewpoint I am a patient not of my doctor or of the doctor aspect of myself, but of my psyche—a sufferer of it and from it. The soul is the patient of its pathologizing, and I am a patient because my soul pathologizes. Treatment attempts to take away the pathologizing, separating it from soul.

If we follow the psychological viewpoint to its ultimate consequences, we come to realize that doing something, approaching helpfully, deciding practically, may all have to be abandoned if we are to take pathologizing psychologically. So long as we are still aiming to alleviate or rectify we are engaged in preventative treatment. By searching for the right treatment we literalize pathologizing into its medical meaning. The model in our thought creates the case before us. Thus the idea of treatment as a literal activity would have to be laid aside, for if we are consistent in our thinking there can be no such procedure as "psychological treatment." The two terms exclude each other: when we are *psychological* about pathologizing we are not treating it; when we are *treating* pathologizing we are not being psychological about it.

For this reason "clinical" psychology is a remnant of the medical model. It may prove its worth in case after case by dismantling pathologized structures. But it does this by forfeiting the psychological viewpoint. For judging by results belongs to medical empiricism; besides, it assumes what is still to be established: that the soul's pathologizings are to be dismantled. By taking the soul's sickness fantasy at face value as clinical pathology, the clinical approach creates what it then must treat. It creates clinical patients.

"Psychological" and "treatment" cannot be conjoined—unless we revise what we mean by treatment and see it as a fantasy. We then would have the drug fantasy, the diet fantasy, the surgical fantasy, the shock fantasy, the vacation fantasy, the group fantasy. These would be psychological modes of imagining about pathologizing. They are each part of psychotherapy, not as treatments but as fantasies that can serve soul-making. Each time I enter into a fantasy about which diet to begin or group to join, my pathologizing is being given a containing field in which to elaborate and validate itself. Pathologizing is given a chance to fantasy itself further. This would cease the moment any of these "treatments" was programmed as a literal therapy. Let us recall here that psychotherapy, in accordance with the root meaning of the words "psyche" and "therapy" means *to serve soul,* not to treat it. The psychology I am working out in these pages may be fundamentally engaged with psychopathology and inseparable from the pathologizing process, but it is not intended as a treatment for it.

Serving soul implies letting it rule; it leads, we follow. Here we adapt Jung's famous dictum that analysis is dreaming the myth onward, transposing it to "pathologizing the myth onward." By following the peculiar disordered activity itself as one of our guides, therapy will have room for the bizarre, decayed, and fantastic. As our model of thought is that "like has an affinity with like," therapy for the abnormal would have to be abnormal as well. Since our occupation is primarily with the failed aspects of life, we would have to put away all ideas of therapeutic success. Since pathologizing is frightening, we are obliged to follow fear, not with courage, but as a path that leads deeper into awe for what is at work in the depths of the soul. Here we must keep from seizing up in panic and coagulating the frightening peculiarities with a literal interpretation of them, giving them a diagnosis that demands treatment. "Pathologizing the myth onward" means staying in the mess while at the same time regarding what is going on from a mythical perspective. We try to follow the soul wherever it leads, trying to learn what the imagination is doing in its madness. By staying with the mess, the morbid, the fantastic, we do not abandon method itself, only its medical model. Instead we adopt the method of the imagination. By following pathologizing onward we are attempting to discover precisely the methods and laws of the imaginal in distinction to the rational and the physical. Madness teaches the method.

Before any attempt to treat, or even understand, pathologized phenomena we meet them in an act of faith, regarding them as authentic, real, and valuable *as they are.* We do not decrease their value by considering them as signs of medical sickness or inflate their value by considering them as signs of spiritual suffering. They are ways of the psyche and ways of finding soul.

Professionalism and Wrong Pathologizing

By regarding our symptoms as the accidents that brought us into therapy rather than as the *via regia* into soul, we neglect their importance in soul-making. Instead, this importance is displaced onto therapy. By carelessly turning over our symptoms to professional therapists, we have reinforced the grip of professionalism upon psychopathology. Here the critics of psychotherapy have much on their side: they note well the dependency of the helping professions upon the fantasy of sickness. Because states of soul need professional help only when they can be found sick, a collusion develops between patient and therapist in regard to psychopathology. They both require it for the therapy game.

The therapy game enacts an archetypal pattern. It was said in antiquity that the same God who constellates an illness is the one who can take it away. The healer is the illness and the illness is the healer. It is therefore of first importance to find out "who," which archetypal person, is involved in the psychopathology, a point discussed in the previous chapter. But as this ancient psychological idea has become translated into modern secular therapy, the "who" is none other than the professional therapist.

By giving the pathologizing a clinical name, the professional therapist makes the first move in this therapy game. The first move is not the pathologizing of the patient. His complaints and oddities are not clinical psychopathology *until so named.* Until then, symptoms are demonstrations of the psyche, a mode of its being and expression, part of its fantasy and its affliction. But as soon as the move is made of professional naming, a distinct entity is created, with literal reality. On the one hand I am protected from this "thing" by separation from it; it now has a name. But on the other hand, I now "have" something, or even "am" something: an alcoholic, an obsessive neurotic, a depressive. Moreover the therapist has become the very God who by bringing the condition is the only one who can take it away. The patient tends to believe in his therapist: "He alone can help me for only he knows really what is wrong." What is "really" wrong means what is "literally" wrong, what has been literalized into wrongness by the professional therapy game.

In this way the analyst and the patient become locked in a long-term analysis, for the analyst is the one, the very God, who has seen into the patient's incurable weak spot, his vulnerable heel, his ruinous secret. The analyst's insight and the patient's wound together embody the archetypal figure of the Wounded-Healer, another ancient and psychological way of expressing that the illness and its healing are one and the same. (In our pathologizing there is indeed a kind of health that has to do with soul, and in our health there is indeed a concealed kind of pathologizing.) But again in modern secular therapy the Wounded-Healer has been divided down the middle: illness is all on the patient's side and health all with the therapist. The archetype is split,[30] and the two halves are bound together compellingly in what is called transference and countertransference. The two halves are locked into endless erotic and power struggles, the sado-masochism of the therapy game. Little wonder therapy speaks so much of "resistance" and that manuals are written explaining how to overcome or break through the patient's "defense mechanisms." Little wonder too that it becomes so difficult to conclude a long-term analysis, since both partners have been caught in this literalized enactment of an archetypal theme. Therapeutic analysis has side effects no less lethal than drugs.

For the wrong pathologizing of the therapy game is killing. Lévi-Strauss has noted that asymmetrical games, such as those between the unequal partners of therapy, end in killing one opponent.[31] The killing of psychotherapy takes place on a psychological level: the neurosis, the problem, is supposedly "got rid of," whereas actually it is soul that is being killed—again through a wrong pathologizing, a wrong understanding of the soul in the symptom.

Wrong pathologizing has spread well beyond the games of the consulting room and clinic, becoming a covert political instrument of the state. Political heretics may be declared mentally ill in order to banish them—and this procedure is smoothly justified with assurances that it is for the "patient's" own good. We may not draw comfort from supposing that this goes on only in the Soviet Union. Wrong pathologizing also enters the social scene when a psychiatric defense is used for justifying revolutionary behavior, e.g., true pathology lies not in the defendant but in the society and institutions that produced him or her, in the law that does not recognize psychological realities, or in the cultural mores that do not allow for subcultural deviation. This sort of psychiatric expertise is not merely employed to get the defendant off or have him committed to therapeutic rather than punitive treatment, but masks an attack upon the institutionalized mores of sexuality, property, and due process of law. Here psychiatric arguments about psychopathology, especially the anarchic ones we saw above (Szasz, Laing), are part of a revolutionary program. Whether such a revolution is called for is one thing; to disguise it in arguments of psychopathology is another.

Most insidious of these abuses of psychopathology is the cover it now gives to a moral philosophy. Ideas of mental health and mental illness are ideas about the psyche, about the soul. When we are told what is healthy we are being told what is right to think and feel. When we are told what is mentally ill we are being told what ideas, behavior, and fantasies are wrong. A specific ideology of compliant middle-class humanism (again as Szasz points out[32]) is propagated by mental health, is policed by professionals and is infiltrated into the community, its courts, clinics, welfare centers, and schools. The avenues of escape are blocked by the professional abuse of pathologizing. To refuse the mental health approach confirms one's "sickness." One needs "therapy," soul sessions at the state church, a community mental health conversion center supported by public moneys. There the young priests of serious good will, whose community influence begins early with "disturbed" children, counsel whole families about divorce, suicide, orgasms, and madness—in short about crucial events of the soul. These professionals are the guardians of the nation's soul, and to whom are they accountable for what takes place during their interventions into the soul's crises?

How can we take back therapy from the killing asymmetry of professionalism and the political abuses of wrong pathologizing, from a system which must find illness in order to promote health and which, in order to increase the range of its helping, is obliged to extend the area of sickness. Ever deeper pockets of pathology to be analyzed, ever earlier traumata: primal, prenatal, into my astral body; ever more people into the ritual: the family, the office force, community mental health, analysis for everyone.

As religion has lost hold partly because it neglected the significance of the soul's pathologizing, and as therapeutic psychology spreads in religion's place, analysis has claim to being the major viable method for redeeming the condemned areas of the psyche. Therapy has become the way of soul-making. Its practice may differ—groups, or individuals, short or long term, physical or verbal, meditation, drama, behavior-conditioning, or imagination—but the premise is the same. The work of making soul requires professional help. Soul-making has become restricted by therapy and to therapy. And psychopathology has become restricted to therapy's negative definition of it, reduced to its role in the therapy game.

But how lift the therapeutic restriction on soul-making without at the same time making the transcendental leap clear of psychopathology altogether? How retrieve psyche from professional therapy and still keep psychopathology as source and base of our insights? The question turns on pathologizing, for it has been the goad driving us to the professional. *We cannot recover soul from its alienation in professional therapy until we have a vision of pathologizing which does not require professional treatment in the first place.* We need a new vision of the soul's pathologizing process and a new background for its frightening phenomena.

Psychopathology as an Archetypal Fantasy

Regardless of how one denies psychopathology in the various theories we have discussed, regardless of how one cures it by medical means or ennobles it through religious interpretations, and regardless of how wrongly psychopathology is employed in the abuses of therapy and politics, we never rid ourselves of pathologizing as a psychological idea. A fantasy of it remains in the systems that would deny or cure it as well as in those that misuse it. The fantasy attests to its reality as a psychic factor. This reality of psychopathology must be kept distinct from how we interpret it and what we do about it. And since this fantasy is the first reality of psychopathology, a psychological view of psychopathology must begin by considering it as one of the many archetypal fantasies of the soul.

As there are archetypal fantasies of health and of growth, of being saved and of coming home, so there are similar imaginal motifs of falling ill, being wounded, and going mad. Although falling sick may belong to medicine, the fantasy of it belongs to the soul, which can present us with illnesses in fantasy, in fears, and in symptoms without any medical actualities whatsoever. And even where the fantasy may connect with actual illnesses in what is called psychosomatics, the fantasy itself may not be taken with medical literalism.

As the fantasy of illness is first of all fantasy (and not illness), so treating the fantasy requires a therapy that focuses on fantasy (and not illness). Pathologizing must be met by imaginal thinking rather than clinical thinking. Because pathologizing is primarily a psychological reality it needs psychological insight. The *psychological* approach always begins with the same premise: every fantasy says something about the soul regardless of the content of the fantasy. Whether incest, torture, or murder, whether love, revelation, or bliss, every fantasy is first of all a psychological event aside from its literal content. Fantasy can use any sort of content, divine or morbid, and *none of this content should be taken literally until all of it is recognized as fantasy.* Before we examine the pathologized content of a fantasy we must recognize the archetypal fantasy of pathologizing.

Psychopathology as an archetypal fantasy means that the soul produces crazed patterns and sicknesses, perversions and decay, within dreams and behavior, and in art and thought, in war and politics, and in religion, because pathologizing is a psychic activity per se. Psychic sickness remains as an archetypal category of existence independent of its contents. It does not matter how we define psychic sickness from period to period or culture to culture: the fantasy itself is continuous. The contents by which it is defined and recognized change, but they should not be confused with the category itself. Definitions of mental illness that vary according to the society offer a specific content for the archetypal idea of pathology. These notions of what a crazy person is provide *images* of psychopathology, but these notions are not the true description of madness. For we have seen that the description is variable and its contents are partly dependent upon which ruling idea of sanity prevails.

The definitions of psychopathology can never stand up universally across time and space. One man's meat is another man's poison, inasmuch as madness, like wisdom, like goodness, like beauty, is an archetypal category. It is the archetypal fantasy of madness that gives the definitions of psychopathology their persuasive power; but they cannot be taken as positivistic statements that define true madness. This true madness we do not know and can never know, for it is a false issue. All we can know is that the psyche always defines some aspect of itself as mad, the reasons for which become one of the eternal questions for psychological reflection. Pathologizing provokes psychologizing. Like love, God, death, and the nature of soul itself, madness is one of the psyche's fundamental thematic fantasies.

The pathologizing fantasy governs above all the practice of psychotherapy. We cannot investigate the idea of healing or its archetypal background unless we first examine the patient who manifests the

pathological fantasy. It is the patient who, by embodying the pathologizing fantasy, makes possible practice of whatever sort of style. Without the archetypal fantasy of pathology there would be no shaman, no
medicine man, no psychopharmaceutica, no analyst. Again, the fantasy
comes first.

Even in straight medical practice today, just as Thomas Sydenham
supposedly observed in the seventeenth century, at least two-thirds of
the persons whom the physician sees have nothing organically sick; but
they have the experience and fantasy of sickness. They are pathologizing. Medicine calls this "psychosomatics" or "functional disorder," and
treats the pathologiz*ing* as patholog*y,* for instance by prescribing pills.
By taking that primary pathologizing process with clinical literalism,
medicine and pharmacy develop their professions. They live more from
the pathological fantasy than they do from organic pathology. Thus a
medical model for understanding pathologizing begs the question, since
the medical model is itself a result of the primary process of pathologizing. The soul's fantasy of sickness necessitates subsequently the persons
and systems and *materia medica* for meeting the fantasy. The medical
model is merely one of the modes for engaging the pathologizing fantasy. We shall shortly come to other modes which do not take the
fantasy as clinical fact.

Because the reality of the fantasy comes before the reality of the
illness, illness too requires looking at with a psychological eye. Concrete, medically diagnosed illness with organic pathology is not only a
clinical event. It is also, if not first and foremost, a psychological event
whose physical aspects require a psychological examination. We may
no longer make a cleavage between organic pathology and psychopathology, following the old Cartesian division between physical and
mental. Everything matters to soul and expresses its fantasies, whether
ideas in the head or bones in the body. The body has its home in the
soul and every organic pathology is a cooperation between pathogenic
agent and the human person as host. An infection must find the host
receptive, unresistant, perhaps even welcoming. Even parasite-caused
diseases, or those brought on through accidents, epidemics, or degener-
ative processes, seemingly organic and so external and "unpsychological," represent the pathologizing fantasy and are absorbed by the
psyche and reflected in it. The components of any illness—affected
organ or system, causal agent, style of disease process—all have their
significances in the language of pathologizing fantasy as well as that of
pathological facts. Heart, skin, and joints, whether congenital, chronic,
or acute, whether accidental, infectious, or hereditary—each and all of

these have psychological significance, are metaphors too; they are foci of fantasy as well as of disease.

More subjectively, within each of us pathologizing takes place even without diseases. We each have a predilection for pathologizing. It shows in our spontaneous fantasies. Whenever a symptom appears, or an anxiety about our state of mind or physical welfare, it is immediately carried by fantasy into its worst potential, into the incurable possibility: the stiff neck becomes immediately the incipient meningitis; the little lump, cancer; and the nightmare a presentiment of madness, accident, or ruin. There is the feeling of something "deeply" wrong, something "deeper" going on that needs immediate attention. With pathologizing comes the feeling of dark forces in the depths, and so it appears in the fantasies of latent psychosis, latent homosexuality, latent criminality: that given the circumstances I would crack, and out of the crack would crawl my pathological demons.

Whether we bear the symptom like a hero, deserve it like a martyr, or treat it like a doctor, we are pathologizing as well by enacting the role of patient. The symptomatic event cannot be left soberly as it is: we begin to ritualize it. It becomes symbolic of something beyond itself as we fall into various odd behaviors, suddenly dependent like a child or anxious about weakness and death. Pathologizing is at work.

The psyche's natural movement in fantasy toward the diseased condition has already been labeled by the language of psychopathology, where it is called hypochondria. But what is hypochondria? What events in the soul does this term refer to?

Freud's statement that nothing is more foreign to the ego than the symptom is brought closer by the experience of hypochondria. For what superstars of arrogance we would be without the inbuilt fantasy of defectiveness! Hypochondriacal complaints act like negative feedback, guarding the ego from its delusions of grandeur. Who is more suspect than the one who says: "I am perfectly all right," "never sick," "nothing wrong at all"? Hypochondria opens a door out of the ego which the ego continually complains of but cannot close. To put the matter another way around and not from the ego's perspective: heroic consciousness has no place for complaint. During the Trojan War the heroes could not abide Philoctetes, who though one of their number complained of a continuously suppurating wound on his foot. They put him off on an island isolating him from them. But was his never-healing wound his complaint, or was complaint (hypochondria) his "wound" which set him apart from the heroic style. To the hero a wound either kills or mends, but it does not remain perpetually open.

We have often been told that hypochondria means suffering from imaginary ills, but does it not rather mean suffering the ills of the imagination? Hypochondriacal complaints refer to the ego's wounds received through the imagination, and hypochondria reflects a process of pathologizing which forces the ego to grow aware of the imaginal working not only in the images of the mind but also in sensations of the body, in the somatic psyche. Hypochondria makes the imaginal painfully real, makes us recognize that the imaginal includes physical life and speaks in it and through it. Therefore we can understand the special role hypochondria played in the development of the idea of neurosis,[33] of purely psychological disorders. It is the prototype of the psychological complaint, the complaint of the psyche against being taken only physically—and also not somatically enough.

Pathologizing as Metaphorical Language

The psyche uses complaints to speak in a magnified and misshapen language about its depths. We know this change of pulse is not a heart disorder, that we did not contract syphilis unawares years ago. The fears are foolish, we laugh them off; but they are there. Something keeps telling us these weird tales. So let us start our revision of pathologizing by considering it a manner of telling, a way in which the psyche talks to itself. Let us see pathologizing as a mode of speech.

The psyche uses many languages for describing itself. We see these best in dreams because they are the best model for the actual structure of the psyche (see above, pp. 33f). Dreams tell the soul's tales in persons and they also use the language of animals and landscapes, much as the Gods told of their different archetypal qualities through persons, animals, and landscapes. The soul may speak of itself as a desert, an island, an airport. It may be a cow or a tiger. Dreams also use parts of the body as parts of dream speech in which feet and teeth and heart do not refer to actual body parts. And dreams use the family as a mode of symbolic speech—where "brother" and "father" and "son" convey emotional messages beyond the factual family members.

In addition to these modes, dreams speak with psychopathological imagery: the idiot child, the boy with infantile paralysis, the figure with queer psychotic eyes or on the operating table having her womb cut out. Here we need the same symbolic understanding that has taught us that dream modes of speech do not refer to actual geographies and animals, to actual body parts and family members. The psyche is using a particular metaphorical language system which is very detailed and concrete and seems to accomplish a specific end. Sick figures—crippled, with venereal disease, hurtling toward an accident, locked in a closed ward —have an *exceptionally moving power*. We start up, afflicted, haunted through the day, psychologically on edge. The pathologized images have moved the soul in several ways: we are afraid; we feel vulnerable and in danger; our very physical substance and sanity appear to be menaced; we want to prevent or rectify. Especially this last seizes us. We feel protective, impelled to correct, straighten, repair. For we have confused something sick with something wrong.

Pathologized images do indeed bring guilt, and not only because of the long historical tradition linking sin and illness. The guilty feelings are more than historically caused; they are psychologically authentic because affliction reaches us partly through the guilt it brings. Guilt belongs to the experiences of deviation, to the sense of being off, failing, "missing the mark" *(hamartia)*.[34] It is indeed questionable whether guilt and pathologizing could be so severed from each other that we could feel pathologized and vulnerable without at the same time feeling guilty.

However the true missing of the mark is taking the guilt literally, where failings become faults to be set right. This places the guilt on the shoulders of the ego who "should not" have failed. Then pathologizing reinforces the ego's style and guilt serves a secondary gain, increasing the ego's sense of importance: ego becomes superego, drivenly busy with repairing wrongs. A guilty ego is no less egocentric than a proud one.

But we can let go of this style of guilt, seeing through it as a defensive business that prevents archetypal fantasies from coming through. For from the archetypal point of view, the matter is less that one feels guilty than *to whom:* to which person of the psyche and within which myth does my affliction belong, and does it bespeak an obligation? Which figures in which complexes are now laying claim? From this perspective the guilt brought by pathologizing takes on radical importance. It leads out of the ego and into a recognition that through a pathologized experience I am bound to archetypal persons who want something from me and to whom I owe remembrance.

A sickened image of course vitally afflicts us, for pathologizing touches our sense of life. It both vitiates and vitalizes, a quickening through distortion. The sense of vital affliction we feel leads us into a natural response. Because the fantasy or dream image is so concretely vivid and we feel it so vitally, we match it with a concrete, medical-style move. But we forget that the image is part of dream speech and that the sense of affliction, too, is as a necessary part of that speech as the feeling aspect of the metaphor. The affliction reflects a *pathos,* a being moved, or movement, now taking place in the psyche. Categories of positive and negative, health and disease, do not apply. Instead we assume that something essential for the psyche's survival, its very life, and death, is being expressed in this manner and cannot be expressed with the same subtle and vital impact in any other way. We would save the phenomena just as they are, untreated, uncured. The fantasies of sickness are assumed from the outset and in entirety to be part of the psyche's depth—and we are depth psychologists by virtue of these pathologized enigmas which provide the subjective stuff of psychological reflection. Though pathologizing uses the language of natural events, this does not imply that we are to take these events naturalistically.

An Excursion on the Naturalistic Fallacy

By the naturalistic fallacy, I mean the psychological habit of comparing fantasy events with similar events in nature. We tend to judge dream images to be right or wrong (positive or negative) largely by standards of naturalism. The more like nature an image appears, the more positive; the more distorted the image, the more negative. Rather like its sister fallacy in philosophy, the naturalistic fallacy in psychology also claims that the way it *is* in nature is the norm for how it *should* be in dreams.

But nature cannot be the guide for comprehending soul. To understand dreams in terms of their likeness to nature simplifies both nature on the one hand and the spiritual and psychic meaning of dreams on the other, by finding analogies for what is presented in dream images only in the realm of nature. One event in nature can indeed be compared with another, and thereby we do see deformities and pathologies. A diseased elm in the street is rightly compared with standards drawn from other elms. But a blighted tree in the mind must be compared with other mental phenomena, with blighted trees in the realms of psyche and spirit. For the dream tree is an imaginal one, and the fields for its comparison are in the imagination: painting, literature, poetry, vision, myth, dream.

The naturalistic fallacy is common because it requires least effort on the part of an interpreter. He need only look around him at natural everyday events for his models. The very easiness is itself part of the fallacy—the inertia of following nature.

Naturalism soon declines into materialism, a view which regards the way things are in the perceptual world of things, facts and sense-realities to be the primary mode. It insists that material reality is first and psychic reality must conform with it: *psyché* must obey the laws of *physis* and imagination follow perception.

But this perspective cannot do justice to the compressed quality of dreams, to their peculiar ways of denying the principles of matter: space, time, causality. Like poetry, psychic speech is condensed and distilled. This speech is on another level, raised from natural meaning to imaginative meaning. Condensation heightens and intensifies significance. So do the other terms Freud used for describing dream speech: distortion, displacement, overdetermination. These are not merely inferior kinds of thinking (looked at from the naturalistic viewpoint) but ways of speaking poetically, rhetorically, and symbolically. Though the dream, and the symptom too, may be "the most natural thing in the world," occurring even in animals, they are not nature but culture. These events are nature that has gone through a process within the imagination. To return dreams to nature by measuring their images against natural events misses the extraordinary intensification of fantasy. It misses the fact that *dream and fantasy, and symptoms too, are making soul in the very midst of nature.*

Unlike naturalism in aesthetics or in philosophy and natural science, the naturalistic convention used by therapists has never been subject to critical scrutiny. The word *nature* has never even been properly reflected upon by the practitioner who relies habitually upon one or another of its more than sixty connotations.[33] The many meanings of the word betray the possibility of differing archetypal influences. The naturalism of the great Goddess of corn and crops has other psychological implications than does nature to the hero, a world of outer things or inner impulses to be conquered and harnessed. And these "natures" differ again from the virginal pristine nature of Artemis, the nature of Pan, the nature of Dionysus, or the mechanistic rational nature of Saturn. Therapeutic practice tends to be nature's child, seeing only its own face of simplicity and trust, unaware that nature takes on the face of the God who is determining what we see through our subjective viewpoints. If we look at it with the worshipful Romanticism of a nature nymph, it looks back at us with the same face.

Owing to the simplistic idea of nature used in therapy, the natural tends to be idealized. It becomes a nature without deformities, irrationalities, and individual idiosyncracies. This ideal standard is used moralistically to find fault with dreams and dreamers for what deviates from nature. In this manner the naturalistic fallacy releases a whole chain of further ones: a nomothetic fallacy (interpreting particular dream images through general laws); a normative fallacy (interpreting particular images through idealized standards, i.e., how an image should have appeared, correctly); a moralistic fallacy (interpreting unnatural images as also immoral). All these moves neglect the fundamental fact that the events of imagination do not occur in empirical nature. A multicolored child, a woman with an erected penis, an oak tree bearing cherries, a snake becoming a cat who talks, are neither wrong, false, nor abnormal because they are unnatural. Tigers of the imagination are not restricted to jungles and zoos; they can crouch upon my bookshelf or stalk the corridors of last night's motel. Pathologized images need to be read in the same way: a drowned baby, a flayed animal that is yet alive, or loss of teeth, hair, or fingers do not refer to similar events in empirical nature.

For example, a patient dreams of a racehorse with a broken leg. First the naturalistic fallacy looks for a memory horse from yesterday or from childhood to learn about the dream horse from personal associations with natural horses. Then it compares the dream horse with natural horses in general. Because a natural horse with a broken leg would be seriously sick, so the dream horse is sick. Besides, the dream horse "should" not have a broken leg. Since a natural broken-legged horse would most likely be killed, the dream horse represents the danger of death, or the wish to kill, or self-destruction. The more literalistic the naturalism, the more likely an interpretation in terms of serious illness and danger. Therapy will work at saving the horse (the medical fallacy), where "horse" means anything from the patient's vitality, his very life, to an unspecific libidinal charge carried by some aspect of his life.

In contrast, the racehorse may be interpreted by amplifying it with other themes: the horsepower of Wotan, of Poseidon; the space-conquering hero-horse of Hun, Mongol, Crusader, Arab, Spaniard; the motifs of speed, racing, winning; the Roman and Vedic horse sacrifice; the death horse; nursing-the-animal. The dream horse tells us more than the horse of memory or of nature. A series of symbolic, mythic, and cultural paths of insight are opened through the wound of affliction. Then we may see the afflicted horse to be the "carrier" of the dreamer's vulnerability. He is now stopped, opened, asking for meaning. The wound is that which enables the psyche to move him from his former position—riding to win —to one of awareness through breakdown. The broken leg is the focus of this change from nature into culture.

If we assume the horse should be on its feet again, restored to health, we forsake the actual image and move counter to the dream itself. But if we remain with the broken-legged horse as it is, then the dreamer gains insight by means of the pathologized image; for instance, that he has been "flogging a dead horse," abusing his physical vitality by racing to win proud on a thoroughbred charger. The pathologized image makes possible a new reflection, one that the dreamer feels poignantly because it is coupled with affliction, touching the soul at the point of death. The wound is the very focus of this movement from the former position high on his horse going swiftly with the natural flow of energy to the present one of recognizing other, psychic realities. The image itself represents the sudden shift in perspective from life to death, from physical reality to psychic reality, from nature to imagination.

The Breakdown of Normal Psychology

So to understand the metaphorical language of pathologizing we may not look at the twisted in terms of the straight, the failed in terms of the ideal, the dying in terms of life. To take a perspective different from that presented in the images and fantasies sets up a polarity. This polarity between straight and twisted, enacted by doctor and patient, further contributes to the killing asymmetry of the therapy game.

Having refused the assumptions of wrongness, we may not for a moment entertain the notion that images of sickness should not be there, or that they require action because they are diagnostic of danger. If there is anything wrong or dangerous in regard to pathologized fantasies it is in how we treat them; our attitude may turn them into the very events we fear. Our attitude toward the pathologizing may be more destructive than the pathologizing itself.

Nonetheless it can be argued that we do perceive the twisted against the norms of the straight. Even if psychopathology speaks an alien tongue and deserves the respect we give to any language not our own, this language is not only alien; it is distorted. Somewhere an ideal or norm is indeed presumed. If there were no natural position for comparison, how could there be the fallacy; if there were no literalism, how would we recognize the metaphorical symbolic perspective? To speak of distortion and deviations implies normal standards.

Here we need to make a distinction. Ideals and norms provide means for *seeing* pathologizing but they are not to be taken as means for *measuring* pathologizing. From the psychological viewpoint neither the statistical norm nor the ideal norm can offer the least relevance regarding the inherent value of a pathologized fantasy or experience. My nightmares, compulsions, anxieties may be essential to my work, my life-style, and my relations with others. Norms are perceptual modes for seeing contrasts; they are staining methods which help us notice deviations more sharply. By realizing how strongly pathologized an event is, we more immediately sense its importance. But the psychological worth of what is going on is stated not by the norm or the deviation, but by the affliction itself. It reports its own interior significance in its accompanying fantasy-images.

Pathologizing thus afflicts the very fantasy of norms themselves, the idea that there are objective standards, bench marks for the soul, its fantasy, its madness, its fate. When a therapist insists that no two cases are alike, he means this not merely in the detail of its accidents but in the profound sense that human being is essentially "differing" being, and that individuality is given with the particular mix of soul, the complexity of its composition. Therefore, when Jung defines individuation as a "process of differentiation"[36] and differentiation as "the development of differences, the separation of parts from the whole,"[37] it means realizing our differences from every other person.

But it also means our internal differences deriving from our internal multiple persons. Therefore an individual cannot provide a norm *even for himself.* The many persons which play their parts through an individual have differing paths to follow, different moments of rise and decay, different Gods to obey. The doctrine we saw in the last chapter about two or more kinds of soul (in China, Egypt, and Greece) also presents these souls as undergoing different destinies. Some ascended, others sank into the earth or below the earth, or joined ancestors, etc. The falling apart of the individual at death, the dissolution of his complexity, which the Buddha taught in his last cautionary enigma—"Decay is inherent in all composite things. Work on your salvation with diligence."—points to the absolute non-normality of each individual person. *If the fundamental principle of psychological life is differentiation, then no single perspective can embrace psychological life, and norms are the delusions that parts prescribe to one another.* A standard for one figure may be pathology for another, and pathology for one part may be normal from another perspective within the same individual.

Anarchy, the absolute relativism of this insistence on differences, can only be resolved in terms of a deeper perspective that takes full account of the ceaseless interconnections and fantasies going on among the persons of the psyche. I mean here the polytheistic perspective described in myths where norms are the myths themselves in their structuring and governing of experience. They tell us where we are, but not where we should be; and *they themselves are never the same,* but vary and deviate so that there is no single basic standard of any single myth, only variations upon it. But we have already touched on the place of myth in the organization of the psyche and we shall return to it again. Now the issue is one of recognizing the impossibility of laying down measures for psychic events. Heraclitus, Plotinus, Augustine, Kant, and Hegel have each held, in his own way, that soul—its depth, imagination, subjectivity, interiority—is immeasurable. Measureable norms and soul are incommensurables. We can speak only of the measurement fantasy and the normative fantasy as ways the psyche tries to become aware of its differences by looking in mirrors that are unable to reflect a true replica.

We are compelled to step away altogether from an ideal norm of man and a statistical norm of man. To take pathologizing thoroughly means the collapse of any normative psychology that is derived from external standards. Studies, experiments, research results, typicalities, have no bearing on soul-making except to provide materials for fantasy, and ideal types of behavior drawn from saints, sages, or statistics have value, not for behavior, but as metaphorical models for the personified imagination.

So we leave the normative ideals of health as balanced wholeness which derives either from statistical averages or idealizations of a sound mind in a sound body, a superman image of God-man who dominates our ego's fantasies of itself as a hero in marble without hurt or blemish, carved of one solid piece, perpetually balanced upon its center of gravity. For our concern is with the symptom, that thing so foreign to the ego, that thing which ends the rule of the hero—who, as Emerson said, is he who is immovably centered. Pathologizing moves the myth of the individual onward by moving him first of all out of the heroic ego.

We understand this pathologized language to be intentionally not speaking of human perfection, or even about the complete human being carrying his wounds and his cross; rather the psyche is telling us about its lacunae, its gaps and wasteland. And we believe that the tale told in these images is not even about us, men and women, not about human being mainly, but about itself, about psychic being; so that the deformation of human images with maimings, breaks, and suppurations decomposes our humanistic icon and our spiritual vision of the perfectibility of man, cracks all normative images, presenting instead a psychological fantasy of man to which neither naturalism nor spiritualism can apply. Both spiritual man and natural man are transformed by being deformed into psychological man.

Pathologizing is an iconoclasm; as such it becomes a primary way of soul-making. It breaks the soul free from its identification with ego and its life and the upperworld heroes of light and high Gods who provide the ego with its models, and who have cast our consciousness in a one-sided, suppressive narrowness regarding life, health, and nature. Pathologizing forces the soul to a consciousness of itself as different from the ego and its life—a consciousness that obeys its own laws of metaphorical enactment in intimate relation with death.

Imaginal Backgrounds to Pathologizing: 1. Alchemy

Psychology can look elsewhere for a background to pathologizing. There are fields where bizarre fantasies and afflicted figures are the norm. These fields do not expect the psyche to comply with other perspectives—medical, religious, humanistic, or whatever. By remaining wholly within the realm of the imagination they offer a psychological viewpoint to pathologizing.

When we look at alchemy as our first example, let us bear in mind that this was the depth psychology of an earlier age. It is a prestage of psychological analysis rather than of chemical analysis.[38] The alchemist projected his depths into his materials, and while working upon them he was working also upon his soul. The means of this work was the imagination: alchemy was an imaginative exercise couched in the language of concrete substances and impersonal objective operations. It is because alchemy presents such precise, concrete, and rich examples of the imaginative process of soul-making that I refer to it so often in this book.

The materials, vessels, and operations of the alchemical laboratory are personified metaphors of psychological complexes, attitudes, and processes. Every one of the alchemist's operations upon things like salt, sulphur, and lead were also upon his own bitterness, his sulphuric combustion, his depressive slowness. The fire he tended and regulated with careful exactitude was the intensity of his own spirit, his failing or burning interest. By means of concretely physical fantasies, the alchemical psychologists worked at the same time on both the soul in his materials and the soul in himself. In the depths of the soul there was also psychopathology, and in fact the substances and processes themselves were conceived in pathologized language, so that in alchemy we find pathologizing as an integral, necessary aspect of soul-making.

So much is this the case that when we enter the thought of alchemy these events lose their stigma of sickness and become metaphors for necessary phases of the soul-making process. So we find: processes of dismemberment, torture, cannibalism, decapitation, flaying, poisoning; images of monsters, dragons, unipeds, skeletons, hermaphrodites; operations called putrefaction, mortification, pulverizing, dissolution. The woodcuts and drawings of the alchemists display the processes with every sort of bizarre and obscene configuration.

Fundamental to these strenuously pathologized images and activities was one basic idea: the soul is lost in its literal perspective, its identity with material life. It is stuck in coagulations of physical realities. This perspective of reality needs to break down and fall apart, to be skinned alive and sensitized, or blackened by melancholic frustration. Habits and attitudes that obscure psychic insight and have lost psychic significance need to be dissolved, or made to stink, becoming monstrous and repulsive, or grindingly rubbed away.

These operations were part of what was called in alchemy the *opus,* the work that today in psychology is referred to as "working through resistances." In the consulting room we have personalized the resistances, whereas in the laboratory of the alchemist they were regarded as necessary qualities of the material itself, an aspect of the materialism and naturalism in which the psyche is imprisoned. Freeing the psyche from its material and natural view of itself and the world is an *opus contra naturam,* a work against nature. Essential to changing the soul's viewpoint are the experiences of pathologizing, for they express the decomposition of the natural; they present images that do not and cannot take place in the natural world. Although working with natural materials such as urine, quicksilver, or antimony, alchemy changed these substances into fantasies. It recognized the substantial nature of fantasy and the fantasy aspect of all natural substances. This was its true *opus contra naturam:* the transmutation, within the alchemist himself, of the natural viewpoint into the imaginal viewpoint. For this creative act pathologizing was indispensable.

Pathologizings, in fact, were necessary states of the soul as it went through the transmuting process. The alchemical process *was pathologizing:* transformation is a pathologizing experience. And none of these conditions were imagined morally or medically. So it is first of all to alchemy we must look to understand comparable destructive and disfigured events taking place within the psyche today. Alchemy as a psychological discipline came to an end long ago, but the alchemical processes within the psyche go on as before. Having lost the alchemical model, we are obliged to classify many of these processes now as psychopathology.

2. The Art of Memory

The art of memory affords a second example of a technical and objectified system of imagination where pathologizing is called for. This art was an extraordinary technique employed from classical times through the Renaissance for ordering the memory (or imagination—for these terms referred to each other and at times were interchangeable, much as our term "the unconscious" tends to cover both today).

The human memory was conceived as an internal treasure-house or theater rather than as an alphabetical or chronological filing system. Whereas an encyclopedic filing system is a *method* by which *concepts* are *written,* available one page at a time; a theater is a *place* where *images* are *envisioned,* available all at once. In the art of memory events belong together in clusters or constellations because they partake of the same archetypal meaning or pattern, and not merely because these events all begin with the letter *A* or *B* or happened on the same day or in the same year. The organization of the mind was based on inherent meanings, not on arbitrary nominalistic labels. In this arena of memory all the information of the universe could be stored, so that this art provided a means for having universal knowledge present to anyone mastering the techniques. It was both a retrieval system and a structural model for laying out the groundwork and hierarchies of the imagination on archetypal principles. The ordering rubrics that provided the categories were mainly the planetary Gods and themes from classical myths.

Essential to recollecting (which idea or topic or natural event belonged where) was distortion, a "tortured psychology"[39] as Frances Yates has called it. Visages, postures, and dress of figures to be remembered were twisted into odd, unnatural shapes, becoming "strikingly hideous and horrible."[40] They were pathologized. The masters of the art used bodily representations for conceptual ideas.[41] Notions are most vivid when they are concretely personified, especially those corporal likenesses which are comic, monstrous, bloodied, and diseased. These *metaphorica* (as they were called by Albert the Great) move the memory more than do usual images. Pathologized images were *imagines agentes,* active images, true soul-movers.

If we replace the word *memoria* with "imaginal soul" or "the realm of unconscious memories, fantasies, and emotions" as it later came to be called, we are better able to understand what was going on in this art. Then, by transposing the art of memory into a lesson for soul-making, we learn that if the soul is to be truly moved, a tortured psychology is necessary. For the soul to be struck to its imaginal depths so that it can gain some intelligence of itself—or, as we would say more dryly today, "become conscious of the unconscious"—pathologizing fantasies are required. A bloodied or obscene image in a dream, a hypochondriacal fantasy, a psychosomatic symptom, is a statement in imaginal language that the psyche is being profoundly stirred, and these pathologized fantasies are precisely the focal point of action and movement in the soul.

The importance of the horrifying image is still recognized in psychology. It is still to the *trauma* (castration threats, primal scenes, patricide, rejecting mothers, hideously jealous siblings, and other such vividly shocking fantasies) that psychoanalysis looks for the prime movers of the soul, the sources of its psychodynamics.

The art of memory is relevant in another way. It also suggests something about the care of interior images. When going into the imagination, it seems one should keep close to the images, for as Albert the Great says, this art should not "distend the soul" by carrying it through "imaginary spaces as a camp or a city."[42] The exploration of the imaginal of which we spoke in the last chapter here finds a very different interpretation.

Both alchemy and the art of memory work within minimal space. The alchemical process is imagined to happen within a closed vessel. Giulio Camillo puts the entire imaginal universe into a small wooden room, his Renaissance memory theater.[43] Albertus Magnus suggests that the distance one travels between images be no more than thirty feet.[44] According to him the most effective interior space for vivifying the imagination is in places "solemn and rare." These are the most "moving."[45]

We learn that one need not soar and plunge on grand shamanistic journeys in order to affect the soul to its depths. These would be trips of the spirit which distend the soul, filling it with air or gas, inflation. The soul is not moved by our moving through it; this is but another heroic voyage of the ego now translated into interior space. Instead, the pathologized image held solemnly is what moves the soul. One dwells upon the affliction or dwells with it, in bed with the leper, in its embrace. And as in alchemy or in memorizing, one goes over and over the same ground again. This *iteratio*, as it was called, is the itinerary, fantasy ever returning to the same complex, moving it now this way, now that. A virtue of pathologizing is that it does not let us escape the closed space required for soul-making, the heat and oppression and intensity—all of which are the antidote for spiritual inflations.

Yes we do need to extend our psychological space. This is one of therapy's main concerns. The soul has shrunk because its imagination has withered, and so we have little psychological space for fantasying, for holding things and mulling, for letting be. Events pass right through us, traceless. Or they press us into tight corners, no room to maneuver, no inner distance. We can hold more in mind than in soul, so that the contents of our minds are largely without psychological significance, input without digestion. "We had the experience but missed the meaning" (T. S. Eliot).

Imaginal geography, as described in the preceding chapter (pp. 38f), is not the only way of differentiating the imagination into qualitative regions or of extending nonphysical space. "Know thyself" means also know thy peculiar images, holding them in an interior void, close and familiar, without doing anything to them or for them. It is an inactive imagination and sometimes this is enough, for as we put events inside to carry and hold and digest, space is created to contain them.

For the art of memory warns against extension becoming distention. It is as possible to overreach and over-grow inwardly as in the world. Then we have myriads of images, the soul a supermarket with a little of everything or a vast continent that urges us to superficial interior flights, tourists in the soul. But this is less likely to happen when we remember that the idea of interiority refers to the vessel of the body and the psychological space is the realm of depth and not extension.

Paradoxically, we gain breadth of soul and wider horizons through vertical descent, through the inwardness of the image. Its puzzling peculiarity draws us down and in. The art of memory is an art of time, as work with memory always is. Unlike spiritual space travel that goes farther and farther "out," with freaking and peaking, highs and speed, the deepening of psychological space increases through slowness. The alchemists spoke of patience as a first quality of soul and considered soul-making the longest journey, a *via longissima*. The language is digestion, a vegetable love, depression into still waters.

I am aware that alchemy and the art of memory present difficult ideas. A reason for their difficulty is that we have lost touch with these two fields. And a reason for this loss returns us precisely to our main theme: psychopathology. Having supressed from our imagination the pathological strands and taken this part either medically or theologically, we have weakened the power of the imagination. It has dwindled to "mere fantasies"—because it no longer touchs us through the shock of pathologizing. Imagination has paled, no longer seems fully real, and so alchemy and the art of memory which rely upon and delight in the pathologized no longer seem valid disciplines.

As these fields faded, and with them the peculiarly twisted imagery of the medieval and Renaissance periods, the gruesome and grotesque lost touch with soul. Pathologizing was forced to make its appearance dissociated from the main imagery of the culture, through the Marquis de Sade or the Gothic novel, Victorian pornography, yellow journalism, the diseases and cruelties of social realism, surrealism, horror films, and now more recently by means of televised images in natural color soberly reported "live" from the war fronts.

But alchemy and the art of memory do reach us across the centuries by speaking to our distress. When an alchemical process or a tortured image is the relevant background to our psychopathology, then we see our distortion in the mirror of these distortions. Therefore, too, the best way to approach these fields is through our individual distress. Then they are no longer abstract studies of past centuries, but ever-present vehicles of soul-making.

And yet these ideas are not so difficult. Our Western psychological history has always recognized the central importance of pathologizing, for pathology has provided the central image of our culture. Christ—who began iconologically as a healer and teacher, as a shepherd, as *bambino* on Mother's knee—was some centuries later pathologized gruesomely onto the cross. The increasing emphasis upon the crucifixion image may be interpreted in any number of ways—historically, medically, theologically—but psychologically it confirms the truth that the soul is moved most profoundly by images that are disfigured, unnatural, and in pain.

An Excursion on Pathology as Crucifixion

The tremendous image of Christ dominates our culture's relation to pathologizing. The complexity of psychopathology with its rich variety of backgrounds has been absorbed by this one central image and been endowed with one main meaning: suffering. The *passio* of suffering Jesus[46] —and it is as translation of Jesus' passion that "suffering" first enters our language—is fused with all experiences of pathology. The crucifixion presents pathologizing first of all in the guise of emotional and physical torment. We read this suffering in the story (the days leading up to the crucifixion and the act itself) and we see it in paintings (the distressed agony in the scene). The allegory of suffering and its imagery has functioned so successfully to contain the pathologizing that one tends to miss the psychopathology that is actually so blatant in a configuration at once distorted, grotesque, bizarre, and even perverse: Golgotha, place of skulls; betrayal for money, Barabbas the murderer, the thieves and gambling soldiers; the mock purple robes and scorning laughter; the nails, lance, and thorns; the broken legs, bleeding wounds, sour sop; persecutory victimization along the route; women lovingly holding a greening corpse and their post-mortem hallucinatory visions. Quite an extraordinary condensation and overdetermination of psychopathological motifs.

Let me not be misunderstood. I am neither suggesting a psychiatric study of Jesus nor reducing the Christian mystery to psychopathology. This sort of foolishness belongs to the nineteenth-century's *folie raisonnante*. I am simply pointing out an obvious truth: religions always provide containers for psychopathology.

Our psychopathologies can be held within the narrative structure of a religious allegory. What is similar in us to events taking place in the story receives meaning by being linked with and finding place within a central myth. We recognize the ability of religion to contain psychopathology usually only when a religion breaks up. Then the complexes search for new Gods, or revert to old ones dormant within their patterns, and history books write of religious decline accompanied by moral degeneracy and barbarism.

But psychopathology is always present within religion, and we do not see it to the degree that the religion functions successfully. When critics like Marx, Nietzsche, and Freud stress that religion makes us unconscious, they mean more precisely that religion protectively covers psychopathology.

To press this further: the more successful a religion, the more psychopathology can be sheltered under its aegis, given rationale in its dogma and allowed operation by its ritual. But once one is outside the sphere of a religion, the psychopathology within it stands out. When cannibal confronts missionary, who is religious and who insane? Each has his own religious cosmos in which his styles of insanity—the one eating people, the other converting them—are well contained. From the viewpoint of another religious culture the crucifixion seems a sick and horrible image, just as from ours the central place of the yoni and lingam in Hindu religious practices or its hideous figure of Kali-Durga seem obscene psychopathological indulgences. To understand something about a culture's patterns of pathologizings, how they are lived and how they are justified, one turns first to that culture's religion. For religion, its odd minor sects especially, is an enormous treasury retaining and effectively organizing delusional systems, stereotypical behaviors, overvalued ideas, erotic obsessions, and sado-masochistic cruelties. The less religion, the more psychopathology spills out in the open and requires secular care.

However—by containing pathologizing, religion constricts it to the significance established by the allegory. The crucifixion model holds pathologizing to the one narrative and its governing idea of suffering, the theology of the passion. Therapy in our culture eventually comes up against the Christian allegory, whether the pathologizing is going on in an individual who is consciously Christian or not.

As part of working through the effects of this structure, let us distinguish three strands which have been identified: *(a)* specific pathologized contents and motifs (paranoid persecution and martyrdom, sado-masochism, illusions and hallucinations belonging to miracles of resurrection and the denial of death, psychopathy of betrayal, thieving and murder); *(b)* the emotion of suffering coloring the entire pattern; *(c)* theological allegorization (condemnation of enemies' behavior styles, value of suffering, rebirth through victimization, and the many other exegeses drawn from the central image).

With these strands distinguished we might be able to view *(a)* pathologized phenomena without at once going into *(b)* the emotion of suffering and *(c)* the allegorical interpretations. In other words, we might be both less victimized by pathologizing and less theological about its virtue. We might be less exaggerated about our loving, not having to be crucified to feel it truly, and about our dying, having to deny it or be a martyr to it. We would be returning to the crucifixion as an extraordinary image distinct from its allegorization.

I am suggesting here that we return to the original meaning of *pathos.*[47] In Greek this word meant most basically "something that happens," "experiences," a being moved and the capacity to be moved. The movements of the soul are *pathe,* and if we follow Aristotle, they show a capacity for change or qualitative changes actually going on. Of course these alterations can be painful and felt as afflictions, which Aristotle also noted. Nevertheless, *pathos* and suffering can be distinguished; the soul can go through its changes, even pathologizing changes, without these alterations in its quality having necessarily to be identified with suffering. Then we might be in a better position to envision soul-making in direct relation with pathologized images and experiences without having to sustain and overvalue them by the suffering of the Way of the Cross, and to realize—further—that even the crucifixion image is but one of many possible fantasies of pathologizing.

The Christ image was once better able to offer a variety of reflections even to its own myth. In the early centuries of Christianity Christ had various pagan identifications, principally Hercules,[48] and was in competition, so to speak, with both that hero and Mithra. Christ was imagined as well, against the backgrounds of Perseus, Asclepius, Orpheus, and Dionysus, and then later as Eros, Apollo, and also Jupiter. The advantage of imagining these pagan persons as faces of the Christ figure is that then one was better able to see which fantasy of Christ was dominating. Now with these pagan images absent, Hercules, Apollo, or Eros may subtly infiltrate the Christ idea and an individual's *imitatio* altogether unbeknownst to him. Then the Christian path becomes an imitation of Hercules, say, enacted and justified by the heroic ego, but called "Christian" action, or cleanliness, reform, or crusade.

If, as some report, the Christ vehicle no longer carries our culture's religious requirements, then it can no longer contain our pathologizings either. Fantasy no longer rests content with the *imitatio Christi* (where sin means pain or pain sin, where love means torture and goodness means masochism, but all is redeemable for there is no real death, and so on). Instead, fantasies escaped from this vessel begin to look for other reflections for psychological messes and pathological distortions. It is, therefore, imperative to be as iconoclastic as possible toward vessels that no longer truly work as containers and have become instead impediments to the pathologizing process.

By iconoclasm, I do not mean breaking the tremendous pathologized imagery of crucifixion, but rather shattering its crusted *allegorization* into a too-specific meaning which impedes us from recognizing the other figures within the Christ image and the other voices speaking through our pathologies, telling us neither of sin nor of suffering, necessarily presenting neither testimonies of love nor gates of resurrection.

As one instance: depression. Because Christ resurrects, moments of despair, darkening, and desertion cannot be valid in themselves. Our one model insists on light at the end of the tunnel; one program that moves from Thursday evening to Sunday and the rising of a wholly new day better by far than before. Not only will therapy more or less consciously imitate this program (in ways ranging from hopeful positive counseling to electroshock), but the individual's consciousness is already allegorized by the Christian myth and so he knows what depression is and experiences it according to form. It must be necessary (for it appears in the crucifixion), and it must be suffering; but *staying* depressed must be negative, since in the Christian allegory Friday is never valid *per se*, for Sunday—as an integral part of the myth—is preexistent in Friday from the start. The counterpart of every crucifixion fantasy is a resurrection fantasy. Our stance toward depression is a priori a manic defense against it. *Even our notion of consciousness itself serves as an antidepressant:* to be conscious is to be awake, alive, attentive, in a state of activated cortical functioning. Drawn to extremes, consciousness and depression have come to exclude each other, and psychological depression has replaced theological hell.

In Christian theology the heavy sloth of depression, the drying despair of melancholy, was the *sin* of *acedia*[49] (as it was called in Church Latin). It is just as difficult to manage today in therapeutic practice because our culture on the New Testament model has only the one upward paradigm for meeting this syndrome. Even though the Christ myth is supposedly no longer operative, tenacious residues remain in our attitudes toward depression.

Depression is still the Great Enemy. More personal energy is expended in manic defenses against, diversions from, and denials of it than goes into other supposed psychopathological threats to society: psychopathic criminality, schizoid breakdown, addictions. As long as we are caught in cycles of hoping against despair, each productive of the other, as long as our actions in regard to depression are resurrective, implying that being down and staying down is sin, we remain Christian in psychology.

Yet through depression we enter depths and in depths find soul. Depression is essential to the tragic sense of life. It moistens the dry soul, and dries the wet. It brings refuge, limitation, focus, gravity, weight, and humble powerlessness. It reminds of death. *The true revolution begins in the individual who can be true to his or her depression.* Neither jerking oneself out of it, caught in cycles of hope and despair, nor suffering it through till it turns, nor theologizing it—but discovering the consciousness and depths it wants. So begins the revolution in behalf of soul.

3. Myths

On the assumption that a psychological sickness is an enactment of a pathologizing fantasy, archetypal psychology proceeds to search for the *archai,* the governing principles or root metaphors of the fantasy. Archetypal psychology would attempt to lead the pathologizing into meaning through resemblance with an archetypal background following the principle stated by Plotinus, "All knowing comes by likeness,"[50] and following the method he also initiated called "reversion" *(epistrophé)*—the idea that all things desire to return to the archetypal originals of which they are copies and from which they proceed.[51] Pathologizings, too, would be examined in terms of likeness and imagined as having the intentionality of returning to an archetypal background.

What archetypal pattern is like my present behavior and fantasy? Who am I like when I do and feel this way? "Likeness" here refers to the idea that what is concretely manifested in an individual psyche has its likeness in a cluster of archetypal resemblances where the pathologizing I am undergoing finds place, makes sense, has necessity, and to which the pathologizing can "revert." These archetypal resemblances are best presented in myths in which the archetypal persons I am like and the patterns I am enacting have their authentic home ground.

It is to this mythical realm that I return all fantasies. The authentication of the fantasies of sickness is not in nature but in psyche, not in literal sickness but imaginal sickness, not in the psychodynamics of actual configurations past or present, but in mythical figures which are the eternal metaphors of the imagination,[52] the universals of fantasy.[53] These mythical figures, like my afflictions, are "tragical, monstrous, and unnatural,"[54] and their effects upon the soul, like my afflictions, "perturb to excess."[55] Only in mythology does pathology receive an adequate mirror, since myths speak with the same distorted, fantastic language.

Pathologizing is a way of mythologizing. Pathologizing takes one out of blind immediacy, distorting one's focus upon the natural and actual by forcing one to ask what is within it and behind it. The distortion is at the same time an enhancement and a new clarification, reminding the soul of its mythical existence. While in the throes of pathologizing, the psyche is going through a reversion into a mythical style of consciousness. Psychoanalysts have seen this but condemned it as regression to magical, primitive levels. But the psyche reverts not only to escape reality but to find another reality in which the pathologizing makes new sense.

In recent years I have made several forays into the idea of reversion as a primary method of archetypal psychology. A new *method* had become urgent. If a psychology refuses to borrow the developmental and historical, the natural scientific, and the religious approaches to psychological events, then it must find another fundamental method of understanding. Understanding psychological events through the general principle of opposites—depth psychology's main method—is too mechanical. It presents all soul events within a compensatory system of pairs: mind and body, ego and world, spirit and instinct, conscious and unconscious, inner and outer, and so on interminably. But soul events are not part of a general balancing system or a polar energy system or a binary information system. Soul events are not *parts* of any system. They are not reactions and responses to other sorts of events at the opposite end of any fulcrum. They are independent of the tandems in which they are placed, inasmuch as there is an independent primacy of the imaginal that creates its fantasies autonomously, ceaselessly, spontaneously. Myth-making is not compensatory to anything else; nor is soul-making.

So I began by examining various psychological syndromes as if they were mythical enactments, as if they were ways in which the soul is mimetic of an archetypal pattern. Of course this approach in modern times started with Freud. He imagined psychopathology against a background of the Oedipus myth. But Freud's method of reversion took a positivistic course; it became reduction. Instead of leading events back to their base in myth and seeing that pathologizing was ultimately mythical behavior—the soul's return to myth—Freud tried to base the myths on the actual behavior of actual biological families, ultimately reducing the mythical to the pathological.

My first essay in this method was an attempt to deliteralize suicide by grasping the pathologizing fantasy there going on as a metaphorical search for death by a soul caught in a naturalistic literalism called life.[56] The more I went into the subject, the less satisfactory were the positivistic explanations of it and the more it seemed that the pathologizing in suicide fantasies and behaviors were evidently of compelling necessity to the soul. I came to realize that we could do nothing whatsoever therapeutically about the literal act of suicide unless we understood very closely the fantasy and its intentions of returning the soul from life to death as a metaphor for another sort of existence.

But the task of referring the soul's syndromes to specific myths is complex and fraught with dangers. It must meet the philosophical and theological arguments against remythologizing, arguments which would see our approach as a backward step into magical thinking, a new daemonology, unscientific, un-Christian, and unsound.[57] It must meet as well its own inherent pitfalls, such as those we find in Philip Slater's work, *The Glory of Hera.*[58] Though he indeed recognizes that mythology must be related to psychology for myths to remain vital, his connection between psychological syndromes and myths puts things the wrong way round. He performs a wrong pathologizing upon mythology by explaining Greek myths through social culture and family relations. His is the sociological fallacy: i.e., one reads Greek myths for allegories of sociology. I would read sociology as an enactment of myths. And just here is a redeeming value of Slater's work. It offers an insight into the archetypal background—not of myths, but of his own sociological perspective. His theme is Hera, Goddess of family, state, and society; his approach is that of sociology, the discipline which in our day is a tribute to this Goddess, a Glory of Hera.

But the chief danger lies in taking myths literally even as we aim at taking syndromes mythically. For if we go about reversion as a simple act of matching, setting out with the practical intellect of the therapist to equate mythemes with syndromes, we have reduced archetypes to allegories of disease; we have merely coined a new sign language, a new nominalism. The Gods become merely a new (or old) grid of classificatory terms. Instead of imagining psychopathology as a mythical enactment, we would, *horribile dictu,* have lost the sense of myth through using it to label syndromes. This is the diagnostic perspective rather than the mythical, and we are looking not for a new way to classify psychopathology but for a new way of *experiencing* it. Here the Homeric and classical Greeks themselves provide a clue: their medical diagnoses were not in literal terms of myths and Gods, even though their thinking and feeling about affliction and madness was permeated with myths and Gods.[59] So we must take care, remembering that mythical thinking is not direct, practical thinking. Mythical metaphors are not etiologies, causal explanations, or name tags. They are perspectives toward events which shift the experience of events; but they are not themselves events. They are likenesses to happenings, making them intelligible, but they do not themselves happen. They give an account of the archetypal story in the case history, the myth in the mess.

Reversion also provides a new access to myths: if they are directly connected to our complexes, they may be insighted through our afflictions. They are no longer stories in an illustrated book. *We* are those stories, and we illustrate them with our lives.

Despite the risk of losing precisely the mythical perspective we are trying to gain, we can point to some of the potentialities in this approach. We can refer the manifestations of depression together with styles of paranoid thought to Saturn and the archetypal psychology of the senex.[60] Saturn in mythology and lore presents the slowness, dryness, darkness, and impotence of depression, the defensive feelings of the outcast, the angle of vision that sees everything askew and yet deeply, the repetitious ruminations, the fixed focus on money and poverty, on fate, and on fecal and anal matters.

Later I explored hysteria and the myths of Dionysus to show the God in that syndrome.[61] I hoped I might grasp why hysteria has always been associated with women, young women especially, and why this women's God, in whose troop were raving dancing girls, was also called Lord of Souls and associated with the depths of the underworld. I suggested that similar mythical phenomena were taking place in the beginnings of depth psychology, for it was hysteria in young women patients that led to the discovery of the unconscious psyche.

In a third study I explored the mythopathology revolving around the figure of Pan and the phenomenology of instinctual drives such as masturbation, rape, and panic.[62] Through the myths of Pan's behavior, especially in relation with retreating anima figures of reflection (Echo, Syrinx, and the Moon), we can learn much about the compulsion-inhibition patterns of human impulsiveness.

Eros in relation with Psyche, a myth which has been depicted in carvings and painting and tales for more than two thousand years,[63] offers a background to the divine torture of erotic neuroses—the pathological phenomena of a soul in need of love, and of love in search of psychic understanding. This story is particularly relevant for what goes on in the soul-making relationships which have been technically named "transference."

In addition to these examples, it is also possible to insight the ego, and ego psychology, by reverting it to the heroic myths of Hercules, with whose strength and mission we have become so caught that the patterns of Hercules—clubbing animals, refusing the feminine, fighting old age and death, being plagued by Mom but marrying her younger edition—are only now beginning to be recognized as pathology.

There are many avenues open for bringing mythology and pathology together. How little we understand, for instance, about the relation of sensual love and battling activity, the pathologized cycle of battle to bed to battle. But the Mars-Venus myths could give insights. What for instance would the myths of Hera tell about the pathologizings of marriage; and what background can be found in Hera's sons—Ares of battle-rage and Hephaistos the crippled smith—for a woman's angry attempts to smash the marriage bond to create on her own. (Hera brought forth these sons, by the way, without benefit of Zeus, in revenge and on her own.) Or we could look at the high-flying young champions —Bellerophon falling from his white winged horse, Icarus plunging into the sea, Phaëthon hurtling in flames, unable to manage his father's chariot of the sun—to understand the self-destructive behavior of the spirit and the young men in whom the spirit is strong.[64] The tales are endless and so are their possibilities, but no more endless than our pathologies and their possibilities.

This first entry into myth needs an important correction. It commits the ego fallacy by taking each archetypal theme into the ego. We fall into an identity with one of the figures in the tale: I become Zeus deceiving my wife, or Saturn devouring my children, or Hermes thieving from my brother. But this neglects that the whole myth is pertinent and all its mythical figures relevant: by deceiving I am also being deceived, and being devoured, and stolen from, as well as all the other complications in each of these tales. It is egoistic to recognize oneself in only one portion of a tale, cast in only one role.

Far more important than oversimplified and blatant self-recognitions by means of myths is the experiencing of their working *intrapsychically* within our fantasies, and then through them into our ideas, systems of ideas, feeling-values, moralities, and basic styles of consciousness. There they are least apparent, for they characterize the notion of consciousness itself according to archetypal perspectives; it is virtually impossible to see the instrument by which we are seeing. Yet our notion of consciousness may derive from the light and form of Apollo, the will and intention of Hercules, the ordering unity of the senex, the communal flow of Dionysus. When any one of these is assumed by the ego as its identity and declared to be the defining characteristic of consciousness, then the other archetypal styles tend to be called psychopathological.

This leads to a conclusion: psychopathology from the archetypal perspective means that *specific* psychopathologies belong to the various myths and operate as inalienable functions and images within them; psychopathology, as a *general* term, refers to the intervention into polytheistic consciousness of the monotheistic standpoint, forcing the literalizations and identifications that we still commonly call ego. Psychopathology, in general, refers to singleness of vision or an ignorance of fantasies that are always playing through all behavior.

Pathologizing: A Peroration

We are now in a position to form three ideas about the necessity of pathologizing. These ideas also express the dominant themes of this chapter, and the entire book presents variations upon them.

First, archetypal psychology can put its idea of psychopathology into a series of nutshells, one inside the other: within the affliction is a complex, within the complex an archetype, which in turn refers to a God. Afflictions point to Gods; Gods reach us through afflictions. Jung's statement—"the gods have become diseases; Zeus no longer rules Olympus but rather the solar plexus, and produces curious specimens for the doctor's consulting room"[65]—implies that Gods, as in Greek tragedy, *force themselves symptomatically into awareness.* Our pathologizing is their work, a divine process working in the human soul. By reverting the pathology to the God, we recognize the divinity of pathology and give the God his due.

From the archetypal perspective the Gods manifest themselves in and through human life, and therefore Greek polytheism, as W. F. Otto said, "contradicts no human experience."[66] Everything belongs—nothing is denied or excluded. Psychopathologies of every sort become part of the divine manifestation. "The gods" writes H. D. F. Kitto, "are never transcendental, external to our universe . . . they are some force within ourselves, some divine instinct. . . ."[67] They are the very sources of our acts and our omissions, according to Kerényi, present not only when invoked or praised.[68] To find them we look to our complexes, recognizing the archetypal power in the complex. For as Jung says, "It is not a matter of indifference whether one calls something a 'mania' or a 'god.' To serve a mania is detestable and undignified, but to serve a god is full of meaning. . . ."[69]

A complex must be laid at the proper altar, because it makes a difference both to our suffering and perhaps to the God who is there manifesting, whether we consider our sexual impotence, for example, to be the effect of the Great Mother's Son who may be served thereby, or Priapus who, neglected, is taking revenge, or Jesus whose genitality is simply absent, or Saturn who takes physical potency and gives lascivious fantasy. Finding the background for affliction calls for familiarity with an individual's style of consciousness, with his pathologizing fantasies, and with myth to which style and fantasy may revert.

To study the complex only personally, or to examine only personally the psychodynamics and history of a case is not enough, since the other half of pathology belongs to the Gods. Pathologies are both facts and fantasies, both somatic and psychic, both personal and impersonal. This view of pathology brings with it a view of therapy such as we find in the Renaissance with Paracelsus, who said:

> . . . The physician must have knowledge of man's other half, that half of his nature which is bound up with astronomical philosophy; otherwise he will be in no true sense man's physician, since Heaven retains within its sphere half of all bodies and all maladies. What is a physician who knows nothing of cosmography?[70]

"Cosmography" here refers to the imaginal realm, the archetypal powers bearing the names of the planets and the myths portrayed by the constellations of the stars. Neglect of this "half," the imaginal or psychic component, the God in the disease, fails the human. To deal fully with any human affair, one must devote half one's thoughts to what is not human. "Maladies" lie also in the archetypes and are part of them.

If Gods reach us through afflictions, then pathologizing makes them immanent, opening the psyche for them to enter; thus pathologizing is a way of moving from transcendental theology to immanent psychology. For immanence is only a doctrine until I am knocked back through symptoms by these dominant powers, and I recognize that in my disturbances there really are forces I cannot control and yet which want something from me and intend something with me.

Of all my psychological events my pathologizing seems at times to be the only happening that is peculiarly mine. Afflictions give me the convincing delusion of being different. My hopes and fears, and even my loves, may all have been put upon me by the world's directions, or by my parents as residues and options of their unlived lives. But my symptoms point to my soul as my soul points to me through them.

Yet the symptoms and quirks are both me and not me—both, most intimate and shameful and a revelation of my deeps, steering my fate through character so that I cannot shrug them off. Yet they are *not* of my intention; they are visitations, alienations, bringing home the personal/impersonal paradox of the soul: what is "me" is also not "mine" —"I" and "soul" are alien to each other because of soul's domination by powers, daimons, and Gods.

The pathological experience gives an indelible sense of soul, unlike those we may get through love or beauty, through nature, community, or religion. The soul-making of pathology has its distinct flavor, salty, bitter; it "skins alive," "wounds," "bleeds," making us excruciatingly sensitive to the movements of the psyche. Pathology produces an intensely focused consciousness of soul, as in undergoing a symptomatic pain—sobering, humbling, blinding. It gives the hero a little twinge of heel, the soft spot that reminds the ego of death, of soul. Do you remember Zooey's remark (in Salinger's story) when his sister asks him about his symptom? "*Yes,* I have an ulcer, for Chrissake. This is Kaliyuga, buddy, the Iron Age. Anybody over sixteen without an ulcer's a goddam spy."[71] In my symptom is my soul.

What pathologizing does for the individual's psychology it does as well for the field of psychology: it keeps us close to the actuality of the psyche, preventing metaphysical and scientific escapes. Already a generation ago Erwin Minkowski pointed out:

> . . . Psychopathology has had the great merit of leading me and my philosopher-psychiatrist colleagues back to the concrete reality of our patients' lives again and again . . . thus protecting us from the dangers of pure philosophy. It was never a question of transposing purely and simply the data and methods used by a given philosophy into the realm of psychopathological facts. That would have led to a 'hyperphilosophizing' of psychopathology . . . it would have risked deforming psychopathology entirely.[72]

This sensate, concrete physical reality of soul was refound in this century through the psychological occupation with pathologizing. The descent into soul via pathologizing is what the last three score years and ten of analysis has taught. It has been the chief lesson of the entire psychotherapeutic movement. Any postanalytical hermeneutic for the soul must have learnt this lesson so as to include its meaning. The rediscovery of soul through psychopathology reigns supreme over all psychotherapy's other achievements: cultural, social, methodological, philosophical. Where earlier psychology tried to see through religion for its psychopathological content, we are now trying to see through psychopathology for its religious content.

Our complexes are not only wounds that hurt and mouths that tell our myths, but also eyes that see what the normal and healthy parts cannot envision. André Gide said that illness opens doors to a reality which remains closed to the healthy point of view. One understands what he meant about the psychological acuity and richness of culture during periods of historical decay; but why is the same phenomenon of psychological depth in periods of personal decay—ageing, neurosis, depression—not recognized with the same respect?

The soul sees by means of affliction. Those who are most dependent upon the imagination for their work—poets, painters, fantasts—have not wanted their pathologizing degraded into the "unconscious" and subjected to clinical literalism. ("The unconscious," and submitting the pathologized imagination to therapy, found favor with less imaginative professions: nurses, educationalists, clinical psychologists, social workers.) The crazy artist, the daft poet and mad professor are neither romantic clichés nor antibourgeois postures. They are metaphors for the intimate relation between pathologizing and imagination. Pathologizing processes are a source of imaginative work, and the work provides a container for the pathologizing processes. The two are inextricably interwoven in the work of Sophocles and Euripides, Webster and Shakespeare, Goya and Picasso, Swift and Baudelaire, O'Neill and Strindberg, Mann and Beckett—these but an evident few.

The wound and the eye are one and the same. From the psyche's viewpoint, pathology and insight are not opposites—as if we hurt because we have no insight and when we gain insight we shall no longer hurt. No. Pathologizing is itself a way of seeing; the eye of the complex gives the peculiar twist called "psychological insight." We become psychologists because we see from the psychological viewpoint, which means by benefit of our complexes and their pathologizings.

Normal psychology insists that this twisted insight is pathological. But let us bear in mind that normal psychology does not admit pathologizing unless dressed in its patient's uniform. It has a special house called abnormal. And let us also bear in mind that the ego's normative view of the psyche is a cramped distortion. If we studied soul through art, biography, myth; or through the history of wars, politics and dynasties, social behavior and religious controversy; then normal and abnormal might have to switch houses. But normal academic psychology eschews these fields and compiles its statistics so often from undergraduates who have not yet had the chance to experience the range of their madness.

The deeper reason for steering clear of analysis is that it may disturb the myth in the madness by excising its pathological parts in the name of clinical improvement. If our psychological lives are under the governance of mythical patterns because Gods are moving in our complexes, then the pathologizing going on in our lives cannot be extracted without deforming the myth and preventing reversion to it. The implication is that each archetype has its pathological themes and that each pathological theme has an archetypal perspective. Archetypal psychopathology finds the pathological inherently necessary to the myth: Christ must have his crucifixion; Dionysus must be childish and attract titanic enemies; Persephone must be raped; Artemis must kill him who comes too close.

Myths include the phenomena that are discredited in normative psychology, where they are called abnormal, bizarre, absurd, self-destructive, and sick. If we pursue this difference between usual psychology and mythology, we see clearly how *mythology saves the phenomena of psychopathology.* Psychology finds place for these phenomena of the soul only by discrediting them; mythology credits them just as they are, finding them necessary to its account. It makes no excuse, for it presents nothing wrong. It is not the myth that is wrong but our ignorance of its workings in us. The fallacies are circumvented; they do not even arise—neither the normative, the clinical, nor the moralistic. Because archetypal psychology looks to myth for its base, it too regards the pathologized phenomena of the psyche as necessary to a complete account of any psychic complexity. Without psychopathology there is no wholeness; in fact, psychopathology is a differentiation of that wholeness.

The healthy, normal parts of the soul—or what might better be called its unimaginative and literalistic fantasies—are never quite able to accept the ultimate reflection each of us makes about our individual course of depth analysis.

There is an irreversible trend of pathologizing in the soul. I am curiously dependent upon it, and when it is lost to me, my sense of soul too wavers and fades. I experience the necessity of pathologizing as a need of soul. It is like an immutable and incorruptible core, for though it moves and goes through changes, it is never transformed, is permanently bound to all my psychological life, providing the base ground, the primal material for all my psychic processes, for soul-making itself. It is irredeemable because the category of redemption does not here apply; it belongs authentically to the soul's mythical essence; as such, pathologizing is essential to my myths and my soul.

Second, these conclusions about pathologizing reflect our historical culture. Although these ideas are drawn from the same sources as Freud and Jung and in the main follow their thinking, yet these ideas reflect the movement of pathologizing beyond Freud and Jung.

Consciousness today is closer to its pathology. Psychopathology is no longer held behind asylum walls. The sickness fantasy is now so dominant that one sees disintegration, pollution, insanities, cancerous growth, and decay wherever one looks. Pathology has entered our speech and we judge our fellows and our society in terms once reserved for psychiatric diagnoses. And the ego falls apart.

No longer is ego able to cope by *will power* with tough problems in a *real* world of *hard* facts. Our falling apart is an imaginal process, like the collapse of cities and the fall of heroes in mythical tales—like the dismemberment of Dionysian loosening which releases from overtight constraint, like the dissolution and decay in alchemy. The soul moves, via the pathologized fantasy of disintegration, out of too-centralized and muscle-bound structures which have become ordinary and normal, and so normative that they no longer correspond with the psyche's needs for nonego imaginal realities which "perturb to excess."[73]

Is it history or culture or society that has forced the recognition of pathologizing on us? It seems the psyche itself insists on pathologizing the strong ego and all its supportive models, disintegrating the "I" with images of psychopathic hollowness in public life, fragmentation and depersonalization in music and painting, hallucinations and pornographies in private visions, violence, cruelty, and the absurd surrealisms of urban wars, racisms, causes, freakishness in dress and speech. These images, like the pathologized *metaphorica* in the memory art, alchemy, and myth, twist and shock the "I" out of its integrative identity, out of its innocence and its idealization of human being, opening it to the underworld of psychic being. It is not the psyche itself that insists upon a revision of psychology in terms not of peaks but of parts?

Falling apart makes possible a new style of reflection within the psyche, less a centered contemplation of feeling collected around a still point, thoughts rising on a tall stalk, than insights bouncing one off the other. The movements of Mercury among the multiple parts, fragmentation as moments of light. Truth is the mirror, not what's in it or behind it, but the very mirroring process itself: psychological reflections. An awareness of fantasy that cracks the normative cement of our daily realities into new shapes.

This style, with which we are engaged in both the form and the content of these chapters, could not have come into being had the normal control apparatus of the old ego not fragmented, making possible a new sophistication of multiple mirroring, where beginning and end do not matter, where premises are themselves conclusions and conclusions open into discontinuities, repetitions with variations. The very style of doing psychology—of thinking and feeling and writing it —incorporate pathologizing. And so it must, if a psychology book is to reflect and evoke the psyche.

The style of consciousness today is pathologized and draws its awareness from the pathography that is our actual lives. "Consciousness" means psychic reflection of the *psychic* world about us and is part of adaptation to that reality. As that reality darkens and divides, consciousness can no longer be described with heroic metaphors of light, decision, intention, and central control. *Ego consciousness as we used to know it no longer reflects reality.* Ego has become a delusional system. "Heightened" consciousness today no longer tells it from the mountain of Nietzsche's superman, an overview. Now it is the underview, for we are down in the multitudinous entanglements of the marshland, in anima country, the "vale of Soul-making."[74] So heightened consciousness now refers to moments of intense uncertainty, moments of ambivalence. Hence the task of depth psychology now is the careful exploration of the parts into which we fall, releasing the Gods in the complexes, bringing home the realization that all our knowing is in part only, because we know only through the archetypal parts playing in us, now in this complex and myth, now in that; our life a dream, our complexes our *daimones.*

I mentioned earlier how our fantasies carry events to an incurable possibility, to meningitis or cancer, or to suicide. The "incurable possibility" is nothing less than death. So for a *third* reason pathologizing is a royal road of soul-making. It takes each complex to its ultimate term, to its final unknown, the depths where we can penetrate no further, never knowing what's "the matter." The complex that gnaws and makes us peculiar also makes us particular distinct individuals— for that is what "peculiar" means. For life, the complex is but a symptom to be rid of. But because the inhibition, the distortion, and the affliction point to death, the complex becomes a center around which one's psychic life constellates. It is not upon life that our ultimate individuality centers, but upon death.[75] Its kingdom, Greek myths of Hades and Tartarus say, is the world under and within all life, and there souls go home.[76] There, psychic existence is without the natural perspective of flesh and blood, so that pathologizing by taking events to death takes them into their ultimate meaning for soul. One has one's death, each his own, alone, singular, toward which the soul leads each piece of life by pathologizing it. Or perhaps it is pathologizing that unerringly leads the soul into the deepest ontological reflection. Symptoms are death's solemn ambassadors, deserving honor for their place, and life mirrored in its symptoms sees there its death and remembers soul. Pathologizing returns us to soul, and to lose the symptom means to lose this road to death, this way of soul.

Plato and his followers presented three main modes of soul-making: eros, dialectics, and mania.[77] There is a fourth: thanatos. We find a basis for this connection between soul-making and death in Plato's own description of the dying Socrates in a dialogue *(Phaedo)* which examines the nature and reality of *psyché* even while dwelling upon the pathologized details of hemlock poisoning. The soul is led to knowledge of itself (to true ideas in Platonic language) through love, through intellectual discipline, and as Hegel too saw, through madness.[78] But equal with these is pathologizing as the mode of reflection in terms of invisibles and unknowables, the fantasies of psychic existence, what is below and after the actions of life and is deeper than they—that is, what is symbolically attributed to death.

Like Socrates in the *Phaedo,* although for a period which extended through his whole adult life, Freud examined the nature and reality of the psyche, all the while reflecting upon his own death and that of his friends and family, on the nature of death, on the physical pathology of his body, and the pathologizing going on in his patients and colleagues.[79] His pathologizing was contemporaneous with the creation of depth psychology, which laid the groundwork for soul-making again in our era.

By beginning with the symptom, "a thing that is more foreign to the ego," pathologizing turns the entire psyche upon a new pivot: death becomes the center, and with it fantasies that lead right out of life. Pathologizing is not only a metaphorical language but a way of translation, a way of turning something literally known, usual, and trivial like the psychopathologies of everyday life into something unknown and deep. As such, pathologizing is a hermeneutic which leads events into meaning. Only when things fall apart do they open up into new meanings; only when an everyday habit turns symptomatic, a natural function becomes an affliction, or the physical body appears in dreams as a pathologized image, does a new significance dawn. As the psyche is never invulnerable to these movements, so it is never cured. Therewith archetypal realizations may enter. So too an archetypal psychology can never leave its base in pathography.

The deepening and interiorizing that goes on through pathologizing lends neurosis an extraordinary feeling of significance, that through it we are elected, separated from merely ordinary people. This appraisal, deriving itself from neurosis, is of course neurotic (nothing makes us more commonly normal than our "abnormalities"). But the sense of significance points beyond neurosis, beyond this symptom and that complaint which so many others have too.

The feeling of election through the complex is above all a psychic statement, which says that a pathologized awareness is fundamental to the sense of individuality. It tells of a difference, not between kinds of people, but between styles of consciousness, natural and psychic, literal and imaginal. Having forced the reality of the imaginal upon one, pathologizing leaves one marked by its imprint. A piece of the person has been struck by the Gods and drawn into a myth and now cannot let go of its mad requirements. The boar has wounded Ulysses' thigh; the daemon of the crossing point has broken Jacob's hip. I am an individual, by virtue not of my common wounds but of what comes through them to me, the archetypes of my myths in which lie my madness, fate, and death.

By clinging faithfully to the pathological perspective which is the differential root of its discipline, distinguishing it from all others, depth psychology maintains its integrity, becoming neither humanistic education, spiritual guidance, social activity, nor secular religion. By refusing the temptations and sentimentalities that would leave sickness and queerness behind, depth psychology retains even the disparaging terms of its textbooks. For to abandon the words so weighted with sickness, so negative in connotation, would again split the psyche from its pathology. The value of these words lies precisely in keeping psyche pathologized. Neither literalistically real, nor the empty nomina of a professional convention, these words are metaphorical expressions for our psychic condition, sources of reflection, ways of finding oneself into a myth.

By remembering its own genealogy myth—that it was born from the psychopathology of French and Austrian hysteria and Swiss schizophrenia, outcast afflictions which then made no sense and were held in disrepute—depth psychology keeps in touch with souls *in extremis,* with the afflicted, the abnormal, the refused. By maintaining itself in this perspective through pathologizing, in touch with the fantasy of sickness that everyone else would prefer to cure or to deny, depth psychology is inevitably both traditional and revolutionary.

We are traditional because we return all things to their deepest principles, the *archai,* the limiting roots holding down and in. They determine by recurring with fatalistic regularity, little caring for place or time. We are revolutionary because these same *archai* are the radicals of existence. They will out, always. They force the claims of the dispossessed soul upon the ruling consciousness of each place and time.

Three / Psychologizing or Seeing Through

> *Our general instinct to seek and learn will, in all reason, set us inquiring into the nature of the instrument with which we search.*
>
> PLOTINUS
> *Enneads* IV, 3, 1.

Psychological Ideas

The question before us in this chapter is even more essential to the psyche than those with which we have been engaged. Now we shall be asking not only what is psychology itself, that discipline named for the soul, but what is *psychologizing*—the soul's root and native activity. Our inquiry will now proceed by means of ideas rather than persons, although the archetypal connection between persons and ideas should emerge in the course of the chapter.

By emphasizing ideation, we shall be assuming the passionate importance of psychological ideas. We shall be showing that the soul requires its own ideas, in fact, that soul-making takes place as much through ideation as in personal relationships or meditation. *One aim of this book is the resuscitation of ideas* at a time in psychology when they have fallen into decline and are being replaced by experimental designs, social programs, therapeutic techniques.

There seems to be nothing more astounding in the field of psychology than its scarcity of interesting ideas. Whole schools are built upon one book, and one book upon one idea, and that often a simplification or a borrowing. The ideational process in psychology is far behind its methodology, instruments, and applications—and far, far behind the psyche's indigenous richness. In this century since Freud and Jung and the wealth of ideas they introduced—from libido, projection, and repression to individuation, anima/animus, and archetype, to pick but a handful—how few have been the ideas generative of psychological reflection! Technical concepts proliferate in the jargon of a profession, but these are short-lived fruit flies feeding on the sound fruit.

Ideas decline for many reasons. They too grow old and hollow, become private and precious; or they may detach from life, no longer able to save its phenomena. Or they may become monomanic, one particular idea crediting itself with more value than all others, and in opposition to them. Today action is thought of within this polarity, which at its extreme would make action blind and ideas impotent. An old cliché, the bodiless head of academic psychology, is converting into a new cliché, the headless body of therapeutic psychology—a current demonstration of action against ideation.

French thought, especially, has long been concerned with the relation between idea and action, between writer and fighter. To "descend into the street" or to be "above the *melée*" occupies the fantasy of French intellectuals such as Sartre as much as in the days of the Dreyfus affair. Indeed, French thought is paradigmatic for this problem, for whenever ideation and action become separate and opposite, we find ourselves in the tradition of Descartes, where the realm of thinking is cut off from that of the material world. Ideas have no effect, being only in the head, and actions become materialistic mechanisms whether described by modern Marxists or Monod. The struggle to reunite the parts, or to go around them, fully occupies modern French thought. When it turns to Freud and to the body, as in the cases of Merleau-Ponty, Ricoeur, and Lacan, or when these same writers consider words and language equal to action itself, we see that the old Cartesian dualism has reappeared in these attempts to overcome it. Their fascination with the connection between ideation and action, their approaches and solutions, are relevant mainly for those occupying the same split psychological situation that Cartesianism represents.

We are used to contrasting idea and action, believing that subjective reflection restricts action, sickling it over with the pale cast of psychological thought. We tend to believe that psychologizing opposes participating, that instead of doing something about the world, psychology sees through it with interpretations. But when this opposition does occur in our lives, it is not because of an inherent enmity between idea and action; but rather because the action has a blind antipsychological component and is being used to dodge psychological reflection. *Sometimes we act in order not to see.* I may well be actively doing and taking part in order to avoid knowing what my soul is doing and what interior person has a stake in the action. Depth psychology has perceived this pattern of avoidance, this flight into activity, and has condemned it as "acting out." A good deal of pathologizing takes place disguised as looking for action, going where the action is, getting a piece of the action. It is against this manic hyperactivity that some of our fears of ideas, reflection, and even depression need to be considered. Without ideas the soul is more easily compelled, more compulsively active.

But action and idea are not inherent enemies, and they should not be paired as a contrast. On the one hand, psychologizing, as we shall soon be describing it, is an action. The soul's first habitual activity is reflection, which in old-fashioned language belongs to the essence of consciousness as wetness to water, as motion to wind. And reflection by means of ideas is an activity; idea-forming and idea-using are actions. On the other hand, action always enacts an idea. To forget this is to take action literally, to fall prey to the ideology of activism (action sicklied over with a big bulge of muscle). *Action itself is an idea,* and there are many ideas of action. It depends upon our idea of action whether it must be blind and opposed to ideation or, as political activists insist, must come first and reflection later, after the act. Psychological ideas do not oppose action; rather they enhance it by making behavior of any kind at any time a significant embodiment of soul. And it is *to bring soul into action and action to soul* by means of psychologizing that is this chapter's aim.

So we shall be affirming that the work of psychological ideation is not divided from action. Psychological ideation is relevant to action of any sort and is itself an action of a class within which other actions can be subsumed.

I have slipped in one qualification which ought not to go unnoticed. Not just any ideas are passionately important, not just any ideas are worthwhile to the soul; the kind for which I make this claim are psychological ideas, for it is by means of them that the psyche reflects upon itself and furthers soul-making. By psychological ideas I mean those that engender the soul's reflection upon its nature, structure, and purpose.

Unlike such terms as intelligence, behavior, motivation, reinforcement, Freud's and Jung's ideas of depth psychology are internal to the psyche. They are less about man and his functioning and parts than about soul and its functioning and parts. (This distinction between man and soul we shall have to reserve for the last chapter in order to treat it fairly.) Freud's and Jung's ideas are both based in psyche and are for the psyche. An idea such as *exchange* may be useful for the psyche, but it is based outside, in economics. Or an idea such as *repression* may be based in the psyche but useful outside for understanding society. True psychological ideas circulate within a psychic field, arising from the psyche and returning to it. They self-reflect. That is their internality and is what gives them their ability to interiorize events. An event that is psychologized is immediately internalized; it returns to the soul.

Moreover, major psychological ideas echo the deepest questions of the soul, bringing it to reflect profoundly about its nature and destiny. These ideas can more readily be called archetypal because they perpetually recur with powerful fascination both in the history of psychology and in our individual psychological history, where we meet them as crucial insoluble problems. Some of these archetypal ideas arise from the soul's relation with death, the world, and other souls; with its body, its gender and generation; with virtue and with sin, with love, beauty, and knowledge; with Gods, with sickness, with creation and destruction, with power, time, history, and future; with family, ancestors, and the dead. Archetypal ideas are primarily speculative ideas, that is, they encourage speculation, a word which means mirroring, reflecting, visioning. As archetypal ideas are rather like mythical fantasies, so psychologizing by means of them is a fantasying activity, seeing into things and speculating about them by means of fantasies.

Archetypal ideas or fantasies appear in a wide range of material—in art, religions, and scientific theories; in delusional systems of the insane and in the personal organization of our lives. But we cannot consider an archetypal idea in itself psychological unless it has been psychologized—that is, considered primarily as a manifestation of the psyche, as first of all an archetypal problem of the soul. This reflective moment keeps ideas connected with soul and the soul in connection with its ideas.

A psyche with few psychological ideas is easily a victim. It has meager means for orientating itself as a soul in a psychological field. It also loses the ability of seeing through ideas that are imposed upon it. It asks the wrong questions and forgets itself as soul; it turns to ideas from other areas and is blinded by the dazzling illuminations coming to it through notions of nature, of history, or of religion. Such concepts as evolution or energy or salvation, by lighting up and making clear the obscurities of history, religion, philosophy, or the physical world, tend to take in more than the area of their derivation—they tend to take in the psyche, too. Then the soul forgets its distinct nature, that it requires its own ideas, and that evolutionary development, transformations of energy, a dialectic of opposites, or a theology of salvation are borrowed coin from alien realms. Then we begin to consider the soul to be the reflection of political and economic processes—Marxist psychology, or spiritual evolution—Chardinesque psychology—or we imagine the psyche to be like a piece of electronic machinery or comparable to a scant-haired primate.

Let me recapitulate how this alienation comes about: First we refuse the importance and value of ideas—usually by placing them in opposition to actions. This leads to unreflecting action at the expense of ideas, fostering an overactive soul without an idea of itself. Then we borrow alien perspectives, regarding ourselves as consumers, computers, or apes.

The borrowing of alien perspectives starts a process of alienation in which the soul, having no adequate idea of itself, loses touch with itself. *We have not only lost soul; we have lost even the idea of soul.* Where do we find "soul" in a psychology book or lecture or a psychotherapy session? "Modern man in search of a soul" also means that man is in search of an idea of the soul, ideas that can give soul, soul-making ideas. Without them nonpsychological ideas become invested with soul values, and we become infiltrated by ideologies.

Ideologies do not originate in the strength or truth of ideas; they do not require important ideas at all, and may be based more on slogans than on articulated systems. Their true source is in souls that have lost valid psychological perspectives. An idea turns into an ideology owing to the conviction it receives, the passion with which a soul lost to itself invests it.

Not only does the psyche without ideas turn to alien fields and to ideologies. It turns as well to other people, asking for an idea about this or that problem, in search of insight, religious truth, spiritual guidance. A psyche without sufficient ideas becomes in need of persons, unable to distinguish between persons and the ideas they embody. In its victimization it looks for masters. Hence the dependency upon every sort of psychological teacher from psychiatrist to guru and all the blind alleys of false loves for the sake of ideas, where falling in love is a search for ideas, and the battle between lovers turns out ultimately to be an incompatibility of fantasies and a contest between psychological perspectives.

Our proclivity for alien ideas, our possession by ideologies that we can die for, and our fascination with persons who might open our eyes to psychological awareness, demonstrate that the soul must have ideas. The passionate importance of psychological ideas is evidenced by the psyche itself in its search for and clinging to notions, insights, principles, and persons by which to see itself. To use the metaphor of instinct,[1] the soul hungers for ideas. It is as if the instinct to reflect could not function without ideas, as if ideas were our means to reflect and were instinctually required. The psyche seems to be driven to ideation in order to exercise its reflective function, and this drive or function means as much to its survival as do reproduction, aggression, and play.

Does this not imply that a primary obligation of the psychologist— and particularly the therapeutic psychologist, whose first concern is *psychēs therapeia* or care of soul, and who is the devotee or servant of

Psyche—is to admit this need of soul for ideas. A psychologist serves Psyche by elaborating her ideas, and a psychologist is not a psychologist unless he has elaborated a *logos* of the *psyche*, his own web of psychological ideas which attempt to do justice to the soul's variety and depth.

If today we are sick from loss of soul, and if this alienation arises partly from the paucity of psychological ideas, then part of our healing proceeds through ideation. A part of working on one's psyche is working out one's psychology, building ideational modes for more differentiated reflection about its processes. As the soul goes through processes its ideas change, and the discussion of ideas must keep pace with these changes. The discussion of ideas in therapy is therefore not necessarily a defense against emotion but the preliminary to emotion and the carrier of it. This holds true for the individual and for the field itself, which dries and ages when it lacks new ideas to advance its emotional life. Ideation thus becomes a psychotherapeutic activity, part of archetypal psychology's method of treatment. We shall see how this works as we proceed.

In therapy a most essential idea to discover is which idea of soul the patient is enacting: is it material and physiological, Christian and immortal, personal and self-owned? Equally important: what ideas of soul has the therapist? Under what archetypal idea concerning the nature of the psyche are they together enacting the therapy? If therapy is soul-making, what fantasy of soul are they making?

The Vision of Ideas

I have continually been using the metaphor of vision, speaking of perspectives, of seeing, viewing, blinding, reflecting. This visual metaphor is appropriate to ideas. For ideas are not mere residues of empirical investigations, concepts abstracted from operations. They are not, as Locke believed, "founded in particular things." Neither are they the reason in or of things, as Aquinas and Hegel thought. Nor need we take ideas to be Kantian innate categories of reason, fixed principles predetermining all psychic experience. We may leave to one side such philosophical questions as whether ideas are built or given, whether they are induced, deduced, or abduced (Pierce). Because we are not looking at them within a fantasy of process, we do not have to examine their origins and their development. Especially, we may refrain from calling them eternal objects in the manner of Whitehead and from examining their locus in an immanent realm of transcendental consciousness in the manner of Husserl, for I do not want ever to separate ideas from psyche.

I would remove discussion of ideas from the realm of thought to the realm of psyche. It is their appearance in the psyche, their significance as psychic events, their psychological effect and reality as experiences relevant for soul, that demand our attention as psychologists.

For us ideas are ways of regarding things *(modi res considerandi)*, perspectives.[2] Ideas give us eyes, let us see. The word idea itself points to its intimacy with the visual metaphor of knowing, for it is related both to the Latin *videre* (to see) and the German *wissen* (to know). Ideas are ways of seeing and knowing, or knowing by means of insighting. Ideas allow us to envision, and by means of vision we can know. Psychological ideas are ways of seeing and knowing soul, so that a change in psychological ideas means a change in regard to soul and regard for soul.

Our word idea comes from the Greek *eidos,* which meant originally in early Greek thought, and as Plato used it, both that which one sees —an appearance or shape in a concrete sense—and that by means of which one sees.[3] We see them, and by means of them. Ideas are both the shape of events, their constellation in this or that archetypal pattern, and the modes that make possible our ability to see through events into their pattern. By means of an idea we can see the idea cloaked in the passing parade. The implicit connection between having ideas to see *with* and seeing ideas themselves suggests that the more ideas we have, the more we see, and the deeper the ideas we have, the deeper we see. It also suggests that ideas engender other ideas, breeding new perspectives for viewing ourselves and world.

Moreover, without them we cannot "see" even what we sense with the eyes in our heads, for our perceptions are shaped according to particular ideas.[4] Once we considered the world flat and now we consider it round; once we observed the sun rotate around the earth, and now we observe the earth turn round the sun; our eyes, and their perceptions did not change with the Renaissance. But our ideas have changed, and with them what we "see." And our ideas change as changes take place in the soul, for as Plato said, soul and idea refer to each other, in that an idea is the "eye of the soul," opening us through its insight and vision.[5]

Therefore the soul reveals itself in its ideas, which are not "just ideas" or "just up in the head," and may not be "pooh-poohed" away, since they are the very modes through which we are envisioning and enacting our lives. We embody them as we speak and move. We are always in the embrace of an idea. Therapy has as important a job to do with ideas as it has with symptoms and feelings, and the investigation of a person's ideas are as revealing of his archetypal structure as are his dreams and his desires. No one concerned with soul dare say, "I am not interested in ideas" or "Ideas are not practical."

Ideas remain impractical when we have not grasped or been grasped by them. When we do not get an idea, we ask "how" to put it in practice, thereby trying to turn insights of the soul into actions of the ego. But when an insight or idea has sunk in, practice invisibly changes. The idea has opened the eye of the soul. By seeing differently, we do differently. Then "how" is implicitly taken care of. "How?" disappears as the idea sinks in—as one reflects upon *it* rather than on how to do something with it. This movement of grasping ideas is vertical or inward rather than horizontal or outward into the realm of doing something. The only legitimate "How?" in regard to these psychological insights is: "How can I grasp an idea?"

Since psychological ideas, or insights as I have sometimes called them, reflect soul, the question of comprehending them turns on one's relation with soul and how the soul learns. The answer to this has always been "by experience," which is tantamount to turning the question back upon itself, since one of the main activities of soul as we defined them at the beginning of this book is precisely that of changing "events into experiences." Here we are specifying how events become experiences, saying that the act of seeing through events connects them to the soul and creates experiences. Simply to participate in events, or to suffer them strongly, or to accumulate a variety of them, does not differentiate or deepen one's psychic capacity into what is often called a wise or an old soul. Events are not essential to the soul's experiencing. It does not need many dreams or many loves or city lights. We have records of great souls that have thrived in a monk's cell, a prison, or a suburb. But there must be a vision of what is happening, deep ideas to create experience. Otherwise we have had the events without experiencing them, and the experience of what happened comes only later when we gain an idea of it—when it can be envisioned by an archetypal idea.

The soul learns less in psychology than in psychologizing—a difference we shall soon be explaining in detail. It learns by searching for itself in whatever ideas come to it; it gains ideas by looking for them, by subjectivizing all questions, including the "How?" To give any direct answer to "How?" betrays the activity of soul-making, which proceeds by psychologizing through all literal answers. As it gains ideas by looking for them, the soul loses ideas by putting them into practice in answer to "How?"

There is in fact a direct relation between the poverty of ideas in academic and therapeutic psychology and their insistence upon the practical. To work out answers to psychological questions not only immediately impoverishes the ideational process, but also means falling into the pragmatic fallacy—the assumption that ideas are valued by their usefulness. This fallacy denies our basic premise: that ideas are inseparable from practical actions, and that theory itself is practice; there is nothing more practical than forming ideas and becoming aware of them in their psychological effects. Every theory we hold practices upon us in one way or another, so that ideas are always in practice and do not need to be put there.

Finally, psychological learning or psychologizing seems to represent the soul's desire for light, like the moth for the flame. The psyche wants to find itself by seeing through; even more, it loves to be enlightened by *seeing through itself,* as if the very act of seeing-through clarified and made the soul transparent—as if psychologizing with ideas were itself an archetypal therapy, enlightening, illuminating.[6] The soul seems to suffer when its inward eye is occluded, a victim of overwhelming events. This suggests that all ways of enlightening soul—mystical and meditative, Socratic and dialectic, Oriental and disciplined, psychotherapeutic, and even the Cartesian longing for clear and distinct ideas —arise from the psyche's need for vision.

Archetypal Psychologizing

There must of course be a link between alien ideas from other fields and the psyche's indigenous structures, else we would not fall prey to ideologies and alienation. Let us now examine some of these pseudo-psychological ideas. At the same time we can show the process of psychologizing actually at work.

When for instance we view psyche as life, defining soul as the life-principle within each organic individual, and also consider life to be evolutionary—as a complex developmental growth from less to more —the idea of growth could not infect our understanding of soul unless it found the host willing, unless there were a structure of ideation that could welcome a formulation of soul in closest link with animal and vegetable life, a blurring of distinctions between development of individuals and species, between growth and movement upward ("growing up"), and a trust in an obscure material causation which has no origin but *is* origin. I mean the archetypal perspective of the Great Mother and her growing child. In other words, when we conceive of psychic life mainly developmentally and conceive the purpose of soul mainly in terms of growth, our ideas, though filled with evolutional terms from Darwinian biology, resonate with the person of the mother archetype.

She it is who prefers a slippery intertwined holism to distinctions among parts. She it is, as vegetation Goddess, who nourishes an idea of psyche among a welter of confusing similars—organism, life, *élan vital, bios, zoē,* the feminine, nature—as well as keeping tangled and buried the subtle differences between growth, increase, differentiation, development, evolution, progress, individuation, change, transformation, metamorphosis, and the like.

This mother's perspective appears in hypotheses about the origin of human life, the nature of matter, and the generation of the world.[7] The Great Mother's viewpoint also appears in theories concerning the genesis of religion. The work of Margaret Murray,[7a] for example, finds the life-giving creative power which is at the basis of all belief in God to refer ultimately to the mystery of pregnancy and child-bearing. Her book is exemplary for demonstrating the archetypal background to thought. The arguments she uses, the facts she adduces, the situations she imagines in the prehistoric past and in the minds of mothers and children today, and the language itself (mystical power, growth, animals, search for origins) as well as her concrete modes of expression all belong to the very archetypal structure (Great Mother) she is attempting to establish. We should have a new category for this sort of fallacy, perhaps, "archetypal *petitio principi.*"

A second example of alien ideas of the psyche might be drawn from Christian theology, where the soul is conceived to stand primarily in love because, as Augustine said, "No one is who does not love"; "love and do what thou willst"; for the first commandment is love, since love is the essence of God, in whose image the human soul is made; through love alone is the soul redeemed, for love comprehends all other ideas —truth, justice, and faith too, all virtues and sins, and this love gives to soul its immortal fire and the arrow of its mission to increase love's dominion through ever-widening unions. Even as it recurs in a variation in Freud's idea of libido, this idea could not have taken hold so effectively unless it echoed an archetypal structure which images and experiences a cosmos ruled by Gods of love—Eros, Jesus, Aphrodite. Just as growth can be seen through as an archetypal fantasy, so too can the psyche see through the dogma of love, recognizing its archetypal validity as a metaphor rather than as the literal truth.

Or as a further example: could the soul have so readily formulated itself in borrowing from philosophy the idea of the *tabula rasa*—that there is nothing in intellect or imagination or heart that has not come from outside through the doors of sensation—if the soul had not already lost sight of itself as a reminiscing, interiorly sensuous and imaginative complexity of propensities, rich with the gifts of given a prioris. The empty slate idea of the psyche's nature, so dominant in our culture, could be accepted as a true image only by a deprived psyche with no mirror in which to see itself. *Tabula rasa* and the association of sensory bits of information—and also the therapeutic hopes of starting afresh, wiping the slate clean, crying forth and emptying out— betray a poverty of psychological ideation, the very problem we are here involved with, in a culture which has long considered this fantasy of passive emptiness to be the true description of soul. Again there is an archetypal person influencing our idea of soul, the person of the innocent nymph, the virgin anima to whom nothing has happened, a Cinderella, a Sleeping Beauty, who generates nothing within herself— unlike the rich Pandora fantasy of the Platonic soul who comes into the world filled with gifts of all the Gods.

An Excursion on the Idea of the Empty Soul

The idea of an empty soul is not only modern: cf. Plato, *Republic* IX, 585ᵇ, for a comparison of the emptiness of the soul with folly and ignorance; also his *Gorgias* 493–94, where the empty vessel is again compared with the porous soul of the foolish. The Socratic work of curing ignorance means also curing the soul of its ignorance in regard to itself, bringing it to realize (e.g., *Meno*) that it is *not* an empty jar or a *tabula rasa*.[8] The work of therapeutic analysis, both Freudian and Jungian, the former with its emphasis upon memory, the latter stressing the imagination, can be seen as recapitulations of Platonism. Recognition of the "reality" of the "unconscious" is a re-cognition of the depth, fullness, richness of psyche, that it has contents, that it is not a *tabula rasa*. The task of coagulating the psyche or building the vessel or developing inner space through internalizing is also Platonic. The metaphor is similar to that of the jars in the *Gorgias*. In analysis we learn *to hold* psychic contents—emotions, fantasies, urges—to retain our dreams, not to let our psychic life leak out.

There have been *refutations* of Locke, associationism, mechanism, and the empty soul in philosophy. But there have been no *methods* as effective as depth analysis for experientially dispelling the condition of a porous soul, which is the psychic premise of the clean slate idea. A direct counterpart of the *tabula rasa* is the mystique of soul our society is currently undergoing. Suddenly soul has been refound, and with it a psychological perspective on everything from astrology, psychedelic hallucinations, Eastern religions, and ethereal vibrations to medicine, food, and dung. The *massa confusa* of elements in our new use of the word "soul" cannot be sorted out until we work out afresh our *idea* of soul, which means nothing less than elaborating an adequate psychology based on the soul metaphor. This in turn requires a discipline of closing the jars, initiating a psychic containment in which the psyche may separate the elements and coagulate its fantasies of itself into psychological insights.

In these three instances—the growth, love, and *tabula rasa* ideas of the psyche—we see what our idea lets us see. The evidence we gather in support of a hypothesis and the rhetoric we use to argue it are already part of the archetypal constellation we are in. Again, the "objective" idea we find in the pattern of data is also the "subjective" idea by means of which we see the data.

We see repression in the world around us most clearly when we are assumed by the archetypal role of its redeemer. The liberating hero sees repression everywhere, while the old king sees the very same events as order, duty, and tradition. He has a different role to play in events because he has a different idea; both role and idea are archetypally governed. Should we, on the one hand (and as another example), participate in Hera's perspective, we can convincingly see within all creative impulses—so exciting to the maiden anima, Zeus' mortal nymphs—the lawless and promiscuous aspect of Zeus who is supposed to be lawgiver and husband, but who takes what he wants where he wants it, all the while inwardly unsettling family and society. On the other hand, the same constellation of Zeus and Hera, now from the Zeus perspective, sees family and social life as the yoke of Hera, inhibiting the possibility of procreative fantasy and the free-ranging imagination that fathers new structures. Perspectives of these sorts lie at the back of our judgments and actions. And without these kinds of perspective we remain in a monotheistic model of consciousness which must be one-sided in its judgments and narrow in its vision, for it is unaware of the wealth and variety of psychological ideas.

So too might we proceed with basic psychological ideas about the nature of the soul: that the soul is a harmony or a multiple and varied unity, that it is born in sin, that it is divine and immortal, that it is a quest for meaning or self-knowledge, that its essence is life and warmth, that its essence is death, that it is structured in three or more parts which enjoy a *psychomachia* in a strife of oppositions, that it is in enigmatic relations with the body, that it is fundamentally an element like air or water or a vaporous mixture of them. Each of these classical ideas of psychology about the psyche should be examined for its archetypal significance rather than merely taken in the terms in which it presents itself. These are statements about the soul by the soul; they are self-descriptions which tell of the many ways the psyche looks at itself, and that it must tell its tale in many ways. Its nature drives us to the polytheistic position which gives a variety of patterns to the psyche's phenomena. The persistence and ubiquity of these classical psychological ideas and their ability to compel generation after generation in psychology indicates something more at work in these ideas than merely the content they pronounce. For one thing, the very richness of ideas about the soul tells us how rich is its phenomenology. It is as if Psyche were naturally pagan because of the soul's natural polytheism.

These last few pages have been demonstrating the method of archetypal psychologizing. Psychologizing has been shown to mean analyzing not only our personalities and psychological material, such as dreams and problems, but the ideas with which we regard our personalities and psychological material. More: *archetypal psychologizing means examining our ideas themselves in terms of archetypes.* It means looking at the frames of our consciousness, the cages in which we sit and the iron bars that form the grids and defenses of our perception. By re-viewing, re-presenting and re-visioning where we already are, we discover the psyche speaking imaginally in what we had been taking for granted as literal and actual descriptions. There is a psychic factor, an archetypal fantasy, in each of our ideas which may be extracted by insighting for it.

This psychological questioning, this *reflexio* which turns ideas back upon themselves in order to see through to their soul import, makes soul. Psyche appears where it had not been noticed. Psyche becomes more clearly separated from its literal identifications, making clearer the mirror by which life is reflected. I take this psychologizing activity to be the primary work of my field.

Hence psychologizing, as it converts alien ideas into psychological ones, subsumes all other actions. *Through psychologizing I change the idea of any literal action at all—political, scientific, personal—into a metaphorical enactment.* I see the act and scene and stance I am in, and not only the action I am into. I recognize that through my ideas I apprehend and am apprehended by my inmost subjectivity, entering all actions in the role of an idea.

There Are Gods in Our Ideas

Archetypal psychology envisions the fundamental ideas of the psyche to be expressions of persons—Hero, Nymph, Mother, Senex, Child, Trickster, Amazon, Puer and many other specific prototypes bearing the names and stories of the Gods. These are the root metaphors.[9] They provide the patterns of our thinking as well as of our feeling and doing. They give all our psychic functions—whether thinking, feeling, perceiving, or remembering—their imaginal life, their internal coherence, their force, their necessity, and their ultimate intelligibility. These persons keep our persons in order, holding into significant patterns the segments and fragments of behavior we call emotions, memories, attitudes, and motives. When we lose sight of these archetypal figures we become, in a sense, psychologically insane: that is, by not "keeping in mind" the metaphorical roots we go "out of our minds"—outside where ideas have become literalized into history, society, clinical psychopathology, or metaphysical truths. Then we attempt to understand what goes on inside by observing the outside, turning inside out, losing both the significant interiority in all events and our own interiority as well.

The weaker and dimmer our notions of the archetypal premises of our ideas, the more likely our actions are to become stuck fast in roles. We become caught in typical problems, missing the archetypal fantasy we are enacting. Even with the best moral intentions, political goals, and philosophical methods, we will exhibit a psychological naïveté. Even that precious instrument, reason, loses its freedom of insight when it forgets the divine persons who govern its perspectives.

I have tried elsewhere, in one instance, to show this psychological naïveté in our beliefs in futurism, our worship of development, maturity, and independence, our search for origins or for a lost childhood in historical, linguistic, or primitive beginnings, as well as the peculiarly feeble reasoning which attempts to advance these ideas—all of which is appropriate to the child archetype.[10] In another study I examined another specific structure: the archetypal background of scientific masculine consciousness, which I called Apollonic and which blinds the eye of observation when it looks at female anatomy, conception and reproduction theories, embryogeny, and hysteria—always seeing the same female inferiority despite, and because of, its scientific methods and "objective" intentions.[11] There, too, we see reason in the service of an archetypal perspective. Another example is given by W.K.C. Guthrie.[12] He connects "the idea of progress" with "the fully personalized mythological character" of Prometheus, "God of Fore-thought." Other examples of disclosing the archetypal person within a set of ideas have been worked upon by Stein, by Miller, and by Mayr.[13]

Yet where else can we be but in one or another of these mythical patterns, these visions which govern human beings as the world believed itself ruled from Olympus and by daimons, powers, and personified principles which we now call "the unconscious"—perhaps because we have become so unconscious of them. The scene of our actions and we the actors are ontologically necessitated, and limited, by these envisioning ideas which depth psychology calls "unconscious projections" or "actings-out" when the blindness they occasion is seen through by someone else: "Can't you see what you are doing?" we shout. "Can't you see my point of view?" But we cannot, because we are in the grip of a particular vision, and this vision is given not merely by a set of values, by a cultural or sociohistorical condition. Within and behind these ideas, making them so instinctually certain, so libidinally charged with excitement and endurance, so universally familiar, so few in number and repetitive in history, are the archetypes which form the structures of our consciousness with such force and such possession that we might, as we have in the past, call them Gods.

Preliminary Resumé and Implications

We have come to a clearing where we can look around and take our bearings. We have gradually been exposing the psychology of the archetypes in order to show the nature of archetypal psychology. In Chapter 1, which was mainly a reflection from the imaginative psyche, the *phantasia* of the archetypes emerged. We saw there the many images of their persons, their appearances as mythical figures, as *daimones* and Gods. Chapter 2, mainly a reflection from the affective psyche, brought out the *pathos* of the archetypes. We saw there that Gods are in the styles of our suffering, in the *casus,* the way things fall, shaping our case history into their myths. Now this chapter, mainly a reflection from the intellectual psyche, presents the *logos* of the archetypes so that we may recognize the Gods and their myths in our ideas.

The implications of this chapter so far are extensive. In the first place, should the Gods express themselves in the psyche through its ideas, then our occupation with ideas is at least partly a religious occupation, a means of addressing the ideational face of the Gods and redressing our mirroring of this face. Through ideas we keep the Gods in mind, keep mindful of them. In the second place, if the Gods are immanent in the soul in its ideas, then psychologizing ideas involves us with the divine. Here I am but reaffirming an old idea of the holiness of intellect and the supreme gift of ideation in a society gone ape over feeling.

And third, if we consider the Gods as expressing themselves each in a specific mode of being, each with symbolic attributes, landscapes, animals and plants, activities and moralities and psychopathologies, then part of the specific mode of being of each God is a style of reflection. *A God is a manner of existence, an attitude toward existence, and a set of ideas.* Each God would project its divine *logos,* opening the soul's eye so that it regards the world in a particularly formed way. A God forms our subjective vision so that we see the world according to its ideas. As Saturn will shape order slowly through time, so the puer eternus, winged and fiery, will turn matters into spirit—"quick now, here now, said the bird." The child will see the future in each event and thereby force its coming, while each of the Goddesses will form a distinctly different vision of relationship, nurture, and interiority.

Finally, since ideas present archetypal visions, I do not ever truly have ideas; they have, hold, contain, govern me. Our wrestling with ideas is a sacred struggle, as with an angel; our attempts to formulate, a ritual activity to propitiate the angel. The emotions that ideas arouse are appropriate, and authentic, too, is our sense of being a victim of ideas, humiliated before their grand vision, our lifetime devotion to them, and the battles we must fight on their behalf.

Psychologizing, Psychology, Psychologism

In affirming psychologizing, let me insist that this affirmation is not relativistic. I shall be adamant, even arrogant, in my claim for psychology. But we shall have to see what is meant by that word.

There are many academic departments, as there are many faculties within the human soul. Our house has many mansions and even more windows; we perceive from a multiplicity of perspectives, ethical, political, poetic. But the psychological perspective is supreme and prior because the psyche is prior and must appear within every human undertaking. The psychological viewpoint does not encroach upon other fields, for it is there to begin with, even if most disciplines invent methods that pretend to keep it out.

Though it might be less offensive to consider psychology one department among many and one interest among others, any such eclectic and relativistic presentation of the psychological viewpoint is vicious: it refuses the very duty of psychology, which is to speak for the psyche. Whether psychologists can stand for it or not, psychology inherently assumes superiority over other disciplines, because the psyche of which it is the advocate does indeed come before any of its compartmental activities, departmentalized into arts, sciences, or trades. These departments are each reflections of one or another face of the psyche. In this sense they each reflect psychic premises at the foundation of their viewpoints and their knowledge. But psychology cannot be one department among others, since the psyche is not a separate branch of knowledge. The soul is less an object of knowledge than it is a way of knowing the object, a way of knowing knowledge itself.

Prior to any knowledge are the psychic premises that make knowledge possible at all. Most disciplines try, as Jung says, "to forget their archetypal explanatory principles, that is, the psychic premises that are the *sine qua non* of the cognitive process."[14] These premises keep knowledge humbly situated within psychic precincts, where it is linked with all the follies of human subjectivity, the ironies of pathology, but also the imaginative richness of the soul. These psychic premises, or "inalienable components of the empirical world-picture" as Jung calls them, are a discomfort to the intellectual spirit, which would think them away in order to have *intellectus purus* (St. Augustine), "pure act" (Aquinas), "pure reason" (Kant), "pure Being" (Hegel), "pure logic" (Husserl), "pure prehension" (Whitehead), or "pure science." But the archetypal premises of cognition manifest themselves in styles of consciousness which include our complexes as well as our modes of thought. We may not forget that philosophical thinking, for instance, must speak in terms of purity. Its abstract asceticism is part of the puritan dignity of the philosophical style itself.

Ideation and psychopathology are indissolubly married, for better and not for worse. This was one of Freud's most fruitful insights. Order, purity, defensiveness, and economy—and anality—belong together as Freud first implied. And, archetypal psychology has since added, the entire character complex, as well as its mode of thought, belong to the psychic premises of the senex archetype, or Saturn.[15]

The archetype is a psychic premise with many heads: one we see in our dream imagery, another in emotion and in symptoms, another styles our behavior and preferences, while still another appears in our mode of thought. We may not cut off the ideational head and call it "pure" reason, denying its archetypal body and collateral attachments. The same archetype dominates our individual choices, our messes, and our ideas.

This interconnection between idea and psychopathology by no means reduces ideas to sickness; we are not engaged in a psychoanalysis which would expose the higher forms of culture as sublimated pathology. Rather, the connection between idea and pathology is for the mutual benefit of both.

Because ideas express our complexes and their archetypal cores, ideas always have a psychopathological aspect. Some are more depressive, others more paranoid, others more divisively schizoid. However, because they express ideas, complexes have philosophies in them and can be worked upon philosophically. Also, ideas shore up and contain our complexes. They provide shields that protect us from their onslaught. Ideational systems, such as worked-out religious beliefs or ethical and scientific attitudes, are means for keeping complexes in an order. When a person's or a nation's belief falls apart there is a general psychic disorder. The ideas that held the complexes no longer function as adequate containers.

The archetypal position implies that all knowing may be examined in terms of these psychic premises. It suggests nothing less than an archetypal *epistēmē*, an archetypal theory of knowing. Were we to begin in this direction, this theory of knowledge would follow the implicit connection between *epistēmē* and *eidos* in Plato, that is, we would start off by looking at all knowledge as the expression of ideas that have psychic premises in the archetypes.

A perspective of this kind would help us rethink the moral problem in science. If scientific ideas were connected with their psychological significance, the two realms of objective science and subjective ethics could no longer be so dramatically opposed. By recognizing that a style of thought expresses an archetypal mode of consciousness *including its style of behavior,* the sort of morality to be expected by the psychic premises of scientific theory would belong as corollary to the theory. The idea of science as objective and amoral (or moral only internally, in regard to obeying the requirements of its methods and conventions) has itself an archetypal premise in Apollo, where detachment, dispassion, exclusive masculinity, clarity, formal beauty, farsighted aims, and elitism are basic fantasies. These have been literalized by science, becoming its belief and behavior.

It is not our aim to dwell on the psychology of science or scientists, philosophy or philosophers, or on epistemology in general. Rather our aim is to remember that all knowledge can be psychologized. And that by being psychologized, it also becomes a means of psychological reflection. Therefore all teaching is relevant to the soul as long as its literalism is psychologized. Every statement in every branch of learning in every university department is a statement made by the psyche through men and women and is a psychological statement. Psychology is taught not only in the department that bears its name. It is going on everywhere. Indeed it may be going on best where it is noticed least, as in "negative learning," as an underground interior reaction of "dissonant learning," in which the sourness of the student eats through the established positive statements, corroding their face value, yielding an acerbic learning that is *against* what is given, a countereducation. Psychologizing sees through what is taught; it is a learning beyond any teaching.

If psychology can be learned everywhere, then it has no field of its own. Rather it is a perspective on all fields, parasitical to all fields, drawing from everything in the universe for its insights. It is limited, however, wholly by the individual who carries it and the points of view each person brings to bear. Psychology never transcends its subjective premises in the psyche. Or, as Jung said in his Terry Lectures, the psyche is both the object of psychology and also its subject. Psychology gains its definition less through the development of an objective field than through the defining limits of the subjective person upon whose developments it depends.

So it is not surprising that the depth psychology of Freud and Jung could not fit into universities as one department among others. The teaching of depth psychology had to go on in private, and in separate training institutions. It still does. This points to the difference between psychologizing and other activities. Psychologizing is not one among others, and a psychology which attempts to reflect the soul in its depth can never be limited to experimental, social, clinical, or philosophical qualifiers, for it is itself a *universitas*.

We should hasten to qualify that psychologizing does not mean *only* psychologizing, or that statements may not have content, merit, and import in the area of their literal expression. Philosophical and scientific assertions are, of course, not only psychological statements. To reduce such assertions wholly to psychology commits the psychologistic fallacy, or "psychologism." This point is important.

Psychologism means *only* psychologizing, converting all things into psychology. Psychology then becomes the new queen and—by taking itself and its premises literally—becomes a new metaphysics. When the insights of psychologizing harden into systematic arguments, becoming solid and opaque and monocentric, we have the metaphysical position of psychologism: there is only one fundamental discipline and ultimate viewpoint, psychology.

One can detect this whenever religious, moral, aesthetic, or logical events are given (1) a *literalized* account in terms (2) of underlying psychological processes only, and (3) when these processes are made personally *human;* the psychologistic fallacy requires all three legs. Archetypal psychologizing performs the first two acts by seeing through statements for their psychological significance and by connecting ideas to their psychic premises in the archetypes.

However, it avoids the psychologistic fallacy because these psychic premises, the archetypes, remain the perspectives of mythical persons who cannot be reduced to human beings or placed inside their personal lives, their skins, or their souls. Archetypes are psychic structures, but *not only this,* for they are also Gods who cannot be encompassed by anyone's individual soul. We keep from psychologism by remembering that not only is the psyche in us as a set of dynamisms, but we are in the psyche.

Therefore psychologizing does not mean making psychology of events, but making psyche of events—soul-making. So psychologizing methods may be applied to psychology itself. Psychology's statements may be questioned in terms of their theological or political implications. Herbert Marcuse, for instance, has indeed seen through some psychology by means of political tools, showing up many of psychology's assumptions.[16] But he has literalized his tools and cannot see through his own ideas about politics and the archetypal fantasy of Dionysian liberation.

It is not the conceptual tool or the specific language that makes soul, but the manner and purpose with which the tool is employed. Hence what is entailed thus far is a recognition that *every statement in whatever field is made by the psyche and has an implication for the soul, and for its psychopathology.*

What is Psychologizing: Some Distinctions

Now what is the activity of psychologizing? How may it be more narrowly characterized? We have considered it necessary, hence legitimate; we have pointed out that it occurs unprompted; and we have concluded that it seems to be an attempt of the psyche to realize itself wherever it can. Thus it takes place in many ways and at many levels, from the simplest "figuring out," questioning curiosity, and paranoid afterthoughts about "What do they mean?" and "What else is going on here?" to reflection in tranquility, the most sophisticated scrutiny of signification, and scientific doubting. *Psychologizing goes on whenever reflection takes place in terms other than those presented.* It suspects an interior, not evident intention; it searches for a hidden clockwork, a ghost in the machine, an etymological root, something more than meets the eye; or it sees with another eye. It goes on whenever we move to a deeper level.

Psychologizing tries to solve the matter at hand, not by resolving it, but by dissolving the problem into the fantasy that is congealed into a "problem." In other words, we assume that events have an outer shell that we call hard, tough, real, and an inner matter that is epiphenomenal, insubstantial, strange. The first we call problems, the second fantasies. Problems are always "difficult" and "serious." One is stuck with them; they don't go away. Whereas fantasies are hard to catch. They are said to be "just fantasy" or "mere fantasy," "silly" or "far-fetched." They are never considered "thorny," "weighty," or "basic" like problems.

The etymology of "fantasy" connects them with visibilities, light, showing forth, like a procession of images presented to the mind's eye. The word "problem" means originally something that sticks out or projects into one's view, a barrier, an obstacle, a screen. The word in Greek could refer to armored defenses and shields. So problems do challenge the heroic ego, presenting it with projects and projections. By means of problem-solving the ego partly defines itself. Heroic ego and hard problems require each other; they toughen each other in the coping game called "reality."

Our style of consciousness is hero-based and ego-centered. We give credit to problems and disbelieve fantasies, so that fantasies present themselves first projected as problems, which are literalized fantasies. To make a problem of something appeals to the heroic ego, who needs his fantasy of problems. To make problems or to solve them reinforces the defensive literalistic screen against fantasies. But whenever we make a fantasy of something, we make it, as the word itself says, visible, bringing to it light. Where problems call for will power, fantasies evoke the power of imagination. Those who work professionally with imagination recognize the value of fantasies and resist having them turned into psychological problems to be analyzed. It threatens their imaginal realities. Similarly, those who work professionally through practical reason—scientists or social workers—resist having their problems turned into fantasies. This threatens their ego realities. By seeing through the illusion of problems into the reality of fantasies, we shift from the heroic ego to the ego of the imaginal.

But psychologizing may take many paths. It may proceed by means of historical examination of underlying causes, by linguistic analysis, by rehypothesizing empirical data, by philosophical dialectic. It may also proceed through irony and humor that expose, or by means of art that takes one through the evident. Love, too, can be a method of psychologizing, of seeing into and seeing through, of going ever deeper.

Seeing through does not depend on the field of psychology nor require the language of psychology—neither its terms nor its tools; for psychologizing is not confined by any single method, since it is the native activity preceding and within all methods just reviewed. Critical, historical, experimental, artistic reflections are each an expression of the psyche's hungry eye which would see through. Essential to it are qualities of reflection which are conscious, intentional, subjective, signifying, interior, and deep.

Like all activities of the psyche, psychologizing has its shadow in a psychopathological exaggeration: paranoia. The squint that suspects interior intentions, that subjectivizes events and is always on the lookout for hidden meanings, indeed takes its paranoid pleasure in psychologizing. But the paranoid vision is such precisely because it does not see through. It stops with a literal answer, more solid and unshakable than the first-level matter at hand. It "knows" where true psychologizing never knows. The paranoid eye does dissolve the evident into a fantasy, but it takes the fantasy for literal truth. By connecting psychologizing with paranoia we gain a new perspective on its vision: paranoia would see through; as its very name says, it is a noetic activity that would go beyond what is given. To correct it by arguing against its reason or by pointing to the facts fails its psychologizing intention. The paranoid tendency rather needs to be encouraged to see through further and further until it can see through itself.

Although seeing through is a process of deliteralizing and a search for the imaginal in the heart of things by means of ideas, we should not assume that it is mainly intellectual or a work of intuitive abstraction. Psychologizing does not mean merely moving from the concrete to the abstract. Here we should clear up a distinction between the literal and the concrete.

First of all, literalness can appear in highly abstract ways. We may take abstractions literally, as truths, rules, laws. Metaphysical thinking is one such example of abstract literalness; so too is theological thinking, where the most abstract notions about divinity are taken as literal dogmas. It is for this reason that metaphysics and theology so easily become ways of avoiding psychologizing. Even at the very moment they are talking of soul they may be escaping from it into a literalness about its problems, its truth, its redemption. Whenever we say "the soul is" this or that, we have entered upon a metaphysical venture and literalized an abstraction. These metaphysical assertions about the soul may produce psychology, but not psychologizing, and as avoidances of psychologizing they are an abstract acting-out. We act out not only by running away into concrete life; we act out equally in the flight upward into the abstractions of metaphysics, higher philosophies, theologies, even mysticism. The soul loses its psychological vision in the abstract literalisms of the spirit as well as in the concrete literalisms of the body.

Secondly, however, though body life is always concrete, it is not necessarily literal. We perform concrete acts of all sorts, eating and dancing, fighting and loving, which signify beyond their literalism. Soul and body are distinct, but not necessarily opposed. Nor are soul and concrete events opposed.

Alchemy provides an excellent example of soul-making by means of concrete events. The alchemists were engaged daily with the concrete —fires and mixtures and liquids—and yet were doing a psychic work. They kept their eye on the psyche in the concrete materials they were working with, so as not to take the salt and the sulphur, the heating and the dissolving, only physically, only literally. They warned, "Beware of the physical in the material." The concrete materials were indispensable; however, to take them physically, literally, was to lose the psyche.

The physical, which appears as well in the metaphysical, refers to a literalism, the fantasy of a real stuff, matter, or problem that *is* what it is and cannot be seen through. The enemy of *psyché* is *physis,* however it appears, concretely or abstractly. The enemy of psyche is never material things or concrete life unless we forget that these, too, are always subject to seeing through.

The distinction between concrete and literal, so important to alchemy, is the essential distinction in ritual. The ritual of theater, of religion, of loving, and of play require concrete actions which are never only what they literally seem to be. Ritual offers a primary mode of psychologizing, of deliteralizing events and seeing through them as we "perform" them. As we go into a ritual, the soul of our actions "comes out"; or to ritualize a literal action, we "put soul into it." Here not only can the priest and the alchemist point the way; so too can the actor, the entertainer, and the ball-player. They are able to divest the concrete of its literalism by the psychological style they bring to an action. Ritual brings together action and idea into an enactment.

Why, How, What—and Who

Returning again directly to our inquiry "What is psychologizing?" we see that it asks the question of meaning differently and probably more deeply than the philosophical *Why?* and the practical *How?* Psychologizing asks "What?"

We ask, "What happened?" "What do you feel?" "What do you want?" These questions then proceed to: "What does this mean?" in terms of "What idea is this?" "What pattern is going on?" We seek to identify the constellation of events by a precision of their nature. We inquire precisely into the dream, its actual sequences, the feeling of its movements, the details of its images.

"What?" proceeds straight into an event. The search for "whatness" or quiddity, the interior identity of an event, its essence, takes one into depth. It is a question from the soul of the questioner that quests for the soul of the happening. "What" stays right with the matter, asking it to state itself again, to repeat itself in other terms, to re-present itself by means of other images. "What" implies that everything everywhere is matter for the psyche, matters to it—is significative, offers a spark, releases or feeds soul.

Why, how, and what, together cover a good many of the impulses within psychologizing. But there are strong differences between these questions. *Why* takes one toward explanations or purposes; *how* takes one toward a set of conditions, or causes, or solutions, or applications. Both take us away from what is at hand, away from what is present and actually taking place. Some philosophers dislike the *what* question, and others do not even ask it.[17] Scientific thinking would prefer to resolve all *what*'s, and *why*'s too, into *how*'s. *What* belongs to the essentialist tradition extending from Aristotle through Husserl, the father of modern phenomenology. But the psychological *what* differs even from this background. This difference between phenomenology and archetypal psychologizing needs clarifying.

When we turn to events themselves and let them tell us what they are, our work is phenomenological. And our work is phenomenological when we search for the essence of what is going on in terms of an essential idea or style of consciousness, putting to one side all *why*s and *how*s. But here our paths part because phenomenology stops short in its examination of consciousness, failing to realize that the essence of consciousness is fantasy images. Archetypal psychology carries the consequences of fantasy through to their full implications, transposing the entire operation of phenomenology into the irrational, personified, and psychopathological domain, a transposition from the logical to the imaginal. Phenomenological reduction becomes an archetypal reversion, a return to mythical patterns and persons. We see through the logical by means of the imaginal; we leave the intentional for the ambiguous. This is what depth psychology has always insisted upon: look at conscious events and intentions from the unconscious, from below. Look at the daylight world from the night side, from fantasy and its *archai.*

Freud, Jung, and Husserl see through phenomena differently. Freud began in neuropathology, Jung in archeology and psychiatry, and Husserl in mathematics. Their methods and the essences they arrive at betray their starting points.

Moreover archetypal psychologizing, unlike phenomenology, does not use concepts for the categories of its vision. Psychologizing's *what* dissolves as it specifies, first into "Which?"—which among the many traits and moods are here being demonstrated at this moment?—and then ultimately into "Who?"—who in me says I am ugly, makes me feel guilty; who is it in my soul that needs you so desperately? Seeing through to this *who* dissolves the identification with one of the many insistent voices that fill us with ideas and feelings, steering fate on its behalf. At first these persons, who are at the core of what we feel, say, and do, seem interiorized bits of our personal history. But soon they show their impersonality. For in the last instance the *who* refers to an archetypal figure within the complex, the dream, and the symptom.

By dissolving *what* into *who,* we follow one of the main styles of questioning used with the oracles at Delphi and Dodona: "To what god or hero must I pray or sacrifice to achieve such and such a purpose?"[18] The questions of why things are as they are, how they came about, and how to settle them—even those of what is going on and what it means —find ultimate issue in revelation of the particular archetypal person at work in the events. Once we know at whose altar the question belongs, then we know better the manner of proceeding. If the Goddess of love has the main hand in a present turmoil, we best find our way through with her perspective, temporarily leaving aside Hercules' heroic career, Hera's reliable marriage, or Athene's wise reflection. What the Gods notoriously want is remembrance of them, not choice among them, so that every conflict—and the very question "Who?"—by asking which among many, indicates them all. All are implicated and all remembered. Awareness that, as there are many complexes in our conflicts, there are many Gods imaged in our souls, shifts an issue from a matter of choice to that of sacrifice, where sacrifice means remembrance of one because there are many.

Once this psychological task of discovery belonged to the poet. "He sees events through and through even when the participants see only the surface. And often when the participants sense only that a divine hand is touching them the poet is able to name the god concerned and knows the secret of his purpose."[19]

The Process of Seeing Through

Let us now condense the process of psychological discovery into a series of steps. First there is the psychological moment, a moment of reflection, wonder, puzzlement, initiated by the soul which intervenes and countervails what we are in the midst of doing, hearing, reading, watching. With slow suspicion or sudden insight we move through the apparent to the less apparent. We use metaphors of light—a little flicker, a slow dawning, a lightning flash—as things become clarified. When the clarity has itself become obvious and transparent, there seems to grow within it a new darkness, a new question or doubt, requiring a new act of insight penetrating again toward the less apparent. The movement becomes an infinite regress which does not stop at coherent or elegant answers. The process of psychologizing cannot be brought to a halt at any of the resting places of science or philosophy; that is, psychologizing is not satisfied when necessary and sufficient conditions have been met or when, testability has been established. It is satisfied only by its own movement of seeing through.

Moving from outside in, it is a process of *interiorizing;* moving from the surface of visibilities to the less visible, it is a process of deepening; moving from the data of impersonal events to their personification, it is a process of subjectivizing.

Second, psychologizing *justifies itself.* As we penetrate or try to bring out, expose, or show why, we believe that what lies behind or within is truer and more real, powerful, or valuable than what is evident. It is a justification in terms of depths; we justify the activity by appealing to an ultimate hidden value that can never fully come out but must remain concealed in the depths in order to justify the movement. This ultimate hidden value justifying the entire operation can also be called the hidden God *(deus absconditus),* who appears only in concealment.

Third, the present event, the phenomenon before us, is given a *narrative.* A tale is told of it in the metaphors of history, or physical causality, or logic. We tell ourselves something in the language of "because." The immediate is elaborated by fantasy, so that a metamorphosis occurs as the immediate becomes part of an account. It is a process of mythologizing. And all explanations whatsoever may be regarded as narrative fantasies and examined as myths.

Fourth are the *tools* with which the operation proceeds. Here we return once again to ideas, for ideas are the soul's tools. Without them we cannot see, let alone see through. Ideas as the eyes of the soul give the psyche its power of insight, its means of prying open, stripping bare, going through. Again, without ideas the soul is a victim of literal appearances and is satisfied with things just as they present themselves. It has no idea of anything further, is without doubt or prompting to see through.

Yet the disrepute of psychologizing may be blamed mainly upon the confusion of the tools—ideas—with the activity. Psychologizing becomes illegitimate by simplifying into psychologisms, when it loses the distinction between the activity of seeing through and the specific ideas by means of which it sees. For example: by means of the idea of the unconscious we are able to see into, behind, and below manifest behavior. But the unconscious is merely a tool for deepening, interiorizing, and subjectifying the apparent. Should we take the unconscious literally, then it too becomes a husk that constricts the psyche and must be seen through, deliteralized. Without the idea of the unconscious we could not see through behavior into its hidden unknowns. But we do not see the unconscious.

The problem here is the ancient one of hypostasizing an idea into a literal thing. However, this is more than slipshod thinking, for it is inherent in *eidos,* idea, itself. As the discussion above has shown, idea implies both the tool by which we see and the thing we see. Psychologizing is in danger when it forgets that literalism is inherent in the very notion of idea. Then we begin to see ideas rather than seeing by means of them.

Before I go on I want to go back. There are some additions to these four steps that may help keep them from being imagined too narrowly. The most important is that seeing through requires all four so-called steps, and all four may simultaneously proceed. We tell ourselves a justifying story as we penetrate inward by means of ideas. Or an idea may start us off psychologizing, or a fantasy about an event may prompt the moment of reflection and the search for something deeper.

In regard to the first step, dreams—which are themselves attempts to gain a vantage point other than the usual daily one—show the reflective moment by any of several motifs. Changes of physical position and attitude can be metaphors for seeing through. To psychologize we need to "get closer" or even to "back off" for a different perspective or to look at things from a new angle. Other motifs are: turning lights on or off, entering, descending, climbing up or fleeing to gain distance, translating, reading or speaking another tongue, eyes and optical instruments, being in another land or another period of history, becoming insane or sick or drunk—all of which are concrete images for shifting one's attitude to events, scenes, and persons. Watching images on a screen or making images with a camera also present modes of psychologizing. But best of all is glass. Glass in dreams, as windows, panes, mirrors, presents the paradox of a solid transparency; its very purpose is to permit seeing through. Glass is the metaphor par excellence for psychic reality: it is itself not visible, appearing only to be its contents, and the contents of the psyche, by being placed within or behind glass, have been moved from palpable reality to metaphorical reality, out of life and into image. Only when the alchemist could put his soul substances in a glass vessel and keep them there did his psychologizing work effectively commence. Glass is the concrete image for seeing through.

In regard to the second and third steps, it is well to realize that *justifying* our psychological insights and *mythologizing* them into an account does not mean that we now know more fully or surely what is actually taking place. Although we justify our moving through the given by believing that what we come upon is more real or true, this justification and the myth we tell are not to be taken as literally true and real. If I see through your behavior by means of the idea of the Savior complex, believing that this account is more basic and valid than appearances, there is no surety that it *is* the Savior complex and that now I know it because I have seen it.

Mythologizing events and behavior into stories, accounts, and explanations does not lead to more validity, to more certitude about what is; there is no "more" of any kind. That is the language of objectivity; but psychologizing goes inward, subjectivizing. The revelation of myth within events confirms ambiguity, it does not settle it. Myth moves into meaning merely by taking one out of literal objectivities, and the place to which myth carries one is not even a central meaning, or the center of meaning where things are supposed to feel certain. Instead, we hover in puzzlement at the border where the true depths are. Rather than an increase of certainty there is a spread of mystery, which is both the precondition and the consequence of revelation. Therefore the more clearly I see the myth that is taking place in the events I am psychologizing, the more mysterious and enigmatic they become, even as they become more and more revealed.

Further, concerning the third step, there is a distinction between the narrative of psychologizing and the kinds of accounts called *Sprache* (language game) by Wittgenstein and *la parole* (meaningful word) by Merleau-Ponty. *Sprache* is primarily an analytical account that situates an event in a nexus of verbal relations; *la parole* is primarily a syntactical account that draws meaning out of words in their relationships within sentences. Whereas a narrative is primarily a poetic fantasy. The tale and its sentences are carried by an archetypal pattern, a mythologem.

Where the first two steps tend to be linguistic in their concern, furthering analytical consciousness, the third—mythologizing—tends to be dramatic and ritualistic. The inherent rhythm of the narrative movement transposes and transforms events, even invents them. We are different at the end of the story because the soul has gone through a process during the telling, independent of its syntax and full understanding of its words. Moreover, a narrative account is irreversible: once an event is told into a tale it cannot easily be dislodged from its home there, always bearing with it echoes of its first telling. Through the telling of events—which is what *mythos* originally meant—the soul takes random images and happenings and makes them into particular lived experiences. The soul needs something more than language games, more than words and speech. Psychological living implies living in a fantasy, a story, being told by a myth.

Fantasy need not always be verbal, nor must there be visual imagery. The account which translates an event into experience may be incorporated bodily through style, gesture, or ritual, like entering into a more subtle or skilled way of going about things. We feel we are getting into the secret of cooking, fingering an instrument, playing ball, as we fantasy ourselves into a new style. Psychologizing breaks up repetitiveness; it is particularly effective when we perform one activity as if it were another, writing novels as if they were music (like Thomas Mann).

We come now to some of the consequences of the fourth step—using ideas as tools for seeing through. Tools, too, belong to Gods. All instruments have a life beyond our modern technological fantasy of tools as cold, passive implements. An ideational tool may possess its possessor, turning all events into the shape and likeness of the tool, fixing us in its own literalism. When the tool is simpler than the matter to which it is being applied, there results *psychological reduction*. When I use the idea of development to grasp the many varied themes that go on in the soul during adolescence, the ideational tool organizes the events of youth at the expense of simplifying them so that they can be handled by the idea. Then complexities become simple, the rich becomes poorer and the difficult easy, because we have confused what we find with the instrument that finds it. So if my ideas are Freudian, say, or Jungian, I shall find that what I uncover conforms to the ideas that have revealed it, reducing the matter I am probing to the scale of the tool.

A corollary to psychological reduction is *psychological dogmatism.* An idea which is at first a *modus res considerandi,* a way of regarding, becomes a form which strikes its imprint upon the insight. We begin to regard things typically: in types, then stereotypes. Forgetting the gentle caution of Bishop Butler—"everything is what it is, and not another thing"—we reply to the question "What?" with precast form responses. To see what a thing is requires a fresh perception for each image, whereas types conveniently mold everything into their own image. Only the image can free us from type-casting, since each image has its particular peculiarity that fits no preconceived frame. There can be no dogmatism of the image, and the greatest enemy of dogma is the imagination's spontaneous freedom.

When we neglect the image for the idea, then archetypal psychology can become a stereotypical psychology. Then the precise detail of an image, just as it is, is replaced by a general idea of it. For instance, each younger woman in each dream is not the anima any more than every older man is a father figure. We do indeed see these imaginal persons in our dreams: the one wading at the river bank, beckoning; the other masterfully demonstrating chemistry in an amphitheater. Though their image, behavior, and mood leads us to recognize them as "anima" and "father," and though we even gain insight through this archetypal recognition, we do not literally see the anima or the father. These are psychological ideas by means of which we see and which tend to cast what we see inescapably into molds. Ideas are inevitably dangerous for psychologizing.

This has wide repercussions beyond the dangers in dream interpretation. For example: to psychologize modern political history as an instance of the repression of instinct in a Freudian sense may release insights, because it dissolves a literal political problem into a psychological fantasy. The psychologizing process is stopped, however, by a new literalism, that of sexual politics. Instead of psychologizing both politics and sexuality by means of the idea of repression, we politicize sexuality and sexualize politics the moment the idea of repression changes from a mode of seeing through events into a description of events. The fallacy lies in identifying the psychologizing activity with a specific psychology (the theory of repression); for we do not see repression, we see by means of the idea of repression. When we forget to psychologize the tools by means of which we see, the insights we receive blur and dull and coagulate into a new literalism. Psychologizing rigidifies into psychology.

Psychologizing Psychology

Thus psychology is its own worst enemy, for it is easily caught in its tools, its psychological methods and insights. Psychology's task therefore has to start on home ground: seeing through its own tools—the unconscious, the ego, the case history, the diagnostic label—each of which can obstruct the soul by its literalism.

Any psychology that believes itself, that takes itself at its own word, no longer reflects the psyche or serves soul-making. The more hard evidence and solid backing a psychology finds for its hypotheses, the less its ideas open the soul's eye toward concretely specific insights. The righter it becomes, the wronger its effects; the more tested, the less true. Our tools construct theologies in an idolatry of concepts and methods.

Perhaps there can be no *discipline* of therapeutic psychology, only an *activity* of psychotherapy. Perhaps therapeutic psychology is self-defeating; once insights become "psychology," serving as an interpretative tool, a reliably steady mirror throwing light on all events from the same angle—then the particularity, multiplicity, and spontaneity of the soul's reflections become codified. An articulated, all-worked-out psychology is better spoken of as a theology or a philosophy or a movement, and the activity performed in its name and called "therapy" (Freudian, Jungian, Rogerian, Reichean) is more truly indoctrination or conversion. It is more likely to be ideology than psychologizing.

Psychologizing is often a brief act that shocks, quickens, and warms. But we do not need to literalize this dynamic experience into the energetics of forces, nor do we need to demonstrate the psyche's *dynamics* by psychodynamics. The process of seeing through requires neither a system of thermodynamics (entropy) such as we find in Jung, or hydrodynamics (damming, channeling, flooding) such as we find in Freud. Nor do we need electrical fields (charges, conversion, transformation), nor a system of teleological energetics with all parts drawn like iron filings by the magnet of the goal. These superstructures of psychodynamics also need to be seen through for their root metaphors and for what inactivity or fear of inertia they may be masking. To phrase one's psychic life in a highly dynamic language of forces and powers and charges in no way guarantees that movement is taking place. In fact, the dynamic fantasy may provide a deceptively comfortable armchair for the Stygian stasis of six or seven years of weekly therapy.

Let us reimagine psychodynamics as mythical tales rather than as physical processes; as the rise and fall of dramatic themes, as genealogies, as voyages and contests and respites, as interventions of Gods. But if we must call upon physical analogies in order to be convinced of the substantial reality of the psyche's dynamics, then let us reduce the scale.

Let us imagine a "micro-psychics" and speak of seeing through as quantum jumps of mini-insights. If our model for the movements of the soul were reduced, our therapeutic expectations might show less hope and less despair—and more accuracy in regard to what is actually going on. Our reflections then might show more personified proportions. Instead of the language of land reclamation and icebergs (Freud) or archeological excavations and positive/negative poles (Jung) our reflections would correspond with the modesty of the soul. Since the psyche is so often depicted as a little bird, a butterfly, a tiny figure within the breast or emerging from a nostril, its movements require description in like degree.

Analysis has been gorgeously extravagant in the mythical thematics or "mythemes" of its work, more like the grandiose tasks of Hercules or Theseus than the needlework and basketwork and alchemical slow stewing that goes on in actual soul-making, where not only the hero reigns, but Athene and her weaving, Demeter and her digesting, Artemis and her nursing, and Priapus and his gardening mainly govern its long days.

By discarding psychodynamics as necessary for a description of the psyche, archetypal psychology shares a viewpoint with existential psychology. But there are major differences between existential and Jungian therapies. First, the substructures in existential therapy, those receiving the capital letters, are concepts, not images and persons. Existential psychology makes small daily events—by adding the German suffix "keit" or "heit" or "sein" (-hood or/-ness or/-dom)—into big nouns able to carry whole realms piled on their heads. Without Gods or archetypes or other divine substantials it divinizes substantives. Such existential therapy cannot help but be essentially a metaphysical activity, as is appropriate for anyone following Heidegger; it cannot be a psychological activity, appropriate for anyone following Jung.

Second, existential therapists do not relish "symbology" to the same degree as do Jungians, who emphasize the amplification of images through myth, religion, art, and folklore. Jungians, however, do not relish "situations" in the manner of existential therapists, who amplify and explore them for significance much as Jungians do symbols. Third, and of main concern here, Jungian therapy is definitely conceived in a developmental processional manner, whereas existential therapy does not link situations of existence together into an individuation process or a narrative of becoming conscious. Alchemy, fairy tales, myth—so important in Jungian thought—are all personified *processes* rather than conceptualized *situations.*

Here archetypal psychology, which I am working out in these chapters, diverges from both existential and Jungian perspectives in regard to the stasis/process issue, the issue sometimes put in terms of being versus becoming. The existential model is static. With its emphasis upon states and situations of being, it neglects the evidence of process within archetypal patterns and does not acknowledge that process is itself an archetypal idea. We find it expressed in descriptions of nature and of history, and in philosophical systems as contrasting as Aristotle, Comte, Hegel, Whitehead, and Teilhard. Process is also apparent in the patterning of drama and story, in the experience of dreams as a narrative chain, and in the movement of dream figures through situations.

Where existentialists neglect process, Jungians literalize it. Because the process of individuation is an archetypal fantasy, it is of course ubiquitous and can be "demonstrated" in texts and cases, just as any archetypal fantasy has its manifestation in historical events. But this process is not the axiomatic law of the psyche, the one purpose or goal of ensouled beings. To assert this even as an hypothesis or to establish it with instances is to desert psychologizing for metaphysics. It is to literalize and systematize one psychological idea, forgetting that *individuation is a perspective.* It is an ideational tool: we do not see individuation, but by means of it. Moreover, the descriptions of this process are archetypally determined, so that the notion of individuation may show the child and fantasies of developmental maturation, or the hero and fantasies of enlightening and strengthening, or the mother and fantasies of cyclical nature. We can take process into account without elevating it to the major explanatory fantasy of the soul, either as individuation or as development, forgoing the comforting teleological fallacy which holds that we are carried by an overall process on a rocky road onward to the Great End Station.

A more precise way of taking process into account without taking it literally (and speaking of linear, dialectic, or spiral models) is to explore the processional characteristic of the archetypes. Their tales and their figures move through phases like dramas and interweave one with another, dissolve into one another. Whether expressed as instincts or as Gods, archetypes are not definitely distinct. One instinct modifies another; one tale leads to another; one God implicates another. Their process is in their complication and amplification, and each individual's psychic process involves attempting to follow, discriminate, and refine their complications. Here is an ongoing Protean movement, which ceases however if it is fixed by identifying these movements as transformation, as progression or regression, or by overrefining them into clearcut sureties. All we can say is that the archetypes are structures in process; this process is many-formed and mythical; neither "psychodynamics" nor "individuation" can do justice to it.

Psychodynamics and the process of individuation are only two of the many fundamental ideas that can be re-visioned by psychologizing. The classical questions of psychology—the mind-body relation and the God-soul relation, whether nature (biology) or nurture (society) is primary, what is conscious and what the definition of true madness, what is emotion and how explain human differences, what is perception and extrasensory perception—these are not issues to be approached in their own literal terms. They are insoluble except within the limited sense of each particular system of psychology, and these literal approaches lead to a conflicting array of answers. These questions by becoming problems are also statements about areas where psychologizing has got stuck. We have come to take them literally and look for solutions.

But is the solution to these problems *as problems* what the soul seeks? Or is it trapped in the activities of a psychology department (where metaphorical riddles are taken as empirical problems to solve), perhaps for a psychological reason? Possibly these very places where psychology sticks in spite of generation after generation of research, experiment, and theorizing, offer the primary fantasy material for psychologizing. Out of these obdurate, intractable problems comes the history of psychology, a continuous flow of psychological ideas. The psyche seems more interested in the movement of its ideas than in the resolution of problems. Therefore no classical psychological problem can ever be solved, nor can it be made, by any means, to disappear from the scene.

Psyche's obstinate problems offer focus for fantasy. They are the unchanging ground to which psychologizing returns ever again, like Antaios, to draw its strength. The particularized problems of each of us, problems we call our own—what is it to be truly human, how to love, why to live, and what is emotion, value, justice, change, body, God, soul, and madness in our lives—these too are insoluble. Are they meant to be solved? Are we meant to be free or master of sexual, money, power, family, health, moral, religious problems? They bring us to psychologize, to go deeper into caring for the soul, which is psychotherapy, care of soul. And the purpose of these eternal psychological problems? To provide the base of soul-making.

Psychologizing: Moving Through the Literal to the Metaphorical

It would seem I have been talking from both sides of my mouth, saying that psychology is the most important of fields because it speaks for psyche—and, at the same time, that it cannot speak for psyche; that its first concern is therapy, and that a therapeutic psychology defeats itself; that psychological ideas are essential to the eye of the soul, and that they block its vision. In short, I have been saying that psychology is its own worst enemy. The cause of these internal oppositions is literalism. Literalism prevents psychologizing by making psychology of it.

Here I join Owen Barfield and Norman Brown in a mafia of the metaphor to protect plain men from literalism. Barfield writes: ". . . the besetting sin to-day is the sin of literalism."[20] And Brown says: "The thing to be abolished is literalism; . . . the worship of false images; idolatry. . . . Truth is always in poetic form; not literal but symbolic; hiding, or veiled; light in darkness . . . the alternative to literalism is mystery."[21]

Now mystery is not a class of events different from literal events, but is those same literal events regarded differently, when they are seen to be ambiguously concealing and start us psychologizing. As Wittgenstein says: ". . . no phenomenon is, in itself, especially mysterious, but every one can become so to us, and just this is the characteristic of an awakening spirit in people."[22]

Literalism prevents mystery by narrowing the multiple ambiguity of meanings into one definition. Literalism is the natural concomitant of monotheistic consciousness—whether in theology or in science—which demands singleness of meaning. Precisely this monotheism of meaning prevents mystery, as Brown says. It also hardens the heart, preventing deeper penetration of the imagination, as Barfield says. And both say that literal meanings become new idols, fixed images that dominate our vision, and are inherently false because single.

Furthermore, Barfield carefully shows that "literalness is a quality which some words have achieved in the course of their history; it is not a quality with which words were first born."[23] By treating the words we use as ambiguities, seeing them again as metaphors, we restore to them their original mystery. Seeing through our literalisms is a process of resacralization of the word.

But let us not take literalism itself literally. After all, idols too are images of Gods, and for psychology there are no "false" images, no false Gods, only fallacious approaches to them. Literalism is itself one kind of mystery: an idol that forgets it is an image and believes itself a God, taking itself metaphysically, seriously, damned to fulfill its task of coagulating the many into singleness of meaning which we call facts, data, problems, realities. The function of this idol—call it ego or literalism—is to keep banality before our eyes, so that we remember to see through, so that mystery becomes possible. Unless things coagulate there is no need for insight. The metaphorical function of the psyche depends on the ever-present literalist within each of us.[24]

So it would seem that an adequate psychology must be one that cannot take itself or any of its ideas literally. Its fantasy of itself must be one that allows psychologizing to continue as an open process of ideation. It may not be based upon axioms and laws, or even rely upon hypotheses. Instead it will have to consist of fictions. Whereas hypotheses can be hardened with evidence and tried by experience, becoming truths because they may be verified or falsified, fictions are distinguished by their "inconceivability." They are full of contradictions and "logical impossibilities."[25] They can never be taken literally in their own terms, but carry on their calling card the prefix of their class mark, "as-if."

An Excursion on Fictions

A fiction cannot be proved wrong: ". . . neither its contradiction of experience nor even logical objections can disturb it."[26] "Fictions . . . are assumptions made with a full realization of the impossibility of the thing assumed."[27] The main characteristic of fictions is "the express awareness that the fiction is just a fiction, in other words the consciousness of its fictional nature and the absence of any claim to actuality."[28]—so far the German philosopher Hans Vaihinger, who thoroughly worked out the role of fictions in thought.

Vaihinger sees fictions as "mental structures" and "the fictive activity of the mind [as] an expression of the fundamental psychic forces."[29] But then he performs a psychologism. Because they are psychic, they are personal, human. And because they are personally human they are only expedient, enunciating only practical and relative truths, valid only in relation to the person using them.[30] For Vaihinger they become *mere* fictions, subjective inventions of a human mind.

But the very fiction of the archetypes is that they posit themselves to be more than personal and human, because the psyche is both immanent in persons, and between persons, and also transcends persons. Archetypes are mental structures, but not only mental structures. Our archetypal fictions keep their mythopoeic, their truly fictional, character beyond what we do or say about them. We can never be certain whether we imagine them or they imagine us, since creation myths always place Gods prior to mankind. All we know is that we seem unable to imagine without them; they are the precondition of our imagination. If we invent them, then we invent them according to the patterns they lay down.

We must keep on the edge of this sort of paradox to be truly thinking in an "as-if" manner. We may not, like Vaihinger, literalize fictions too, and take too seriously their "inconceivability" and "impossibility," stuffing them solid with scholarly German examples. The very evidence he accumulates for their nonexistence gives them a metaphysical status. In other words, even his "as-if" needs to be seen through, for it tends to become a new model and models tend to solidify, substantiate. As Braithwaite says about scientific explanatory models: ". . . 'the last trace of the old, hard, massy atom has disappeared'; but it lies latent whenever a model is used. Thinking of scientific theories by means of models is always *as-if* thinking. . . . The price of the employment of models is eternal vigilance."[31]

So, we may not use "as-if" fictions as explanatory principles, as an obverse to axioms or truths, for they then become another variety of axioms or truths. This would be to give them a substantial power. It would turn them into models which must be seen through. Our desire for a solid backstop somewhere needs to be reconciled with Heraclitus' idea of depth of soul which stops nowhere. By calling upon "as-if" thinking to provide the backstops, we are obliged to accept, as Black points out, that "as-if" models and "as-if" thinking have less explanatory power.[32] But our search is not for explanations, since these satisfy anyway only in terms of the archetypal premises they bring with them.

Fictions are not supposed to have great explanatory power, so they do not settle things for a mind searching for fixity. But they do provide a resting place for a mind searching for ambiguity and depth. In other words, fictions satisfy the aesthetic, religious, and speculative imagination more than they do the intellect. Personifications should always be taken in this ambiguous light: even should they appear vividly, the definition of their reality remains open. Or, from the "as-if" perspective, the kind of reality we attribute to the personifications of the archetypes will depend upon "who" is defining reality and "what" archetypal fantasy is now operating in the psyche. An ultimate, absolute, definite reality transcendent to one or another archetypal perspective is again another fiction.

As truths are the fictions of the rational, so fictions are the truths of the imaginal. Fictions satisfy the need of psychologizing, providing a wholly psychological base, an altogether psychic invention which posits itself as such and hence cannot take itself literally. None, not a single one, of its premises is an actuality, a demonstrable happening, a fact of the world, belonging to the fantasy of objectivity, positivism, empiricism.

Moreover these premises, having a wholly metaphorical existence, cannot be mistaken for metaphysical existence. They are envisioned figurations, constellations,[33] or personified psychological ideas, but not metaphysical reals or spiritual substances. Our premises present a world that escapes both the demands of logic for definition and the demands of empirical science for demonstration. Fictions take their place in the realm traditionally reserved for the soul, between the world of spirit (metaphysics and intellect) and the world of nature (science and sense perception). They furnish psychology with its own psychic premises, not borrowed from metaphysics and the sciences, which offer a mode of seeing through metaphysics and the sciences. By acceptance of the imaginative fictional factor in all intellect and sense perception, these two faculties of the soul can become instruments rather than antagonists of psychologizing. No longer must we pit "pure" thought and "objective" observations against psychological thinking and observations. All activities of the psyche, whatever psychic faculty they originate in or whatever academic faculty they are manifested in, become means of soul-making.

Although we are pressing to the extreme the personified archetypes' impossible fictional nature, their very impossibility provides the ground of possibility for psychologizing. By virtue of their inconceivability, their enigmatic and ambiguous nature, these metaphorical premises elude every literalness, so that the primary urge of seeing through everything fixed, posited, and defined begins archetypally in these fictional premises themselves. Here I am seeking to ground possibility in the impossible, searching for a way to account for the unknown in the still more unknown, *ignotum per ignotius.* Rather than explain I would complicate, rather than define I would compound, rather than resolve I would confirm the enigma.

Let us recall here what Paul Ricoeur said in his Terry Lectures: "Enigma does not block understanding but provokes it. . . . That which arouses understanding is precisely the double meaning, the intending of the second meaning in and through the first."[34] Moreover we have at our side in this stance against definition a responsible rationalist, Karl Popper, who writes that "outside mathematics and logic problems of definability are mostly gratuitous. We need many undefined terms whose meaning . . . will be changeable. But this is so with all concepts, including defined ones, since a definition can only reduce the meaning of the defined term to that of the undefined terms." And ". . . all definitions must ultimately go back to undefined terms."[35] Perhaps our recourse to *ignotum per ignotius* is no mere mercurial trick of the alchemist, no mystification at all, but has indeed its intellectual justification.

The comprehensive metaphor, answering our requirements for intellectual puzzlement and explanation through enigma by providing as-if fictions in depth, complexity, and exquisite differentiations, is myth. Particularly in classical mythology the metaphorical mode exhibits itself in vast display and precise detail. These myths present the archetypal dramas of the soul, all its problems portrayed as fictions, "the tragical, monstrous, and unnatural"[36] given sense and importance, providing a heaven for as it is on earth.

The infinite regress of psychologizing, its interiorizing process from visible to invisible which we have just described (and which we described above in Chapter 2 as the pathologizing that speeds fantasies toward death, the last term and the prime metaphor)—this infinite regress here comes to rest because here it meets the *permanent ambiguity of metaphor,* where "rest" and "permanence" are also as-if fictions. For these intellectual concepts, like all intellectual concepts, "rest" or find "permanent ground" and "base" in metaphor and can only be "established" by consent of metaphor. It is the imaginal that gives certainty to our intellectual sureties, augmenting the intellect beyond itself—despite its attempts to constrain with definitions—to connote and imply and suggest always more than its terms would denote. For the intellectual too expresses fantasies that are rooted in myths, and these fantasies can be exposed by the psychologizing eye of the soul.

Nunquam enim satiatur oculus visu, said Cusanus. "The eye, as a sense organ, is neither satiated nor limited by anything visible; for the eye can never have too much of seeing; likewise, intellectual vision is never satisfied with a view of the truth. . . . The striving for the infinite, the inability to stop at anything given or attained is neither a fault nor a shortcoming of the mind; rather it is the seal of its divine origin and of its indestructibility."[37]

So the infinite regress should not bother us; it occurs even in empiricism when one tries to follow a sequence of ideas back to their "origin" in an observation of a "hard fact."[38] Psychologizing by means of the infinite regress is also regressing toward the infinite, the God within. Each step in the process yields insight. It is like peeling the mystic's onion, but here not for the sake of an esoteric void at the core but for the sake of the perpetual movement inward, much as Ficino said that "perpetual ratiocination" was the proper activity of the soul.[39] By perpetually moving inward and bringing out hidden fantasy images, psychologizing becomes, not an esoteric activity, but the activity that makes events esoteric. By the searching out of what lies within and behind events, their literal sense becomes evident, exposed, and dull. At the same time, when events are turned inward they gain the element of significance for soul.

Within the metaphorical perspective, within the imaginal field, nothing is more sure than the soul's own activity following its wayward inertia from insight to insight; nothing truer, more firm, or eternal than soul itself and its fantasy, exercising this fantasy in freedom from logical, sentimental, or moral restrictions, extending its comprehension by seeing through the coagulations of every sort of fixated form. Thus the soul finds psyche everywhere, recognizes itself in all things, all things providing psychological reflection. And the soul accepts itself in its mythical enactments as one more such metaphor. More real than itself, more ultimate than its psychic metaphor, there is nothing.

Psyche and Myths

Myths talk to psyche in its own language; they speak emotionally, dramatically, sensuously, fantastically. Through the mythical perspective we perceive significances and persons, not objects and things: "Primacy of expression-perception over thing-perception is what characterizes the mythical world-view."[40] Concrete particulars become universalized through myth; myths also tell of universals in specific images of figures and places, exact happenings which have never happened but always do happen.[41] Happenings need reflection and patterning in something that is beyond happening and of another ontological order, where the wonders of nonevents are the events. Or, as Karl Otto Müller said, myth is where "the marvellous is truth,"[42] so that its extraordinary, strange wonder stands behind all kinds of truth. "Myth," says Hermann Broch, "is the archetype of every phenomenal cognition of which the human mind is capable. Archetype of all human cognition, archetype of science, archetype of art—myth is consequently the archetype of philosophy too."[43] So, too, myth is metapsychology and metapsychopathology. This Jung and Freud each showed: Jung simply by describing his own psychological ideational processes as "mythologizing"[44] Freud by creating what Wittgenstein called "a powerful mythology" which one must "see through."[45] We see through it first in the obvious—Oedipus, Eros, Thanatos. We see it more subtly and significantly in the mythical "child" on whose mighty little shoulders rests the huge hydraulic machine of psychoanalysis.

Let us recall that Freud's theory of infantile sexuality is not squarely based on the empirical child. Freud never analyzed children, and the memories of childhood which confirmed his theory were taken from adults whose reminiscences were fictions or myths, that is, "expression-perceptions" rather than literal "thing-perceptions." The figure of a polymorphous perverse infant that is depicted in his *Three Essays on the Theory of Sexuality* (1905) is thus a mythical (contraposed to empirical, factual, literal) creation. This child is not only mythical but mythic, for it has been believed in, its reality has been "confirmed" by "studies" and by personal revelation (witness), and it gives support to a school of teaching and a view of the world, as does any mythic person. The myth that is alive is not noticed as mythical until seen through.[46]

We practitioners go on mythologizing, deriving our tough-minded empirical facts from an extraordinary form of fiction: the case history, the anamnesis, the "write-up," by means of which the details of a life are composed into a story, receive a vision, and thereby a mythical person becomes the personification of a fate which issues into the therapeutic process.

One beauty of mythic metaphors is that they elude literalism. We know at the outset that they are impossible truths. Like metaphor itself, the power of which cannot satisfactorily be explained, a myth also speaks with two tongues at one time, amusing and terrifying, serious and ironic, sublimely imaginative and yet with the scattered detail of ridiculous fancy. The metaphors of myth condense past and present together, so that the past is always present and the present can be felt from the detachment of the past.[47] Myths also make concrete particulars into universals, so that each image, name, thing in my life when experienced mythically takes on universal sense, and all abstract universals, the grand ideas of human fate, are presented as concrete actions.[48] And always a myth is the psyche telling of itself in disguise, as if it had nothing to do with psychology, as if all myths were "really" about cosmogony, or quest and adventure, or the origins and sins of dynasties, or slaughters and loves, as if myth were speaking literally of the guises it wears that hold its psychic interiority.

My view of metaphor starts from Vico, who takes the metaphor to be a mini-myth, "a fable in brief."[49] Because metaphor "gives sense and passion to insensate things," it is a manner of personifying, and thus mythologizing. By condensing myth and metaphor in this way, Vico shelters under his superb mind my frequent lack of distinctions between myth and metaphor. In my approach to metaphor I consider it to be like the as-if fictions of Vaihinger, but less semantically as a figure of speech and more ontologically as a mode of being, or psychologically as a style of consciousness. Metaphors are more than ways of speaking; they are ways of perceiving, feeling, and existing.

I have been considering metaphor as particularly psychological because, as it were, it sees through itself. The binary opposition (Lévi-Strauss on myth and Harald Weinrich on metaphor) contained within it is contained *by* it. Conflicts become paradoxes. The positions it states are inflected by a voice that sets it off in inverted commas. At one and the same time it says something and sees through what it says. We can never take a metaphor from one side only, nor can we be sure which side it means. Is Richard the lion a lion in a cage named Richard? Or, is Richard the lion a courageous king? We are perturbed; there are echoes of schizophrenic thinking; fantasies are rising. This well-known example is too simple, for many kinds of metaphors have been distinguished and named; but it serves to illustrate the basic idea: psychological consciousness, because it sees through, because it flourishes in ambiguity, is metaphorical.

Archetypes are semantically metaphors. They have a double existence which Jung presented in several ways: (1) they are full of internal oppositions, positive *and* negative poles; (2) they are unknowable *and* known through images; (3) they are instinct *and* spirit; (4) they are congenital, yet not inherited; (5) they are purely formal structures *and* contents; (6) they are psychic *and* extrapsychic (psychoid). These doublings, and many others like them in the description of archetypes, need not be resolved philosophically or empirically, or even semantically. They belong to the internal self-contradiction and duplicity of mythic metaphors, so that *every statement regarding the archetypes is to be taken metaphorically,* prefixed with an "as-if."

This Jung says himself: "Every interpretation necessarily remains an 'as-if.' "[50]

The ground principles, the *archai,* of the unconscious are indescribable because of their wealth of reference. . . . The discriminating intellect naturally keeps on trying to establish their singleness of meaning and thus misses the essential point; for what we can above all establish as the one thing consistent with their nature is their manifold meaning, their almost limitless wealth of reference, which makes any unilateral formulation impossible.[51]

Mythic metaphor is the correct way of speaking about the archetypes because, like Gods, they do not stand still. Like Gods they cannot be defined except through and by their complications in each other.

Archetypes are the skeletal structures of the psyche, yet the bones are changeable constellations of light—sparks, waves, motions. They are principles of uncertainty. Since they cannot be confronted directly, they become defined, as Jung always insisted, as "unknowable in themselves." But their unknowability depends only on the method by which we would "know" them. We have no clear and distinct knowledge of them in themselves and by themselves in the Cartesian sense of certainty; but we know them indirectly, metaphorically, mythically. We meet archetypal reality through the perspective of myths, since "fading into uncertainty belongs to the very nature of myth."[52] We speak of archetypes as Plato did of myths: "This or something of the kind is true," and "I would not stand up for it completely," so that what one says "does not become encased in rigid armor."[53]

Mythical consciousness does not need an "as-if." So long as ideas are not fixed into singleness of meaning, we do not need to pry them loose with the tool of "as-if." Vaihinger after all derives from Kant and in reaction to Kant's categorical monotheistic mind. "As-if" is a necessary philosophical step for recognizing the metaphorical character of all certainties in what we see, say, and believe. But if we begin in mythical consciousness we do not need the prefix. It is implied throughout, always.

If myths are the traditional narratives of the interaction of Gods and humans, a dramatic account "of the deeds of the *daimones,*"[54] then our way of finding Gods in our concrete lives is by entering myths, for that is where they are. "Entering myths" means recognizing our concrete existence as metaphors, as mythic enactments. The initiation of this way is through the *daimones,* the "little people" of the complexes of whom we spoke in the first chapter.

This multiple perspective finds expression in the polytheistic Gods who intermarry, whose realms intermingle and interpenetrate. In the sophisticated psychology of Orphic and Neoplatonic mythology in the Renaissance, the duplicity and triplicity of each image and each theme was a tenet in all mythic understanding.[55]

Thus the discerning question, which keeps consciousness aware in the welter and profusion, is the eternal "Who?" that is answered never by one single archetype or one God, but always by this one in its particular constellation with others. These constellations are precisely what mythologems describe: they are descriptions—not of Gods, but of patterns, interactions, of Gods in their complexities. *Gods apart from myths are abstractions* made by monotheistic consciousness that imagines Gods and archetypes as monolithic units. But Gods are relations and always imply each other; only when a God or archetype is conceived by monotheistic consciousness does it appear as one alone. Then we speak of the mother archetype, or of Dionysus, say, but the mother archetype does not exist phenomenologically without either a consort or a child or a daughter as well as a place and set of attributes, and Dionysus appears either with a crowd or with a wife, or with Hermes or with Zeus or with Titans, as well as with those specific accoutrements by which he is recognized.

By presenting all this, myths offer the multiplicity of meanings inherent in our lives, while theology and science attempt singleness of meaning. Perhaps this is why mythology is the mode of *speaking* religion in polytheistic consciousness, and why monotheistic consciousness *writes* down theology. Polytheistic consciousness is ever reminded by myth of the ambiguity of meanings and the multiplicity of persons in each event in each moment.

Despite their graphic description of action and detail, myths resist being interpreted into practical life. They are not allegories of applied psychology, solutions to personal problems. This is the old moralistic fallacy about them, now become the therapeutic fallacy, telling us which step to take and what to do next, where the hero went wrong and had to pay the consequences, as if this practical guidance were what is meant by "living one's myth." Living one's myth doesn't mean simply living *one* myth. It means that one lives *myth;* it means *mythical living.* As I am many persons, so I am enacting pieces of various myths. As all myths fold into each other, no single piece can be pulled out with the statement: "This is my myth." Remember, the mythic is a perspective and not a program; to try to use a myth practically keeps us still in the pattern of the heroic ego, learning how to do his deeds correctly.

Myths do not tell us how. They simply give the invisible background which starts us imagining, questioning, going deeper. The very act of questioning is a step away from practical life, deviating from its high-road of continuity, seeing it from another perspective. But—could this shift of perspective happen if there were not some other place, some other hidden ground to stand on, a mythical place that gives another vantage point, thereby placing us in two ontological positions at once, ourselves divided and yet conflict contained, ourselves already metaphors? As metaphors speak with inverted commas, giving a new double interiority, an echo, to a plain word, so when we begin to mythologize our plain lives they gain another dimension. We are more distanced because we are more richly involved.

A semantic definition of metaphor is "deviant discourse,"[56] and its corresponding opposite term is "literal." The dictionary says that metaphors transfer meaning. If psychologizing proceeds by seeing through the plainly literal, then the psychologizing activity will continually enliven, by transferring meaning into and out of direct discourse. Psychology then refers less to a body of knowledge than to a perspective parallel to other bodies of knowledge, a running commentary to their direct and literal discourse. Psychology will not be straight and well-structured. It will be scattered, not direct, not a Hero on his course, but a Knight Errant picking up insights by the way.

An Excursion on Errancy

Before we follow the Knight Errant to the chapter's end, let us look at errancy and error. The "errant fantasy" makes its first important appearance in Plato (*Timaeus* 47e–48e), where we find two opposing principles at work in the universe: Reason *(nous)* and Necessity *(anánkē)*, also called the Errant Cause. Francis Cornford, one of the great commentators on Plato, describes *anánkē* as "rambling," "aimless," "irresponsible."[57] Reason cannot bring the errant principle or necessity altogether under its control. Errancy seems opposed to intelligent order and purpose, and according to Cornford we meet it in coincidences and spontaneity; it points to the irrational element in the soul.[58] Paul Friedländer, another master of Plato's thought, suggests that *anánkē* can even be imagined as having physical location in the center of man and the universe where it operates as the principle of indefiniteness, unreason, and chaos.[59] The soul has some special relationship to this errant principle of aimless necessity, since as Plato says in the *Republic* (621a), souls enter the world by passing beneath the throne of the Goddess, *Anánkē*, whose three daughters govern the destiny of every soul.

For Plato the truth of intelligent reason was not enough to account for man and the universe. Something else was necessary, especially in accounting for what governs the psyche. Some wandering necessary force also comes into play, and in fact, it is through errancy that we see Necessity at work. Thus the archetypal background to error is Necessity; through error-caused events Necessity breaks into the world. If this errant cause, necessity, is the principle in errors, then let us consider error necessary, a way the soul enters the world, a way the soul gains truths that could not be encountered through reason alone. Psychological awareness rises from errors, coincidences, indefiniteness, from the chaos deeper than intelligent control.

This approach to error is a cornerstone of depth psychological method: it is basic to Freud's investigations of the slips and errors of daily life and to Jung's examination of the errors of attention in the association experiments. Necessity breaks through the control of reason and reveals in a chance moment the "errant cause" operating in the soul. Historically, depth psychology starts from this perspective and in principle continues to look for its truths in errors in which deeper, more central necessities lie. Moreover, it regards reason itself from a viewpoint built upon errors, and it takes all duplicities—fabrications, half-truths, lies—as a mendacious discourse that is psychologically necessary.

An equivocation is an *opus contra naturam,* a place where the psyche is speaking against the natural flow of reasonable, predictable expectations, the truth of the ways things are. Hermes, who cheats his father Zeus as soon as he is born, is the congenital deceiver bringing equivocation into the world with divine authority. He is God of equivocation as he is guide of the soul. And we each sense him when we would speak most deeply of our souls, for just then we feel the error, the half-truth, the deception in what we are telling. This is not bad faith, unless we forget that Hermes works as well through the messages of lies as through truths. No one can tell the real truth, the whole truth about the soul but Hermes, whose style is that of duplicity. Psychology is thus not a discipline of truth, as is science or philosophy or theology. From the psychological perspective, lying and telling the truth are invalid categories; both call for psychologizing, and truths more than lies for they are even harder to see through.

In other words error is not only where truth went wrong but where another sort of truth, a fictional one, is going on. Vaihinger himself notes "the linguistic similarity of the fiction to error . . . error is marked by the same formula, and psychologically it has the same formation as the fiction. Fiction is, after all, merely a more conscious, more practical and more fruitful error."[60] Fictions, too, follow the errant path; requiring, says Vaihinger, a "circuitous" and "deviant" style of consciousness.

Of course a psychology that thinks in this style about truth and error, that does not correct errors to get nearer truth, abandons both the idea of empirical psychology and that of psychological progress. Popper writes: "And we make progress if, and only if, we are prepared to *learn from our mistakes:* to recognize our errors and to utilize them critically instead of persevering in them dogmatically. Though this analysis may sound trivial, it describes, I believe, the method of all empirical sciences."[61] To put this in our terms: the fantasy of progress and the fantasy of empiricism require the fantasy of *rectifying* error.

Rather than place error within the empirical fantasy of trial-and-error, which employs progressive corrections toward eradicating itself (reducing the errant factor and increasing the rational factor), where error must always be doomed to play the shadow enemy of truth, let us instead place error within the "errant fantasy." We do this because, as Dufrenne says, "fictitious vagabonds are true by the very fact that they are witnesses of an errant world."[62]

The Knight Errant

The Knight Errant is a wanderer, and his path has been deviant ever since Parmenides decried loose-limbed wandering as the way of error, deceptive opinion, going astray.[63] For the grand rational tradition, the way of psychologizing is too close to *phantasia* and the *senses*, having wandered off course and away from the true logos of intellectual reasoning, intuitional revelation, and the eternalities of spirit. The Knight Errant follows fantasy, riding the vehicle of his emotions; he loiters and pursues the anima with his eros, regarding desire as also holy; and he listens to the deviant discourse of the imagination. His arguments make use of the "straw man"; he personifies, makes the other position come alive, so that he can meet it as body and not only as thought. As one of the Knight Errant's main tasks was helping the poor,[64] so does psychologizing liberate the parts of the soul trapped in the poverty of materialistic perspectives. But the Knight Errant is also an outcast, a renegade wandering like Cain, never quite able to return within the structures of literalism, seeing through their walls, their definitions, and so excluded by their norms—like Bellerophon, who having fallen from his white winged horse of direct ascent, limped through "the Plain of Wandering," having to move on, from hero to vagabond to rogue. The Knight Errant of psychology is partly picaresque rogue, of the underworld, a shadow hero of unknown paternity, who sees through the hierarchies from below. He is a mediator betwixt and between, homeless, of no fixed abode. Or his home, like that of Eros, is in the realm of the daemons, of the *metaxy* (the middle region), in between, back and forth. Or his home is in the ceaselessly blowing spirit, as Ficino placed the home of thought in soul and the home of soul in spirit. "That is why man alone in this present condition of life never relaxes, he alone in this place is not content. Therefore man alone is a wanderer in these regions, and in the journey itself he can find no rest. . . ."[65]

On the road like the Knight Errant and the picaresque rogue, psychologizing is always questing after something while it wanders without goal; the narrative of its process is episodic and not epic. All the while it sees through the hypocrisies, the fixed positions of every convention, as the classic Spanish rogues Lazarillo and Guzman and the figures of Cervantes see through justice and bravery, through family and charity, through class and money, through religion and love.[66] This wandering spirit within becomes the private teacher of negative learning, and one's psychopathy is given a psychic function.

For indeed wandering is a psychopathic trait. The mocking discordant shadow who must see through because he is also a Knight Errant, passionate and idealistic, is indeed a figure of psychopathy. It is he within who is driven out of stable connections, who cannot settle, cannot conform, because he is driven to unsettle all forms. But this fugue in the soul need not be condemned to play the antisocial criminal, since precisely his mordant insights are those that can awaken the callow unpsychological innocent—who also lives within us—to discern among ideas, discover new perspectives, and survive. This the rogue errant can teach—psychological survival. Thus may our psychopathic shadow become a guiding psychopomp and bring about a reformation of the innocents from below, through the shadow—of the lamb by the wolf.

Now we return again to Plotinus, who conceived the soul as the "wanderer of the metaphysical world," whose place was in between.[67] So psychologizing brings the soul's insights from in between: interlinear, interspersed, intermittent, a running commentary below the line, footnotes accompanying the work of the hand.

To see into the depths and look from below and beneath yields that picaresque taste for the psychological which we find in both Freud and Jung—for bitter irony in the midst of all noble therapeutic endeavors and despite dedication to consciousness, culture, and soul. Like the Knight Errant, psychologizing is exceptionally individualistic, speaking in the first person, as does the rogue, both the author of psychology and the psychology itself fundamentally subjective. And this rogue is anarchic, a law breaker, knowing no bounds of proprium. Not criminal —no—but not moral either. Despite the depth of the spirit's quest, or because of it, psychologizing appropriates from theology, from science, from literature, from medicine, parasitical and penetrating everywhere, playing the thieving renegade among the faculties, always both illegitimate and arrogant, and yet, too, a servant of many masters, now the ancilla of philosophy or theology, now of physiology or biology.

Is Hermes the God within it? Hermes, who guides thieves, and dreams and souls, who relays the messages of all the Gods, the polytheistic hermeneutic? Does he not appear where fields meet and paths intersect or thoughts cross over into quick light? Hermes is the connector-between, Apollo's brother yet Dionysus' first carrier. Because of Hermes, psychologizing is always moving between opposing views such as the Apollonic and the Dionysian attitudes, standing at either end of its spectrum,—partly Apollonic Knight, partly Dionysian Rogue, both and neither. Each sees in psychologizing the fault of its opposite. To the Apollonic perspective, psychologizing seems tricky, shadowy, nocturnal, without objective distance, and without concern for either healing or beauty. In the Dionysian perspective, psychologizing seems too individualistic, intellectual, elitist, without enough nature, community, and abandon. Hermes holds this bridge, and connects, too, to night, to death, and the hidden hermetic message in all things.

"The world of Hermes is by no means a heroic world."[68] Nor can psychologizing make it, either, with the heroic ego. Its phallic power is in the word rather than the sword, proceeding by luck and timing, opportunity, where *opportunas* once meant the swift movement of seeing through an opening. Seeing-through, insighting, is an activity that opens; anything becomes an opportunity for soul-making.

Psychologizing is always at variance with the positions of others; it is a countereducation, a negative learning, moving all standpoints off balance toward their borders, their extremes. At the borders Hermes rules, and in these regions of no-man's-land there can be nothing alien, nothing excluded. Psychologizing thus knows no bracketing-out, no *epoché* as the phenomenologists call it. To bracket out puts square walls around a metaphysical or scientific content, providing a sacred precinct for ideas to remain literally intact, closing them off from psychologizing. But every statement is made by the psyche and offers an opportunity for soul-making. Here errors are as fruitful as truths, since each and every sentence tells a tale of the soul. Hermes, who is not bound by the moralistic fallacy, can understand the confabulations and circumlocutions of deceptive fictions. They are ways of making metaphors, for errors and deceptions say "this" as if it were "that."

Psychologizing arrives at no conclusions, for to make a point is to come to a stop. So the errant path also follows Plato's and Plotinus' description of the course of the soul as circular.[69] Psychological reasoning tends to be circular, thriving on the repetition compulsion and cycles of return to the same insoluble themes. If its learning is through error, here error does not mean rectifying mistakes and improvement, but rather learning through what is deviant, odd, off in oneself, where psychologizing is pathologizing.

The errant way leads to the less known for sure, to less knowledge as established, as accumulated into security. It even dissolves the known into doubt, into the freedom of uncertainty. Is not knowledge supposed to free one? *Knowledge makes us able to leave it behind,* able to take off down the road of pitfalls in full foolishness, risking even greater windmills still further out, an old knight more and more bold, an old rogue more and more peculiar, ageing into the freedom of our pathology.

Psychological reflections always catch light from a peculiar angle; they are annoying at the same time as they are perceptive. Psychologizing sees things peculiarly, a deviant perspective reflecting the deviance in the world around. The psychological mirror that walks down the road, the Knight Errant on his adventure, the scrounging rogue, is also an odd-job man, like Eros the Carpenter who joins this bit with that,[70] a handyman, a *bricoleur*—like "a ball rebounding, a dog straying or a horse swerving from its direct course"[71]—psychologizing upon and about what is at hand; not a systems-architect, a planner with directions. And leaving, before completion, suggestion hanging in the air, an indirection, an open phrase . . .

Four/Dehumanizing or Soul-making

And what we long for and have need of is soul—soul of bulk and substance.

MIGUEL DE UNAMUNO
Tragic Sense of Life

Prologue: Polytheistic Psychology,
or a Psychology with Gods, Is Not a Religion

By speaking of Gods as we are doing all through this book, it seems as if we had lost the distinction between religion and psychology. Because the movement of our archetypal psychologizing is always toward myths and Gods, our psychologizing may seem actually a theologizing, and this book as much a work of theology as of psychology. In a way this is so, and must be so, since the merging of psychology and religion is less the confluence of two different streams than the result of their single source—the soul. The psyche itself keeps psychology and religion bound to each other. Therefore our talk of Gods is not merely a trespass; nor is it merely the use of personified hyperbole for heightening the value of archetypes, which as psychic functions and structures could as well be described more conceptually, or with analogies to physiological organs, physical forces, or philosophical categories. No— we speak of Gods because we are working toward a *nonagnostic psychology,*[1] a psychology which does not have to operate in the hollow left from the separation of Sunday and weekday, church and interior state of mind.

Later in this chapter when we explore the Renaissance we shall find that it is possible to have a psychology that is theistic and yet different from religion. This polytheistic psychology within which we are working, and which derives from Renaissance and Greek attitudes, cannot fall into splits between religion and psychology. By starting and staying with the soul's native polycentricity, the multiple archetypal powers, psychology must always keep in mind the governance of the Gods. By keeping our focus upon soul-making, we cannot help but recognize that the Gods in the soul require religion in psychology. But the religion that psychology requires must reflect the state of soul as it is, actual psychic reality. This means polytheism. For the soul's inherent multiplicity demands a theological fantasy of equal differentiation.

Religion in our culture derives from spirit rather than from soul, and so our culture does not have a religion that reflects psychology or is mainly concerned with soul-making. Instead, we have a psychology that reflects religion. Since the religion in our culture has been monotheistic, our psychologies are monotheistic. As we have seen, the prejudices against fragmentation, self-division, and animism are religious in their fanatical intensity. Always psychological thought enjoins the plethora of psychic phenomena to follow the laws of unified models. The monotheistic model may be overtly religious, as is Jung's self, or disguised, as in Freud's attempt at a comprehensive system. Organicism, holism, unified-field theory, monistic materialism, and other psychologies express their fundamental monism through insistence upon clarity, cohesion, or wholes.

By turning to polytheism we leave behind the riddling conundrums built upon monotheism—either religion or psychology, either one or many, either theology or mythology. We enter a style of consciousness where psychology and religion are not defined against each other so that they may more easily become each other.

If we look at those profoundly psychological and religious periods, the Renaissance and Greece, we find that the Renaissance had no field called psychology and the Greeks had no theology—not even a word for religion. But both Florentines and Athenians had *anima, psyché,* myths and images, and they had Gods. Perhaps this is the reason religious questions as separate theological perplexities tend to fall away when one sticks closely to the soul and its psychologizing process. The theological reality of the Gods no longer seems paramount, as they become more psychologically evident in the images and myths of our lives.

Psychologizing moves psychology to a place where it does not belong only to Sunday or to weekdays, to religious or secular thought. A polytheistic vision implies that all days refer to Gods, as the names of the days themselves attest, and that the Gods are in daily life. Psychology is therefore always religious and theistic; theology, the study of the Gods, is always psychological, bound to the actualities of the secular, where myths are daily taking place.

In other words, polytheistic thinking shifts all our habitual categories and divisions. These are no longer between transcendent God and secular world, between theology and psychology, divine and human. Rather, polytheistic distinctions are among the Gods as modes of psychological existence operating always and everywhere. There is no place without Gods and no activity that does not enact them. Every fantasy, every experience has its archetypal reason. There is nothing that does not belong to one God or another. The idea of a secular psychology becomes impossible.

The idea of the secular versus the religious is responsible for the *science fantasy of psychology.* In order to move toward a nonagnostic psychology we must first see through psychology's dominant belief in itself as a science. Clearly, from the ideas we have been shaping, archetypal psychology does not imagine itself or the psyche as belonging to science, even social or behavioral science. A mythologizing that prefers many perspectives to operational definitions, a psychologizing that asks *Who?* and *What?* rather than *How?* and *Why?*—a personifying that subjectifies, a circular errancy that is not to be corrected, and a pathologizing that is not to be treated (to say nothing of the naturalistic, pragmatic, and empirical as "fallacies")—all make it impossible for a psychology based on psyche to imagine itself as science.

The science fantasy with its reliance upon objectivity, technology, verification, measurement, and progress—in short, its necessary literalism—is less a means for examining the psyche than for examining science. Our interest lies not in applying the methods of science to psychology (to put it on a "sound scientific footing"), but rather in applying the archetypal method of psychologizing to science so as to discover its root metaphors and operational myths.

Science is not soulless at all. It too is an activity of the psyche and of the archetypes in the psyche, one of the ways of enacting the Gods. By psychologizing scientific problems, methods, and hypotheses we can find their archetypal fantasies.[2] For science, also, is a field for soul-making provided we do not take it literally on its own terms.

The difference between psychology and religion boils down to the same as between psychology and science: literalism. Theology takes Gods literally and we do not. But this is to use a cleaver, whereas the distinction requires more subtlety. Another way of putting it would be that the difference between religion and psychology lies not in our description of the Gods but in our action regarding them. Religion and psychology have care for the same ultimates, but religion approaches Gods with ritual, prayer, sacrifice, worship, creed. Gods are *believed* in and approached with religious methods. In archetypal psychology Gods are *imagined.* They are approached through psychological methods of personifying, pathologizing, and psychologizing. They are formulated ambiguously, as metaphors for modes of experience and as numinous borderline persons. They are cosmic perspectives in which the soul participates. They are the lords of its realms of being, the patterns for its mimesis. The soul cannot be, except in one of their patterns. All psychic reality is governed by one or another archetypal fantasy, given sanction by a God. I cannot but be in them.

Whereas this view of Gods does not infringe upon their reality for the theology-fantasy—which, like science, is a fantasy of the soul—this view does put in doubt their theological substantiality and literal existence, their absolute ultimacy beyond the reaches of the soul.

Because our polytheistic psychology is not making theological claims, because it is not approaching Gods in a religious style, theology cannot repudiate psychological polytheism as heresy or false religion with false Gods. We are not out to worship Greek Gods—or those of any other polytheistic high culture, Egyptian or Babylonian, Hindu or Japanese, Celtic or Norse, Inca or Aztec—to remind us of what monotheism has made us forget. We are not reviving a dead faith. For we are not concerned with faith or with the life or death of God. *Psychologically, the Gods are never dead; and archetypal psychology's concern is not with the revival of religion, but with the survival of soul.*

A new theological polytheism does not automatically come into being when soul phenomena are led into a psychological relation with Gods.[3] Nor does archetypal psychology become religion by talking of archetypes as if they were Gods. For it is possible to imagine in one style and worship in another.

Greek psychological philosophers, for example Socrates, practiced polytheistic religion by offering prayers to Gods, while imagining monotheistically about the One, the Beautiful, and the Good. Similarly, but in reverse, Renaissance philosophical psychologists practiced monotheism. Both Petrarch and Ficino (whose roles in the tradition of polytheistic psychology I will discuss later) were ordained members of the Church offering their prayers to Christ while they imagined by means of polytheism's images and myths.

So let us not get caught in a choice between two styles of religion or between psychology and religion. A choice between alternatives already presumes dualism, which archetypally brings with it the divisive sword. (No Greek Olympian, by the way, had a sword for emblem; the spear of deeply penetrating insight, yes; but no sword to cut in two.) The fantasy of dualism ultimately refers to monism and is therefore very different from polytheism. Dualities are either faces of the same, or assume a unity as their precondition or ultimate goal (identity of opposites). Even a radically irreconcilable dualism is merely the struggle between parallel Ones. Monism and dualism share the same cosmos.

The fantasy of polytheism permits no single one to be elevated to The

One in a literalistic manner. Zeus posits himself above all others, for the archetypal idea of oneness presents itself as first, superior, progenitor. But Zeus is only one among other equals, a *primus inter pares,* and myths show him limited by the others. In this polytheistic vision the struggle between the one and the many, good and evil, and all the either-or problems of the monotheistic fantasy become irrelevant. Polytheistic mythical thinking seems quite nonchalant about binary oppositions. When Lévi-Strauss raises the idea of binary opposites to be the single explanatory principle of mythical thought, is he speaking with the true voice of myth or of Descartes and his dualism?

Let us imagine an unworried blending of polytheistic and monotheistic styles as in the Renaissance. Even for medieval Christianity "the pagan gods were as truly existent as the Trinity or the Virgin Mary."[4] They were of course generally evil because pagan. But a characteristic virtue of Renaissance thought was that an interplay could go on between images from different myths without theological considerations, and that the psychological significance of polytheistic images could stand forth without blame for their "paganism." This attitude is profoundly psychological because it allows the diverse perspectives of myths and their figures to see through one another. None can be taken as literally real; none can claim precedence. As in the Renaissance, there can be "an easy ambivalence of pagan humanistic and Christian values without attempting to reconcile the differences."[5]

There will always be attempts at reconciliation between Christian monotheism and pagan polytheism, between theology and psychology, when the archetypal perspective of unity and systematic order dominates. The polytheistic perspective requires no "reconciliation" since there is place for all from the beginning. But monism cannot take the ambiguity of diversity. It experiences it as a tension of opposites which must be accommodated through a higher single principle and resolved. This synthesizing operation, by moving higher, is always an inflating exercise, an identification with a one high God who creates a firm order out of many viewpoints. But this chapter leaves such concerns behind. As an essay in polytheistic psychology, the discussion that follows attempts to move soul-making away from the preconceptions of monotheistic psychology.

Archetypal Psychology Is Not a Humanism

As archetypal psychology is not a science or a religion, so too it is not a humanism, and that is the theme we shall develop in this chapter. In the customary division of academic powers science is placed on one side, the humanities on the other, and psychology falls somewhere between the two or is given a monstrous joint title such as "human science." Even during the Renaissance, when natural science and human studies entered our culture, they were two brothers in opposition to a third: theological religion, which tried to prevent science from turning to nature and the humanities from turning to the polytheistic past. Three distinct fantasies with three separate foci emerged in this conflict—a logos of nature (science), a logos of man (humanities), a logos of God (theology). But what about the logos of psyche?

Where does psychology belong? According to the history of our field, the term *psychologia* first presents itself in theological surroundings. Textbooks always say it was introduced by Melanchthon, Luther's close friend and co-worker.[6] It makes its appearance together with the new terms of the Reformation: *self-regard, self-love, self-conceit, self-destruction.* The new word selfness, and the self as a reflexive intensive pronoun, expressed a new reflective style, a new interiority and intensification of the person.

Melanchthon would have assigned psychology to the natural sciences by grouping the study of soul under *physiologia* together with physics and mathematics.[7] But the religious milieu of its birth prevailed, and the inward and personal direction of *psychologia* was reinforced during the next centuries, especially by the introspection of German pietism and Kant's elaborately argued fantasy of the moral person, the human soul as focus of the creation. Psychology had slipped away from theology and had joined the human studies. Kant called it anthropology.

Today, after a long period during which medical, experimental, and statistical psychology have tried to make a science of it, the study of soul is once again considered to be the study of man. Archetypal psychology however departs from that notion—in fact from all three positions—and conceives the study of soul to have a way of its own. One can still share the perspectives of religion, science, and humanism, but one need not assume their premises or come to their conclusions: it is possible to personify and imagine about divine persons without being a theologian, to pathologize and examine symptoms without being a medical scientist, and to psychologize about language and images, history of ideas and method of knowledge, without being a humanist or philosopher. But if forced into an alliance with any of the three, then archetypal psychology is as close to the service and study of Gods as it is to the service and study of man.

Much of the close interplay between archetypal psychology and polytheistic religion has been exposed in earlier chapters. Now the crucial emphasis is upon the distinction between psyche and the human. This does not, however, imply a division between the human and psyche, separating actual man from actual soul.[8] The distinction, radical as it sounds, merely repeats the honored religious idea that a man may lose his life and not his soul, or lose his soul and keep his life. It is supported by other religious traditions which speak about disembodied souls; about external souls (such as we discussed under animism); about human beings who sell or ransom their souls or have never had soul at all. These traditions emphasize the distinction further by saying that soul is immortal or is weighed in an afterlife, i.e., has an existence beyond life and apart from the human being.

Philosophy, from Plato and his Neoplatonic followers (especially Plotinus) and from Hegel and his neo-Hegelians, also supports this idea. Its tradition is that even if psyche refers to an individual soul here and now lived by a human being, it always refers equally to a universal principle, a world soul or objective psyche distinct from its individuality in humans.

However, of these notions, psyche and human, psyche is the more embracing, for there is nothing of man that soul does not contain, affect, influence, or define. Soul enters into all of man and is in everything human. Human existence is psychological before it is anything else— economic, social, religious, physical. In terms of logical priority, all realities (physical, social, religious) are inferred from psychic images or fantasy presentations to a psyche. In terms of empirical priority, before we are born into a physical body or a social world, the fantasy of the child-to-come is a psychic reality, influencing the "nature" of the subsequent events.

But the statement that soul enters into everything human cannot be reversed. Human does not enter into all of soul, nor is everything psychological human. Man exists in the midst of psyche; it is not the other way around. Therefore, soul is not confined by man, and there is much of psyche that extends beyond the nature of man. The soul has inhuman reaches.

That the soul is experienced as my "own" and "within" refers to the privacy and interiority of psychic life. It does not imply a literal ownership or literal interiority. The sense of "in-ness" refers neither to location nor to physical containment. It is not a spatial idea, but an imaginal metaphor for the soul's nonvisible and nonliteral inherence, the imaginal psychic quality within all events. Man can never be large enough to possess his psychic organs; he can but reflect their activities.

Soul and Body

To take the sense of in-ness literally is to be caught in the ancient dilemma about the soul's location: is it in the heart, the humors, or the nervous system? Is it in the pineal gland, the carotid artery, or dispersed through the cells of living tissue? Is it information inside genes? These questions, seemingly so foolish and outdated, were crucial for psychologizing because they led to deeper interiorizing. As we saw in the third chapter, the sense of in-ness is fundamental to all psychologizing. The soul draws us through the labyrinth of literalisms ever inward, realizing itself through retreat. The retreating nymph is a perennial anima image in myth.

The fact that psyche can never be identified with any of its locations or incorporations and that it must always be distinct from body is not a tragic disaster, the result of man's two natures. We are engaged here neither in a theology of man placing him between ape and angel, nor a philosophy or science of man dividing him between mind and matter. Soul is distinct from body because soul may not be identified with any literal presentation or perspective. As the perspective that sees through, the psyche cannot itself be another visibility. As connecting link, or traditionally third position, between all opposites (mind and matter, spirit and nature, intellect and emotion), the soul differs from the terms which it connects. Its distinction from body is only in terms of literalism, the literal notion of body, encased in skin, out there. This notion also distorts soul into some sort of pious ghostly vapor, running the physiological machine as a little invisible subject in a control tower.

But the moment we realize body also as a subtle body—a fantasy system of complexes, symptoms, tastes, influences and relations, zones of delight, pathologized images, trapped insights—then body and soul lose their borders, neither more literal or metaphorical than the other. Remember: the enemy is the literal, and the literal is not the concrete flesh but negligence of the vision that concrete flesh is a magnificent citadel of metaphors.

Putting soul inside man also neglects that man, too, is a personified literalism—no more an actual real container than soul. In Chapter 1 the realization grew that a human life is actually a personification of the soul, a projection of it, contained by it. Although we readily accept the notion that human energy, and nature, life, and Gods are not specifically human privileges and that they exist "outside" human beings, we curiously balk over distinguishing soul from human being. Is this because we do not allow anima her independence? Is this the fundamental intolerance of human psychology: its inability to admit the distinct reality, the full reality, of soul, so that all our human struggle with imagination and its mad incursions, with the symptoms of complexes, with ideologies, theologies, and their systems, are in root and essence the unpredictable writhing movements of Psyche freeing herself from human imprisonment?

Our distinction between psyche and human has several important consequences. If we conceive each human being to be defined individually and differently by the soul, and we admit that the soul exists independently of human beings, then our essentially differing human individuality is really *not human at all*, but more the gift of an inhuman daimon who demands human service. It is not my individuation, but the daimon's; not my fate that matters to the Gods, but how I care for the psychic persons entrusted to my stewardship during my life. It is not life that matters, but soul and how life is used to care for soul.

This bears upon dreams. Dreams, we said earlier, are the best model of the actual psyche, for they show it personified, pathologized, and manifold. In them the ego is only one figure among many psychic persons. Nothing is literal; all is metaphor. Dreams are the best model also because they show the soul apart from life, reflecting it but just as often unconcerned with the life of the human being who dreams them. Their main concern seems not to be with living but with imagining.

Even if dreams have this "unreal" focus, they are no less valuable and emotional. But their value and emotion is in relation with soul and how life is lived in relation with soul. When we move the soul insights of the dream into life for problem-solving and people-relating, we rob the dream and impoverish the soul. The more we get out of a dream for human affairs the more we prevent its psychological work, what it is doing or building night after night, interiorly, away from life in a nonhuman world. This lifelong activity of nightly imaging is distinct from what we do in the day with these images, applying all the humanistic fallacies—egoistic, naturalistic, moralistic, pragmatistic. Dream activity might better be conceived as soul-making, or in D. H. Lawrence's words, building the Ship of Death.

Dehumanizing Emotion and De-moralizing

If our souls are not ours, it further follows that our psychological afflictions and emotions too are not truly ours. They come and go, not by our will or unconscious wish, but by factors independent of our potency. They belong to archetypes, as these affect us through the emotional core of the complex. So therapy of affects will never be encompassed only by the examination and care of human life, but will be forced by the nature of psychic affliction into an archetypal therapy. One turns to archetypes, not so much for getting to the causes or roots of pathology, but to come upon the background reasons that give pathology significance. We look to archetypes for the formal meaning and purpose in events rather than their causal origin or material base.[9]

Of course if our aim is medical, then relief, treatment, and cure are uppermost; background reasons are relevant only where they can help these intentions. But if our aim is psychological—that is, connecting what happens with soul—then we will search for the most fundamental significance of the events in their archetypal or mythical patterns.

Like afflictions, emotions put me in the center of things, giving importance and existential assurance to human being.[10] They seem so centrally mine. Yet they are external to the individual person. We share in emotions and hold them in common; they transcend history and locality; we read them in another's face beyond language and culture, feel them in the gestalt of landscapes and natural things, receive them from images buried thousands of years ago and from the sounds and shapes and words of inorganic art objects. Grief, jealousy, comedy have their images that require no interpretative apparatus; they bear archetypal significance beyond your or my personal experiences of them.

Scientific psychology has sometimes called the transpersonal background of emotion instinct, a term (or fantasy) we have reviewed (p. 244n). By showing emotion's phylogenetic sources and parallel expressions in animals, psychology was indirectly recognizing the nonpersonal background of human affect.[11] In theological accounts of emotion it has been attributed to a sinful essence or a cataclysmic prehuman event (the Fall), or to the generative principle of the beast, only accidentally rather than essentially attached to man. This perspective toward emotion which in one way or another keeps its origin or its essence distinct from human being has led to many practical methods which further support the fantasy of the separability of emotion from man. *Ataraxia* (tranquillizing), *apathia* (freeing from passion), and *katharsis* (casting off or washing away) are all methods which work from the premise of this distinction: the psychic events of emotion can be discriminated from human being.

We need not use these guises of concealment for what we want to say. They are in any case pejorative, their way of making the distinction is in value language: emotion is archaic, inferior, sinful, disordering.

Whereas our distinction between human and emotion treats it as a "divine influx," to use the poetical language that appealed to Blake.[12] Emotion is a gift that comes by surprise, a mythic statement rather than a human property. It announces a movement in soul, a statement of the process going on in a myth which we may perceive in the fantasy images that emotion accompanies. This means that human beings are not responsible for their statements of emotion. Aesthetics recognizes this, finding emotion an incomplete artistic statement which requires personal shaping to be considered valid art. Law, too, recognizes this, and so does common speech. We are not altogether ourselves in undergoing strong affects and so not humanly accountable for what is not our property.

But clinical therapy, which trades in emotions, insists that they belong to human nature; therapy makes its patients individually responsible and personally guilty for universal archetypes. We are made accountable not only for ourselves, but also for the doings of the Gods. Archetypal therapy, in contrast, attempts to envision emotions less personally, less as resultants of human forces. For when freed from human centricity, reverted to fantasies, and then to mythic patterns, emotions have a different quality of experience. The family quarrels, the lovers' enthusiasms, the office explosions, all have profound backgrounds; whether epic, tragic, or comic they are always mythic, far larger than life and at a distance from life.

Let us not take our "human faculties" for granted as human. Let us keep in perpetual question whether what we experience is truly human property, part of the *proprium* as psychology calls it.[13] At least by keeping this an open question there is less risk of taking possession of what may ultimately not belong to human nature at all. This also implies keeping open about the registrar of experience. Is the experiencer a human, or a psychic faculty who is "as-if" human—an interior person who intends and selects and organizes experiences but is also in a mythical fantasy which "I" call "my" subjectivity? Scholastic psychology going back to Aristotle always based the registration of experience upon an interior unifying sense linked with imagination. Imagination is the organizer. If so, then our experiences are organized by mythical images, for it is by means of the imagination that the imaginal realm of archetypes plays through the psyche.

If human nature is a composite of multiple psychic persons who reflect the persons in myths, then the experiencer is also in a myth. He or she is not one but many, a flux of vicissitudes. A fixed recording center in their midst is the archetypal illusion of self-identity. This illusion results from experiences which at the first, prepsychologized level always appear literal, to be literally just what they are. The literalization of experience results in literalizing the experiencer. But if experiences can be seen through as archetypal fantasies, then the subject of them has no more fixed identity than they.

I am suggesting further that we entertain the extreme view that the notion of human being as centered in the moral person of free will is also a mythical fantasy, an archetypal perspective given by a single Hero or a single God; our freedom to choose, our moral center and decisiveness, our free will—all is the code of a transpersonal dominant. Moral codes, including those which attempt the simplification of universality (the Judaic, the Christian, the Kantian, or the Delphic), are the literalization of an archetypal position.

Here I am attempting to de-moralize the psyche from the moralistic fallacy which reads psychic events in terms of good and bad, right and wrong. This requires the fiction of a fixed subject, the Chooser, or a choosing subject, the Fixer, who can repair, amend, atone. The moralistic fallacy is central to the myth of man in the middle, humanism's psychology of a self-identified ego, the Hero whose decisive sword divides in two so that he may choose between good and evil.

Moralism plagues psychology, as it must if we remember psychology's origins in the Reformation and Melanchthon's attempt to bring about the ethical culture of Germany. Even empirical psychology has its moralistic tone, tending to be both descriptive and normative together. Whether in the fantasy of Watson, Skinner, and Mowrer or in Freud, Maslow, Laing, and Jung, psychology wants to show in the same demonstration both how we are and how we should be—the "should be" disguised by saying, "This is how mankind really is; here is our basic nature; this is what it is to be human." What does not fit in becomes inhuman, psychopathic, or evil. Every student of psychology is forced into moralistic positions and every patient of psychology caught in moral judgments about the soul.

Again we find Blake seeing through the moralistic fallacy. Kathleen Raine writes of his view as follows: "Satan's first step is to invent a moral code based upon the false belief that individuals can of themselves be good or evil. This is in direct contradiction to the real nature of things, by which the proprium is merely the recipient of the divine influx. The morally 'good' specter is as satanic in every way as the morally 'evil,' since what is alike in both is their negation of the Imagination."[14]

Like emotions, morals too are "divine influxes." They are effects of

Gods who structure our consciousness according to definite principles. There is a morality of Hermes where cheating belongs, of Ares where raging destruction belongs, of Dionysus where victimization belongs. The necessity that rules the Gods gives a necessity to each of their imaginal positions and prevents any single one from overstepping the limits presented by the images themselves. The principles of one mythical perspective do not go beyond the myth itself and are not general rules for all conduct.

Conflicts between these perspectives are the themes of the human comedy and its tragedy. There is no place we can stand beyond good and evil, beyond the reach of myths which involve us in their positions. So-called amorality is also an archetypal enactment, whether of Cain, Prometheus, the Trickster, or another. The archetypal viewpoint attempts to shift our intense monocular focus from the question of good and evil altogether. We need to see through the question itself, since whether "beyond it" or struggling with it one is reinforcing heroic ego psychology. *Rather than looking at myths morally, archetypal psychology looks at moralities mythically.*

By considering morals as the claims of the imaginal powers, morality itself becomes imaginal. Morality is rooted in psychic images and psychic images are moral powers. These images remind us that we are not alone, choosing and deciding, but that in our choices and decisions we are always reflecting mythic stances. To follow a morality literally is the fallacy that forgets morality's imaginal background; it is even an immoral or impious stance, for it forgets the God in the morality. So, when Blake says that choosing in terms of good and evil negates Imagination, it is implied that the first step in recovering the imaginative perspective is to set aside all moral points of view toward the images of fantasy, dream, and pathology. Images are to be left free of judgments, good or bad, positive or negative.

We have been so dominated by the heroic ego that questions of free will and self-determination have become central concerns of Western thought. Let us return morality to the imagination, and instead become concerned with its free play and free workings in order to understand the soul's images and changes exempt from taxing burdens of moralisms.

Part of the movement to demoralize psychology is *disowning* responsibility. Again Melanchthon raises his preceptorial finger, and we have come to believe that responsibility, commitment, standing for our every word and deed are psychological notions, whereas they are moral ideologies. As we saw in the first chapter, the persons of the psyche are not mine. I do not own them, and so I do not own their feelings and actions either. These other persons give me ethical dilemmas and crises of conscience; but when I own up to all their events as mine in the name of moral responsibility, I commit the even greater sin of satanic self-hood, the ego who owns what is archetypal. The very recognition of the "others" as not mine, disowning them, limits their scope of action. They can be heard but not literally obeyed. The knowledge of "who" is involved in an urge already inhibits the urge through the image aspect of it. So too for moral judgments, whose voices also reflect non-ego images and persons. Disowning thus prevents another psychological "sin," identification.

Psychology's one obligation is to see through, to think and feel psychologically. That obligation alone it may not forego and still retain the name of psychology. Archetypal reflection of each psychic movement returns the morality of actions to the Gods from whom all morality supposedly comes. Reverting moral issues to their archetypal base deepens one's moral sense by recalling that moralities are transpersonal.

Finally, how can we call the soul human when its fantasies, emotions, morality, and death are beyond our human reach. Soul may be lent us by our ancestors as we live out their patterns in our genealogy myth; or by the Gods as we enact their pathologically bizarre dramas; or by our dreams, thereby reminding us at the fresh day's start of the soul's different and underworld existence; or by something yet to happen that is making its way through us—the *Zeitgeist,* the evolutionary process, *karma,* the return of all things to their makers—but our lives are on loan to the psyche for a while. During this time we are its caretakers who try to do for it what we can.

A Critique of Modern Humanism's Psychology

Psychology as an independent field is possible only if we keep our focus upon psyche, not upon what we today believe is human. When we lose this focus on psyche, psychology becomes medicine or sociology or practical theology or something else, but not itself. Notoriously, in all these fields, the soul is secondary or absent; psyche is reduced to a factor or a function of something more literal. Psychology collapses into these different frames of humanism when it loses the courage to be itself, which means the courage to leap qualitatively out of its humanistic presuppositions, out of man in the personal sense, out of psyche in the humanistic sense. Soul-making means dehumanizing.

Should we dehumanize psyche, we would no longer speak so possessively and with such clinging subjectivism, about *my* soul, *my own* feelings, emotions, afflictions, dreams. And we might stop drawing only upon persons for insights, seeing pathography only in lives, using only human beings for psychologizing. The psyche displays itself throughout all being. Present and past, ideas and things, as well as humans, provide images and shrines of persons. The world is as much the home of soul as is my breast and its emotions. Soul-making becomes more possible as it becomes less singly focused upon the human; as we extend our vision beyond the human we will find soul more widely and richly, and we will rediscover it, too, as the interiority of the emptied, soulless objective world.

The horizon of the psyche these days is shrunk to the personal, and the new psychology of humanism fosters the little self-important man at the great sea's edge, turning to himself to ask how he feels today, filling in his questionnaire, counting his personality inventory. He has abandoned intellect and interpreted his imagination in order to become one with his "gut experiences" and "emotional problems"; his soul has become equated with these. His fantasy of redemption has shrunk to "ways of coping"; his stubborn pathology, that *via regia* to the soul's depths, is cast forth in Janovian screams like swine before Perls, dissolved in a closed Gestalt of group closeness, or dropped in an abyss of regression during the clamber up to Maslovian peaks. Feeling is all. Discover your feelings; trust your feelings. The human heart is the way to soul and what psychology is all about.

1. FEELING AS GOD

The faith in human feeling is nothing other than a new religion, a religion with teachers and terms, rituals and doctrines, but without Gods. Where did it come from and where does its central fantasy of feeling belong in our understanding of psyche?

The historical base of humanistic religion is not the humanism of the Renaissance, as we shall soon see, but the intellectualism of the Enlightenment. When the Goddess Reason was enthroned, subjective feelings were reduced to her inferior, irrational opposite. They are still as ideationally vacuous today as when they first saw daylight in Rousseau's arms. Hegel saw feeling quite differently:

> Feeling and heart is not the form by which anything is legitimated, moral, true, just, etc., and an appeal to heart and feeling either means nothing or means something bad. . . . "From the heart proceed evil thoughts,

murder, adultery, fornication, blasphemy, etc." In such times when "scientific" theology and philosophy [and therapy] make the heart and feeling the criterion of what is good, moral, and religious, it is necessary to remind them of these trite experiences. . . .[15]

Hegel is here remembering the shadow side of feeling which contemporary humanism, so long suffering from the shadow side of scientific intellect, has forgotten in its conversion to a new extreme. The terrorist and the girl who kills for her cult-hero (Charles Manson) also trust their feelings. Feeling can become possessed and blind as much as any other human function when it is taken literally. Feelings too are metaphors, expressions of fantasy, indicative of psychic images. They are not immune to ego and its literalizations; feelings are no more truths than are ideas, no more facts than are perceptions. Feelings too are subject to archetypal powers that govern their ethical values, their aesthetic judgments, their styles of relating, expressing, and absorbing. Feelings are not a faultless compass to steer by; to believe so is to make Gods of them, and then only Good Gods, forgetting that feeling can be as instrumental to destructive action and mistaken ideologies as any other psychological function. It prevents our pathologizing, and so can be pathogenic to others—certainly the fantasies in studies on "bad mothers" and "schizogenic families" have told us that. Organizational loyalties can make us commit perjury; class solidarity and military pride can make us intolerant and cruel; and feelings of personal attachment can make us defensive, possessive, and sentimental. Here I am not judging good and bad feelings, but unraveling further Hegel's thought.

His remarks will surely be seen through and put down as a typological reaction of a thinker against feeling. But if left at that, we remain in a psychologism which leaves the content of his insight unheard. The opposition of thinking and feeling itself must be seen through, especially since this opposition has plagued Western thinking about feeling, and feeling about thinking, from the Enlightenment (when these faculties first came into prominence as opposites),[16] through Jung's system of types in the 1920's, into today. For as certain sorts of feeling emerge from long repression they set up a new style of repression in the name of feeling, this one against "head," "words," and detached reflection. Instead of being caught by typology into these contradictory opposites we can see typology as a tool for relativizing positions, a way of making a metaphor out of any function, so that it can no longer posit itself one-sidedly and single-mindedly. A typology then becomes freed of the literalism in which it presents itself, becoming a metaphor for psychic ambivalence in the form of a systematic explanation.

Even Nietzsche, a philosopher of feeling, or at least one who spoke from his feelings, can be skeptical about them, subjecting them to a critique as Kant did with reason. Nietzsche said: " 'Trust in your feelings!' But feelings comprise nothing final, original. . . . Trusting in our feelings means obeying our grandfather and grandmother more than the gods within ourselves: our reason and experience."[17]

Nietzsche here recognizes the Gods in our ideas and psychic events. But he misses that they also govern feelings which he presents as the clichés of a civilization, its ingrained attitudes, handed down and inculcated from earliest childhood. Insights and perceptions flash suddenly; ideas move after them more slowly; but feelings are conservative. They are embedded in tastes, styles, values, manners, which have their surface vogues and revolutions but last as the basic warp of a civilization, determining its particular twist and recurring patterns. The eternal recurrence of history happens right in our feelings. What seem most personally differentiated and individualized are variations through time of ancestral, ethnic, geographical, and religious feeling determinants: our grandmothers and grandfathers in Nietzsche's terms, archetypes in ours.

The recurrence of history through feeling is demonstrated by the new therapy of the new humanism and its faith in feeling, especially by its Californian branches with its weekend missions and its traveling parsons. The very notion that feeling is good and healthy, that the appearance of feelings in therapy is a wondrous subjective event and a sign of objective improvement, and that following feeling leads one through— these valuations are expressions of the Christian tradition. Sincerity, openness, communion with others in the midst of others all belong there, as do insistence on the heart, on the goodness of inner nature, and the child archetype. The faith convinces; there is witness to its effects—less because it is the New Therapy than because it is the New Testament, the recurrence of an archetypal pattern.

2. THE INSUFFICIENCY OF LOVE

Some humanism has carried its feeling deeper to the centrality of love, finding there the meeting point of man and soul. But what sort of love is meant? Here the archetypal psychologist tries to distinguish among love's many patterns. Eros, Jesus, Aphrodite, Magna Mater—just who has sent the Valentine? No doubt that love is divine, but just which divinity is governing its course?

When archetypal psychology speaks of love, it proceeds in a mythical manner because it is obliged to recall that love too is not human. Its cosmogonic power in which humans take part is personified by Gods and Goddesses of love. When cosmogonies about the creation of the world place love at the beginning, they refer to Eros, a daimon or a God, not just to a human feeling. Love's cosmogonic power to structure a world draws humans into it according to styles of the Gods of Love.

Besides, there are styles of loving that appear in Gods seeming to have nothing to do with love: Athene loves Ulysses by advising and protecting him and rejoining him with Penelope, and Hermes loves Priam by furthering a surreptitious deal in dead of night for the slain body of his son. Each God loves according to his fashion: when Zeus visits love upon a human there is a magnificent disaster with an extraordinary result, and this differs again from the disastrous results of Apollo's chases. Ariadne's love can embrace both battle-hardened Theseus and wine-softened Dionysus. What we need is an archetypal psychology of loving, an examination of love in terms of myth.

Even if we stay only with Aphrodite, or Venus as she has been called since the Romans, we find her love to be a complicated group of myths, now enmeshed with Ares, now with the heights of Uranos, the waves of Poseidon, the concrete artifacts of Hephaistos; now in opposition to Artemis or to Hera and Athene, now in a triangle with Eros and so an enemy of Psyché. She has remarkable progeny—Priapus with the grand erection is a son of her love (as is Eros himself), and Hermaphroditus, who carry her business into extremes. But she has her own odd sides, sometimes appearing black, bearded, and helmeted, secretly in love with war, and her loving is complicated further by her genealogy, which reveals her deepest kinship connections, what she is truly most "like." There we discover that she is born out of the froth of emotions when the old man Uranos' genitals are cut off (the repressed sexuality of any stern senex attitude); there we see her passion for revenge, her sisters Nemesis and the Furies; there we see too her enactment in the Queens of Beauty, the Helens of this world, their thousand avenging ships, their wars that drag on for ten years, the rages and treacheries.

To comprehend the logos of love, even if only the one presented through Aphrodite, one must follow the whole course through. The train of her myths tells more of psychic reality than do the defining statements of love in philosophy, theology, and psychology. Love's images are multitudinous and yet precisely characterized by the locations of her temples, by her festivals and her favorite landscapes, localities, animals, plants, and mythical persons. Other languages at least sometimes try to catch some of these differentiations with several terms for love. We have but one. So when we say God is Love, just whom do we mean?

The God within the beautiful illusions of humanistic therapy may well be Aphrodite. Her role in psychotherapeutic thinking has not yet been adequately examined. Let us recall that from the earliest days of depth psychology in Charcot's Parisian clinic the content of the repressed was Aphroditic: "la chose génitale."[18] Freud, who watched these demonstrations of girls in their trance postures, returned to Vienna germinating his erotic theory of the neuroses. The word he chose for the soul's movement and energy, "libido," comes from the Dionysiac-Aphroditic vocabulary referring originally to *lips,* the downpouring of sexual liquids.[19]

Aphrodite continues to appear in therapeutic work, not only in the roses and sparrows of transference, in the *porne* of therapy (the sexual storytelling, the relished details), but also as Aphrodite *kalon,* the beautifying sweet illusions that cosmetically cover pathologies. We can trace her through two more of her classical epithets: *peitho,* an insinuating gentle persuasion that has led some critics of psychoanalysis to see all therapy as a refined method of rhetorical suggestion; and *praxis,* the practical advice of counseling human relationships, especially regarding bed, body, and infighting.

In the tale of Eros and Psyche (to which I have referred several times because it presents a long series of themes and images for the relationship of love and soul[20]) Aphrodite impedes Psyche. She wants to keep Eros for herself, keep him from Psyche, from becoming psychological. Is this because Aphrodite is too literalistic, too much in love with the sensate surface and visibility of things, too concerned with harmony (also one of her children), and with practicality? If so, then therapy that follows her style may teach us much about enjoying and managing the literal problems, while at the same time preventing eros from finding soul. And their union is essential for soul-making.

Despite the richeries that can be dug out of Aphrodite's myths, neither all of love nor all of therapy can be awarded to one God. Psychotherapy, beginning with Freud's introduction of death into its purview, has come to realize that soul-making leads beyond the pleasure principle and that love is not enough. As Norman Brown has written, "Love is a little moment in the life of lovers; and love remains an inner subjective experience leaving the macrocosm of history untouched. Human history cannot be grasped as the unfolding of human love."[21] Love develops its own history and counterhistory, in groups, in families, in transference, in the *histôire* of an affair, with dates and keepsakes in its museum of memorabilia. This history stands outside the arena of events and sets up its private, oppositional calendar with anniversaries and festivals, commencing at the hour when love was born.

Love meets the needs of soul only within specific archetypal patterns in particular instances. Then one or another of its mythical fantasies speaks directly to my situation. It could be Hera eternally embraced with Zeus in their marriage bed, or Eros sulking and blind to the soul's actual plight, or Jesus vivid and morbid on the cross. It is love in one or another of these imaginal forms that works on us. But to take love as *the* principle of psychotherapy is again to find a monotheistic panacea for the imaginative complexity of our psychic life.

Blake must have sensed the insufficiency of love as the redeemer, for he called Jesus the Imagination,[22] implying love of imagination, or love working in and through imagination. Love, then, is no longer an end but a means for the return of soul through the human and by means of the human to the imaginal, the return of the human psyche to its nonhuman imaginal essence. Love, in this view, is one of the many modes of archetypal emotion and fantasy, one style of madness, no more privileged than any other. Therapy is not for love's sake but for the soul's sake; the game is not that psyche should find eros, with love as goal, but that eros should find psyche—soul as aim. Love's arrow, then, is to strike the soul, hit its vulnerability, in order to begin that state of deep pathologizing we call being-in-love.

The psyche would not be loved out of its pathology, nor forgiven. Grace, yes, and *caritas,* send down what you will, but do not forgive me the means by which the divine powers connect and become real: my complexes, which are my sacrifices to these powers. Until I sense them in my confusions, the Gods remain abstract and unreal. Forgiveness of the confusions in which I am submerged, the wounds that give me eyes to see with, the errant and renegade in my behavior, blots out the Gods' main route of access.

3. THE EGOISM OF FORGIVENESS

Forgiveness is the other side of the guilt we discussed in Chapter 3. Forgiveness belongs also to ego, as ego's cry for relief from carrying the whole world on its shoulders. We would be forgiven because we are overloaded, and humanism's psychology would heap even more upon our personal capacity, strengthening the ego, increasing the regions of our responsibility and commitment, developing our concern, growing new feelings and new sensitivites, radiating ever new connections, wholeness as the great globe itself. We are the center of existence, or as Sartre describes existential humanism: "Man is nothing else but that which he makes of himself. . . . Man is responsible for what he is. Thus, the first effect of existentialism is that it puts every man in possession of himself as he is, and places the entire responsibility for his existence squarely upon his shoulders."[23] Of course we fail, and since there is no power to call upon other than this ego, we beg forgiveness. And of course human interactions cannot bear these superhuman burdens. The more attention we feed into them in accordance with the instructions of humanism's psychology, the more they demand. For their demands are superhuman, archetypal. Our human relations, overcharged with archetypal significance, break down. We cannot carry the Gods because we are human. Were we not alone responsible, but supported by their persons and sharing in their myths, then burdens, blame, and forgiveness would no longer be so central.

As it is now, of course our mothers fail, for they must always be Great, having to be each an archetype, having to supplant the dead depersonified world and be the seasons and the earth, the moon and the cows, the trees and the leaves on the trees. All this we expect from persons when we have lost the myths. And who can be a God? Of course our lovers fail, having to be Heroes, to release us from the dragon, to be Eros and flames of fire, to be marvellous wise, or quickening with the divine word. All fail and all are guilty and all would be forgiven. Into the vacuum left by the lost pantheon of archetypal reality, we pour our human hearts of personal feelings, reactions, expectations. Of course we fail, and the consequent guilt we also personalize, taking it squarely upon the shoulders of the responsible ego, repairing and seeking forgiveness within human relatedness. Yet the issue is not human at all.

As we work out a psychology that is not centered in the ego, not centered anywhere, we will move away from the ego's guilt fantasy, and its forgiveness fantasy too. The classical background to which we revert psychic events simply had no concepts for "sin" and "redemption."[24] There, forgiveness tends to mean forgetting. Rather than a virtue, it borders upon the impiety of neglect.

The Gods forgive little and rarely. Aphrodite's love does not forget. She lays her claim on those who forget her, she retaliates through her relatives, the Furies, who—like the return of the repressed, as they are called in psychoanalysis—forget nothing. The Gods want to be remembered, and they do not ask forgiveness for their havoc, so that their havoc is also remembered. Both Hebrews and Greeks nursed their remembrances through generations. The continuity of a curse and a grievance keeps in consciousness the value of ancestors, of enemies and friends, and of the archetypal nature of disputes and wrongs. To be forgiven wipes out all this and erases history. One starts like a child with a clean slate, ignorant of the nature of man, of the depths of soul, of the Gods.

Humanism's psychology starts off by forgiving and forgetting. Its very use of the word "human" forgets what it means. By making it mean "humane," the shadow in the word is forgiven. But the human touch is also the hand that holds the flame-thrower and tosses the grenade. Correctly speaking, to humanize means not just loving and forgiving; it means as well torturing and vengeance and every cravenness history will not let us forgive. (Of course the Love Children insist on keeping innocent of history; history, having replaced all former repressions, has become today the primordially repressed. No one wants to look back, except with sentimental nostalgia, for in that mirror we see Vietnam, Algeria, concentration camps—all human phenomena.) Hitler was human, and Stalin too, and the soldiers banging at Christ's legs were as human as their victim, and they knew what they were doing.

The contemporary euphemistic word "human" perversely neglects this misanthropy that is also human. Even if we dismiss history and look merely at contemporary events, our view of the human must include how humans actually behave; it must include their psychopathology. If we are to fulfill the humanistic ideal by becoming fully human, then we are obliged to remember that the process of that becoming means saving the unforgivable. By saving, I mean remembering, keeping the pathologized experience and its images safe in memory. The process of individuation or the work of soul-making is the long therapeutic labor of lifting repression from the inhumane aspects of human nature. This process eventually embraces psychopathology untransformed. Self-realization involves the realizing in consciousness of the psychopathic potential one prefers to call inhuman.

By embracing this psychopathic potential within a wider field of psychic space, we can tie its rampant nature to fantasy images. There are fantasies in our inhumanities and when we recognize these images we discover just what it is our psychopathic propensities are striving to enact. Psychopathy too has its mythical background; our inhumanity can be tamed by dreaming.

In other words, making soul means putting events through an imaginal process. Whether this be art, alchemy, mythical speculation, the pathologizing of depression, or the free run of fantasy through the corrals of psychic space, this process requires *imaginative work*. None of the humanistic solutions face up to this requirement. Forgiveness misses the horror altogether and feeling loses the imaginative aspect of the task. Feeling therapies, which divert images into relationships and exploit them for emotional intensites, violate the imagination as much as intellect that converts images into ideas. Neither pursue fantasy for its own sake. And love is not enough; or rather, love is just one more form of imaginative labor. Love then can be seen as neither the goal nor the way, but as one of the many means of putting our inhumanity through a complicated imaginal process.

The Proper Measure of Mankind Is Man; of Psychology, Soul

If I have hammered hard at humanism in psychology, it has been in order to remember the border between psyche and the human. There is a fine line between them, and our notions of man tend to encroach upon psyche. The soul and its afflictions, its emotions, feelings, and varieties of love are all certainly essential to the human condition. But they are all archetypally conditioned. We cannot come to terms with them merely as human, merely as personal, without falling into humanistic sentimentalities, moralisms, and egocentricities. Then soul-making becomes making better human connections, while the real issue of feeling—discriminating among and connecting to archetypes—is ignored. Humanistic sentimentality softens and deadens our sensitivity to archetypal realities and keeps our perception too shortsighted, focused only on ourselves and neighbor.

Moreover soul-making gets falsified. Soul is made in the valley of the world, as Keats romantically wrote. But it is not that valley, not that world. Nor is soul-making aimed directly at the betterment of persons in society. Such events, should they occur, are by-products, the result of re-visioning and ensouling the world. The path of depth psychology still remains the individual psyche. The Freudian "left" of social- and culture-oriented depth psychology works on the world and the valley, literalized into the ghetto as the residence of soul rather than as the place of its making.

Soul-making is also distinct from improving personality. The notion of personality development trains its focus upon man and the increase of his potentials, and here the ideals of human growth, human resources, and creativity again keep soul bound to the movement of feelings within the human horizon.

All areas of feeling shrivel in significance when man becomes the measure, when feeling becomes only a problem to work on and grow from. Feeling that is a merely human function loses its power to reflect psyche beyond the human to the unknowns of the soul. Therefore it is necessary to dehumanize, depersonalize, and de-moralize the psyche in order to deepen the meaning of its human experiences beyond the measure of man.

Ever since Aristotle, the essence of man has been defined by his prime mover, the soul. In our tradition the essence of psyche is not man, for the soul's prime mover is expressed in a fantasy of transhuman powers. And so to start with man is to begin the wrong way round. Or to put it more logically: the human is necessary to psychology, but it is not sufficient.

The insufficiency of the humanistic approach shows most seriously in the reduction of great transpersonal events to personal dynamics: myths become man-made. This misunderstanding of myth runs through humanism from its beginning in Protagoras the Sophist (to whom is attributed the phrase "man, the measure of all things") through the Enlightenment's allegorization of myths as humanistic lessons, to its dying fall in Sartre's humanistic existentialism. So much is the depotentiation of myth the continuing concern of humanism that this becomes its definition: humanism's psychology is the myth of man without myths.

Myths that shape human lives become in humanism instruments which the mind invents to explain itself to itself. The inherent otherness of myth in an imaginal other realm, the creative spontaneity of these stories and the fact that they are tales of *Gods* and their doings with humans—all become something a man makes up. We lose the experience of their primary reality and of ourselves as passing through them, of being lived by them, and that "myths communicate with each other through men without their being aware of this fact."[25]

As the perceptive philosopher Charles Hartshorne has noted, the rise of humanism correlates with "the downfall of primitive animism, which is the mythological form of man's fellowship with nature."[26] Whether or not this is historically demonstrable, the fantasy of a compensatory relation between humanism and mythical personified thinking is precisely our point. Loss of the mythical sense and thus of the Gods begins with Protagoras, the prototypical humanist for whom "thought completely dominates myth."[27] Myth becomes a way of speaking about human mentations, an allegory of our psychodynamics; thought molds myth as it will. Where archetypal psychology would see Hercules or Oedipus making my soul enact and fulfill a mythical pattern, demythologizing humanism would see my making Hercules or Oedipus out of my personal psychodynamics. From this stance, myths teach man about man and nothing about Gods.

Such a demythologized vision leads straight into the humanism of our day. "Existentialism is nothing else but an attempt to draw the full conclusions from a consistently atheistic position," says Sartre.[28] But the Gods come back willy-nilly under the cover of heroic man-centeredness, infiltrating the structure of humanistic consciousness itself, its ideals, and its formulations about man's world-shouldering responsibility and his ego choices that create existence.

The Inhumanity of Greek Humanism

If we look beyond Protagoras to the wider context of Greek culture, we see clearly that soul does not depend on personal life, nor do personal relationships provide any guarantee against psychological tragedy. The personal relationships in the family of Theseus, Phaedra, and Hippolytos, or the family of Alcestis, and even between Oedipus and Jocasta, are not lacking in the humanistic values of charity, dignity, concern, and humaneness. But tragedy comes, and it comes from the Gods.

The human in this Greek view of man depends not upon personal relationships but on relationships with archetypal powers which have their inhuman aspects. Greek humanism always "remained to some degree inhuman, not in the sense of barbarian, but in the sense of the Gods."[29] They provide the inhuman perspective, so that the acute insights of the Greeks derive from a psyche, and a psychology, in which divine inhumanity has its place. A study of man can never give a sufficient perspective, for man is fundamentally limited; he is a frail *brotos, thnetos,* a poor mortal thing, not fully real.[30] Gods are real. And these Gods are everywhere, in all aspects of existence, all aspects of human life. In this Greek view—and "Greece," as we have seen, refers to the polytheistic imagination—there is no place, no act, no moment where they are not.[31] The Gods could not absent themselves from existence in a Protestant theological manner; they *were* existence. There could not be two worlds—one sacred, one profane; one Christ's, one Caesar's—for the mundane was precisely the scene of divine enactment.

Today we can put this psychologically, saying we are always in one or another archetypal perspective, always governed by one or another psychic dominant. The profane also carries soul, since the profane too has its archetypal background.

This perspective begins in a polytheistic consciousness, whether that of Greek religion or of archetypal psychology. Our difficulty with grasping the Greek world view is that while we begin always with an ego, the Greeks always began with the Gods. When the Delphic oracle or Socrates or a modern analysis exhorts one to "know thyself," this knowledge is of human limits, a humanity limited by the powers in a soul that are inhuman and divine. To care for these powers is the calling of the *therapeutes.*

This term means originally "one who serves the Gods."[32] (It refers also to "one who attends to anything" and to "one who attends to the sick.") The therapist is the one who pays attention to and cares for "the God in the disease," but we cannot define him in the humanistic manner of Laing: "Psychotherapists are specialists, in human relations"[33] —unless we add to this definition what Laing further says: "I am a specialist, God help me, in events in inner space and time, in experiences called thoughts, images, reveries, memories, dreams, visions, hallucinations. . . . We live equally out of our bodies, and out of our minds."[34] Here human relations are *not* the specialty of the therapist. The specialty is interiority and the psychic realities that are beyond the body and the mind in its narrow human sense.

Therapy of soul necessarily leads away from personal life with persons. A man or woman in Greek polytheistic psychology placed the personal in perspective through cult, initiation, and sacrifice, or through activities in the civic world, or through the catharsis of tragedy, or erotic mania and its discipline, or through overcoming the ignorance and opinion of the personal through reason and dialectic— but never, *never was human relationship an end in itself.* The closeness of persons with each other in the smallness of Greek life, and even the stress of love and friendship in Plato and Aristotle, is not for its own sake. Man and his love could not save, because man was not divine. Man had not become the Great God, front and center, perhaps because God had not become a man.

Moreover, as Dodds writes:

Aristotle denies that there can be such a thing as *philia* between man and God, the disparity being too great; and . . . one of his pupils remarks that it would be eccentric *(atopon)* for anyone to claim that he loved Zeus. Classical Greece had in fact no words for such an emotion: *philotheos* [love-of-God] makes its appearance for the first time at the end of the fourth century and remains a rarity in pagan authors.[35]

To this we can add observations from Otto: "The image of divinity directs man away from the personal" and emphasizes "superiority of the essential over the personal." The inhumanity of the Greek Gods "must always disappoint souls hungry for love who desire an intimate bond" with a divine person.[36]

In this perspective the human task was to draw the soul through recognition closer to the Gods, who are not human but to whose inhumanity the soul is inherently and priorly related. To neglect or forget these powers—to believe one's life was one's own, or that one's feelings were personal, or that personal relationships alone could provide community or substitute for relationships with Gods—meant loss of humanity. The human was unthinkable without its inhuman background. To be cut off from personified archetypal reality meant a soul cut off.

Greek humanism reflects this pagan polytheism. For psychology, this polytheistic paganism means a dehumanized psyche, cognizant above all of human limitation, where to know myself means to know that they, the "little people" of my psyche, are at the same time *megalo theoi,* the Great Ones. It is their participation in the soul's complexes that gives banal complexes their power, enabling them to set limits to "me" and at the same time expand the scope of the psyche so that it can reflect the immense mythical universe of the polytheistic imagination.

Toward a Psychology of the Renaissance

Here, where the psychology of soul-making reaches out to the polytheistic imagination, the major themes of this book now gather to a head. The place of their gathering is the Renaissance, where we find ourselves also at the heart of humanism, for it is to the Renaissance that all humanistic disciplines turn for their modern origin and inspiration. Since our aim of dehumanizing conceals an attempt to *re*humanize in another, more classical sense of "human," we need to explore Renaissance psychology, where the term human is so important. To do this we need to understand what is implied by their sense of this term.

The first question is one that has been avoided for centuries. Just how was this efflorescence in art, literature, music, politics, science, discovery—this new vision of man and the world, to which we still turn today for our sources and models—how was this renaissance *psychologically* possible? That era, in terms of economic and political history and history of art and science, has been thoroughly surveyed, but there is still no scholarly work called *The Psychology of the Renaissance.*[37] In fact, the word "psychology" in connection with Renaissance studies rarely appears. Yet until we touch the psyche of the Renaissance, we cannot penetrate below its surface.

We must ask what interior ferment made possible such a revival in so many fields. I believe that psychology is missing from Renaissance studies because it is their very content, the latent unconscious ground upon which all else has been erected. I also believe that *were we better able to understand the psychology of the Renaissance, we might find both base and inspiration for a renaissance of psychology.*

Whether or not there is such a thing as "the Renaissance," and if so what it means, when it began, and why, are questions subject to intense scholarly controversy;[38] scholarship seems to reenact the Renaissance warfare among petty principalities. Psychologically this must be so, since the very term for the period belongs not only to history but to psychology. Unlike some other period terms (classical, modern, medieval, Norman) "renaissance" touches the soul in its rebirth fantasy, around which a good deal of passion and symbolism always constellates.[39] The Renaissance idea is a fantasy rooted archetypally in the psyche. It occurs in language before the modern scholarship of Burckhardt[40] and before fourteenth-century Italy itself. It is not a historian's invention: Renaissance is a word used by the very people of that time about themselves, as we use rebirth about ourselves.

A second question fundamental to the exploration of Renaissance psychology is, What did the Renaissance mean by "humanitas?"[41] At first glance its meaning seems restricted—simply *studia humanitatis,* the study of humane literature, the works of classical writers who had been neglected because of the Church's concentration upon Aristotelian-based theology. The Italian humanists (as we call them now), especially the Florentines, loved classical poetry, moral essays, history and biography, and Platonic philosophy. But if we psychologize their love, we will see that within the overt subject matter was a latent and powerful psychological content: the pagan myths. Overtly, they were studying rhetoric, style, and the material of language. But from the very beginning in Petrarch the inner content of the materials was the mythical persons and ideas from a pre-Christian polytheistic world.

Renaissance humanitas began among readers and writers as a *care for the contents of the intellectual imagination.* This humanitas was in fact an exercise of imagination, an exploration and discipline of the imaginal, whether through science, magic, study, love, art, or voyages.

It sought the development of the imaginative mind and its power of imaginative understanding, in contradistinction to both the theological mind of Church philosophy and the feeling heart of mendicant and monastic Church orders.

Feelings, compassion, *philanthropia,* personal relations (in our modern sense) were of course significant elements in their concerns, but these were not their primary source of inspiration in the way that words and images were. The realms of feeling and caritas had already been widely developed in Christian contexts, so that the new humanitas did not mean humaneness. Nor does Renaissance humanitas mean "humanism"—a word coined in 1808 by a German schoolteacher.[42] Since words bring with them the aura of their origins, our "humanism" still exhales this pedagogical and Romantic feeling about a Mediterranean and classical world from which it is always far removed. Renaissance "care of soul" looked less to social context and human experiences for its models and insights into soul than to the archetypes of the imagination disguised in the antique texts.

From the beginning, again in Petrarch, Renaissance study of ancient writers was considered to be "care of soul."[43] It was, therefore, a psychotherapy. Petrarch has been considered the first modern man, which perhaps means the first psychological man. In this psychology soul-making is indissolubly bound with the search for an imaginal world represented by the fantasy of antiquity. These two—soul and antiquity—were his prime concerns.[44] It was as if the world of the past was the imaginal space in which he built his interior life. Even his meticulous scholarship and passion for style were for the sake of soul. Right expression and right psyche were one: "Speech can have no dignity unless the soul has dignity."[45] His interest in man followed from his interest in soul. Psyche, not "humanism," came first. So, too, his life-long love for Laura was almost wholly imaginary—he had seen her once in her girlhood, at a distance. It was love for an imaginal figure, a true devotion to anima. Although not literalized into an actual love, her image vivified his entire life and its many deep human connections.

An Excursion on the Beginnings of the Renaissance, April 1336

Petrarch is of major importance for us. The muddle of psyche and human which it is the express aim of this chapter to relieve begins at that symbolic moment when the Renaissance itself "begins," Petrarch's descent from Mont Ventoux (April 1336, and he not yet 32).

At the top of the mountain, with the exhilarating view of French Provence, the Alps, and the Mediterranean spread before him, he had opened his tiny pocket copy of Augustine's *Confessions.* Turning at random to book X, 8, he read: "And men go abroad to admire the heights of mountains, the mighty billows of the sea, the broad tide of rivers, the compass of the ocean, and the circuits of the stars, and pass themselves by. . . ."[46]

Petrarch was stunned at the coincidence between Augustine's words and the time and place they were read. His emotion both announced the revelation of his personal vocation and heralded the new attitude of the Renaissance. When, soon after, he wrote an account of this experience he said that men neglect themselves *(relinquunt seipsos).* Similarly in his *Secretum,* written later, the character Augustine speaks of the uselessness of knowing all things if one remains ignorant of oneself. Petrarch draws this crucial conclusion from the Mont Ventoux event: "Nothing is admirable but the soul" *(nichil preter animum esse mirabile).*

Not only does the Renaissance begin symbolically with Petrarch's turning inward, but so does the Renaissance scholarship fantasy. Commentators and translators interpret the "soul" and the "self" in his writing as "man"; to them the event on Mont Ventoux signifies the return from God's world or nature to man.[47] This is where the humanistic fallacy begins. It is crucial to remember this fact.

If one looks again at the passage Petrarch was reading which so stunned him, one finds that Augustine was discussing *memoria.* Book X, 8 of the *Confessions* is important to the art of memory. It is about the soul's imaginative faculty.

> Great is this force of memory [imagination] excessive great, O my God; a large and boundless chamber! who ever sounded the bottom thereof? yet is this a power of mine, and belongs unto my nature; nor do I myself comprehend all that I am. Therefore is the mind too strait to contain itself.[48]

These sentences immediately precede the passage Petrarch opened on the mountain. In them Augustine is wrestling with the classical problems, beginning with Heraclitus, concerning the measureless depth of the soul, the place, size, ownership, and origin of the images of *memoria* (the archetypal unconscious, if you prefer). It was the wonder of this train of thought that struck Petrarch, the wonder of the interior personality, which is both inside man and yet far greater than man. Moreover, this interior personality, subject to the control of remembering, can, in Augustine's words, bring forth and drive away images "with the hand of my heart"[49]—and yet I can enter into it as a boundless chamber and even encounter myself as an image among others.[50] Augustine's dilemma was the paradoxical relationship of man and soul. The revelation on Mont Ventoux opened Petrarch's eyes to the complexity and mystery of the man-psyche relationship and moved him to write of the marvel of the *soul,* not the marvel of man.

Our chapter continues in the tradition of Petrarch, accepting the nature of paradox which affirms two factors together as similar and yet distinct, with a tension between them. There is a me and a *memoria;* this psychic region is both in me and I in it. There is both man and soul, and the two terms are not identical, even if internally and inherently related. Aside from them, there is the external world of nature. Augustine and Petrarch imply three distinct terms: man, nature, and soul. Man may turn outward to the mountains and plains and seas or inward to images corresponding with these, but neither those out there nor those in here are mine, or human. Renaissance psychology begins with a revelation of the independent reality of soul—the revelation to Petrarch on Mont Ventoux of psychic reality. The physical mountains were not his by virtue of his seeing them; the internal images of mountains were not his by virtue of his imagining them. Imaginal events have the same objective validity as do the events of nature. Neither belong to man; neither are human. The soul is not mine; there is an objective, non-human psyche.

The humanistic fallacy, which most Renaissance interpreters share for want of a more adequate psychology, continues to identify both imaginal events and Petrarch's "soul" and "self" with "man." It cannot hold the Augustinian paradox that keeps psyche and human as two factors "in" each other by virtue of imagination. Therefore the humanistic fallacy fails to acknowledge what Petrarch actually wrote: Soul is the marvel. *It is not the return from nature to man that starts the Renaissance going, but the return to soul.*

Petrarch's experience is called the Ascent of Mont Ventoux. But the crucial event is the *descent,* the return down to the valley of soul. He deliberately refused the spiritual path (represented to him by Saint Augustine), remaining loyal to his attachments to writing, the image of Laura, and his reputation among men—unable "to lift up," as he says, "the inferior parts of my soul." This is further confirmation, I believe, of our reconstruction of the psychology of the passage, of Petrarch's experience on the mountain, and of the root metaphor of the Renaissance.

Renaissance Neoplatonism and Archetypal Psychology

Often in the course of a therapeutic analysis a revolution in experience occurs. Soul is rediscovered, and with it comes a rediscovery of humankind, nature, and world. One begins to see all things psychologically, from the viewpoint of the soul, and the world seems to carry an inner light. The soul's freedom to imagine takes on preeminence as all previous divisions of life and areas of thought lose their stark categorical structures. Politics, money, religion, personal tastes and relationships, are no longer divided from each other into compartments but have become areas of psychological reflection; psyche is everywhere.

This revolution in experience took place on a grand scale during the

Renaissance, and was embodied in the philosophy of Neoplatonism;[51] it was a "panpsychism," psyche everywhere. There are striking likenesses between the main themes of Neoplatonism and archetypal psychology. Most important, the style of fantasying of the two is similar. In part this similarity is, of course, due to the fact that traditional Neoplatonism has influenced archetypal psychology, and in part because we interpret Neoplatonism in the light of our needs for a traditional background. But mainly the coincidences between Renaissance Neoplatonism and archetypal psychology rest upon a common starting point: soul. Neoplatonism treats "of the nature of man by means of the concept of Soul, conceived as something substantial. . . ."[52]

This body of thought gives full answer to the longing for "a soul of bulk and substance," the opening cry of this chapter. It is subtle, complex, and ambiguous, a composite of thinking, erotic feeling, and imagination. It is more mythic and exhortative than expositional and discursive;[53] it persuades through rhetoric rather than proving through logic, preferring to be evocative and visionary rather than explanatory.

Neoplatonism abhorred outwardness, the literalistic and naturalistic fallacies. It sought to see through literal meanings into occult ones, searching for depth in the lost, the hidden, and the buried (texts, words, leftovers from antiquity). It delighted in surprising juxtapositions and reversals of ideas, for it regarded the soul as ever in movement, without definite positions, a borderline concept between spirit and matter. All the while this philosophy remained close to alienation, sadness, and awareness of death, never denying depression or separating melancholy from love and love from intellection. It was often contemptuously negligent of contemporary science and theology,[54] regarding both empirical evidence and scholastic syllogisms as only indirectly bearing on soul. Instead, it recognized the signal place of imagination in human consciousness,[55] considering this to be the primary activity of the soul. Therefore any psychology that would have soul as its aim must speak imaginatively. It referred frequently to Greek and Roman mythical figures—not as allegories, but as modes of reflection.

Renaissance Neoplatonists also evoked ancient thinkers in their personified images. The great men of the past were living realities to them because they personified the soul's needs for spiritual ancestors, ideal types, internal guides and mentors who can share our lives with us and inspire them beyond our personal narrowness. It was a practice then to engage in imaginative discourse with persons of antiquity. Petrarch wrote long letters to his inner familiars, Livy, Vergil, Seneca, Cicero, Horace, and sent regards to Homer and Hesiod. Erasmus prayed to divine Socrates. Ficino set up an academy similar to the one in Athens and reenacted the Symposium in honor of Plato's birthday, supposedly November 7. Machiavelli sought solace in the company of ancient heroes, poets, and legendary figures such as Moses, Romulus, and Theseus. He wrote:

> On the coming of evening, I return to my house and enter my study; and at the door I take off the day's clothing covered with mud and dust . . . and put on garments regal and courtly; and reclothed appropriately, I enter ancient courts of ancient men where, received by them with affection, I feed on that food which only is mine and which I was born for, where I am not ashamed to speak with them and ask them reasons for their actions; and in their kindness answer me; and for four hours of time I do not feel boredom, I forget every trouble, I do not dread poverty, I am not so frightened by death; I give myself entirely over to them.[56]

Today, Machiavelli's habits on homecoming might be said to require the services of a psychiatrist; then, Neoplatonic psychology supported him. Not only did Neoplatonism give place to the imagination within man and his psychology, but the Renaissance in general recognized that the imagination must have a place, a realm for envisioning, like Machiavelli's "ancient courts of ancient men."

Imagination's place might be the night sky of Renaissance astronomers or astrologers, or the geographical continents of its explorers. It might also be the gigantic mythological construction of Dante's worlds, the complex stoves and vessels of alchemists' laboratories, the memory theater of Giulio Camillo, or the imaginal past of Greek and Roman antiquity. Imagination must have space for differentiated unfolding. This immeasurable depth of soul or endless cavern of images, as Augustine called it, or "black pit" in Hegel's words, must have a container. If we today would restore imagination to its full significance, we too need some sort of enormous room that can act as its "realistic" vessel.

For us, the Renaissance itself provides one such magnificent theater for the imaginal soul. As we approach it, both as a period of history then and there and as a story about the psyche here and now, we are embracing it in much the same manner as Renaissance men did ancient history. In their study they too were living a metaphor: the myth of classical antiquity. They too were in a then . . . and now, there . . . and here. This myth of classical antiquity in which the imaginal world of the archetypes was placed allowed a "present" life to be built upon archetypal models located in the "past." It was not history as such that supported their present lives, since their awareness of history and their interest in archeology—in the classical world of Roman civilization among whose actual ruins they lived—were at first negligible.[57] It was a *fantasy* of history in which were true models of persons, images, and styles. History gave the Renaissance imagination a place to put archetypal structures—gave it a structure within which to fantasize.

The philosophical container of their metaphor, as we have noted, was Neoplatonism, including the belief that their texts were teachings of a God or sage, Hermes, "older"—and therefore prior to and purer—than Plato and perhaps the Bible.[58] By giving a culturally deep and intellectually immense psychology to the psyche's fantasies, Renaissance Neoplatonism enabled the soul to welcome all its figures and forms, encouraging the individual to participate in the soul's teeming nature and to express soul in an unsurpassed outburst of cultural activity.

Here we have a first answer to the essential question: How was the Renaissance possible? It was possible because the new life experienced in northern Italy during the fifteenth century had its source in the rediscovery of the imaginal psyche; the discoveries about man, nature, art, and thought arise from the rebirth of soul as formulated by Neoplatonism.

Marsilio Ficino: Renaissance Patron of Archetypal Psychology

Renaissance Neoplatonism is mainly the work of one man: Marsilio Ficino—a loveless, humpbacked, melancholy teacher and translator who lived in Florence, still one of the most neglected important figures in the movement of Western ideas. An exploration of why he is important and neglected will perhaps help us to understand more about the psychology of the Renaissance.[59]

Every psychological system rests upon a metapsychology, a set of implicit assumptions about the nature of the soul. Behaviorists require the associationist theory of mind developed from Aristotle through Locke and today's information theory; Jungians depend upon Kant and the Protestant tradition of a transcendent unknowable, and Freudians on a metapsychology derived from the nineteenth century's assumptions about science, matter, and evolution. Renaissance metapsychology, Neoplatonism, was based mainly on Ficino's translations and reformulations of Plato and Plotinus, Proclus, and other Neoplatonist writers in Greek. Ficino himself noted the parallel between his revival of Platonism and "the rebirth of grammar, poetry, rhetoric, painting, sculpture, architecture, music, and astronomy which had been accomplished in his century."[60]

To make Ficino the only source of the *quattrocento* rebirth goes too far, but there is no doubt that he was the formulator of its central idea. This was soul, and for Ficino the soul "was all things together . . . the center of the universe, the middle term in all things."[61] Psyche, not man, was the center and measure. "The fascination of Ficino's work lies precisely here: in the invitation to look beyond the opaque surfaces of reality . . . in seeing not the body but the soul . . . as only the one who sees this soul sees man, so all things have their truth and this is their soul, whether they be plants or stones or stars in heaven."[62] "Ficinian philosophizing is in essence only an invitation *to see* with the eyes of the soul, the soul of things . . . an incentive to plumb the depths of one's own soul so that the whole world may become clearer in the inner light."[63]

Ficino's invitation to see psychologically is a revolution in philosophy. Because of the centrality of soul, all thought has psychological implication and all is soul-based. We think as our souls would have us think, so that philosophy is a reflection of what goes on in the soul and a way of working on the soul's destiny. Just as "human experiences lead to certain philosophical conclusions,"[64] so philosophical conclusions lead to certain human experiences. Philosophy is a psychological activity.

Therefore the ground of philosophical education becomes a reeducation in terms of soul. This in Ficino's eyes is a countereducation, or "the introspection of an interior experience which teaches the independent existence of the psychic functioning."[65] Events are related first and foremost to soul rather than to theology of God, science of nature, or humanistic disciplines of language, poetics, and history. The question that asks what bearing this event has upon soul sees through and interiorizes, and so Ficino's thought has been called a "philosophy of immanence." It is also a psychologizing. But it is even more accurate to call his countereducation a psychotherapy, since it is addressed to the soul.

The immanence of soul in all things and areas of study dissolves the borders between faculties and deliteralizes their contents. When we turn to the psychology in a philosophy, theology, or science, we no longer study the field literally, for this psychological activity educates away from the literal content and the literal notion of separate fields and departments. Hence the psychologizing method is especially threatening to any strict construction of a field that takes its body of knowledge as doctrinal truth. Ficino's "triumph of decompartmentalization"[66] was opposed by every vested interest in science, traditional academic philosophy, and religion.[67] Neoplatonism dangerously relativized the absolute superiority of Christian revelation, which because of Neoplatonic psychology became one perspective among many.

Historically, this extraordinarily influential method of Ficinian thought and the Ficinian Platonic Academy in Florence are best conceived as a flourishing underground movement. It was developed in a short period of time by a small group of talkers and writers who lived in close geographical proximity, maintaining a tenuous connection with the vicissitudes of political life going on around them. The doctrines of the Church, except for an occasional capitulation,[68] and the indoctrination of education, except for some new texts and translations, were little affected by Ficino's activities. The official Aristotelian orthodoxies of psychological education continued as before, as do the psychological orthodoxies today, unable to incorporate into academic structures the viewpoint that puts psyche first.

Nonetheless, as Eugenio Garin has written: "After Ficino there is no writing, no thought, in which a direct or indirect trace of his activity may not be found."[69] His ideas spread throughout Renaissance Europe like a movement. This fifteenth-century movement, nourished by a clique surrounding one man and maintained through talk and letter-writing and fierce hard work in the face of depression and thoughts of death—its revolutionary content and its impact upon the soul of subsequent generations—all compare with twentieth-century psychoanalysis.[70]

Precisely here lies Ficino's importance: he was a Doctor of Soul, the very term he himself used for Plato[71] and the very vocation announced to him by his patron Cosimo de' Medici, who supposedly said at their first meeting, when Marsilio was a youth, that as Ficino's father was a physician of the body, Marsilio would heal the soul.[71a] And it is as Doctor of Soul that Ficino is neglected, for his thought in its deepest sense is a depth psychology, both in its construction of a systematic viewpoint for understanding the soul and in its treatment of that soul through relations with archetypal principles personified by the planets of the pagan pantheon.[72] Ficino was writing, not philosophy as has always been supposed, but an archetypal psychology. His basic premise and concern was *anima,* and so he must be read from within his own perspective, psychologically.

Hitherto anima had only been one subject of a great summa; soul one facet in the summation of the universe. But through Ficino's Neoplatonism psyche gained the honor of no longer being only a subject for study but also being the subject who studies. Psyche is a universe, and all study, as we said in Chapter 3, is ultimately psychology.

Renaissance Pathologizing

Perhaps the Renaissance's most popular figure from myth was Proteus.[73] His ceaselessly changing image that could take on any shape or nature represented the multiple and ambiguous form of the soul. "We have seen," said Pomponazzi, "that human nature is multiple and ambiguous," and this nature "comes from the form of the soul itself."[74] (Pomponazzi himself delighted in ambiguity, having inscribed on his personal medallion a *gloria duplex,* the double image of eagle and lamb.) "The soul may be shaped into all varieties of forms . . . and the soul profits from everything without distinction. Error and dreams serve it usefully . . .," wrote Montaigne.[75] Man's Protean nature derives from inherent polyvalence of the psyche, which includes the grotesque, the vicious, and the pathological. Inasmuch as a mythical image is a containing presence, a means of giving form and sense to fantasy and behavior, the Protean idea could keep the soul's many *daimones* in inherent relation. It was like another favorite image, Fortuna, on whose great wheel were innumerably different directions, which multiplicity was given cohesion by the Goddess.[76] Proteus and Fortuna were exaltations of the principle of the Many.[77]

For the soul's multiplicities need adequate archetypal containers, or —like fallen angels in a maze—they wander in anarchy. Anarchy begins when we lose the archetype, when we become an-archetypal, having no imaginative figures to contain the absurd, monstrous, and intolerable aspects of our Protean natures and our fortunes. In Proteus and in Fortuna everything has place: no shape or position is inherently inferior or superior, moral or immoral, for the wheel turns and the soul's ambiguity means that vice and virtue can no more be separated from each other than the eagle and lamb.

Again and again we find historians speaking of Renaissance immorality. In a pathologized image worthy of the art of memory, Voltaire writes: "This courtesy glittered in the midst of crime; it was a robe of gold and silk covered with blood."[78] A fantasy of decay and degeneracy belongs with the archetype of *renovatio:* rebirth appears together with rot. The imagination of rebirth, the fantasy that a Renaissance is taking place, begins in the rebirth of imagination for which pathologized images are the strongest agents. Thus it is no surprise to hear from Northrop Frye that "Renaissance writers, when they speak of the imagination, are interested chiefly in its pathology, in hysteria and hallucination. . . ."[79] Statistically favored themes in art were seduction, rape, and drunkenness.[80]

Pathologizing was a root metaphor of the condition of life, providing a passionate existential base for psychology without which, as Nietzsche said, it becomes mere introspection or observation.[81] Nietzsche also noted that we cannot speak of the Renaissance unless we can reimagine the closeness of each individual to the feelings of survival and death. History books always put this pathologized awareness into literal terms: the black plague; perennial malaria; syphilis that suddenly appeared in Naples in 1485; pirates, brigands, and mercenaries; the threat of the Turks in the East.[82] But pathologizing was an essential part of the Renaissance fantasy appearing in all sorts of *imaginary* forms such as the paranoid concerns with new defense systems which occupied some of the best minds of the age (Albrecht Dürer, Leonardo da Vinci) with city walls and artillery. There were the political intrigues, complicated suspicions and actual persecutions, especially the fear of witches and the beginning of the Inquisition (*Malleus maleficarum,* 1486). Depression, which cannot be blamed upon "hard times" which every age suffers or upon a melancholic character trait which every person carries, seems to have shadowed the lives of such successful and creative Renaissance individuals as Dürer, Savonarola, Machiavelli, Ficino, Leonardo, and Michelangelo. Petrarch confesses in his *Secretum* that depressive *acedia* could rack him for days and nights, plunging him into infernal darkness and a "hatred and contempt for the human state." Montaigne writes: "Since my earliest days, there is nothing with which I have occupied my mind more than with images of death."

To imagine the Renaissance psyche we must enter a fantasy of street-knifings and poisonings, murder at High Mass, selling daughters, incest, torture, revenge, assassination, extortion, usury amid magnificence. Hostility was studied and enemies cultivated as necessary to the complete psychic phenomenology of being human.[83] We find no more evidence of humaneness and humanitarianism than of enmity. Shakespeare set much of his villainy in Italy, perhaps because he was also a social realist, merely a reporter of what was going on: Petrarch's father was sentenced to have a hand chopped off; Cesare da Castel Durante was knifed to death in St. Peter's; Antonio Cincinello, whose father and grandfather were imprisoned, was himself hacked to pieces in his house by a mob; Cola di Rienzo was killed by another mob; Peruzzi, the architect, was poisoned by a jealous confrere; Dante was threatened with mutilation and fled into exile and Michelangelo fled Florence in panic for his life; Campanella was imprisoned for heresy and Torrigiano sentenced to death for blasphemy. Bruno and Savonarola were burned,

Cellini twice imprisoned, Galileo menacingly interrogated, and Tasso —mad—incarcerated in a cell. Pope Alexander VI had three cardinals poisoned.

To go beyond Italy: Cervantes lost a hand in war and was sold as a slave by pirates; Camôes lost an eye; Valdés died of the plague. John Hus was burned, as were Servetus, and Vives' father; Thomas More was executed. Columbus was shipped home in chains, Zwingli cut down in battle, Marlowe stabbed in a brawl. Psychologizing was not a "mere fantasy," not a method, not a research project, but a matter of survival. One had to see through into the depths of everything and everybody, keeping one's death and one's soul before one's eye. It was a way of living life.

Hades, Persephone, and a Psychology of Death

Within a world of such dark depths, it is not surprising to find Hades playing a significant role in Neoplatonic fantasy.[84] In this fantasy the hidden God *(deus absconditus)* who rules the underworld of death and shadows all living existence with the question of final consequences, comes also to mean the God of the hidden, the underworld meaning in things, their deeper obscurities. Underworld, secrecy, hiddenness, and death, whether in the chambers of plotters or the psychic interiority of scholars, reflect the invisible God Hades.

It is against this background that we must place also such major Renaissance concerns as reputation *(fama)*, nobility, and dignity. They take on further significance when envisioned within a psychology that bears death in mind. To consider *fama* merely as fame in our romantic sense puts Renaissance psychology into the inflated ego of the very important person or pop star. But when death gives the basic perspective, then magnificence, reputation, and nobility of style are tributes to soul, part of what can be done for it during the ego's short hour on the stage. Then fame refers to the lasting worth of soul and psychology can afford to treat of the grand themes: perfection of grace, dignity of man, nobility of princes. With death in the background—and Hades is equally called Pluto, Riches, or Wealth-Giver—Renaissance magnificence celebrates the richness and marvellousness and exotic otherness of the soul and its far-flung imagination. How difficult for us in our northern tradition to consider soul together with fame and splendor! How maidenly pure, how wood-washed and bare has become our notion of soul!

Let us pause here to recall that the idea of rebirth refers to a wholly psychic phenomenon, unequalled in animal nature. Renaissance is a potentiality of the soul, not of nature, and is thus an *opus contra naturam,* a movement from nature into soul. This movement of rebirth from natural existence to psychological existence requires a preceding or a simultaneous dying. Fantasies of rebirth occur together with death fantasies; Renaissance and death belong together. Scholarship has put the dying fantasy into historical periods, such as Huizinga's "waning" of the Middle Ages, thereby indirectly recognizing that dying is an integral part of the rebirth fantasy, so that renascence belongs archetypally to Hades. I am suggesting that we misapprehend the Renaissance by seeing it as a turbulent tribute to Gods of love, light, life, and nature. I believe the God of the Renaissance and of *all psychological renascences* to be Hades, archetypal principle of the deepest aspect of the soul.

The Renaissance humanists themselves evidently needed a fantasy of misery and catastrophe in order to contain the renascent energy they were riding. Ficino never ceased complaining of pain and melancholy, yet this "bitter desperation" was the source of his psychological philosophy.[85] Petrarch kept before his mind the "great overarching reality of man's life: his death."[86] Yet the more occupied with death, the more these humanists thought, built, wrote, painted, and sang.

This preoccupation with death gives us a clue for understanding why Renaissance humanism had to summon up the figures of Socrates and Plato and to disparage Aristotle. Aristotle's definition of soul, as the life of the natural body inseparably bound with individual lives,[87] does not allow enough place for life's other side, death, or for the relationship of psyche with death. Greek poetic tradition from Homer through Plato conceived of psyche primarily in terms of death, that is, in relation with the underworld or the afterlife. When soul is described only in terms of life and that life identified with individuals, there is no way to "dehumanize" soul, no way to approach psyche other than in the biological and analytical ways Aristotle preferred. The Aristotelian fantasy rules Western psychology as it did Melanchthon's outlook; it does so today whenever psychology assumes the organic biological slant toward the soul's events, or whenever it insists on empiricism.

It is crucial to see through the Aristotelian "organic fallacy" about the psyche. Otherwise the soul remains held within the perspectives of life. Then care of soul means only reverence toward life and respect for individual human beings where soul is embodied. Just here Aristotelianism neglects what the Platonists remember: psyche is indeed the essence of living bodies, but living bodies are also dying bodies. The Platonist's insistence on immortality of soul was an insistence on the soul's disassociation from life and a priori relation with death. From this viewpoint Aristotle's definition of soul can be more psychologically restated: soul is the primary actuality of each body that bears death within it. Soul refers to that fantasy of death going on, in countless ways, in the midst of the organic and natural standpoint.

We come nearer to a psychological renaissance, whether in our individual lives or in the field of psychology, if we recall that Renaissance psychology never lost touch with disintegration and death. Revival emerges from the threat to survival and is not a choice of something preferable. Revival is forced upon us by the dire pathologizing of psychic necessities. A renaissance comes out of the corner, out of the black plague and its rats, and the shades of death within the shadow. Then even Amor becomes a God of death, as he was in Renaissance imagery. His legs crossed, his torch pointing downward, funerary love was a favorite figure, as was Pluto-Hades holding the keys of the kingdom.[88] This indeed is a far cry from the optimistic humanism of our northern psychology, its uplifting love, its peaks and resurrections.

Here Renaissance humanism truly shares the Homeric view of human: *brotos, thnetos.* What is human is frail, subject to death. To be human is to be reminded of death and have a perspective informed by death. To be human is to be soul-focused, which in turn is death-focused. Or, to put it the other way: to be death-focused is to be soul-focused. This is because Hades' realm refers to the archetypal perspective that is wholly psychological, where the considerations of human life—the emotions, organic needs, social connections of humanistic psychology—no longer apply. In Hades' realm *psyché* alone exists; all other standpoints are dissolved.

Greek mythology shows the wholly psychological perspective of Hades by stating that he has no temples on the surface of the earth and that he receives no libations. It is as if the Hades perspective is concerned only with soul, with what happens "after life," that is, the reflections and images and shadowy afterthoughts lying apart from and below life. Death here is the point of view "beyond" and "below" life's concerns, and has been deliteralized from medical death and theological eschatology about heaven and hell. Death in the soul is not lived forward in time and put off into an "afterlife"; it is concurrent with daily life as Hades is side by side with his brother Zeus. The richness of Hades-Pluto psychologically refers to the wealth that is discovered through recognizing the interior deeps of the imagination. For the underworld was mythologically conceived as a place where there are only psychic images. From the Hades perspective *we are our images.*

The imaginal perspective assumes priority over the natural organic perspective.

If humanism's psychology follows Aristotle, identifying psyche with life and psychology with the study of living human nature, archetypal psychology follows Plato and the examination of soul in relation with death, the psychologizing of dying out of life. Not *our* dying out of life or denying life, not literal death at all, but the movement of each event out of its defensive identities with life. It is a movement downward and inward, psychologizing ever further into Hades, for only there does the psyche find "permanence" and "rest." There is a joy in this. For as the soul becomes a vivified reality of its own, an image-finder and image-maker, life becomes relieved of having to be a vast defensive engagement against psychic realities, a manic propitiation to keep Hades at bay. Persephone mythically represents this movement of soul (anima) from defense against Hades to love for him.

Each of us enacts Persephone in soul, a maiden in a field of narcissi or poppies, lulled drowsy with innocence and pretty comforts until we are dragged off and pulled down by Hades, our intact natural consciousness violated and opened to the perspective of death. Once this has happened—through a suicidal despair, through a sudden fall from a smooth-rising career, through an invisible depression in whose grip we struggle vainly—then Persephone reigns in the soul and we see life through her darker eye.

It is as if we must go through a death experience in order to let go of our clutch on life and on the viewpoints of the human world and its Aristotelian psychology. It is as if we do not recognize the full reality of anima until attacked by Hades, until invisible forces of the unconscious underworld overpower and make captive our normalcy. Only then, it seems, are we able to discriminate psyche from human, experiencing in the belly of our intimate being that the psyche has connections far removed from human concerns. Then we see human concerns differently, psychologically.

The rape of Persephone does not happen just once in a life. Because this anima experience, this radical change in soul is a mythical occurrence, it is always going on as a basic pattern of psychodynamics. Because this particular myth is central to the main Greek mystery cult of psychological transformation, that of Eleusis, Hades' rape of the innocent soul is a central necessity for psychic change. We experience its shock and its joy whenever an event is taken suddenly out of human life and its natural state and into a deeper and more imaginally "unreal" reality.

Until Persephone has been raped, until our natural consciousness has been pathologized, our souls project us as literal realities. We believe that human life and soul are naturally one. We have not awakened to death. So we refuse the very first metaphor of human existence: that we are not real. We refuse, too, to admit that human reality is wholly dependent on the realities that take place in the soul. To hold that "we are not real" means to let go of all seemingly irreducible objectifications of human personality, whether it be the organic body, the human personality, or subjective awareness (Descartes), and to realize them as fantasies of the psyche. To hold that "we are not real" means that the reality of persons and every act of consciousness is a reflection of a fantasy-image: for these are the only actual existents that are not reducible to something other than their imagery; only they are as they literally appear; only fantasies are utterly, incontrovertibly real.

By refusing the fantastic nature of our lives, ourselves as metaphors and images made by soul, we have each become fastened into a constant forced literalism, ourselves as real, the Gods dead. By refusing the as-if frailty of our lives and denying that at our essence is an invisibility, like Hades, who is both the only predictable surety and per se indefinable, we locate the Gods within us or believe we make them up as projections of human needs. We presume human needs to be the literalisms of biology, economics, and society, rather than the psyche's perpetual insistence on imagining.

The refusal to recognize ourselves as "unreal" prevents us from psychologizing ourselves. For should we see through, we would shatter the prime literalism, the humanistic illusion in regard to every sense of reality other than psychic. Instead we cling to the naturalistic and humanistic fallacies—facts, materialism and developmental historicism, empiricism and positivism and personalism—anything to shore up and solidify our frailty.

Humanism's psychology partly perceives this unreality at the core of our existence. When humanistic psychology speaks so intently of self-realization and self-actualization, it is stating that we are not altogether real or actual, that we are still unmade. But then humanism's psychology cannot hold onto this shadowed vision of man and rather exhorts him to make himself, to build a reality out of ego or self, countering his frailty. It turns away from the myths that give our unreality a significant context. Ignoring the mythical nature of soul and its eternal urge out of life and toward images, humanism's psychology builds a strong man of frail soul trembling in the valley of existential dread.

When we fail to recognize our human frailty, Persephone, image of soul, must carry it for us. Then it is she who is frail and insubstantial. Then soul is a phantom we can never catch, an ever-fleeting daughter desperately distracted, symptomatic, at the fringe of the field of consciousness, never able to descend to her proper enthronement within and below. Then we go into the dark afraid of the dark, without soul of bulk or substance.

Anima in the Renaissance

Renaissance psychology does not end in death—it only begins there. From this position comes the leap into life and the embrace of shadow and soul. The preoccupation with the shadow, the profound sense of evil, misery, and life's short wick was joined in Florentine philosophy with its ruling idea: *welfare of soul.* What a curious marriage, what extraordinary double truth—inhumanity and soul together! What sharper contrast between human and psyche could there be? Renaissance morality did not divide soul-making from the deep inhumanity and pathologizing processes in the soul itself.

This deeper psychology, in which the pathologized and inhuman shadow were prime movers, worshiped the images of soul with a productive passion we have since come to consider unique in history. Anima reigned in Renaissance Italy. She appears in a superb variety of personifications which both evoke the emotions of soul and present soul embodied to the imaginal eye. The images range from those familiar to us in Renaissance paintings of Mary, especially as the young Virgin, to the Goddess Flora and her counterpart, the Plague Virgin, who spread poison. Boccaccio wrote an instructive compendium of feminism using the biographies of all the legendary women of myth and history as his models. For Petrarch anima appears in Laura, for Dante in Beatrice, and there were those marvelous figures of (pagan) Armida in Tasso and Angelica (who goes off with the pagans) in Ariosto, and the delicious (pagan) divinities whom Botticelli painted "because," as he said, "they were not real"; and the soul passion in Michelangelo's lyrics.

Anima even inspired a mass movement: down the roads of Italy toward Rome came the pilgrim-tourists to see "Julia, daughter of Claudius," the fifteen-year-old wonder uncovered in the spring of 1485 during excavations, who though dead at least a milennium was rumored to be as fresh and fair in lips and hair and eyes as the living, and —because a tangible embodiment of antiquity—far more beautiful than any creature alive.[89]

The reforming religious zeal of Savonarola in Florence recognized the power of anima's fantasy and tried to burn it out. He ordered a great pyramidal funeral pyre: the burning of Joan of Arc repeated, but now in the shape of anima emblems. The foundation of this spiritual furnace was masks and carnival disguises. Then he heaped on the manuscripts of poets, and next cosmetics, mirrors, ornaments, and ladies' false hair, and—rising higher—lutes and harps and playing cards. Crowning the flaming tower were paintings of both mythic and actual female beauties and ancient sculptures of female heads.[90]

The obsessive preoccupation with love and beauty, including the banalities and obscenities in the obsession, the innumerable dialogues on love, and the wide influence of Ficino's commentary on the *Symposium,* can be better understood if we regard these events from the perspective of the soul-making that takes place through the intercourse between anima and eros. Then we may not regard these obsessions merely as a rash of frivolous poetizing and dilettante philosophy, or as Renaissance pornography. They are something we each do. They are inherent in the movement of soul, the activity of the anima, which seeks eros. For the corollary reason, for an eros with soul, for a psychological eroticism which has been correctly called platonic, we may turn to these writings and paintings. This style of love-dialogue and obsession with beauty is no longer our fashion. Instead we suffer from the division between eros and psyche, a soulless eroticism, and an unloved desexualized soul.

Because "the one fundamental human science of the Renaissance was the knowledge of soul,"[91] it is understandable that Renaissance thought has been long ignored as philosophy, actually held in contempt for being scattered, unsystematic, rhetorical.[92] Its thought is not philosophy but psychology, rooted not in intellect but in imagination. It is anima-thinking—thought that reflects the anima. Its aim was soul-making; hence its concentration upon the realm of anima: treatises on love, on beauty, on myth, on political machinations, on life-style and manners and aesthetic expression, and later on music, as well as works such as Ficino's philosophy specifically concerning soul. Its concern with visual perspective, and perhaps with polyphony in music, can also be related to its psychology of ambiguity which arose from *gloria duplex*—having more than one standpoint, seeing behind, seeing through, and hearing the many voices of the soul.

An Excursion on Perspective in Painting and Polyphony in Music

Again we must ask that same question: What made the discovery of perspective possible just at this time in history? There must have been a transformation of consciousness allowing the new vision, the new ability to see differently and more deeply and with shadow. Some have considered this shift in vision to be in line with the new empirical eye toward nature; they make a direct connection between the observing eye developing at that time in the natural sciences with the emergence of perspective in art. They point to Alberti's treatise on painting (1435–36) and stress its mathematical fantasy.[93] But since we know that seeing is not independent of the archetypal ideas of the psyche, we are always obliged to take our analysis a step deeper, examining the perspective that determines perspective.

Therefore I believe there is a psychological background to the new perspective of Renaissance painting. I refer to a new and more complex consciousness within the psyche itself, which is reflected outwardly in depicting and constructing its image of the world. This new complex consciousness requires a double truth in space *(gloria duplex),* just as perspective requires a focusing of two eyes. The "second point of view" that deepened Renaissance vision was that of classical antiquity—pagan, polytheistic, Neoplatonic. This provided another angle to everything seen in the usual and present world.[94] Thus the Renaissance achievement of spatial perspective reflects the main themes of this chapter: *(a)* the depth dimension of soul now entering the subjective structures of consciousness; *(b)* a new relation with the image and closer participation "in" its "reality"; *(c)* the simultaneous apperception of the soul's multiplicity, its several points of view coalescing as perspective. Again, in this development, Renaissance thought believed it was recapturing the past—how the ancients had seen.[95] Perspective did not develop within the progress fantasy of science or its fantasy of objective observation, but rather as an *imitatio* of pagan antiquity.

The relationship between perspective in space and polyphony in sound has been pointed out by Lowinsky, who reminds us that many musical expressions are borrowed from space (high, low, ascending, pitch, scale, etc.).[96] Likewise, many musical problems refer to the relationship between the one and the many, or the relations of multiplicities among themselves (discord, dissonance, harmony, counterpoint, parallel movement), so that their resolutions intimate psychological solutions to the problems of polycentric tensions in the soul. Polyphony, which is said to have reached its perfection through the Church music of Palestrina (1526–1594), can also be regarded as a triumph of polytheistic consciousness in which, despite its overt Christian content and purpose, the structure of the music is such that "it is impossible to decide which voice has the most important task allotted to it, since all are equally necessary to the general effect."[97] Another example of polytheism in music, but now in terms of content, we find in the astrological songs invented and played by Ficino in order to restore harmony with the planets that were ruling his melancholic psychic states.

Two factors contributed to the psychological condition which made the new music possible: one, the ideas of Platonism,[98] another, the myths of the classical imagination. When in 1607 Monteverdi wrote the first true opera of our Western tradition, *Orfeo*, it was with the idea of reconstructing ancient tragedy—and this opera reflects the story of the descent of a lover into the realm of death to find soul.

My viewpoint in this excursion toward painting and music is an attempt to imitate the Renaissance itself. I am trying to understand perspective and polyphony by putting the psyche in the center of my account.

The Rhetoric of Archetypal Psychology

Not unlike this exposition, the style of Renaissance "philosophers" follows a wandering course. If the style is repetitious it is because the way of the soul, according to Plotinus, is the way of the circle. If the style is erroneous in its facts, logic, and conclusions, it is because—as Montaigne said—the soul is served usefully by error. And if this style is self-contradictory it is because, as Montaigne also said, the soul has an innumerable variety of forms, so that "Whoever will look narrowly into his own bosom, will hardly find himself twice in the same condition. I give to my soul sometimes one face and sometimes another. . . . all the contrarieties are there to be found in one corner or another. . . . I have nothing to say of myself entirely, simply, and solidly without mixture and confusion. *Distinguo* is the most universal member of my logic."[99]

This is a style attempting to be precise in distinguishing among the faces of the soul, all the while appealing to that many-sided soul by speaking in figurative language to the emotions, senses, and fantasy, working its persuasion through artfulness, even if at times becoming bombastic, contrived, even piously woolly. This has all been called rhetoric. In Renaissance rhetoric anima appears yet once more, this time as Aphrodite Peitho, the persuasive Venus who turns our head with a well-turned phrase. Rhetoric played such an important part in Renaissance writing because it is the speech form of the anima archetype, the style of words when informed by soul.

Our academic tradition has missed the psychology of the Renaissance partly because it has not been attuned enough to this use of language, excoriating it for lack of solid evidence and marshaled argument. But logic and proof do not convince the anima, neither then nor now, so that really to hear Renaissance language we have to listen through anima, which is brought to life by personified and pathologized figures of speech, by hyperbole and metaphor, by indirection, repetition, allusion, conceit, and innuendo. This speech is forceful, seductive, and convincing—until examined as scientific analysis or theological discourse. Then it is no longer "serious philosophy." Rhetoric's pleading, complaining, and reiterating speaks the way our symptoms speak, the way our dreams speak. It is an argument of mood; or rather, the imagination does not argue, it imagines.[99a] Rhetoric never persuades the mind unless that mind be from the beginning susceptible to passion and images; its main discriminatory concern is not with forming definitions but with shaping the imagination itself into words.

Depth psychology today is heavily entangled in the problem of language, pulled between extremes of basing all therapy upon linguistic structures or leaving speech altogether for preverbal grunts and gestures. Therapy turns back either to Cartesian structuralism which abstracts speech into unutterable root units or to pietistic revivalism where the inchoate sound of feeling is all. Neither those structures nor those feelings can carry psychology toward giving words to the full size of soul, for they lack the main mark of rhetoric: *eloquence.* We need again what was common in the Renaissance—belief in the verbal imagination and the therapeutic incantational power of words.[100] Besides the France of Lacan's intellect and the Germany of Reich's and Perl's feelings, there is the Mediterranean of the imagination, an inland sea of rhetoric from whose froth Venus rises.

Therapy might profit were it to take a fresh interest in rhetoric.[101] If this is the language of Renaissance psychology, then this may be a way to do psychology—rhetoric as method. If the method of psychology no longer belongs to empiricism, theology, or philosophy, then the style in which psychology speaks may abandon its imitation of those styles.

The running battle we have been maintaining between archetypal psychology and the activities closest to it—practical psychiatry and academic philosophy—comes to full clash in the field of language. We cannot speak of cases the way psychiatry does or of ideas as philosophy does, though we may use psychiatric words and philosophical terms. The contents of psychiatry and philosophy are of prime importance, but the language they use to express those contents is soul-killing. Here we react like Petrarch, who etched out the discipline of Renaissance humanism by warring with "physicians" and "dialecticians," the empirical practitioners and the academic thinkers of his day. He too fought the battle over language. Both their empty soulless nominalism and their "infantile inability to speak" appalled his sense of eloquence, where care for words meant care of soul.[102]

The similarities between rhetoric and the style appropriate to depth psychology may be far closer than we have noticed. Panofsky has compared Neoplatonism with the force of psychoanalysis, despite the fact that Ficino's thought is not taken as "serious philosophy." Another huge body of thought, the literature of depth psychology, also cannot be taken as serious philosophy. Again and again it is demolished by philosophical critiques, yet ever continues unscathed. Depth psychology has not only a specific subject matter, the psyche, but its own style of approach, psychological writing: stories of cases, myths of psychodynamics, rituals of confessional hours, family epics, sexual fantasies, and dreams. Psychological writing tries to be scientific and rational, amassing evidence and drawing conclusions. So psychological writing is often misperceived, and misperceives itself, in the fantasy that it is performing a discursive kind of rational explanation. But what we are doing in psychology compares to Renaissance philosophy, of which Kristeller says that "the content and task of philosophy, and its relation to such other disciplines as theology and literature, mathematics and medicine, were conceived in a manner markedly different from other periods of philosophy. . . ."[103]

Here Jung's style is closer to Renaissance rhetoric than was Freud's. Freud's sober clarity remains beautifully consistent, whether he writes on aphasia, cocaine, female sexual experiences, Moses, or Judge Schreber's insanity. But Jung varies. He can write like a Gnostic, an Eastern guru, a statistical scientist, or a Sunday preacher. He has been accused of most of the faults attributed to one of Renaissance humanism's main models: Plutarch—bad philosophy, bad theology, bad history, and bad style.[104] Neoplatonism, like Jung's writing, has been called "that strange medley of thought and mystery, piety, magic, and absurdity."[105] Like Neoplatonism, Jung's thought is rarely studied in a philosophy department. His rhetoric, like that of Neoplatonism, is to the academic mind simply not "serious philosophy" as is the lucidly monocular writing of Descartes, Locke, or Bertrand Russell.

Can we not speak psychology as we think it, rather than translating it into the foreign language of conceptual rationalism? If we think psychology as fantasy, as personifications, pathologizings, and as-if propositions, then our speech needs to become eloquent in these modes. Rhetoric may help us find our way, since its aim like that of depth psychology is to move the images and passions of the soul. To move the thought of psychology, to advance its thinking, we would first move the soul in which the thought has its home.

Perhaps Jung's style is precisely the one required for soul-making. Its variety reflects the need to have different styles for different archetypal constellations. One of the rhetorical methods of the Renaissance differentiated the styles of literary expression according to the seven planets, personifying Beauty, Verity, Speed, Gravity, and so forth.[106] One used different genres to create different effects in the soul. For ultimately the question of rhetoric in psychology is that of "who is talking to whom." If we would engage the many persons of the psyche, and especially the anima, then our words must allow for a variety of archetypal modes, a "strange medley" of thought, piety, and absurdity.

The rhetoric of archetypal psychology would go yet further in its aims. Its interest in speech is not to improve communication among humans, but to follow the intention of Plato when he said that the competence one may develop in the art of language one "should exert not for the sake of speaking to and dealing with his fellow men, but that he may be able to speak what is pleasing to the gods."[107] It is for the relation with the archetypal dominants themselves that one struggles with language.

Rhetoric brings one of the main moods of these chapters into the open, chapters that were originally lectures, spoken and heard; rhetoric also brings to a conclusion the theme of language that has pursued us all along. First it was the personified manner of speaking, next it was the issue of classification and nominalism in psychopathology, then it was the running encounter between the literal and the metaphorical.

We have paid especial attention to speech because we recognize that there is a special relation between soul and word, between psyche and logos, and that their union is our field, psychology. Psychology ideally means giving soul to language and finding language for soul. Depth psychology pays such careful attention to speech because we begin not only with what Freud first called his "talking cure"; we begin in human being itself: *man as voice of soul.* The word is the starting point of Renaissance humanism and of psychotherapy both, because the formation of fantasy in words is a crucial distinction of being human—whether Greek, where "barbarian" meant someone of another speech; whether Renaissance, where he who was without rhetoric was not civilized; or today in the recent thinking about the essential differences between man and ape in regard to the anatomy of the speech and voice areas of mouth and throat.[108]

Even as abstract a metaphysician as Whitehead recognized the primacy of language over gesture for exciting the "intimacies of bodily existence. . . . Thus voice-produced sound is a natural symbol for the deep experience of organic existence."[109] If we would go deep, we must go to the poetics of the soul within the flesh and its cries. Not the flesh or the cries, but their images in words are soul-making. This Christianity has always insisted upon: word as flesh, flesh as word; my words the organs of body and my body an encyclopedia, a summa of words.

Freud's "talking cure" is also the cure of our talk, an attempt at that most difficult of cultural tasks, the rectification of language: the right word. The overwhelming difficulty of communicating soul in talk becomes crushingly real when two persons sit in two chairs, face to face and knee to knee, as in an analysis with Jung. Then we realize what a miracle it is to find the right words, words that carry soul accurately, where thought, image, and feeling interweave. Then we realize that soul can be made on the spot simply through speech. Such talk is the most complex psychic endeavor imaginable—which says something about why Jung's psychology was a *cultural* advance over Freud's style of talking cure, free autistic associations on the couch.

All modern therapies which claim that action is more curative than words (Moreno) and which seek techniques other than talk (rather than in addition to it) are repressing the most human of all faculties—the telling of the tales of our souls. These therapies may be curative of the child in us who has not learned to speak or the animal who cannot, or a spirit-daimon that is beyond words because it is beyond soul. But only continued attempts at accurate soul-speech can cure our speech of its chatter and restore it to its first function, the communication of soul.

Soul of bulk and substance can be evoked by words and expressed in words; for myth and poetry, so altogether verbal and "fleshless," nonetheless resonate with the deepest intimacies of organic existence. A mark of imaginal man is the speech of his soul, and the range of this speech, its self-generative spontaneity, its precise subtlety and ambiguous suggestion, its capacity, as Hegel said, "to receive and reproduce every modification of our ideational faculty,"[110] can be supplanted neither by the technology of communication media, by contemplative spiritual silence, nor by physical gestures and signs. The more we hold back from the risk of speaking because of the semantic anxiety that keeps the soul in secret incommunicado, private and personal, the greater grows the credibility gap between what we are and what we say, splitting psyche and logos. The more we become tied by linguistic self-consciousness, the more we abdicate the ruling principle of psychological existence. That we then turn to the rats of Skinner and the dogs of Pavlov, the geese and wolves of Lorenz—tune into dolphins or consider man a naked ape—in order to find prototypes for human behavior, indicates to what extent we are losing our speech and with it our sense of a distinctly human nature. *It is not animal prototypes we need for discovering our original patterns, but personified archetypes, each of whom speaks, has a name,*[111] *and has its existence in the language world of myth.* Without speech we lose soul, and human being assumes the fantasy being of animals. But man is half-angel because he can speak. The more we distrust speech in therapy or the capacity of speech to be therapeutic, the closer we are to an absorption into the fantasy of the archetypal subhuman, and the sooner the archetypal barbarian strides into the communication ruins of a culture that refused eloquence as a mirror of its soul.

Between the Failure of Psychology and a Renaissance of Psychology: Psychology Re-visioned

Now at the end of our four chapters we have reverted—by turning a cold back upon the humanism of today—to the Renaissance in order to find a vision of the psyche which might also provide a background for a re-vision of psychology. By looking backward to that "creative breakdown" called the Renaissance we are better able to see the psyche now as it goes through similar processes. We have been using history as a means to psychologize the present. We have been projecting the present actualities of the soul onto a distant historical screen, reading today as history and history as today, much as the Renaissance imagined itself against the fantasy of antiquity. Thus the Renaissance and its psychology is a fantasy about the possibilities for a renascent psychology today.

Despite repeatedly disclaiming the hero, the psychologizing in these pages leads us into this final heroic fantasy: We seek in the fantasy of the Renaissance an Archimedean point by means of which we could gain enough purchase upon psychology so as to lift this great encumbered field, drying to a plain of dust—plowed so long by puritan toilers, their animals, and their machines—off and away from its old Reformational foundations to be set down again upon the back of the Mediterranean bull—Ortega's dangerous two-horned bull—its style of madness and its style of fertility.

I am in search of the myth that can carry psychology, enabling psychology to carry soul. For the question I would raise now at the end, when it is too late to answer, is whether the soul that stirs again today can be served by traditional psychology, whether what we today call psychology meets the psyche's needs.

The soul stirs, and the shadow is abroad. Transition, crisis, and the overhanging menace of breakdown, individual and societal, fill the air with questions of survival similar to those of the Renaissance. The psyche can no longer be held by its old containers of Christian culture. There is recrudescence and ebullition of individual fantasy, of pagan myth, of the anima. With her come the same banners raised in the name of soul by its devotees in the Renaissance and by the Romantics: freedom to imagine, to be beautiful, to show pathologized oddity and variety. Enthroned again is communion with soul in unspoiled nature, in the poesis of music, and in the evocation of Eros and the remembrance of death. The revolution in behalf of soul may not demonstrate these qualities, but it demonstrates in their behalf. And with soul's return, the literal may lose its dominion. The imaginal has become real; for many, *the* real. Yet only one generation has passed since Jung gave his Terry lectures, the burden on him then of having to establish the first premise, psychic reality, which today we easily assume. Former definitions of human existence—religious man, political man, scientific man, economic man—have suddenly given way to psychological man, which means soul-making has become again a general concern. The soul has moved back into the midst of the historical scene, quite independently of psychology. The psyche moves; but does psychology? And can psychology move as it now conceives itself?

We have seen that psychology emerged from the Protestantism of northern and western Europe and its extension westward into North America. To read psychology, to find psychologists, to do psychological research has meant coming to this piece of geographical soil. As if the Japanese, the Russians, the Arabs, the Africans, and the Latins had no psychology. Moreover, the soil has mainly been Germanic. Psychology has been mainly a creation of the German language out of the German soul. As William Cullen of Edinburgh, inventor of the word "neurosis," looked to Göttingen in the eighteenth century; as Coleridge, the New England transcendentalists, and the Herbartians of the early nineteenth looked to Königsberg, Wittenberg, and Weimar; as William James went to Leipzig in the late nineteenth century; so our era turned to Vienna and Zürich, and to Husserl, Heidegger, Binswanger, to Rorschach, to Stern, to the theological psychology of Tillich, Bultmann, Brunner, and Barth, or still to Marx and Engels, or to Gadamer's hermeneutics, or to Koffka and Kohler, to Konrad Lorenz, to Marcuse and Reich, to Horney, Moreno, Erikson, Fromm, and Perls, or to Wittgenstein, or to Nietzsche and Hesse. The list is too long to continue.[112] The cosmos which gave birth and continues to give birth to what we call psychology, and from which we gain our psychological perspectives, has always been to the north beyond the mountains, not thoroughly reached by the Mediterranean classical tradition.

"Psychology" results from a vision given by its historical, geographical, and cultural location. When we ask, "What is psychology? Tell me its definition, its stuff and problems and methods," all the answers given by whatever school still refer to the same foundation. Always we encounter the same literalism and voluntarism that appeared with the Reformation. Intentionality, will, drive, motivation are as crucial now as then, and so too is the reflexive self, the anal character, the independent ego in the middle, whether examined in behavior or worshiped as inwardness. There is the same zeal in learning, now become learning-theory, as under Melanchthon—"teacher of Germany" as he was called —who saw his nation's salvation also in the application of correct learning theory. For it does not matter whether we are behaviorists or strict Freudians, whether we are engaged in self-mastery or self-surrender, introspection or statistics, or whether we try to break loose with glossolalia, creative painting, and nude encounters, psychology remains true to its Reformational background.

And this psychology, for which we erect great buildings to which the students flock, with its libraries, lectures, and laboratories, journals and therapies, mental health clinics and mental health grants, has been and still is impotent. Nothing, nothing, nothing. What *therapeia* has it provided for the soul of our civilization in the four hundred years since Melanchthon? What can we psychologists show in regard to the shadow of the civilization, its inhumanity, or in regard to the anima, the decline of its beauty, of its nature, and even of its longings.

Psychology has been unconcerned with myth and imagination, and has shown little care for history, beauty, sensuality, or eloquence—the Renaissance themes. Its pragmatism, whether in clinic or in laboratory, kills fantasy or subverts it into the service of practical goals. Love becomes a sexual problem; religion an ethnic attitude; soul a political badge. No chapters are more barren and trivial in the textbooks of psychological thought than those on imagination, emotion, and the living of life or the dying of death. Psychology has hardly been touched by anima, until recently as the soul stirs and makes claims on it for relevance and depth.

Psychology's origins in the Reformation continue to shape its course. On the one hand, it presents itself as therapy, a way of self-reflection and self-improvement. This introspective subjectivism (whatever the school of therapy) is sustained by deep pietistic hopes of personal salvation and the moral benefit of working on oneself. The weight and seriousness of psychotherapy (even in the Californian sunshine schools) create in its participants new loads of guilt, now in regard to the morality of its therapeutic aims. Now we are called defensive or resistant to the therapeutic process where once we might have been blamed for closing ourselves against God's grace or turning from His will.

On the other hand, against the value judgments and introspection of therapy, yet stemming from the same heroic voluntarism and literalism —for the same North created both psychological pietism and psychological laboratories, both methods for taking the measure of man— there has been a fierce reactive battle to be empirical, physical, and segmental. The animal, the lab, and statistics have become means of saving psychology from the subjectivism and moralizing inherent in every psychological system. Experimental research has offered a manic defense against insearch, as clinical insearch has provided a paranoid retreat from public accountability.

Either way psychology turns, it does not leave its Protestant root. Thus we are brought to this major recognition: *the many schools of psychology belong to the larger realm of Protestantism,* whatever the style, whatever the branch. Psychology's doctrinal systems are secularized equivalents of religious thought about the soul, and psychology's many varieties named after leaders or localities are of a piece with Protestantism's spread of sects.

Therefore the revolution fermenting in the soul of northern monotheism which has occasioned the belief in the death of its God must also be taking place in psychology. It, too, must be afflicted by the death of this same God.

This is therefore a psychological moment when a renaissance in psychology is possible. For we have learned from Renaissance psychology that rebirth is coupled with defeat, failure is its precondition, Hades its deepest secret. To move toward a renascence, a re-visioning, of psychology means first a recognition of the death of psychology's God and the consequent death in the soul of psychology as a viable carrier of soul-making.

Psychology senses its failure and gropes around for new modes of re-visioning itself by means of new religious reflection. But Yaqui hunting wisdom or the Hindu smilings of a divine child are no less simplistic than psychology's former favorite mirrors—machines, monkeys, and infants. The primitiveness of its mirrors reflects the primitiveness of psychology's view of both man and the soul—naïve, inarticulate, uncultured, as if human complexity or the soul's diversity could be held by saws and homilies. Psychology has been so trapped in the literalizations of subtlety that it now looks to stupidity as a way out. For it had hitherto mixed precision with measurement, discernment with segmentation, sophistication with technology, and differentiation with compartmentalization.

In our re-visioning of psychology we have turned instead to the most complex and richest periods of our civilization and their most sophisticated representations—in images, ideas, and persons—in order to return complexity and subtlety to a wholly psychological sense. Crucial in our move has been the insistence on the mythical polytheistic perspective. A renascence of psychology could only come about if the psyche is given a chance to find itself against the fullest of possible backgrounds. Psychic complexity requires all the Gods; our totality can only be adequately contained by a Pantheon.

There must be place for everything—else we begin again in the old fashion, needing bags called pathology, heresy, id, for what does not find place. Moreover, a polychromatic spectrum offers a cultural mode of soul-making. By enlarging and complicating our images and myths we will have more and deeper cultural vessels for the tremendous surge of fantasies in our age. Otherwise barbarianism, anarchy, or monolithic statism.

Reason cannot do it—the mind was already at the end of its tether years ago, according to H. G. Wells—nor can the ego, no matter how strong, developed, and mature. The history of psychology since the Reformation shows the movement of its reason and the strengthening of its ego, but the history of civilization shows as well the movement of unreason, the imaginal powers irrupting into reason, inflating it with ideologies and thereby steering its course. Psychology has had no means of reflecting these imaginal powers, and that is a primary cause of its failure. A psychology with little place for imagination has little place for the images that rule our lives.

By neglecting images it willy-nilly becomes a moralism, stressing reason and will, the old ego. So psychology has been obsessed by one overvalued idea: man—an ideology arising from the Reformational hero, tone-deaf to all but the bugle, battling his way through binary choices, responsible, committed, progressing toward light, casting soul and darkness from him. If our civilization suffers from *hybris*, from ego inflation and *superbia*, psychology has done its part. It has been looking at soul in the ego's mirror, never seeing psyche, always seeing man. And this man has been monotheistic Reformational man, enemy of images.

But to move toward a renaissance, psychology would have to abandon one of its most tenacious Reformational convictions. It would have to move from a concern with the moral to a concern for the imaginal; the image before the judgment, the imagination before the human, Psyche before Prometheus and Hercules, before Moses, before Christ. Psychology cannot shed its history, but it can see through it. Then it need no longer take the moral stand of civilization against the discontent in the soul, but turn to the soul. In its imaginal seeds lie the renaissance, not only of psychology, but maybe also of the civilization. Everything begins in fantasy.

I am here pointing to what I believe to be the archetypal reason for the failure of psychology to meet the needs of the soul. For this contrast —geographical, historical, archetypal—between Reformation and Renaissance,[113] transalpine and cisalpine, between Hebraic monotheistic consciousness and Hellenic polytheistic consciousness, has divided the psyche into halves now called "conscious" and "unconscious." The contrast although symbolized by Europe is within the soul of every member of the Western culture, and psychology has only worked one side of the mountain. Depth psychology, which should be faithful to the activities of the other side, is also a fantasy native to northern and central European soil. We have not yet witnessed a psychology of the depths elaborated from the other side of the mountains, from the imagination of Hellenism, Renaissance Neoplatonism, and polytheism.

What we have come to call "Western" consciousness is in truth northern consciousness. And we falsify the psychological situation by imagining the basic opposition in the soul to be between East and West. Because this pairing is horizontal it tends to project its oppositions outward into the literal geography of external space, catching us in identifications with Orient or Occident and in fantasies of uniting our souls by a meeting of East and West. The other pairing in our souls is that of North and South, light and shadow, conscious and unconscious, a vertical division between what is above and what is below, a reflection in imaginal geography of our cultural history.

Venturing South is a journey for explorers. It is the direction down into depth, different from the Eastern trip, and from the Western rush of golden boys and girls to pacific harmonies, and from the Northern ascents to cool objective observation. Going South means leaving our psychological territory at the risk of archetypal disorientation. Once when Jung tried to venture beyond his psychic borders toward Rome, he fainted at the railroad station.[114] A similar pathologizing event happened to Freud in Athens.[115] "Rome" and "Athens" were beyond the tolerable limits of depth psychology's founders. Venturing South may mean departing from all we have come to consider "psychology."[116]

Imaginal and cultural geography coalesce in the discovery of the unconscious, for when psychology did first move downward into the depths of the psyche, what it first uncovered was a repressed distortion of Renaissance man. His polytheistic Protean nature now was called polymorphous perversity. His need for exploration, festival, and liturgy became acting-out or ritual compulsions; his reversion to antique models for behavior reappeared as regressive archaism, and his eye on death was now, in the terms of depth psychology, the self-destructive attitudes of the death drive. The one major concession to the mythical imagination—Freud's Oedipus fantasy—remained within the realm of monotheism. One myth alone could account for the psyche of all humankind.

But we have not disposed of Renaissance man. He lives with us still, though I do not mean in our ego ambitions. I mean in our dreams. The return of the repressed is also the return of the Renaissance into our Northern consciousness—and this return comes from the other side of any mountain, across any border, as Italian, Arab, Mexican, Jew, Caribbean, or as Renaissance Moor. Darkened from long confinement in the black holes of our Northern consciousness, Renaissance man is now called the shadow, or the id, or the natural, instinctive, creative dark side. In his hands are the keys to the therapeutic kingdom. For the way to wholeness in all schools of modern psychotherapy means lifting the repression from the dark underside. The essential fantasy of rebirth in therapeutic practice is reunion with Renaissance man, his vitality, his liberty, and his other morality.

There can hardly be a more dangerous fantasy. Therapy does not fully realize what it is suggesting. For Protean Renaissance man is none other than Ortega's two-horned bull Dionysus, our Devil, pagan, perverse, psychopathic, all-powerful, once he comes through the mountain wall. The greatest bulwark of Northern consciousness was its now dead God who commanded battalions of light—moral philosophers, preachers, psychologists. But these are all in disarray as the commander's tent flaps in the wind. To let the depths rise without our systems of protections is what psychiatry calls psychosis: the images and voices and energies invading the emptied cities of reason which have been depersonified and demythologized and so have *no containers to receive the divine influxes*. The Gods become diseases. We cannot command the commander, nor replace him with his sergeant, the strong ego. It's too late for that; the nineteenth century is over, and the marauding fantasies do not heed the ego anyhow. To flee to the East, or up in transcendence, or out into futurology leaves the land in dismay, no ground for homecoming, no nourishing soil.

An alternative remains, and that is southward—the fostering of images by returning to Plotinus' suggestion (p. 14) and developing "shrines and statues" for the "portions and phases" and pathologizings of the soul: the elaboration of "appropriate receptacles" for the psyche in the psyche. Then we can place the turmoil of our fantasies within the larger depository of myths, and by giving them the focus of myth take them out of the streets, where they only run riot in sudden impulse. I mean an unceasing attention to imagination from the first story told a child to the last conversations of old age. I mean the recovery of lost psychic space for containing and of lost mirrors for reflecting. Our field needs to build again rich and fantastic psychologies such as classical mythology, the arts of memory and alchemy; such as Jung's, such as the Neoplatonism that organized and gave culture to the madness of the Renaissance and the Romantics. For what happens to our culture is what happens to *our* culture, our individual fantasies and images, whether we moralize and repress them, diagnose and imprison them, exploit and betray them, drug and mock them. The soul of our civilization depends upon the civilization of our soul. The imagination of our culture calls for a culture of the imagination.

We shall have to build new imaginal arenas for the bull, new imaginal circuses for the crowd of persons and theaters for the images, new imaginal processions for the driving mythical fantasies that now overrun us, racing through our night on psychopathic motorcycles. Renaissance man, the shadow, must be met in his style, in his territory. Integration of the shadow is an emigration. Not him to us; we to him. His incursion is barbarism, our descent is culture.

I have drawn so much attention to the Renaissance in order to offer a background adequate to the forces threatening our individual psychic welfare and our civilization. Our time and its consciousness are in many ways like those of the Renaissance, as we imagine it. Now, as then, there is opportunity in the midst of falling apart to re-vision our world. Especially, we have the opportunity to re-vision psychology so that it can offer understanding and shape to the chaos of Northern man's teeming underside. This area has long been cursed by the singleness of vision of monotheistic consciousness, so that Persephone's deepenings and Pluto's riches, Proteus' diversity and Pan's all-of-nature, merged into a single monster figure, the Devil. But now as consciousness disintegrates into many modes of envisioning, its shadow too differentiates into multiple images. As happened during the Renaissance, we are discovering that concealed in the shadow are the old Gods. To recognize these imaginal powers and to find precise, intelligent, and cultural ways of providing for them——"or not to be—that is the question."

"Discern or perish," wrote Nietzsche.[117] To begin that discerning of the images on which our survival may depend, I have been sinking a taproot into a tradition which offers our native polyphony of voices a polytheistic alternative.

Religion and Psychology Again

The occupation—or is it a vocation?—that emerges from our work in these pages is one of *recollecting the Gods* in all psychological activity. This is what archetypal psychology implies at its most fundamental level, and this is why archetypal psychology is necessarily nonagnostic and polytheistic. The images to which it turns and which give faith in psychic reality invoke the powers of religion just as images have always done. By entering the imagination we cross into numinous precincts. And from within this territory all events in the soul require religious reflection.

When we have religious images and persons, when we are aware of ritual, sacrifice, and creedal teachings, then we are less likely to enact them blindly. Without religious ideas we are prey to them elsewhere as ideologies. Precisely because psychology neglected religious reflection it was easily captured from behind by religion and bound to the horizon of Reformational ideologies. It needs the tools of religion in order to psychologize its actions and beliefs. Psychology has failed also because it took its instruments from everywhere *but* religion—scientific technologies, biological observation, economics, and medicine—an astounding neglect in view of the fact that it was always to religion that the soul belonged. Yet not so astounding, since psychology has also forgotten it was the study of soul.

Recollection of the Gods reopens the basic texts of both Freud's and Jung's later lives, *Moses and Monotheism* and *Answer to Job*. These books, by two old men in their seventies who had spent years unraveling the meshes of hundreds of knotted lives, were recognitions that psychological work, because it is the work of soul-making, inevitably leads to religious reflection. But the mode of their reflection has passed. Born in the nineteenth century, Freud and Jung were probably the last psychologists who could develop their insights from the Bible, which is not a mythology but a sacred book, therefore lending itself better to literalism than to psychologizing. Although its figures and tales are many, its viewpoint and God are one. The psyche's main need is no longer support for the unity of personality against the incursions of the Gods in our pluralism. Now we are interested in a style of religious reflection that both widens and differentiates the scope of our discerning.

So again we come to the relation between religion and psychology. This final time we take the cue from William James, whose *Varieties of Religious Experience* treated religion as a phenomenon of soul. He opened a field, "the psychology of religion," by examining religious positions through psychological observations. Then, the later James of *A Pluralistic Universe* (published the year before his death) recognized that psychological enquiry leads necessarily to a variety of subjectively based, self-sufficient, and valid premises.

Should we now imagine, as archetypal psychology does, that Gods are the archetypal premises within all experiences and all attitudes, then polytheistic religion becomes a first principle of psychology. Thus our attempt at the same fantasy that occupied James—the relation of religion and psychology—is the reverse of James. We would examine psychological observations through religious positions: which God is at work. Here we are opening into "the religion of psychology" by suggesting that psychology is a variety of religious experience.

Psychology as religion implies imagining all psychological events as effects of Gods in the soul, and all activities to do with soul, such as therapy, to be operations of ritual in relation to these Gods. Our theories about the soul are then also myths, and the history of depth psychology a kind of Church history: early disciples and tales of martyrs; the search for a prehistory in extraterritorial areas; the struggle with unbelievers and heresies; apologetics and official biographers; the patristic literature, schools of interpretation and commentaries; the ecumenical attempts, the great schism; the holy localities, their legends and their cures; the conversional mission, and above all, depth psychology's impetus to salvation.

That the contemporary ministry is drawn so strongly by psychology toward a new brotherhood of psychology and religion in parish, mental health center, and individual quest reflects the current ecumenical movement, drawing all branches together. It is not a question of religion turning to psychology—no, psychology is simply going home. Whether this home is North or South, monotheistic Reformation or polytheistic Renaissance, we have yet to see. But the wrong way could again be the imprisonment of soul in an imageless universe, the soul again rent between barricades and barbarians.

Also, by means of religion we might become more aware of the nonagnostic aspect of therapy, that it is a work invoking Gods. Little wonder then that it is fraught with magic, charlatanism, and priestly powers. Little wonder, too, that the emotions having to do with begin-ning therapy and ending it, and with its central experience of transfer-ence, have no adequate explanations in psychology books. The level of such accounts is strikingly trivial compared to the depth of the experi-ences.

Religion would not only give us primary images of soul-making but would open depth psychology's eyes to the religious depth of its activi-ties, to the realization that since its inception it has been actively practising religion. Here we need to psychologize more deeply into Freud's move decrying religion as an "illusion" and considering psy-choanalysis to be reality. This step is necessary in the founding of any religion. Also we could reappraise Jung's lifelong effort to reinterpret, not so much science, philosophy, society, or even psychiatry, but theol-ogy. Depth psychology is thoroughly involved a priori with religion because it is a psychology of the soul. As such, psychology is driven by the "will to believe" (as James called it), of which its belief in sexuality, or humanism, or self are each idols. A re-vision of psychology means recognizing that psychology does not take place without religion, be-cause there is always a God in what we are doing. The recognition of the Protestantism of psychology was the first step. Ultimately we shall admit that archetypal psychology is theophanic: personifying, patholo-gizing, psychologizing, and dehumanizing are the modes of polytheiz-ing, the means of revealing Gods in a pluralistic universe.

A Processional Exit

Though this has been a groundwork of irreplaceable insights, they are to be taken neither as foundations for a systematic theory nor even as a prolegomenon for any future archetypal psychology. Soul-making needs adequate ideational vessels, and it equally needs to let go of them. In this sense all that is written in the foregoing pages is confessed to with passionate conviction, to be defended as articles of faith, and at the same time disavowed, broken, and left behind. By holding to nothing, nothing holds back the movement of soul-making from its ongoing process, which now like a long Renaissance processional slips away from us into memory, off-stage and out of sight. They are leaving—even the Bricoleur and the Rogue Errant who put together the work and charted its course; there goes Mersenne in his monk's dress, and Lou, and Hegel; the Cartesians depart, and the transcendent refusers of pathology, and Heroic Ego who had to bear such brunt; now Anima in all her marvellous veils moves off southward smiling; going too are Freud and Jung, side by side, psychologized, into the distance, and the mythical personages from Greece, the Greek words and Latin phrases, the footnoting authorities, the literalistic enemies and their troop of fallacies; and when the last image vanishes, all icons gone, the soul begins again to populate the stilled realms with figures and fantasies born of the imaginative heart.

Abbreviations

CW	*Collected Works* of C.G. Jung (Bollingen Series XX) translated by R.F.C. Hull and edited by H. Read, M. Fordham, G. Adler and Wm. McGuire (Princeton, N.J.: Princeton University Press and London: Routledge and Kegan Paul, 1953–), cited below by volume number and paragraph.
FN	*The Complete Works of Friedrich Nietzsche,* edited by Oscar Levy, various translators, 18 volumes (Edinburgh: T.N. Foulis, 1911–13).
LS	H.G. Liddell and R. Scott, *A Greek-English Lexicon*, 9th edition, (Oxford: Clarendon Press, 1968).
MA	*The Myth of Analysis* by James Hillman (Evanston: Northwestern University Press, 1972).
MDR	*Memories, Dreams, Reflections* by C.G. Jung, recorded and edited by Aniela Jaffé, translated by R. and C. Winston (London: Collins and Routledge and Kegan Paul, 1963).

Notes

INTRODUCTION

1. H. B. Forman, ed., *The Letters of John Keats* (London: Reeves & Turner, 1895), letter dating from April 1819, p. 326. Keats goes on to say: " . . . I say *'Soul making'* —Soul as distinguished from Intelligence. There may be intelligence or sparks of the divinity in millions—but they are not Souls till they acquire identities, till each one is personally itself. . . . How then are Souls to be made? . . . How but by the medium of a world like this? This point I sincerely wish to consider because I think it a grander system of salvation than the christian religion—."

2. The tone and aim of this book is in keeping with the Deed of Foundation, Dwight Harrington Terry Lecture Fund, November 1, 1905:

"The object of this Foundation is not the promotion of scientific investigation and discovery, but rather the assimilation and interpretation of that which has been or shall be hereafter discovered, and its application to human welfare. . . .

"The lecturers shall be subject to no philosophical or religious test, and no one who is an earnest seeker after truth shall be excluded because his views seem radical or destructive of existing beliefs. The founder realizes that the liberalism of one generation is often the conservatism of the next, and that many an apostle of true liberty has suffered martyrdom at the hands of the orthodox. He therefore lays special emphasis on complete freedom of utterance, and would welcome expressions of conviction . . . even when these may run counter to the generally accepted views of the day."

3. J. Ortega y Gasset, *On Love*, trans. T. Talbot (Cleveland: World-Meridian, 1957), p. 121.

3a. Cf. Eric A. Havelock's "Psyche or the Separation of the Knower from the Known," in his *Preface to Plato* (Oxford: Blackwell, 1963), pp. 197–214, although, where he places psyche on the side of the knower, I hold it to be the separating factor, the in-between.

4. J. Hillman, *Suicide and the Soul*, (1964) (New York: Harper Colophon, 1973), pp. 44–47 for implications of the word *soul*.

5. *CW* 6, §§743, 722, 78.

6. Philip Wheelwright, *Heraclitus* (Princeton, N.J.: Princeton Univ. Press, 1959), Fragment 42 (Diels, Frg. 45; Burnet, Frg. 71). M. Marcovich, *Heraclitus* (Merida, Venezuela: Los Andes Univ. Press, 1967), pp. 366–70, gives a succinct discussion of many translations and especially of the meaning of *bathun*, which like the Latin *altus* may also imply height. (Our Christian culture has radically polarized these directions into heaven and hell.) Marcovich emphasizes the difference between depth and the horizontal direction on the earth's surfaces. Soul is not in the surface of things, the superficialities, but reaches down into hidden depths, a region which also refers to Hades and death.

7. *CW* 9, 1, §267.

ONE / PERSONIFYING

1. On Mersenne see R. Lenoble, *Mersenne ou la naissance du méchanisme* (Paris: Vrin, 1971²). For a list of visitors to Mersenne's quarters in Paris see "Note sur la Vie de Mersenne" in *Correspondance du P. Marin Mersenne*, Mme. P. Tannery and C. de Waard, eds., 11 vols. (Paris: Éditions au Centre National de la Recherche Scientifique, 1945), I, 364–78.

2. For a long list of personifications in Renaissance art see E. Panofsky, *Studies in Iconology* (New York: Harper Torchbooks, 1962), pp. 257–59; for a "new" personification (not listed by Panofsky), see A. Perosa, "Febris: A Poetic Myth Created by Polizano," *J. Warburg Courtauld Inst.* 9:74 ff.

3. The attack on alchemy is mainly in *La verité des sciences* (Paris, 1625). For a discussion of his arguments against Robert Fludd, Giordano Bruno, and the Ficino school, see F. A. Yates, *Giordano Bruno and the Hermetic Tradition* (London: Routledge, 1964), pp. 432–39. Miss Yates writes (p. 435): "Mersenne is a modern; he has crossed the watershed and is on the same side as we are; belief in the power of magic images of the stars seems to him quite mad. . . . He does not condemn such images because he is afraid of their power, but because they are meaningless. Mersenne, who completely discards astrology, naturally also discards astral magic, the miraculous virtue of plants, stones, images, and the whole apparatus upon which *magia naturalis* rests."

4. On the import of Mersenne for science (besides Lenoble, *Mersenne*) see L. Thorndike, "Mersenne and Gassendi," chap. 14 of *A History of Magic and Experimental Science*, VII (New York/London: Columbia Univ. Press, 1958). D. P. Walker, *The Ancient Theology* (Ithaca, N.Y.: Cornell Univ. Press, 1972), pp. 189–93, suggests that Mersenne, through his very attacks on the animistic tradition, helped stimulate controversies that kept it alive. Walker also finds (pp. 168–75) a curious Platonist shadow in Mersenne: his secret translation and dissemination of an Indexed (forbidden) book by Herbert of Cherbury.

5. Mersenne, *Correspondance*, V, 283–89. The reduction of "Jacob's Ladder" to a matter for measurement epitomizes the destruction of a traditionally central image of mythical mysticism by asking the wrong sort of question. Cf. C. A. Patrides, "Renaissance Interpretations of Jacob's Ladder," *Theologische Zeitschrift* 18 (1962): 411–19. Similarly, using geometry to resolve the theological mystery of the Trinity (in which of course, as Mersenne knew, remain traces of prior polytheism), again shows the divinization of mathematical science. It is curious to see the Franciscan ideal of *renovatio* here working itself through the Franciscan (Minime) Mersenne into a mechanical scientism and soulless Cartesian psychology.

6. H. Hastings, *Man and Beast in French Thought of the Eighteenth Century* (Baltimore: Johns Hopkins Press, 1936), Introduction and chap. 1.

7. Should a child die before baptism it goes to Limbo. The child's soul does not have full equality with the souls of other baptized persons. The doctrine of Limbo in Protestantism and Catholicism today is still thorny; for a thorough, if older, discussion of the arguments of infant death without baptism see A. Vacant and E. Mangenot, *Dictionnaire de Théologie Catholique* (Paris: Letouzey, 1910), II, 364–78. The heated theological controversies about infant baptism have their psychological background in the *archetype of the child* and what it evokes in the psyche. I have discussed this elsewhere in terms of the latent paganism and polytheism signified by the "child" and today formulated in Freudian language as its polymorphous and perverse nature. Baptism prevented regression of the infantile psyche to its pre-Christian level. See my "Abandoning the Child," *Eranos 40—1971* (Leiden, Brill), pp. 369–70.

8. C. S. Pierce (1903), quoted from R. J. van Iten, ed., *The Problem of Universals*

(New York: Appleton-Century-Crofts, 1970), pp. 152 f.

9. Cf. M. Foucault, *Madness and Civilization: A History of Insanity in the Age of Reason,* trans. R. Howard (New York: Pantheon, 1965).

10. Cf. *Perceval's Narrative,* ed. G. Bateson (Stanford, Calif.: Stanford Univ. Press, 1961), p. 286.

11. C. F. Chapin, *Personification in Eighteenth-Century English Poetry* (New York: King's Crown Press, Columbia Univ., 1955), p. 16; M. H. Abrams, *The Mirror and the Lamp* (1953) (New York: Oxford Univ. Press, 1971), pp. 274–79, 288; D. C. Allen, *Mysteriously Meant* (Baltimore: Johns Hopkins Press, 1970), chap. 10. For a more sympathetic account of Locke's view, see E. L. Tuveson, *The Imagination as a Means of Grace* (1960) (New York: Gordian, 1974).

12. Allen, *Mysteriously Meant,* p. 308.

13. Chapin, *Personification,* chap. 3. This ancient aesthetic idea is discussed brilliantly by Mario Praz in chap. 1, "Ut Pictura Poesis," of his *Mnemosyne: The Parallel Between Literature and the Visual Arts,* Bollingen Series, (Princeton, N.J.: Princeton Univ. Press, 1970).

14. Cf. Frank E. Manuel, *The Eighteenth Century Confronts the Gods,* chap. 5, "The New Allegorism" (Cambridge, Mass.: Harvard Univ. Press, 1959); J. Seznec, *The Survival of the Pagan Gods,* trans. B. F. Sessions (New York: Harper Torchbook, 1961), pp. 263–323.

15. On personifying among the Romantics, when "personification now came to be a major index to the sovereign faculty of imagination," see Abrams, *Mirror and Lamp,* p. 55, also pp. 64–68, 288–93. For a similar attempt among French poets to reimagine the world through personifying, see R. Marquardt, *Die Beseelung des leblosen bei französischen Dichtern des XIX Jahrhunderts* (Halle: Karras, 1906).

16. Mario Untersteiner, *The Sophists,* trans. K. Freeman (Oxford: Blackwell, 1954), p. 243.

17. Three excellent works on the problem of imagination in Western thought are: M. W. Bundy, "The Theory of Imagination in Classical and Mediaeval Thought," *Univ. Illinois Stud. In Language and Literature,* XII (1927); Gilbert Durand, "Defiguration philosophique et figure traditionnelle de l'homme en Occident," *Eranos 38—1969,* pp. 45–94; Edward S. Casey, "Toward an Archetypal Imagination," *Spring 1974* (New York/Zürich, Spring Publ.).

18. Spinoza, *Tractatus theologico-politicus,* III, 83, as quoted by Allen, *Mysteriously Meant,* p. 301.

19. Cf. J. Piaget, *A Child's Conception of Causality* (London: Routledge, 1930). That all personified thinking is a remnant of childhood either of the race or the individual is a tenet of rationalism of every description, even in Plato and Vico, finding its contemporary issue in the Marxist and Freudian derogation of mythic and religious thinking.

20. *Oxford English Dictionary (OED).*

21. Ibid.

22. The position in the thinking about *religion* is best represented by Martin P. Nilsson, "Kuitische Personifikationen," *Opuscula Selecta,* (Lund: Gleerup, 1960), III, 237, who says: "One needed something corresponding to the needs of men, a specific, described power that met specific needs of the human—thus personification arose through which one described what one needed: it was a specific, limited section of Divine power, and named God." In the thinking about *literature* the position is best represented by Edmund Wilson, *Axel's Castle* (New York: Scribner, 1936), p. 176, who writes: "The real elements, of course, in any works of fiction, are the elements of the author's personality. . . . His personages are personifications of the author's various impulses and emotions: and the relations between them in his stories are really the relations between these" (quoted in Abrams, *Mirror and Lamp,* p. 227).

23. Cf. E. Renner, *Eherne Schalen: Ueber die animistischen Denk- und Erlebnisformen* (Bern/Stuttgart: Haupt, 1967), pp. 205–28.

24. Gerardus van der Leeuw, *Religion in Essence and Manifestation*, trans. J. E. Turner (New York: Harper Torchbook, 1963), I, §9, 1.

25. R. Hinks, *Myth and Allegory in Ancient Art* (London: Warburg Inst., 1939), p. 109. An exhaustive list of these personifications together with their places of cult is given by L. Deubner in W. H. Roscher's *Ausführliches Lexikon der griechischen und römischen Mythologie*, III, 2, 2068–69 (Leipzig/Stuttgart: Teubner; Hildesheim: Olms, 1965). For more recent remarks on Greek personification, see T. B. L. Webster, "Personification as a Mode of Greek Thought," *J. Warburg Courtauld Inst.* 17 (1954): 10–12.

26. Plotinus, *The Enneads*, trans. Stephen Mackenna (London: Faber, 1956), IV, 3, 11.

27. Joseph Gantner, "L'Immagine del Cuor," *Eranos 35—1966*, pp. 261–72. Compare Henry Corbin, "Theophanic Imagination and Creativity of the Heart" in his *Creative Imagination in the Sufism of Ibn 'Arabi*, trans. R. Manheim (Princeton, N.J.: Princeton Univ. Press, 1969), p. 221, where we find this passage: "In Ibn 'Arabi as in Sufism in general, the heart (qalb) is the organ which produces true knowledge, comprehensive intuition, the gnosis (ma 'rifa) of God and the divine mysteries, in short, the organ of everything connoted by the term 'esoteric science.' " The parallels with Western mysticism can be found in *Le Coeur* (essays by many hands), Études Carmélitaines (Bruges: Desclée de Brouwer, 1950). For connections with the physiological heart in theories of emotion see my *Emotion: A Comprehensive Phenomenology of Theories and their Meanings for Therapy* (Evanston, Ill.: Northwestern Univ. Press, 1961), pp. 98 f., 153, 62, also p. 182 on Paracelsus and the imagination of the heart.

28. Miguel de Unamuno, *Tragic Sense of Life*, trans. J. E. C. Flitch (New York: Dover, 1954), p. 139.

29. W. Dilthey, *Gesammelte Schriften*, 12 vols. (Stuttgart: Teubner, 1962), especially vols. V and VII; special topics: U. Hermann, *Bibliographie Wilhelm Dilthey* (Weinheim: Julius Beltz, 1969). For works on Dilthey in English see H. A. Hodges, *The Philosophy of Wilhelm Dilthey* (London: Routledge, 1952); H. N. Tuttle, *Wilhelm Dilthey's Philosophy of Historical Understanding—A Critical Analysis* (Leiden: Brill, 1969); R. E. Palmer, *Hermeneutics: Interpretation Theory in Schleiermacher, Dilthey, Heidegger, and Gadamer* (Evanston: Northwestern Univ. Press, 1969).

30. On the Dilthey-Nietzsche relation, see J. Kamerbeek, "Dilthey versus Nietzsche," *Studia Philosophica* 10 (Basel, 1950):52–84, together with a contempuous criticism of it by G. Misch (editor of Dilthey's Works), "Dilthey versus Nietzsche," *Die Sammlung* 7 (Göttingen, 1952):378–95. In their written works Nietzsche never mentions Dilthey; Dilthey mentions Nietzsche rarely.

31. Quoted and translated by Palmer, *Hermeneutics*, p. 115 (from Dilthey, *Ges. Schrift.* V, 212). Although Palmer shows Dilthey laying stress on persons, Dilthey's move still remains within the fantasy of "personalism" (see above, p. 76). His approach is an improvement over the objective methods of positivistic science; however, Dilthey still tends to literalize personification into persons. He has still to take the step into personifying; for that is what helps us understand, rather than persons as such. Yet Dilthey was a precursor of archetypal psychology. He was moving in the direction of the mythopeic, recognizing its role for psychological understanding, his basic concern. But first he had had to struggle with psychology in its positivistic definition. This struggle led him to recognize that psychology, upon which he wanted to base all human studies that employ the method of understanding, stands closer to art, to poetry, biography, and narrative than it does to experimental science. He also recognized "pathologizing of the image" as the nodal point where dream, fantasy, madness, and the poetic mode meet. (Dilthey, "Dichterische Einbildungskraft und Wahnsinn"

[1886], *Ges. Schrift.* VI, 139 and 90 f.) Dilthey was planning in his old age to revise his *Poetik.* It would have had major components of archetypal psychology, for it would have relied upon typicalities, the symbolic mode of apprehension, and it would have led inescapably into a reevaluation of the Romantic position in regard to the nature of poetic imagery, its outlandish, psychopathological aspects. Cf. K. Müller-Vollmer, *Towards a Phenomenological Theory of Literature: A Study of Wilhelm Dilthey's 'Poetik,'* Stanford Studies in Germanics and Slavics, vol. I (The Hague: Mouton, 1963).

32. T. G. Bergin and M. H. Fisch, trans., *The New Science of Giambattista Vico* (Ithaca, N.Y.: Cornell Univ. Press, 1968), p. 74 (bk. I, §205). We must remember when referring to Vico that, despite his notion of historical development from ancient poetic personifications to modern conceptual rationality, for him the mythical and poetic have the highest place. Personification was the mode of original "fantastic speech making use of physical substances endowed with life and most of them imagined to be divine" (§401). This speech presented in myth was *vera narratio* ("telling it like it is"), and poetic logic or poetic wisdom was necessary, true, spontaneous, economical, and universal. See A. R. Caponigri, *Time and Idea: The Theory of History in Giambattista Vico,* chap. 9 (London: Routledge, 1953; Notre Dame, Ind.: Univ. of Notre Dame paperback, 1968). The passages in Vico's *New Science* most relevant for this discussion are §§205–09, 317, 381, 401; on the relation of Vico and Dilthey, cf. the paper by Hodges in G. Tagliacozzo and H. V. White, *Giambattista Vico: An International Symposium* (Baltimore: Johns Hopkins Press, 1969).

33. E. R. Dodds, *The Ancient Concept of Progress* (Oxford: Clarendon Press, 1973), p. 6.

34. E. Cassirer, *The Philosophy of Symbolic Forms,* trans. R. Manheim (New Haven/London: Yale Univ. Press paperback, 1957), III, 71.

35. W. F. Otto, *Mythos und Welt* (Stuttgart: Klett, 1962), p. 261 (translation mine).

36. Giovanni Papini, "A Visit to Freud," *Colosseum* (1934), reprinted in *Rev. Existential Psychology and Psychiatry* IX (1969):130–34.

37. K. M. Abenheimer, "Lou Andreas-Salomé's Main Contributions to Psycho-Analysis," *Spring 1971,* pp. 22–37. The conflict between objective and anthropomorphic approaches is epitomized in the conflict between Lou and Freud over her long tribute to him called *Mein Dank an Freud* (Vienna: Internat. Psychoanalyt. Verlag, 1931). "Freud told her twice that the 'overly personal title must go,' proposing 'Psycho-analyse' for 'Freud'; she twice said *no* because 'the work is really this one word, is my experience of the man so named; what it would have been like as mere objective knowledge without this human experience I simply cannot imagine (Am after all a woman too)." R. Binion, *Frau Lou* (Princeton, N.J.: Princeton Univ. Press, 1968), p. 464.

38. She met Nietzsche when she was a student, traveling and living with him for some time. On the comparison of her ideas with Dilthey's, see Abenheimer, "Lou Andreas-Salomé's Contributions." Binion (*Frau Lou,* p. 465) does not trace a direct connection with Dilthey but recognizes the Diltheyan character of her insistence on "lived experience." However, "Dilthey was the most prominent professor of philosophy in Berlin at the time Lou attended lectures there (1883–87) [and Lou went for prominent men] . . . Lou shared (on a much lower level) all his main interests. . . . All Lou's methodological criticisms of Freud are clearly derived from Dilthey's ideas." (Private communication from K. M. Abenheimer.)

39. The Diotima simile finds suggestive support in a letter to her from Freud (1931), who writes of her "superiority over all of us—in accord with the heights from which you descended to us." S. Leavy in his Introduction to *The Freud Journal of Lou Andreas-Salomé* (New York: Basic Books; London: Hogarth; 1964–65), p. 20. The correspondence between Freud and Lou lasted until 1936 (six months before her death in February 1937, when Freud was eighty years old). Cf. Sigmund Freud/Lou Andreas-

Salomé: *Briefwechsel*, E. Pfeiffer, ed. (Frankfurt a/M: S. Fischer, 1966). She stirred something similar in Martin Buber, who entitled a work of hers *Die Erotik*, declaring it "a fundamental pure powerful piece of work" (Binion, *Frau Lou*, p. 327). Leavy (*Freud Journal*, p. 207) writes: "The association of spirituality and eroticism was integral and all pervasive in her." Nietzsche was said to have addressed to her, at their first meeting (1882) in St. Peter's at the Vatican, these words: "From what stars have we fallen to meet here?" (Leavy, *Freud Journal*, p. 6). According to Binion (p. 464), the Diotima-Lou analogy was noted already in 1932 by Sarasin.

40. Abenheimer, "Lou Andreas-Salomé's Contributions," pp. 26–27.

41. Cf. my note on the etymology and personification of the God Liber (of the Dionysus-Bacchus configuration) in the term libido: *Emotion*, pp. 76–77.

42. Cf. G. Tourney, "Freud and the Greeks: A Study of the Influence of Classical Greek Mythology and Philosophy upon the Development of Freudian Thought," *J. Hist. Behav. Sci.* 1, no. 1 (1965).

43. S. Freud, *New Introductory Lectures on Psycho-Analysis*, trans. W. J. H. Sprott (London: Hogarth, 1933), p. 124.

44. S. Freud, *The Ego and the Id, Standard Edition* (London: Hogarth Press, 1961), vol. XIX, p. 59.

45. Hillman, "The Dream and the Underworld," *Eranos 42—1973*.

46. *L. Wittgenstein, Lectures and Conversations on Aesthetics, Psychology and Religious Belief*, ed. Cyril Barrett (Oxford: Blackwell, 1970), p. 51.

47. *CW* 9, 1, §514.

48. Ibid., 2: "Association, Dream and Hysterical Symptom"; also 8, §203; 9, 1, §507.

49. Ibid., 8, §§593, 217; 9, 2, §25.

50. Aniela Jaffé, "The Creative Phases in Jung's Life," *Spring 1972*, pp. 171–72.

51. *CW* 13, §58.

52. Ibid., 13, §62; 7, §314; 9, 2, p. 11 n.

53. Ibid., 8, §209.

54. Ibid., 13, §§299, 62.

55. Ibid., 8 §623.

55a. Ibid., 13, §75; 11, §§889, 769.

55b. Ibid., 8, §618.

56. Ibid., 6, §78; cf. 6, §743.

57. Ibid., 9, 1, §136.

58. *MDR*, pp. 181–85.

59. It is the *willfulness* of the personified powers that van der Leeuw particularly emphasizes. "What do ye powers desire? And why do ye desire it?" is the question one addresses to them (*Religion in Essence*, I, §19, 4). Cf. Jung's description of the complex, *CW* 13, §48; 8, §580.

60. Freud, *New Introductory Lectures*, p. 106.

61. O. Fenichel, *The Psychoanalytic Theory of Neurosis* (New York: Norton, 1945), p. 19.

62. J. Hillman, "Psychology: Monotheistic or Polytheistic?" *Spring 1971*, pp. 193–208. Cf. A. Brelich, "Der Polytheismus," *Numen* 7 (Leiden: Brill, 1960), p. 129; van der Leeuw, *Religion in Essence* I, §19, 1, for the relation between polytheism and personifying.

63. *CW* 13, §51 (italics mine).

64. G. S. Kirk, *Myth, Its Meaning and Function in Ancient and Other Cultures* (Cambridge, Eng. and Berkeley, Calif.: The Univ. Press and Univ. of California Press, 1970), p. 205.

65. Van der Leeuw, *Religion in Essence* I, §19, 4.

66. Roberto Weiss, *The Renaissance Discovery of Classical Antiquity* (Oxford: Blackwell, 1969), p. 140. On the relationship of the Renaissance to Greece see further works

cited below in Chapter 4; also Deno John Geanakopolos, *Byzantium and the Renaissance* (Hamden, Conn.: Shoe String Press, 1973).

67. J. M. Osborn, "Travel Literature and the Rise of Neo-Hellenism in England," *Bull. N. Y. Publ. Libr.* 67 (1963):300. Osborn reviews the literature on the subject of the "return to Greece" and travelers' reports, especially since the Renaissance.

68. B. Snell, *The Discovery of Mind*, trans. T. G. Rosenmeyer (New York: Harper Torchbook, 1960), pp. 258–61. Cf. J. Ortega y Gasset, *Meditations on Quixote*, trans. E. Rugg and D. Marín (New York: Norton, 1963), p. 76. Further on the history of the relation to Greece, see R. Pfeiffer, "Von der Liebe zu den Griechen," *Münchener Universitätsreden*, n.f. 20 (München: Huber, 1957).

69. *CW* 4, §106.

70. Ibid., 14, §502; 9, 1, §§507–08.

71. Ibid., 14, §671.

72. Ibid., 5, §274.

73. *MDR*, p. 45.

74. *CW* 12, §65.

75. Cf. K. Kerényi, *Asklepios*, trans. R. Manheim (New York: Pantheon, 1959), esp. pp. 18–46; C. A. Meier, *Ancient Incubation and Modern Psychotherapy* (Evanston, Ill.: Northwestern Univ. Press, 1967), p. 59.

76. Cf. W. H. Roscher and J. Hillman, *Pan and the Nightmare: Two Essays* (New York/Zürich: Spring Publ., 1972).

77. *CW* 13, §55.

78. Ibid., 8, §129.

79. Gregory of Nazianzus, "In Praise of Basil" (*Patr. Gr.* 36, 508), quoted in J. Shiel, *Greek Thought and the Rise of Christianity* (London: Longmans, 1968), p. 76.

80. Cf. *MA*, pt. 3, on hysteria and Dionysus.

81. *CW* 8, §280.

82. Ibid., 9, 1, §272.

83. Ibid., §50.

84. This indistinctness among imaginal figures seems basic to the imaginal realm itself. For even a man as carefully discriminate as Plotinus frequently confuses "the Gods" with daimones and with archetypes, cf. S. MacKenna, Plotinus' *The Enneads*, p. xxvii.

85. *CW* 9, 1, §271.

86. The term "imaginal" for the realm of images, which is also the realm of the soul, comes from Henry Corbin. Cf. his *"Mundus Imaginalis*, or the Imaginary and the Imaginal," *Spring 1972*, pp. 1–19.

87. Mary Watkins, "The Waking Dream in European Psychotherapy," *Spring 1974* and her book *Waking Dreams*, in preparation for Gordon & Breach, New York.

88. Cf. (in English) G. Durand, "Exploration of the Imaginal," *Spring 1971*, pp. 84–101. In French his main papers are published yearly in the *Eranos* yearbooks (1964–1973), and *Les Structures anthropologiques de l'imaginaire* (Paris: Presses Univ. France, 1963).

88a. "The image is not *what* is present to awareness—this is the content proper— but *how* this content is presented." E. S. Casey, "Toward a Phenomenology of Imagination," *J. Brit. Society Phenomenology* 5 (1974):10.

89. R. G. Collingwood, "Polytheistic and Monotheistic Science," chap. 20 of *An Essay on Metaphysics* (Oxford: Clarendon Press, 1940); on monotheistic metaphysics see George Boas, "Monotheism," chap. 9 in his *The History of Ideas* (New York: Scribner, 1969).

90. For a thorough review of Anima, see my two-part essay " 'Anima,' " *Spring 1973*, pp. 97–132 and *Spring 1974* pp. 113–46.

91. Cf. A. N. Whitehead's notion of "importance," *Modes of Thought* (1938) (New

York: Putnam Capricorn, 1958), pp. 159–60: "Importance reveals itself as transitions of emotion" and "My importance is my emotional worth now. . . ."

92. Cf. *MA*, pt. 1 for a long discussion of the relation between soul (Psyche) and love (Eros), the literature on this theme, and its relevance for depth psychology.

93. *Depersonalization*, J.-E. Meyer, ed. (Darmstadt: Wissenschaftliche Buchgesellschaft, 1968): a collection of major papers all in German.

94. J. Drever, *A Dictionary of Psychology* (London: Penguin, 1953), p. 62.

95. *CW* 9, 1, §57.

96. Quoted from Émile Male, *The Gothic Image* (1913), trans. D. Nussey (New York: Harper Torchbook, 1958), p. 392; cf. Otto von Simson, *The Gothic Cathedral*, Bollingen Series (New York: Pantheon, 1956), pp. 183–231.

97. E. H. Gombrich, "Personification," in R. R. Bolgar, ed., *Classical Influences on European Culture* (Cambridge, Eng.: Univ. Press, 1971), p. 248.

98. E. Mounier, *Personalism*, trans. P. Mairet (New York: Grove, 1952), p. xi.

99. E. S. Brightman, "Personality as a Metaphysical Principle," in *Personalism in Theology, Essays in Honor of Albert Knudson* (Boston: Boston Univ. Press, 1943), p. 43. The best review of the nuances of the word "personality," together with an historical introduction to the concept and the literature, still remains Gordon Allport's *Personality*, chap. 3 (New York: Holt, 1937). Wilhelm Stern summarizes the German approach in his *General Psychology from the Personalistic Standpoint*, trans. H. D. Spoeri (New York: Macmillan, 1938). Neither Allport nor Stern takes up the question we are exploring, which is fundamentally involved in any discussion of personality: the psyche's tendency to personify and to experience Gods as persons.

100. Cf. Kathleen Raine, *Blake and Tradition* (Princeton, N.J.: Princeton Univ. Press, 1968), 2:215–17.

101. *Laws* I, 644d; VII, 803c; *Rep.* VII, 514b.

102. *CW* 5, §388.

103. Ibid., 13, §61.

104. Gaston Bachelard, *The Poetic Reverie*, trans. D. Russell (Boston: Beacon, 1971), p. 173. The passage reads: ". . . there is established a psychology of capital letters. The dreamer's words become names of the World. They have access to the capital letter. Then the World is great, and the man who dreams it is a *Grandeur*. This grandeur in the image is often an objection for the man of reason." It is difficult for us today to re-enter the "psychology of capital letters." It is part of mythic consciousness, or what Bachelard calls "the dreamer's" consciousness. The use of capital letters has become a purely technical question for printers and copy editors. Not so for the ancient Greeks, who were able to maintain the as-if ambiguity, the "quasi-personal" nature of their archetypal figures. H. J. Rose brings this out beautifully in a passage on Greek personifications. He says that a writer nowadays will "if he writes in English or French, mark off his personifications . . . with an initial capital. A Greek poet, Pindar notably, can in one and the same clause say that Themis . . . is assessor of Zeus and that *themis* without a capital (to the confusion of modern editors, who cannot print the same word in two different ways at once) is practised zealously in Aigina (*Olympia*, vol. 8, 21–22)." Introductory Lecture, in *La Notion du Divin*, Fondation Hardt I (Geneva: Vando-euvres, 1954), p. 26.

105. *CW* 7, §183. On the relation of daimon, fate, and personal experience, see B. C. Dietrich, *Death, Fate and the Gods* (London: Athlone Press, 1967), p. 319; E. R. Dodds, *The Greeks and the Irrational* (Berkeley, Calif.: Univ. of California Press, 1951), pp. 23, 42, 58 with notes; Paul Friedländer, *Plato* 3 vols., trans. H. Meyerhoff, Bollingen Series (New York and Princeton, N. J.: Pantheon and Princeton Univ. Press, 1958–69) vol. 1, chap. 2, "Demon and Eros," and W. K. C. Guthrie (on the daimon in Empedocles) in his *History of Greek Philosophy* (Cambridge, Eng.: Univ. Press, 1965), II, 263f.

106. Cf. A. B. J. Plaut, "Reflections about not being able to Imagine," *J. Analyt. Psychol.* 11 (1966):130; R. Grinnell, "Reflections on the Archetype of Consciousness: Personality and Psychological Faith," *Spring 1970,* esp. pp. 36–37. Grinnell speaks of faith as a "gift of the dove" (referring to one of Jung's own dreams in which a dove transforms into a little girl). This dream confirmed Jung in his faith in his own personality after his break with Freud and his own isolation, during which period he had turned to the persons of his psyche and first experimented with active imagination. As Grinnell suggests, the discovery of personality, as well as faith in it and in the reality of the psyche, is all a gift of the dove-girl. The implication is that *imagining is psychological faith.* It is a faith in images, and acts of psychological faith are imaginative activities.

TWO / PATHOLOGIZING

1. Freud, *New Introductory Lectures on Psycho-Analysis* (Lecture 31), trans. W. J. H. Sprott (London: Hogarth, 1933), p. 78.

2. E. H. Erikson, *Identity and the Life Cycle,* Psychol. Issues, Monograph Series 1 (New York: Internat. Univ. Press, 1959), p. 122.

3. K. Jaspers, *General Psychopathology,* trans. J. Hoenig and M. W. Hamilton (of the 7th German edition) (Chicago: Univ. Press, 1963).

4. E. H. Battenberg and E. G. Wehner, "Terminologische Kommunikabilität zwischen Psychiatern und Psychologen," *Archiv für Psychiatrie und Nervenkrankheiten* 215, 1, 1971, pp. 33–45.

5. For a discussion of the theoretical and methodological problems in the history of psychopathology, see G. Mora and J. L. Brand, eds., *Psychiatry and its History: Methodological Problems in Research* (Springfield: Thomas, 1970); G. H. Frank, *Psychiatric Diagnosis* (Oxford: Pergamon Press, 1973) reviews the entire question of psychiatric classifications; cf. also S. L. Sharma, "A Historical Background of the Development of Nosology in Psychiatry and Psychology," *Amer. Psychol.* 25, 1970, pp. 248–53.

6. E. Fischer-Homberger, "Eighteenth-Century Nosology and its Survivors," *Medical History* 14, 4, 1970, pp. 397 ff.

7. For connections between syndromes and archetypes see my "An Essay on Pan" *Pan and the Nightmare: Two Essays* (with W. H. Roscher) (New York/Zürich: Spring Publ., 1972); *MA,* pt. 2, where also the question of psychopathology and its language is examined in some detail; and above, chap. 1, on depersonalization; also N. Micklem, "On Hysteria: The Mythical Syndrome," *Spring 1974* (New York/Zürich: Spring Publ., 1974), pp. 147–65.

8. FN, *Twilight of the Idols,* "Skirmishes in a War with the Age," §7.

9. M. Foucault, *Madness and Civilization: A History of Insanity in the Age of Reason,* trans. R. Howard (New York: Pantheon, 1965).

10. T. S. Szasz, *The Myth of Mental Illness* (New York: Hoeber, Harper, 1961); *The Manufacture of Madness* (New York: Harper & Row, 1971); *Ideology and Insanity* (Garden City: Doubleday Anchor, 1970).

11. E. A. Ackerknecht, "Psychopathology, Primitive Medicine and Primitive Culture," *Bull. Hist. Med.* 14 (1943):30–67; now with appendix in his *Medicine and Ethnology* (Bern: Huber, 1971), pp. 57–89.

12. Cf. in particular R. D. Laing's "The Schizophrenic Experience" in his *The Politics of Experience* (Harmondsworth, Eng.: Penguin, 1967). Laing says (p. 95): ". . . *without exception* the experience and behavior that gets labeled schizophrenic is *a special strategy that a person invents in order to live in an unlivable situation.*" It is a survival attempt within an insane world called "normal."

13. Ibid., p. 99.

14. G. W. F. Hegel, *Philosophy of Mind* together with the "Zusätze" in Boumann's

text (1845), trans. A. V. Miller (Oxford: Clarendon Press, 1971), p. 124. The passages relevant to Hegel's view on insanity are those added in 1845 by his editor Boumann from lectures of Hegel (1817 and 1820) and from notes of various auditors which are to be found on pages 92, 123–39, and 143 of the aforementioned book. The "Zusätze" are appendices to §§377–577 of Hegel's *Encyclopedia of the Philosophical Sciences* which were not included in the familiar W. Wallace English translation. Cf. Murray Greene, *Hegel on the Soul* (The Hague: Nijhoff, 1972), pp. 121–25, for a presentation of Hegel on insanity.

Hegel's only sister, Christiane, threw herself into an icy river two months after his death from cholera. She had suffered from "nervousness" and was long one of Hegel's concerns for she lived periodically with Hegel and his wife. Shortly before her suicide she had begun to wear odd clothing, believed that doctors were influencing her with magnets and electricity, and had tried to open her veins. Cf. Karl Rosenkranz, *G. W. F. Hegel's Leben* (Berlin: Duncker und Humblot, 1844), pp. 424 f. As Wolfgang Treher (*Hegels Geisteskrankheit oder das verborgene Gesicht der Geschichte*, Emmendingen, 1969), p. 193, points out, this aspect of Hegel's life is covered over by all modern Hegel biographers who extol him as a model of reason and normal bourgeois life. For instance, H. S. Harris, *Hegel's Development—1770–1801* (Oxford: Clarendon Press, 1972), p. 270, accedes nothing more serious than "fits of black depression" during the generally accepted crisis years of his third decade. Treher prefers to see Hegel burdened with a schizophrenic family trait, and his all-encompassing, self-defending systematic philosophy as a typical product of paranoid thought. Hegel's concern with and insights into insanity and the valid place he gives it in the life of the soul deserve further attention in relation with his biography, especially in regard to his relationship with his sister.

15. *Philosophy of Mind*, "Zusatz," p. 92.

16. Laing, *Politics of Experience*, p. 92; *The Self and Others* (London: Tavistock, 1961), pp. 134–41.

17. Hegel, *Philosophy of Mind*, "Zusatz," p. 143.

18. Ibid., p. 124.

19. The key words are printed regularly on the cover of the *Journal of Humanistic Psychology* and find formulation as a manifesto of the "Third Psychology" in Abraham Maslow's Preface to his book *Toward a Psychology of Being* (Princeton, N.J.: Van Nostrand, 1962). Even George A. Kelly in his "Humanistic Methodology in Psychological Research," *J. Human. Psychol.* 9 (1969):53–65 has been captivated by the exuberant fantasy of man, the limitless creative God. He writes (p. 65): "The humanist research looks for what man can do that he has never done before . . . man's actions are best understood in an expanding context of all that is seen to be possible for him, rather than within boundaries of his presumed nature, his reflexes, his brain, his complexes, his chronological age, his intelligence, or his culture." A similar fantasy carried to an extreme appears in H. Bonner, "The Proactivert: A Contribution to the Theory of Psychological Types," *J. Existential Psychiatry* 3 (1962):159–66. Bonner's slogan is *"I am what I will do."* The proactivert has no dread, no neurosis, no symptoms, no defenses. His life is full of peak experiences. "He approaches every challenge and novel condition with the spirit of exultation," and is "his own *primum mobile,* of dynamic psychological energy and movement" (p. 164). Bonner submits this type "as a preface to a humanistic psychology, which places the proactive person at the very center of the study of man" (p. 166). For similar examples of this idealistic, transcendental language, see *Humanitas,* published by Duquesne Univ. Press, Pittsburgh. In K. Menninger, "This Medicine, Love," in his *Love Against Hate* (New York: Harcourt, 1942), pp. 3–6, we discover that pathology is to be met in the style of "combat" with negative forces as one once met the Devil, aggression, and self-destruction. Cf. his *Man Against Himself* (New York: Harcourt, 1938), introductory motto and pp. 367–86. Gestalt therapy includes itself within the humanistic denial (cf. the Introduction to

Gestalt Therapy Now, J. Fagan and I. L. Shepherd, eds. [New York: Harper & Row, 1971], p. 1: "Now we use words such as enhancement, intimacy, actualization, creativity, ecstasy, and transcendence to describe what we wish for ourselves and others." This the authors consider appropriate to a psychology "which concerns itself with man in his humanness. . . .") In the same volume (p. 78) A. R. Beisser explains, "The Gestalt therapist further believes that the natural state of man is as a single, whole being—not fragmented into two or more opposing parts." Others in this tradition are Carl Rogers, Eric Berne, and many who once were Freudians, e.g., Karen Horney, Erich Fromm, Fritz Perls, Abraham Maslow, each of whom identifies Freud with pathology, pessimism, and thanatos, and then leaves him for greener fields. These fields were literalized by the American continent; leaving Freud, thanatos, and pessimism meant finding America, love, and optimism. But pathologizing can be kept distinct from both optimism and pessimism, both America and Europe.

The passages quoted and the works referred to by no means exhaust the malty fermentation that is generated by the word "humanism" as it spews and froths through so many fields. Perhaps it is the dominant *Weltanschauung* of the mid-twentieth century and as such conceals the dominant pathology of that period: manic euphoria. By eschewing such humanism, archetypal psychology would keep closer to depression, believing that there soul is more likely to be served. For a start into the variety of other discussions of humanism, see the bibliography prepared by H. J. Blackham, *A Guide to Humanist Books in English* (London: Ethical Union, 1962) and his (ed.) *Objections to Humanism* (London: Constable, 1963).

20. A. Maslow, "Naturalistic reasons for preferring Growth-Values over Regression-Values under good conditions," Appendix H in *Religions, Values, and Peak-Experiences* (Columbus: Ohio State Univ. Press, 1964).

21. Ibid., p. 76.

22. W. H. Blanchard, "The Psychodynamic Aspects of the Peak Experience," *Psychoanalytic Review* 56, no. 1 (1969):87–112.

23. Cf. ibid., and Maslow, "Naturalistic reasons," p. 62: "The peak-experience is felt as a self-validating, self-justifying moment which carries its own intrinsic value with it."

24. "Already in the New Testament *psyché* is used only fifty-seven times to *pneuma*'s two hundred and seventy-four occurrences. . . . So much is this the pattern that Paul comes to call *psychikoi* bad and *pneumatikoi* good (I Cor. 2:13–15, cf. I Cor. 15: 44–46)." David L. Miller, "Achelous and the Butterfly," *Spring 1973*, p. 14.

25. G. Santayana, *Realms of Being* (New York: Scribner, 1942), pp. 328–54.

26. R. G. Collingwood, *An Essay on Metaphysics* (Oxford: Clarendon Press, 1940), pp. 101–42; *The Principles of Art* (Oxford: Clarendon Press, 1938), p. 164.

27. There are innumerable accounts of the "spiritual path," but a short one which emphasizes just this difference between spirit and soul as a difference between being emptied of imagination (the mystic) and being filled with imagination (the visionary), as contrasted, say, in the differences between St. John of the Cross and William Blake, has been written by Roger Woolger, "Against Imagination: The *Via Negativa* of Simone Weil," *Spring 1973*, pp. 256–72.

28. Lou Andreas-Salomé, *The Freud Journal* (New York: Basic Books; London: Hogarth; 1964–65), p. 64.

29. Ibid., p. 131.

30. Adolf Guggenbühl-Craig, *Power in the Helping Professions* (New York/Zürich: Spring Publ., 1971) has worked out many effects of the split archetype upon therapy, showing that regardless of how well-intentioned the partners may be, the division in the background casts an inevitable destructive shadow on all therapeutic undertakings.

31. C. Lévi-Strauss, *The Savage Mind* (London: Weidenfeld & Nicolson, 1966), p. 32.

32. Szasz, works cited, especially *Ideology and Insanity.*

33. Esther Fischer-Homberger, *Hypochondrie* (Bern: Huber, 1970) thoroughly reviews the vagaries of the term through the ages.

34. *Hamartia,* translated sometimes as guilt or sin, is appropriate to the province of the physician according to one of the fathers of medicine, Galen (ca. A.D. 130–200). Etymologically it means "missing the mark" and belongs among those "errors" that we discuss under "errancy" (pp. 238f below). Cf. Philip Wheelwright, *The Burning Fountain* (Bloomington, Ind.: Indiana Univ. Press, 1968), pp. 174–81 on *hamartia;* on the relationship between pathology and guilt, see Pedro Laín Entralgo, *Mind and Body* (London: Harvill, 1955), pp. 23, 66, 103–12.

35. Cf. Arthur O. Lovejoy and George Boas, "Some Meanings of 'Nature' " in *Primitivism and Related Ideas in Antiquity* (New York: Octagon, 1965), pp. 447–56; R. Lenoble, *Esquisse d'une histoire de l'idée de nature* (Paris: Albin Michel, 1969).

36. *CW* 6, §757.

37. Ibid., §705.

38. I follow Jung's and Bachelard's views of alchemy: that it is primarily a descriptive system of the imaginal psyche. I recognize that the psychological view of alchemy is not the only one. It may be seen also as charlatanism, as early chemical technology, and as an occult spiritual discipline. None of these other perspectives, however, prevents it from being a psychology as well. Jung's idea of alchemy is more clearly put in his autobiography (*MDR,* pp. 193, 197, 210) than in his writings on alchemy. For a recent non-Jungian discussion of the literature of alchemy, see R. P. Multauf's review article "Essays in Gold-making," *Isis* 62, no. 2 (1971):233–38. For an interesting Jungian comparison between the Marxian and alchemical psychology of matter, see D. Holt, "Jung and Marx," *Spring 1973,* pp. 52–66.

39. Frances A. Yates, *The Art of Memory* (London: Routledge, 1966), p. 104. Cf. L. J. Swift and S.L. Block, "Classical Rhetoric in Vives' Psychology," *J. Hist. Behav. Sci.* 10 (1974):74–83 also on the importance of emotionally striking images.

40. Yates, *Art of Memory,* p. 96.

41. Ibid., pp. 64, 66, 74, 110, 193–94.

42. Ibid., p. 63.

43. Ibid., pp. 129 ff.

44. Ibid., p. 63.

45. Ibid.

46. Cf. E. Auerbach, *"Gloria Passionis,"* in *Literary Language and Its Public in Late Latin Antiquity,* trans. R. Manheim (New York: Pantheon, 1965), pp. 67–81. Cf. André Grabar, *Christian Iconography: A Study of Its Origins,* Bollingen Series (Princeton, N.J.: Princeton Univ. Press, 1968), pp. 131–32; Walter Lowrie, *Art in the Early Church* (New York: Pantheon, 1947), pp. 98, 182–84, discusses the earliest iconography of the passion, where the crucifixion is notable by its absence. The earliest crucifixions that have come down to us are probably not before the fifth century (carved ivory box in the British Museum and the carved cypress doors of S. Sabina in Rome); also J. Daniélou, *Les symboles chrétiens primitifs* (Paris: Seuil, 1961), pp. 95–107 on the early image of the plowshare as cross.

47. LS *pathos;* Aristotle, *Metaphysics* 1022b, 15 ff.; F. E. Peters, *Greek Philosophical Terms* (New York: New York Univ. Press, 1967), pp. 152–55; also B. B. Rees, *"Pathos* in the *Poetics* of Aristotle," *Greece and Rome* 19 (1972):11 f.

48. For some of the Hercules-Christ parallels see J. M. Robertson, *Pagan Christs* (London: Watts, 1911) and *Christianity and Mythology* (London: Watts, 1910); also useful are: M.-R. Jung, *Hercule dans la littérature française du XVI siècle* (Geneva: Droz, 1966); M. Simon, *Hercule et le Christianisme* (Paris: Belles Lettres, 1955). For some of the Hercules-Moses parallels and identifications see E. R. Goodenough, *Jewish Symbols in the Greco-Roman Period,* Bollingen Series (New York: Pantheon, 1964), 10:119–25, 136–37. For the Christ-Sol Invictus identification, for which reason Christ-

mas was celebrated on December 25—the day held in honor of Sol Invictus, see: G. H. Halsberghe, *The Cult of Sol Invictus* (Leiden: Brill, 1972), pp. 162–71. D. C. Allen, *Mysteriously Meant* (Baltimore: John Hopkins Press, 1970), pp. 1–20, reviews the patristic discussions of this theme and some of the recent literature on it.

49. Cf. S. Wenzel, *The Sin of Sloth: Acedia in Mediaeval Thought and Literature* (Chapel Hill: Univ. of North Carolina Press, 1967).

50. *The Enneads,* trans. Stephen Mackenna (London: Faber, 1956), I, 8, 1. Compare the idea of resemblance or family in Wittgenstein, cf. F. Zabeeh, "Resemblance" in his *Universals* (The Hague: Nijhoff, 1966), pp. 37–49, where likeness loses its archetypal significance and becomes only a nominalistic language game.

51. Proclus, *Elements of Theology,* Prop. 29 ff. on *epistrophé.*

52. I use the term *metaphorica* as employed by Albertus Magnus in the art of memory, see above, p. 91f, with references to Frances Yates.

53. G. Vico, *The New Science* (1744), trans. T. G. Bergin and M. H. Fisch (Ithaca, N.Y.: Cornell Univ. Press, 1968), pp. 74, 119 (§§209, 381) where Vico speaks of mythical figures as *universali fantastici.*

54. T. Taylor, "An Apology for the Fables of Homer" (1804), translation of Proclus' essay on the fables of Homer, found in *Thomas Taylor, the Platonist,* K. Raine and G. M. Harper, eds., Bollingen Series (Princeton, N.J.: Princeton Univ. Press, 1969), p. 460. Taylor attempts to account (as do many moralists and Christian thinkers) for the apparent paradox of a sublime religious philosophy and poetry (of Homer) riddled with pathologized images. The entire passage reads:

> "It likewise appears to me, that whatever is tragical, monstrous, and unnatural, in poetical fictions, excites the hearers, in an all-various manner, to the investigation of the truth, attracts us to recondite knowledge, and does not suffer us through apparent probability to rest satisfied with superficial conceptions, but compels us to penetrate into the interior parts of fables, to explore the obscure intention of their authors, and survey what natures and powers they intended to signify to posterity by such mystical symbols."

55. Vico, *New Science,* p. 117 (§376). The point of these mythical images, according to Vico, is "to perturb to excess."

56. J. Hillman, *Suicide and the Soul* (1964) (New York: Harper Colophon, 1973).

57. A main attack on remythologizing via depth psychology comes from Jaspers, whose argument is presented and refused in my "Deep Subjectivity, Introspection and Daemonology," forthcoming from Spring Publications.

58. P. Slater, *The Glory of Hera* (Boston: Beacon, 1971).

59. A good deal has been written on the thinking of the ancient Greeks about psychopathology, e.g., E. R. Dodds, *The Greeks and the Irrational* (Boston: Beacon, 1957); George Rosen, *Madness in Society* (London: Routledge, 1968), pp. 71–136; B. Simon and H. Weiner, "Models of Mind and Mental Illness in Ancient Greece," *J. Hist. Behav. Sci.* 2 (1966):303–14.

60. J. Hillman, "On Senex Consciousness," *Spring 1970,* pp. 146–65.

61. *MA,* pt. 3.

62. J. Hillman, "An Essay on Pan," in *Pan and the Nightmare: Two Essays,* with W. H. Roscher.

63. *MA,* pt. 1.

64. J. Hillman, "Senex and Puer," *Eranos 36—1967* (Zürich, Rhein), pp. 301–60, and "The Great Mother, Her Son, Her Hero, and the Puer," in *Fathers and Mothers* (New York/Zürich: Spring Publ., 1973), pp. 75–127.

65. *CW* 13, §54.

66. W. F. Otto, *The Homeric Gods,* trans. M. Hadas (New York: Pantheon, 1954), p. 169.

67. H. D. F. Kitto, "The Idea of God in Aeschylus and Sophocles," in *La Notion*

du Divin, Fondation Hardt I (Geneva: Vandoeuvres, 1954), p. 188.

68. K. Kerényi, *Geistiger Weg Europas* (Zürich: Rhein, 1955), pp. 39–40.

69. *CW* 13, §55.

70. Quoted in J. Seznec, *The Survival of the Pagan Gods,* trans. B. F. Sessions (New York: Harper Torchbook, 1961), p. 58.

71. J. D. Salinger, *Franny and Zooey* (Boston: Little, Brown, 1961), p. 140. Zooey (need I point out that his name means life in Greek?) *did not want his symptom psychoanalyzed into an explanation.* Compare Jung, "The Symbolic Life" (transcript from shorthand notes by D. Kitchin, Guild Lecture 80 [London: Guild of Pastoral Psychology, 1954], p. 17): "And so we dismiss our souls—'Oh, I am bound by a fixation to my mother, and if I see that I have all kinds of impossible fancies about my mother, I am liberated from that fixation.' *If the patient succeeds, he has lost his soul.* Every time you accept that explanation you lose your soul. You have not helped your soul; you have replaced your soul by an explanation, a theory."

72. Eugène Minkowski, *Le Temps vecu: Études phénoménologiques et psychopathologiques* (Paris: Coll. de l'Évolution psychiatrique, 1933), now *Lived Time: Phenomenological and Psychopathological Studies,* trans. N. Metzel (Evanston, Ill.: Northwestern Univ. Press, 1970), p. xxxix.

73. Vico, *New Science,* p. 117 (§376). There is a distinction between *acting out* "shocking truths" which perturb the psyche to excess and the metaphorical mode of imagination. It is not that we have to do violent, excessive things in order to move the psyche. This is the Romantic's way of seeking perturbations and excess—"living dangerously." Nor must the shocking fantasy be literalized by psychiatry into violent physical treatments such as suggested by Celsus (who gave us the term "insanity") in ancient Rome and by Cerletti (who invented electroshock—as well as artillery fuses, by the way) in modern Rome. Curiously, therapy regards physical shocks to be therapeutic while still regarding the shocking events in myth, dreams, and fantasies as pathological. An excessively strong pathologized image that does violence to our nature might be better understood as the psyche's self-induced shock treatment, preferable to coarser modes of its clinical enactment.

74. See above, Introduction, p. i, for origins of this phrase in Keats and also Blake.

75. Cf. M. de Unamuno, *Tragic Sense of Life* (1921), trans. J. E. C. Flitch (New York: Dover, 1954), p. 269.

76. I have presented at length some of the phenomenology of the realm of Hades and its psychological significance in "The Dream and the Underworld," *Eranos 42—1973.*

77. Cf. Paul Friedländer, *Plato,* 3 vols., trans. H. Meyerhoff, Bollingen Series (New York and Princeton, N.J.: Pantheon and Princeton Univ. Press, 1958–69)1:29–31.

78. See above, p. 369a on Hegel and insanity.

79. Cf. M. Schur, *Freud: Living and Dying* (New York: Internat. Univ. Press, 1972). Freud's pathologizings included: fainting spells, colon and bladder difficulties, some heart trouble, his smoking addiction and dreadfully painful cancer of the mouth, his cocaine period, the afflictions reported in his letters to Fliess, his "depersonalization" experience on the Acropolis—and his obsessive ideas about the date of his own death. Beyond all these concrete manifestations was his "pathologized eye"; his speculative imagination required pathologizing.

THREE / PSYCHOLOGIZING

1. By "instinct" I mean native impulsion. I use the word in a larger sense than in ethology ("inborn release mechanisms") since instinct may not always occur in publicly observable behavior but appears intrapsychically in private imagery and other proprioceptive events. I consider instinct to refer to congenitally given, prior to similar experience or behavior, universally human, precisely patterned, affectively charged

psychic events in which "the body" is a paramount referent. (We imagine the body to be either the locus of instinct or of its significance—hunger, reproduction, defense, etc. —so that the term, by conjuring up "body" in one way or another, is part of the body's reverberation in consciousness: the word "instinct" tends to imply "body.")

I follow Jung (*CW* 8, §§371 f., 397 f., 270 f.) in placing instinct on a continuum with archetypal imagery, that is, in connecting the archetypal persons of the imaginal with bodily experience and the idea of physical necessity. The unbroken continuum between instinct and archetype suggests both an inescapable determinism and an unbounded freedom in the body-imaginal relationship: our fantasies are limited by body and our bodies freed by fantasy—and also vice versa.

I further follow Jung in referring to the activities of both reflection and religion (sometimes called in Jung "spirit," "self," and "creativity") as instincts (*CW* 8, §241 f. and my *MA*, pp. 31–40). By this move Jung keeps all so-called higher or sublimated psychic events in immediate connection with so-called lower or animal psychic events. To hold that the mental life of reflection and the spiritual life of religion are instincts means to recognize that we are as compulsively driven in mind and spirit as we are in hunger and rage. Jung's discussion of the instinct to reflect (*CW* 8, §241–43), which he considers determines the richness and essential character of the psyche, has a clear parallel in Konrad Lorenz' description of "flight" reactions in animals. Reflection means bending back from the perceptual stimulus in favor of a psychic image, a "turning inward." By maintaining that mind and spirit are aspects of instinctual nature, we see them being as basic to psychological life as so-called more organic, physical urges —as enmeshed with physiology and as subject to pathologizings as any other patterns of instinct.

We may leave open the classical questions regarding instinct, such as the number of the instincts, their relation to one another, their relation to physiological homeostatic needs, their phylogeny and inheritance, their survival value, their susceptibility to learning. From the viewpoint of archetypal psychology these classical questions require hermeneutical reflection in terms of what they mean to the psyche before they are answered on their own level.

Despite psychology's dissatisfaction with the concept, mainly because it is supposed to imply vitalism and holism, it is less awkward to maintain "instinct" than to abandon it. For with what shall we fill its place? Especially, what other word so well represents the "psyche of the body" in common speech and psychotherapy? "Instinct" represents the problematic animal body in conceptual language, and the debates over it represent the struggles with the animal body. To the degree that we view instinct mechanistically, to that same degree we are Cartesian, splitting consciousness from body and regarding the animal as a machine. Adolf Portmann's emphasis on the noncompulsive nature of instinct (in distinction to Lorenz and the more mechanistic and deterministic animal behaviorists) reflects a consciousness in which body is offered a freer perspective. Finally, to deny "instinct" is to refuse as well a grand tract of psychology's history by means of which we can examine the variations in the psyche's reflection upon its body. For some of this history see S. Diamond, "Gestation of the Instinct Concept," *J. Hist. Behav. Sci.,* VII, no. 4 (1971):323–36.

2. For an elaboration of ideas as perspectives, see J. Ortega y Gasset, *Meditations on Quixote,* trans. E. Rugg and D. Marín (New York: Norton, 1963), pp. 40, 44, 90, and his editor J. Marías' long note, pp. 170 ff.: cf. FN, *The Genealogy of Morals,* pt. 3, §12.

3. Paul Friedländer, *Plato,* 3 vols., trans. H. Meyerhoff, Bollingen Series (New York and Princeton, N.J.: Pantheon and Princeton Univ. Press, 1958–69) 1:16.

4. For a brilliantly convincing appreciation of the role of vision (idea, mental set, perceptual structures) in the observation of data—from which my example of the sunrise is taken—see N. R. Hanson, *Patterns of Discovery: An Inquiry into the Conceptual Foundations of Science* (Cambridge, Eng.: Univ. Press, 1958; paperback, 1969),

chaps. 1 and 2, and his *Perception and Discovery,* ed. W. C. Humphreys (San Francisco: Freeman, Cooper, 1969).

5. Cf. Friedländer, *Plato,* 1:13 f. and notes for a discussion of the "eye of the soul." The metaphor has analogies with "the imagination of the heart" (see above, chap. 1, p. 22). These two expressions for a psychic mode of perception condense in a phrase of Pindar, "blind heart," and in a phrase from the Sophist Gorgias "the eyes of the imagination" (Friedländer, p. 13). Cf. *Iliad* XXI, 61, which LS translate as "to see in his mind's eye," and R. Lattimore as "I may know inside my heart."

6. The desire for clarity in no way implies arid intellectualism or a return to the Cartesian separations that make an opposition between clear distinctions and soul. Intellectual clarity can be in service of soul, not a disturbance of it, unless the soul's fantasy of itself is dominated by a vaporous wood nymph or other twilight nature-virgins still shy of exposure to daylight. Only when clarity takes itself with Apollonic literalism—worshiping itself as Helios, brilliance as God, requiring distant superiority, a killing detachment, and a purified formalism—must it pit itself against Luna, necessitating a defensive mooniness of psychic fluctuations, indefiniteness, and fantasy images. *There is no necessary opposition between clarity and imagination,* no need to believe with Coleridge that deep ideas must be dim, while clearness is founded on shallowness, or with Niels Bohr that there is "a complementarity between the clarity and the rightness of a statement, so much so that a statement which is too clear always contains something false." Quoted (as a questionable apology for Jung) by A. Jaffé, *The Myth of Meaning,* trans. R. F. C. Hull (London: Hodder, 1970), p. 28. The implication is that to be true to psyche or to nature we must be obscure. This not only opens the door to obscurantism; it neglects the desire of soul for spirit, for a concrete and poetic precision about its imagery and emotion, which in no way requires reductions or limitations to singleness of meaning.

7. Cf. W. K. C. Guthrie, *In the Beginning: Some Early Greek Views on the Origins of Life and the Early State of Man* (London: Methuen, 1957), pp. 29–45. For the mother's perspective on the origins of consciousness see the work of Erich Neumann, especially his *The Origins and History of Consciousness* (London: Routledge & Kegan Paul, 1954). The best discussions that I know of the organicism viewpoint are: Owen Barfield, *What Coleridge Thought* (Middletown, Conn.: Wesleyan Univ. Press, 1972), in the chapter "Life," and M. H. Abrams, *The Mirror and the Lamp* (1953) (New York: Oxford Univ. Press, 1971). Both relate organicism to Romanticism, in which a favorite image is the *tree;* by means of the tree idea many of the great mother's perspectives can be represented. One could look at the Romantic philosophies of organicism afresh from the viewpoint of archetypal psychology in order to examine more precisely the person of the great mother in ideas such as: the seeds of individuating genius in the soul-soil of the unconscious, the reverence toward nature and natural unfolding, the indiscriminate enthusiasm for wholeness and growth, the interest in botany, the appreciation of children.

7a. M. A. Murray, *The Genesis of Religion* (London: Routledge, 1963).

8. For a discussion of the vessel imagery, see I. M. Linforth, "Soul and Sieve in Plato's Gorgias," *Univ. Calif. Publ. Classical Phil.,* XII (1944):295–313.

9. The term "root metaphor" was first elaborated by S. C. Pepper, "The Root Metaphor Theory of Metaphysics," *J. Philos.* 32, no. 14:365 ff., and expanded in his *World Hypotheses* (Berkeley, Calif.: Univ. of California Press, 1942; 5th ed. paperback, 1966). The "root metaphor" idea is itself a metaphor, relying on one of the archetypal themes of the imagination: that of *roots.* In the language of Gaston Bachelard, it belongs to the imagination of the element earth, so that when we can discover a root metaphor we gain the conviction that we have come upon an idea that is basic, grounded, solid, and supportive.

10. J. Hillman, "Abandoning the Child," *Eranos 40–1971* (Leiden, Brill).

11. *MA,* pt. 3.

12. Guthrie, *In the Beginning,* chap. 5.

13. Cf. Murray Stein, "Hephaistos: A Pattern of Introversion," *Spring 1973* (New York/Zürich, Spring Publ.), pp. 35–51; David L. Miller, *The New Polytheism* (New York: Harper & Row, 1974); F. K. Mayr, "Der Gott Hermes und Hermeneutik," *Tijdschrift v. Filosofie* 30 (1968):535–625; also my attempts in "An Essay on Pan," "Senex and Puer," and "Dionysus in Jung's Writings," *Spring 1972,* pp. 191–205.

14. *CW* 13, §378.

15. Although Ficino elaborated the relation between Saturn and philosophy in the fifteenth century, and Burton gave special attention to the melancholy of scholarly men in the seventeenth, the idea appears far earlier in a work attributed to Aristotle (*Problemata,* XXX, 1) where Empedocles, Socrates, and Plato are considered to be melancholics; cf. R. Klibansky, E. Panofsky, and F. Saxl, *Saturn and Melancholy* (London: Nelson, 1964), pp. 17 ff. From Plato we can derive a similar notion, but which places philosophy under another God. In *Philebus* 30c-d "wisdom and reason" are attributed to Zeus and in *Phaedrus* 252c-e the "followers of Zeus" choose their lovers and perform as lovers in accordance with their disposition, given by the Zeus principle of "wisdom." Philosophers (lovers of wisdom) are evidently "followers" (or "children" as later ages phrased it) of Zeus. Philosophy's claims to wisdom and to superiority over all other sciences, its imagery of penetrating vision and comprehensive mastery over the phenomenal world and of long-lasting systematic solidity (the eagle and the oak), its compulsion toward all-embracing coherence that would unify, its judicious balance among diverse positions, the apodictic tone of its voice and thundering anathema of its judgments, the literal importance it gives to abstractions of principle, law, and axiom, as well, finally, as its fecund effects on so many areas of existence (the many fertilizations and many offspring of Zeus) are inherent in the psychic premises of philosophy if we read them through the person of Zeus. For Saturn, besides *Saturn and Melancholy,* see my "On Senex Consciousness," *Spring 1970,* pp. 146–65.

16. Herbert Marcuse, "The Affirmative Character of Culture" (on the soul as a bourgeois refuge) in his *Negations,* trans. J. J. Shapiro (Boston: Beacon, 1968).

17. A defense of the essentialist or "what" tradition appears as a note by P. Merlan in his *From Platonism to Neoplatonism* (The Hague: Nijhoff, 1953), p. 7. E. Cassirer in his *The Logic of the Humanities,* trans. C. S. Howe (New Haven: Yale Univ. Press, 1961), pp. 159 ff., discusses "what" and "whence" (and "why") as a difference—even opposition—between the concept of form and the concept of cause. He likes "what"; Karl Popper does not, cf. his *The Poverty of Historicism* (London: Routledge, 1969), p. 29, and *Conjectures and Refutations,* 3d ed. (London: Routledge, 1969), pp. 104 ff. R. B. Braithwaite, in accordance with the title of his book *Scientific Explanation* (1953) (New York: Harper Torchbook, 1960), does not even take up the "what" question.

18. H. W. Parke, *Greek Oracles* (London: Hutchinson, 1967), p. 87; *The Oracles of Zeus* (Oxford: Blackwell, 1967), p. 111.

19. W. F. Otto, *The Homeric Gods,* trans. M. Hadas (New York: Pantheon, 1954), p. 195. Cf. A. Cook, chap. 6, "Theos" in his *Enactment: Greek Tragedy* (Chicago: Swallow Press, 1971), p. 119: "The action in many plays starts from some special situation of a god—as do, for example, the *Prometheus,* the *Hippolytus,* the *Ajax,* and the *Trojan Women*—or from special divine utterance, an oracle." Homer, the tragedians, and Plato too, show that knowledge of events means knowledge of the universals in the events, i.e., knowledge of the Gods. Plato's works could be examined for the Gods in the dialogue—for instance, the *Phaedo* is dominated by Apollo; the *Phaedrus,* set on a grassy river bank, evokes nymphs at the beginning and Pan at the end; the *Symposium,* a drinking party, has for its denouement the Dionysian entry of Alcibiades to flute music and the simile between Socrates and Silenos; Athene and Zeus, both by their more numerous mention and by the style and concern of the dialogue, seem to govern especially the *Laws* (cf. XI, 921c).

20. Owen Barfield, *Saving the Appearances: A Study in Idolatry* (New York: Harbinger, n.d.), p. 162.

21. Norman O. Brown, a response to Herbert Marcuse in his *Negations* (London: Allen Lane, 1968), p. 244.

22. Ludwig Wittgenstein, "Remarks about Frazer's *The Golden Bough*," trans. E. Strauss, K. Ketner, and B. Ketner, from *Synthese* 17, (1967):233–53. (English translation circulated privately.)

23. Owen Barfield, "The Meaning of the Word 'Literal,' " in *Metaphor and Symbol*, L. C. Knights and B. Cottle, eds. (London: Butterworth, 1960), p. 55.

24. For the interdependence of the metaphorical and the literal, see Patricia Berry, "On Reduction," *Spring 1973*, pp. 67–84. This interdependence is further borne out by an observation regarding primitive language. Where the literal meaning of words in our modern sense is absent, so too is the metaphorical. ". . . Statements made by primitive people cannot really be said to be of the one sort or of the other. They lie between these [literal and metaphorical] categories of ours. They do not properly fit." G. Lienhardt, "Modes of Thought" in *The Institutions of Primitive Society* (Oxford: Blackwell, 1959), p. 99. Perhaps the sharp division between literal and metaphorical in our culture is a manifestation of monotheistic consciousness, where something must be wholly "of the one sort or of the other." Perhaps polytheistic thinking has polysignificance throughout its understanding.

25. Hans Vaihinger, *The Philosophy of 'As If,'* 2d ed., trans. C. K. Ogden (London: Routledge, 1935), p. 269.

26. Ibid., p. 89.

27. Ibid., p. 90.

28. Ibid., p. 98.

29. Ibid., p. 12.

30. Ibid., pp. 88, 89, 99, 265 f.

31. Braithwaite, *Scientific Explanation*, p. 93.

32. Max Black, *Models and Metaphors* (Ithaca, N.Y.: Cornell Univ. Press, 1962), p. 228.

33. Barfield, *Saving the Appearances*, p. 24, employs the term "figuration" because it is new, neutral, and free of presuppositions. It is unburdened by the theoretical positions of configurational (gestalt) psychology. I prefer "constellation" because its meaning suggests the presence of archetypal fantasy. In an astronomical constellation of the stars our eyes see only bright points, while our mind imagines their relations into a personified pattern. Whenever we use the word "constellation" there is implied the dark spaces of the infinitely unknown which are filled by fantasy, thereby receiving a precisely particular pattern.

34. Paul Ricoeur, *Freud and Philosophy* (the Terry Lectures), trans. D. Savage (New Haven: Yale Univ. Press, 1970), p. 18.

35. Popper, *Conjectures and Refutations*, p. 279.

36. T. Taylor, "An Apology for the Fables of Homer" (1804), translation of Proclus' essay on the fables of Homer, found in *Thomas Taylor, the Platonist*, K. Raine and G. M. Harper, eds., Bollingen Series (Princeton, N.J.: Princeton Univ. Press, 1969), p. 460.

37. From Cassirer, *The Individual and Cosmos in Renaissance Philosophy*, trans. M. Domandi (Philadelphia: Univ. of Pennsylvania Press, 1972), p. 69 (where the Latin passage of Cusanus [*Excitat*. V. fol. 488] is given).

38. Cf. Popper, *Conjectures and Refutations*, pp. 21–23.

39. Cf. M. Ficino, *Commentary on Plato's Symposium*, VI, 6, and the notes and translation by S. R. Jayne, *Marsilio Ficino's Commentary on Plato's Symposium* (Columbia, Mo.: Univ. of Missouri Press, 1944), p. 189.

40. Cassirer, *Logic of the Humanities*, p. 94.

41. Cf. Sallustius, *Concerning the Gods and the Universe*, A. D. Nock, ed. and trans.

(1926) (Hildesheim: Olms, 1966), p. 9: "All this did not happen at any one time but always is so."

42. K. O. Müller, *Introduction to a Scientific System of Mythology*, trans. J. Leitch (London: Longman, Brown, Green, & Longmans 1844), p. 44. For opinions against this perspective, by eighteenth-century critics who would banish the marvelous and the mythic from poetry so that it should conform truthfully to modern theory of mechanical nature, see "Truth and the Poetic Marvelous" in Abrams, *Mirror and Lamp*.

43. H. Broch, Introduction to R. Bespaloff, *On the Iliad*, trans. M. McCarthy (New York: Pantheon, 1947), p. 15.

44. Aniela Jaffé, "The Creative Phases in Jung's Life," *Spring 1972*, pp. 179, 188.

45. L. Wittgenstein, *Lectures and Conversations on Aesthetics, Psychology and Religious Belief*, ed. C. Barrett (Oxford: Blackwell, 1970), pp. 43, 51; on psychoanalysis, Wittgenstein says (p. 52): ". . . One must have a very strong and keen and persistent criticism in order to recognize and *see through* the mythology that is offered or imposed on one. There is an inducement to say 'Yes, of course, it must be like that.' A powerful mythology." (Italics mine.) I would have preferred to have Wittgenstein say: "to recognize and see through *to* the mythology." But Wittgenstein uses "mythology" rather in an implied contraposition to "scientific explanation."

46. Cf. my "Abandoning the Child" and—concerning Freud and the analysis of children—*MA*, p. 242.

47. Cf. K. Kerényi, *Die Eröffnung des Zugangs zum Mythos* (Darmstadt: Wissenschaftliche Buchgesellschaft, 1967), pp. 234–35.

48. Cf. P. Wheelwright's discussion of concrete universality in *The Burning Fountain* (Bloomington, Ind.: Indiana Univ. Press, 1968), pp. 52–54.

49. Vico, *New Science*, §404, p. 129.

50. *CW* 9, 1, §265; also §143; *CW* 10, §681.

51. *CW* 9, 1, §80.

52. Friedländer, *Plato*, 1:189.

53. Ibid. (from the *Meno* 86b and the *Phaedo* 114d).

54. J. Fontenrose, *The Ritual Theory of Myth* (Berkeley: Univ. of California Press, 1971), p. 55.

55. E. Wind, *Pagan Mysteries of the Renaissance* (Harmondsworth, Eng.: Penguin, 1967), pp. 199–209.

56. P. Ziff, *Semantic Analysis* (Ithaca, N.Y.: Cornell Univ. Press, 1960), chap. 1. Cf. "Metaphor" in *The Encyclopedia of Philosophy* (New York: Macmillan, 1967), 5: 288–89, with bibliography; *OED*; also, Black, *Models and Metaphors*, pp. 25–47; and Wheelwright, *Burning Fountain*, pp. 84–88 on "indirection" and "soft focus."

57. F. M. Cornford, *Plato's Cosmology* (London: Routledge, 1966), p. 164.

58. Ibid., pp. 165–66, 176.

59. Friedländer, *Plato*, 3:382.

60. Vaihinger, *As If*, p. 94.

61. Popper, *Poverty of Historicism*, p. 87.

62. M. Dufrenne, *The Notion of the A Priori*, trans. E. S. Casey (Evanston, Ill.: Northwestern Univ. Press, 1966), p. 238.

63. For a discussion of what Parmenides meant by "much erring" see Popper, *Conjectures and Refutations*, pp. 408–11.

64. James J. Y. Liu, *The Chinese Knight-Errant* (London: Routledge, 1967), p. 4.

65. Ficino, *Theologia platonica*, II, cap. 14, 7 as translated by Trinkhaus, *Image and Likeness*, 2:493. On the home of soul in spirit, see Ficino, *Commentary on Plato's Symposium*, VI, 9 and Jayne, *Ficino's Commentary*, p. 196, where it is also said that "the home of spirit is the body."

66. *Lazarillo de Tormes*, trans. T. Roscoe, and *Guzman d'Alfarache or The Spanish Rogue* of Mateo Aleman, trans. J. H. Brady, together in two volumes (London: Nimmo

& Bain, 1881). Cf. H. Heidenreich, ed., *Pikarische Welt* (Darmstadt: Wissenschaftliche Buchgesellschaft, 1969), a collection of chapters, essays, and excerpts on the picaresque rogue-trickster (mainly in Spanish literature) by F. W. Chandler, J. Ortega y Gasset, Leo Spitzer, Américo Castro, C. G. Jung, et al. Comparable picaresque rogue-figures are in the works of Smollett—and in English literature *only* in Smollett, according to R. Giddings, *The Tradition of Smollett* (London: Methuen, 1967), p. 21. But Smollett spent an important time of his life in Cartegena, Spain, lived on the French Riviera, and is buried in Livorno, Italy.

67. This happy phrase, originating in W. R. Inge, *The Philosophy of Plotinus*, 3d ed. (London: Longmans, 1929), 1:203, is taken up by both H. J. Blumenthal, *Plotinus' Psychology* (The Hague: Nijhoff, 1971) and E. Bréhier, *The Philosophy of Plotinus*, trans. J. Thomas (Chicago: Univ. of Chicago Press, 1958), p. 54. For a reading of Plotinus in relation to archetypal psychology, see my "Plotino, Ficino, e Vico, precursori della psicologia Junghiana," *Riv. di psicologia analitica* 4 (1973):341–64.

68. Otto, *Homeric Gods*, p. 122.

69. *The Enneads*, trans. Stephen Mackenna (London: Faber, 1956), II, 2, 2.

70. I have not been able to track down references to "Eros the Carpenter" other than those given by R. Klibansky, E. Panofsky, and F. Saxl, *Saturn and Melancholy* (London: Nelson, 1964), pp. 308–10 and plate 15. (This Eros does have a Christian echo inasmuch as Jesus was a carpenter, and his father, Joseph, was a carpenter whose honored day in the Church is a Wednesday (Mercurius' day).

71. "Bricoleur," according to C. Lévi-Strauss, *The Savage Mind* (London: Weidenfeld & Nicolson, 1966), p. 16, is "always used with references to some extraneous movement: a ball rebounding, a dog straying or a horse swerving from its direct course to avoid an obstacle. And in our own time the 'bricoleur' is still someone who works with his hands and uses devious means compared to those of a craftsman. The characteristic feature of mythical thought is that it expresses itself by means of a heterogeneous repertoire . . . it has nothing else at its disposal. Mythical thought is therefore a kind of intellectual 'bricolage.' . . ."

FOUR / DEHUMANIZING

1. Gilbert Durand, "Similitude hermétique et science de l'homme," *Eranos 42–1973* (Leiden, Brill), expands upon the importance of the nonagnostic approach for a new epistemology.

2. Cf. G. Holton, "The Thematic Imagination in Science," in *Science and Culture* (Boston: Houghton Mifflin, 1965).

3. Polytheistic theology is treated in an exciting new way in David L. Miller's *The New Polytheism* (New York: Harper & Row, 1974).

4. G. G. Coulton, *Medieval Faith and Symbolism* (New York: Harper Torchbook, 1958), p. 251.

5. Mario Praz, *Mnemosyne: The Parallel Between Literature and the Visual Arts*, Bollingen Series (Princeton, N.J.: Princeton Univ. Press, 1970), p. 81. Cf. George Holmes, *The Florentine Enlightenment 1400–50* (New York: Pegasus, 1969), pp. 106–8. For Renaissance attempts at reconciliation, see Charles Trinkaus, *In Our Image and Likeness* (Chicago: Univ. of Chicago Press), pp. 553–774.

6. Although Melanchthon's invention of the term psychology has been contested, no direct evidence for it having been found (F. H. Lapointe, "Who Originated the Term 'Psychology'?" *J. Hist. Behav. Sci.* 8 [1972]:328–35, and my note *MA*, p. 127), I believe that the "psychology-begins-with-Melanchthon" fantasy is valid. It tells us in what person—personification—and to what historical and geographical condition of the psyche the word and its work belong, and in what style of consciousness psychology has its source. By declaring Melanchthon its father, psychology states that it is a child of the Reformation.

7. Melanchthon reintroduced the Aristotelian rationalistic and naturalistic psychology of the previous centuries, but he gave it a new moral emphasis. He divided the philosophical disciplines into three branches: *artes dicendi* (rhetoric and dialectic), *physiologia* (physics, psychology, and mathematics), and *praecepta de civilibus moribus* (ethics); cf. J. Rump, *Melanchthons Psychologie,* (Kiel: Marquardsen, 1897), pp. 3 f. This system went a long way to achieving Melanchthon's great aim, the "moral education of Germany through an idealistic approach to human events." (W. Dilthey, "Weltanschauung und Analyse des Menschen seit Renaissance und Reformation," *Gesammelte Schriften,* [Stuttgart: Teubner, 1969], II, 163). With psychology grouped along with physics and mathematics, the way was open for later German achievements in physical psychology. With the art of memory removed from the realm of rhetoric, learning became simply learning by rote without imagery or significances. The way was open for an intellect without imagination, for nomina without personae, for concepts without configurations, and for classifications without inherent sense. Psychology in one stroke became deprived of imagination—scientistic, and yoked to an overall moralistic aim.

8. S. T. Coleridge, *The Friend:* "Distinct notions do not suppose different things. When I make a threefold distinction in human nature, I am fully aware that it is a distinction, not a division. . . ." (quoted in Owen Barfield, *What Coleridge Thought* [Middletown, Conn.: Wesleyan Univ. Press, 1972], p. 19). The thought is Neoplatonic, implied in Plotinus (*The Enneads,* trans. Stephen Mackenna [London: Faber, 1956] IV, 3, 2) and stated by W. R. Inge, *The Philosophy of Plotinus,* 3d ed. (London: Longmans, 1929), 1:214: "But in the spiritual world there is distinction without division." The archetypes too must be considered in this manner: distinct but not separated from one another.

9. I am referring here to Aristotle's four causes—Formal, Final, Efficient, and Material—and suggesting that the first two are particularly relevant for conceiving the role of the archetypes.

10. I use "importance" here and throughout following A. N. Whitehead, *Modes of Thought* (1938) (New York: Putnam Capricorn, 1958), pp. 1–17, who presents it as a fundamental irreducible notion, involved with feeling and emotion and crucial to our attention and perspectives, our values and interests. The term "existential assurance" in regard to the value of emotion is from Gabriel Marcel; cf. J. B. O'Malley, *The Fellowship of Being: An Essay on the Concept of Person in the Philosophy of Gabriel Marcel* (The Hague: Nijhoff, 1966), p. 81.

11. For many of these theories of emotion and the root metaphors at the base of their fantasies, cf. my *Emotion: A Comprehensive Phenomenology of Theories and their Meanings for Therapy* (Evanston, Ill.: Northwestern Univ. Press, 1961).

12. The term "divine influx" comes from Swedenborg; cf. K. Raine, *Blake and Tradition,* Bollingen Series (Princeton, N.J.: Princeton Univ. Press, 1968), 1:4–6; 2: 214–16. William James also wrote of emotions as gifts of the spirit in *The Varieties of Religious Experience* (London: Longmans, 1906), pp. 150–51.

13. G. Allport, *Becoming,* the Terry Lectures (1955) (New Haven: Yale Univ. Press, 1971), p. 61: "*Proprium* is a term intended to cover those functions that make for the *peculiar unity and distinctiveness of personality,* and at the same time seem to the knowing function to be subjectively intimate and important." That the proprium can be lost in depersonalization (see above, pp. 70f) indicates that it is not altogether human property and does indeed depend on something very much like the homunculus which Allport in the same paragraph derides. Feelings of subjectivity, importance, and intimacy refer to soul (which Allport avoids or refuses [p. 55]) or, as we have called it, anima. Unfortunate—these circumlocutions like proprium for making soul academically respectable, so that psychology departments can go on having a "psychology without a soul" (cf. Allport [p. 36] referring to Wundt)!

14. Raine, *Blake and Tradition,* 2:229.

15. G. W. F. Hegel, *Philosophy of Mind*, trans. A. V. Miller (Oxford: Clarendon Press, 1971), together with the *Zuzätze* in Boumann's text (1845), pp. 73–74. For a thorough resumé of Hegel's "feeling soul" and its relation with thinking, see Murray Greene, *Hegel on the Soul* (The Hague: Nijhoff, 1972), pp. 103–42.

16. The opposition in modern times between thinking and feeling begins with Moses Mendelssohn (1755). For a discussion of the history of feeling in psychology see H. M. Gardiner, R. C. Metcalf, and J. G. Beebe-Center, *Feeling and Emotion: A History of Theories* (New York: American Book Co., 1937); and on the conservative aspect of feeling, my "The Feeling Function" in *Lectures on Jung's Typology*, with M.-L. von Franz (New York/Zürich: Spring Publ., 1971), especially pp. 114, 125, 142–43.

17. FN, *The Dawn of Day*, §35.

18. Cf. E. Jones, *The Life and Work of Sigmund Freud* (London: Hogarth, 1953), 1:273.

19. Cf. R. B. Onians, *The Origins of European Thought* (Cambridge, Eng.: Univ. Press, 1954), pp. 472–76.

20. Cf. *MA*, p. 56, for references to the literature on the tale of Amor and Psyche in Apuleius' Roman novel, *The Golden Ass.*

21. N. O. Brown, *Life Against Death* (New York: Random House, n.d.), p. 102, referring to Hegel.

22. Raine, *Blake and Tradition*, vol. 2, chap. 24, "Jesus the Imagination."

23. J.-P. Sartre, "Existentialism Is a Humanism" in *Existentialism from Dostoevsky to Sartre*, W. Kaufmann, ed. (New York: Meridian, 1956), pp. 290–91.

24. E. R. Dodds, "The Religion of the Ordinary Man in Classical Greece," in his *The Ancient Concept of Progress* (Oxford: Clarendon Press, 1973), p. 140.

25. C. Lévi-Strauss, quoted in Octavio Paz, *Alternating Current* (New York: Viking, 1973), p. 156.

26. C. Hartshorne, *Beyond Humanism* (1937) (Lincoln, Nebr.: Univ. of Nebraska Press, 1968), p. 132. Hartshorne notes both the narrowing exclusiveness of humanistic thought, because it rationalizes its own narrowness, and its romantic exaggeration of the goodness of man to the neglect of evil. This romanticism we have already discussed under the humanistic approach to pathologizing.

27. M. Untersteiner, *The Sophists*, trans. K. Freeman (Oxford: Blackwell, 1954), p. 58.

28. J.-P. Sartre, *Existentialism and Humanism*, trans. P. Mairet (London: Methuen, 1948), p. 56.

29. K. Kerényi, "Humanismus und Hellenismus" in his *Apollon* (Dusseldorf: Diederichs, 1953), p. 242.

30. Bruno Snell, *The Discovery of the Mind*, trans. T. G. Rosenmeyer (New York: Harper Torchbook, 1960), p. 246.

31. Cf. W. F. Otto, *The Homeric Gods*, trans. M. Hadas (New York: Pantheon, 1954), pp. 231–60.

32. LS, p. 669; cf. *Phaedrus* 252C, *Laws*, 740B.

33. R. D. Laing, *The Politics of Experience* (Harmondsworth, Eng.: Penguin, 1967), p. 46.

34. Ibid., p. 50.

35. Dodds, "Religion of the Ordinary Man," *Ancient Concept of Progress*, p. 140.

36. Otto, *The Homeric Gods*, pp. 236–38.

37. Although no such text (that I know of) exists, we may remember that all books on the Renaissance can be *read* psychologically even if not written as psychology books. The works I have found to have the most value for psychologizing the Renaissance are mentioned in the notes that follow. Truly *psychological* reading is less concerned with a rational doctrine of soul than with the errant course of psychological imagining and insighting. Therefore most fundamental are works dealing with the polytheistic imagi-

nation, the archetypal psychology of the Renaissance: J. Seznec's *Survival of the Pagan Gods*, trans. B. F. Sessions (New York: Harper Torchbook, 1961); the writings of Frances Yates, Erwin Panofsky, Edgar Wind, Ernst Cassirer, D. P. Walker, and also D. C. Allen.

38. For the indispensable background to the "Renaissance controversy" see W. K. Ferguson, *The Renaissance in Historical Thought* (Cambridge, Mass.: Houghton Mifflin, Riverside Press, 1948); also his "The Reinterpretation of the Renaissance" in *Facets of the Renaissance*, W. H. Werkmeister, ed. (New York: Harper Torchbook, 1963), pp. 1–18; Erwin Panofsky, " 'Renaissance'—Self-Definition or Self-Deception?" in his *Renaissance and Renascences in Western Art* (New York: Harper Torchbook, 1969), pp. 1–41; F. Chabod, "The Concept of the Renaissance" and the concise, masterly analytic Bibliography in his *Machiavelli and the Renaissance*, trans. D. Moore (New York: Harper Torchbook, 1965); J. Trier, "Zur Vorgeschichte des Renaissance-Begriffes," *Archiv f. Kulturgeschichte*, 33 (1950):45–63 (useful for tracing the word back into its botanical context in the classical Latin of ancient Rome).

39. Cf. K. Burdach, *Sinn und Ursprung der Wörte Renaissance und Reformation* (Berlin: Paetel, 1918), p. 17, on the Renaissance as a rebirth "fantasy." Unfortunately Burdach had to find literal evidence, narrowing his insight upon St. Francis and the Christian spiritual *renovatio*. Cf. Jung's paper "Concerning Rebirth," (*CW* 9, 1, §§199–258) for more familiarity with the psychological attitudes inevitably occasioned by the idea of a renaissance.

40. The edition I have used of Jacob Burckhardt's irreplaceable and splendidly readable work is the fat seventh, with Geiger's notes, translated by S. G. C. Middlemore: *The Civilisation of the Renaissance in Italy* (London: George Allen; New York: Macmillan, 1914). Usually considered the psychological part of Burckhardt's work are parts II and IV (on individuality and on man); but of more importance for archetypal psychology (because less personalistically and consciously psychological) are parts V (on festivals, especially) and VI (on the moral shadow and disintegration).

41. For literature of the word "humanitas," see Chabod's Bibliography, *Machiavelli*, p. 207; E. von Jan, "Humanité," *Zeitschr. f. franz. Sprache u. Lit.* 55 (1932):1–66. The distortions of the word today range from "humane" societies whose main concern is the easy old age of British donkeys and dogs to the rigid Marxist dogmatism of the French newspaper *L'Humanité*. P. O. Kristeller, "The Philosophy of Man in the Italian Renaissance" in his *Studies in Renaissance Thought* (Rome: Storia e Letteratura, 1969), p. 261, writes: ". . . 'Humanism' has become one of those slogans which through their very vagueness carry an almost universal and irresistible appeal. Every person interested in 'human values' or in 'human welfare' is nowadays called a 'humanist' . . . the humanism of the Renaissance was something quite different from present-day humanism. To be sure, Renaissance humanists were also interested in human values, but this was incidental to their major concern, which was the study and imitation of classical, Greek and Latin literature." Further (p. 264), "Humanism originated and developed within the limited area of rhetorical and philological studies."

42. Snell, *Discovery of Mind*, p. 246.

43. "Petrarch tried to show the way in which eloquence or literary discipline and philosophy or care of souls were related." E. Garin, *Italian Humanism*, trans. P. Munz (Oxford: Blackwell, 1965), p. 19.

44. Petrarch's fellowship with men and concern with political diplomacy and society (even though he was a recluse) was, as his confessional *Secretum* shows (trans. W. H. Draper [London: Chatto & Windus, 1911]), the natural consequent of care of soul and not its precondition. He put as much care into his gardening, his collections of texts, his refuges in Vaucluse and Arquà, his writings addressed to the dead authors of antiquity and to the absent Laura, as he used toward the living friends and events of his time. Despite Garin's emphasis upon the civic and "social character of Petrarch's

humaneness" (p. 20), Petrarch was "for his time, uniquely introspective" (E. H. Wilkins, *Life of Petrarch* [Chicago: Univ. of Chicago Press, Phoenix, 1963], p. 259).

45. Garin, *Italian Humanism,* p. 19.

46. Augustine's *Confessions,* X, 8, 15, trans. E. B. Pusey (New York: Dutton Everyman, 1966), pp. 212–13.

47. Cf. P. O. Kristeller, "Augustine and the Early Renaissance," *Studies,* pp. 361–62, where a translation and discussion of the relevant passages from Augustine are given, and "soul" and "self" interpreted to mean "man." Thus Kristeller says (p. 362) that the event on Mont Ventoux refers to the Renaissance "return from nature to man."

48. *Confessions,* X, 8, 15.

49. *Confessions,* X, 8, 12.

50. *Confessions,* X, 8, 14.

51. The term Neoplatonism covers many authors and many ideas in many centuries (cf. A. H. Armstrong, "Later Platonism and Its Influence," in R. R. Bolgar, ed., *Classical Influences on European Culture* [Cambridge, Eng.: Univ. Press, 1971], pp. 197–201). Nonetheless there are certain main and continuing psychological strands deriving principally from Plotinus, and these are relevant to archetypal psychology if read in its light. We must recall here that Plotinus has mainly been read through Christian theologians (V. Cilento; Dean Inge; Paul Henry and R. Arnou, both Jesuits; Abbé Trouillard). Therefore the metaphysical and spiritual aspects of Neoplatonism have been emphasized. Whereas psychology sees in Plotinus (and in Ficino) mainly a concern with soul. The *Enneads* opens with psychological questions; "The Problems of the Soul" is its most massive section; it is a psychology book. Some have read Neoplatonism in this light: Philip Merlan, *Monopsychism, Mysticism, Metaconsciousness* (The Hague: Nijhoff, 1963), pp. 55 ff.; E. R. Dodds, "Tradition and Personal Achievement in the Philosophy of Plotinus," in his *Ancient Concept of Progress;* Dodds' contributions and also H.-R. Schwyzer's, to *Les Sources de Plotin,* Fondation Hardt V (Geneva: Vandoeuvres, 1960); H. J. Blumenthal, *Plotinus' Psychology* (The Hague: Nijhoff, 1971). Of general value for Renaissance Neoplatonism are Nesca A. Robb, *Neoplatonism of the Italian Renaissance* (London: Allen & Unwin, 1935) and Edgar Wind, *Pagan Mysteries of the Renaissance* (Harmondsworth, Eng.: Penguin, 1967).

Neoplatonism, by the way, does not belong only to specialist scholars. It is alive, if lonely, not only in archetypal psychology, but mainly through the intellectual competence and vigor of J. N. Findlay, who says ("Towards a Neo-Neo-Platonism" in his *Ascent to the Absolute* [London: Allen & Unwin, 1970], p. 249): "And I shall be prejudiced, even to the extent of using abusive metaphors, since the best way to bring home the sense and worth of Platonism and Neoplatonism is to pit it against such inadequate types of thought as Aristotelian individualism, Germanic subjectivism, Semitic-Protestant theology, let alone extreme empiricism and certain forms of atomistic analysis."

52. Kristeller, *The Philosophy of Marsilio Ficino,* trans. V. Conant (New York: Columbia. Univ. Press, 1943; Gloucester, Mass.: Peter Smith, 1964), p. 203.

53. E. Garin, *Portraits from the Quattrocento,* trans. V. A. and E. Velen (New York: Harper & Row, 1972), p. 152: "Ficino loved to express himself in figurative terms, through images and myths, precisely because his philosophy is not abstract reasoning or physical science. . . ." Many of these images are to be found in Wind, *Pagan Mysteries* and in E. H. Gombrich, "Icones Symbolicae: The Visual Images in Neo-Platonic Thought," *J. Warburg Courtauld Inst.* 2 (1948).

54. Cf. Holmes, *Florentine Enlightenment,* p. 106.

55. Cf. E. W. Warren, "Consciousness in Plotinus," *Phronesis* 9 (1964), pp. 88 to end, and his "Imagination in Plotinus," *Classical Quarterly,* n.s. XVI, no. 2 (1966): 277–79. Ficino did not rank imagination as high as did Plotinus. Other basic divergences between Ficinian Neoplatonism and archetypal psychology concern Ficino's emphasis upon light, hierarchy, and love. His was a more spiritual psychology, a height

rather than a depth psychology; for him the downward direction was into darkness. Archetypal psychology recognizes the validity of *all* fantasy, not only of the "higher" sort, and gives to pathologizing a fundamental rather than an accidental role. In Ficino's own life it was also not accidental.

56. The passage (from the letter to Vettori, December 10, 1513) is given in G. Prezzolini, *Machiavelli,* trans. G. Savini (New York: Noonday, 1967), p. 162.

57. Cf. Roberto Weiss, *The Renaissance Discovery of Classical Antiquity* (Oxford: Blackwell, 1969), who shows the curious mixture of historical interest and neglect, of antiquarian care for detail together with fabrication and speculation. See further Peter Burke, *The Renaissance Sense of the Past* (London: Arnold, 1969). On the role of actual Greece in the Renaissance, see above, the *Excursion on the Return to Greece.*

58. The question of the Hermetic texts and the Renaissance belief in their antiquity is discussed by F. A. Yates, *Giordano Bruno and the Hermetic Tradition* (London: Routledge, 1964), pp. 1–16 and by D. P. Walker, *The Ancient Theology* (Ithaca, N.Y.: Cornell Univ. Press, 1972), pp. 1–21.

59. There are only two modern standard works on Ficino: P. O. Kristeller, *The Philosophy of Marsilio Ficino,* trans. V. Conant (New York: Columbia Univ. Press, 1943; Gloucester, Mass.: Peter Smith, 1964) and R. Marcel, *Marsile Ficin* (Paris: Belles Lettres, 1958). Additional papers on Ficino have been published by Kristeller in his *Studies,* and long passages from Ficino's works may be found in English in Trinkaus, *Image and Likeness;* in D. P. Walker, *Spiritual and Demonic Magic from Ficino to Campanella* (London: Warburg Inst., 1958); and in E. Cassirer et al., eds., *The Renaissance Philosophy of Man* (Chicago: Phoenix, 1958). For a complete English translation see S. R. Jayne, *Marsilio's Commentary on Plato's Symposium,* text and translation (Columbia, Mo.: Univ. of Missouri Press, 1944) and R. Marcel's Latin/French *en face* edition, *Theologie platonicienne de l'immortalité des âmes,* 3 vols. (Paris: Belles Lettres, 1964–70). I have drawn further inferences for psychology from Ficino's thought in my "Plotino, Ficino, e Vico precursori della psicologia Junghiana," *Riv. di psicologia analitica* 4 (1973):341–64.

60. Kristeller, *Studies,* p. 266.

61. Ibid., p. 268, where the Latin passage is given. See also Kristeller's discussion of the man-soul relationship in his *Marsilio Ficino,* pp. 328 f. The principal place in Ficino where the idea occurs that man's dignity derives from the soul is *Theologia Platonica* XIII and XIV.

62. Garin, *Quattrocento,* p. 151. When "body" is disparaged in Ficino in order to affirm soul, it can be psychologized to mean the empirical, literal, physical *perspective,* particularly the perspective of practical action which had less significance in Ficino's scheme of things than did Venus and the voluptuousness. (Cf. Wind, *Pagan Mysteries,* pp. 49 ff., 55, 68 ff.) The opposition is less between soul and fleshly sensual joy—for voluptuousness in Ficino was a model for spiritual delight—than between interiority and outwardness, or what we have called the metaphorical and the literal perspectives.

63. Ibid., p. 153. It is this Ficinian notion of *seeing* which influenced Michelangelo. Cf. R. J. Clements, *Michelangelo's Theory of Art* (New York: New York Univ. Press, 1961), pp. 3–13.

64. Trinkaus, *Image and Likeness,* 2:470. Also Kristeller, *Marsilio Ficino,* p. 357.

65. Trinkaus, *Image and Likeness,* p. 471. Cf. Kristeller's chapter "Internal Experience," in his *Marsilio Ficino.*

66. E. Panofsky, *Renaissance and Renascences,* p. 183.

67. R. H. Bainton, "Man, God, and the Church in the Age of the Renaissance," in W. K. Ferguson et al., *Renaissance: Six Essays* (New York: Harper Torchbook, 1962), p. 87, observes the dangers for traditional Christian theology of Neoplatonic immanentism—the psychological view of God or God in the soul. Similar charges are brought today against Jung's psychology.

68. Only after Ficino's death (1499) did Florentine philosophical psychology capture

Rome. At the Lateran Council of 1513 the Roman Catholic Church promulgated the dogma of the soul's immortality. This dogma, one of the essential fantasies of Renaissance Neoplatonism and subject of Ficino's main writing, by granting the soul eternality affirms the psyche as the equivalent of a God. It is the apotheosis of soul, from human to divine.

69. Garin, *Quattrocento,* p. 156.

70. Panofsky twice compares the impact of Neoplatonism with the psychoanalytic movement, cf. *Renaissance and Renascences,* p. 187, and his "Artist, Scientist, Genius: Notes on the 'Renaissance Dämmerung' " in Ferguson et al., *Renaissance: Six Essays,* p. 129.

71. Marcel, *Marsile Ficin,* p. 161 (Ficino, Preface to his *de Triplici Vita*).

71a. From Jayne, *Marsilio's Commentary,* pp. 16–19.

72. Ficino's treatment of the soul is discussed, with relevant references, by Miss Yates in her *Giordano Bruno and the Hermetic Tradition* (London: Routledge, 1964), pp. 62–83.

73. Cf. A. B. Giamatti, "Proteus Unbound: Some Versions of the Sea God in the Renaissance" in P. Demetz, T. Greene, L. Nelson, eds., *The Disciplines of Criticism* (New Haven: Yale Univ. Press, 1968), pp. 437–75. Cf. *CW* 9, 2, §§338–39 on Proteus; *CW* 14, §50 and 13, §218 where he is identified with Mercurius, and §§239–303 on Mercurius. In that essay Jung (§299) considers Mercurius as "the archetype of the unconscious," stating that "instead of deriving these figures from our psychic conditions, [we] must derive our psychic conditions from these figures." Thus the concept of the unconscious is our way today of formulating Proteus-Mercurius. The connotations of this term, "the unconscious," are descriptions of Proteus-Mercurius, and our relation to "the unconscious" presents the ways we now relate to and conceptualize this figure.

74. Pietro Pomponazzi, *On the Immortality of the Soul,* chap. 2, trans. W. H. Hay, in *The Renaissance Philosophy of Man,* E. Cassirer et al., eds. (Chicago: Phoenix Books, 1956), p. 283. Pomponazzi (1462–1525) was not one of the academy of Ficino, yet even he, an Aristotelian and the "last Scholastic" as he has been called, took this polyvalent position. Cassirer pays him special attention, *The Individual and Cosmos in Renaissance Philosophy,* trans. M. Domandi (Philadelphia: Univ. of Pennsylvania Press, 1972), pp. 80–83, 103–09, 136–40.

75. Montaigne, *Apology for Raymond Seybond,* quoted from D. M. Frame, "Montaigne on the Absurdity and Dignity of Man," in Robert Schwoebel, *Renaissance Men and Ideas* (New York: St. Martin's, 1971), p. 132.

76. Some bibliography on, and images of, Fortuna may be found in: Wind, *Pagan Mysteries,* in the index; R. S. Lopez, "Hard Times and Investment in Culture," in Ferguson et al., *The Renaissance: Six Essays,* p. 44; E. H. Gombrich, "Personification," in Bolgar, ed., *Classical Influences,* pp. 255–56; E. E. Lowinsky, "The Goddess Fortuna in Music," *Music Quarterly,* 29, 1943, pp. 45 ff. Montaigne, in the same chapter cited above, considers the soul mistress of fortune because it is able to transform (a protean idea) all incoming events according to its own light. The soul psychologizes, turning to its own use every twist of fate and fortune. The wheel of Fortune expresses radical relativism: each position is as valid as every other. At the same time all positions are transcendent to human will. It provides a comprehensive vision for holding all the archetypal multiplicity in a containing image that allows each its place. When the "pathological gambling" of the Renaissance is placed against the background of this powerful image, obsessive gambling may be seen through to what it offers man, the gambler: a way by means of Fortune to organize one's life in relation with all the possibilities of the cosmos and to discover at any moment just where one is.

77. The change of view regarding the pantheon of many Gods is exemplified by the change of view in regard to the Roman building, the Pantheon, which in the Middle

Ages was considered a demonic building whose extraordinary dome could have been finished only with the help of the Devil. In the Renaissance there was a radical change of attitude (initiated by Petrarch); it was soon (1446) considered Rome's most beautiful building, and Raphael "decided to be buried not in the Vatican, but in the Pantheon." (T. Buddensieg, "Criticism and Praise of the Pantheon in the Middle Ages and the Renaissance," in Bolgar, ed., *Classical Influences*, p. 267.)

78. Quoted by Ferguson, *Renaissance in Historical Thought*, p. 95. Nietzsche made the most of the depraved view of the Renaissance, turning it around the other way in order to use it triumphantly against his enemies: weakness, the Reformation, and Christian morality (pp. 207–8). Huizinga gave the immorality theme a different twist, finding it less a sign of the Nietzschean virility of the new age than a symptom of the waning, decaying Middle Ages (p. 375).

79. Northrop Frye, *Fables of Identity* (New York: Harbinger, 1963), p. 137. The grotesque came to play an important role in art, particularly in the fifteenth century; cf. N. Dacos, *La découverte de la Domus Aurea et la formation des grotesque à la Renaissance* (London/Leiden: Warburg Inst./Brill, 1969). "Grotesque" derives etymologically from *grotto*, referring specifically to the underground ruins of antiquity where, on the walls of excavated buildings, Renaissance men discovered fantastic figures of sirens, sphinxes, centaurs, and other hybrid unnatural creatures. The authority of the past gave authenticity to "these calculated freaks" of the imagination, as Wind, *Pagan Mysteries*, p. 237, calls them. They depicted the grotesque realities of the Renaissance soul—and Ficino himself made this connection between grotesque images and troubled states of soul (Dacos, p. 74). Whereas ancient grotesques "were regarded by the Renaissance as the classical style for burial and mystery chambers" (Wind, p. 237), mediaeval Christianity had attributed similar imagery to the Devil's kingdom. The sixteenth century returned to this orthodox viewpoint, seeing grotesques as monstrous, animal, and pagan, suitable only for the decor of hell.

80. Seznec, *Survival*, p. 5 and n. 6. Giamatti, "Proteus," presents others. On the lurid excitements of public execution and its place in Renaissance pathologizing, see S.Y. Edgerton, "*Maniera* and the *Mannaia*: Decorum and Decapitation in the Sixteenth Century," in F.W. Robinson & S.G. Nichols, eds., *The Meaning of Mannerism* (Hanover, N.H.: Univ. Press of New England, 1972), pp. 67–103.

81. Cf. FN, *Twilight of the Idols*, "Skirmishes in a War with the Age," §37, p. 91: "This at least is certain, that we should not dare to stand amid the conditions which prevailed at the Renaissance, we should not even dare to imagine ourselves in those conditions . . . do not let us doubt that we moderns, wrapped in the thick cotton wool of our humanitarianism which would shrink from grazing a stone, would present a comedy to Caesar Borgia's contemporaries which would literally make them die of laughter." See further Charles Trinkaus, *Adversity's Noblemen: The Italian Humanists on Happiness* (New York: Columbia Univ. Press, 1940), on the interrelation between psychological attitudes toward life and the poverty, adversity, and insecurity of the humanists' actual lives. Renaissance writers composed treatises and dialogues with these titles: *On the Misery of Human Condition, On the Life of Solitude, On Unhappiness of Men of Letters, On the Unhappiness of Princes, On Earthquakes, On the Causes of Our Calamities, Adversities to be Borne, Sermons on the Stupidity and Misery of Men.*

82. Cf. E. R. Chamberlin, "The Violent World" in his *Everyday Life in Renaissance Times* (New York: Capricorn, 1967), pp. 129–60.

83. The humanist models—Cicero, Seneca, and Plutarch—wrote on enmity, and Erasmus translated the latter's "On the Usefulness of Having Enemies," dedicating it to Cardinal Wolsey of England. Enmity is one more of the neglected themes in today's humanism, which degrades it to the animal fantasy of "aggression" or places it within the mother's sphere of envy and frustration, neglecting that enmity belongs to the phenomenology of eros, whereas Plutarch insisted it is a necessary counterpart to

friendship: we cannot have one without the other.

84. Cf. Wind, *Pagan Mysteries,* pp. 280 f., 262; my "The Dream and the Underworld," *Eranos-42 1973,* discusses the psychological significance of Hades in more detail.

85. Garin, *Quattrocento,* p. 146.

86. J. E. Seigel, "Renaissance Humanism: Petrarch and Valla," in Schwoebel, *Renaissance Men and Ideas,* p. 10.

87. Cf. Aristotle, *De anima* II, 1 and 2. As J. H. Randall says for Aristotle: *"Psyche* obviously cannot exist without a living body" (*Aristotle* [New York: Columbia Univ. Press, 1962], p. 62).

88. Cf. Wind, *Pagan Mysteries,* pp. 280–81, 218–35, 251; Orphic Hymn 18, "To Pluto"; Allen, *Mysteriously Meant,* p. 172.

89. This story can be found fully in Burckhardt's *Civilisation,* pt. III, §2. On the Renaissance anima from a classical Jungian point of view see Linda Fierz-David, *The Dream of Poliphilo,* trans. M. Hottinger (New York: Pantheon, 1950); also Petrarch's *Secretum* which opens with the vision of and dialogue with "a very beautiful Lady."

90. Condensed from Burckhardt's superb paragraph, *Civilisation,* pt. VI, §2.

91. Robb, *Neoplatonism,* p. 43.

92. The depreciation of Renaissance thought has come mainly from the two directions we sketched at the beginning of this chapter: the logos of God (theology), for instance, Étienne Gilson in modern times; the logos of nature (natural science), represented by George Sarton and Lynn Thorndike. Mersenne attacks from both fronts at once. Those who favor a logos of man (Dilthey and Cassirer, for example) rally to defend Renaissance philosophy. R. R. Bolgar, *The Classical Heritage and Its Beneficiaries* (Cambridge, Eng.: Univ. Press, 1954), p. 287, rakes Ficino's thought with vituperous fire: ". . . the more we read Pico and Ficino, the more evident it becomes that their philosophy was merely an apologia for contemporary attitudes. The behaviour patterns they exalt are precisely those which Petrarch had glorified. . . . All this was valueless as philosophy. . . . This preoccupation with mystical fancies and social behaviour weakened the impact of Florentine Platonism as a serious philosophy" (p. 288). Bolgar's argument is just our point: it is valueless to read it as philosophy.

93. Leon Battista Alberti, *On Painting,* trans. J. R. Spencer (New Haven: Yale Univ. Press, 1971).

94. On the role of Neoplatonism in the development of perspective in painting, see E. H. Gombrich, *Art and Illusion,* 2d ed., Bollingen Series (Princeton, N.J.: Princeton Univ. Press, 1961), pp. 52–56.

95. On the role of classical antiquity see G. C. Argan, "The Architecture of Brunelleschi and the Origins of Perspective Theory in the Fifteenth Century," *J. Warburg Courtauld Inst.* 9 (1946):96–121. Earlier literature is mentioned in the notes of these two authors.

96. E. E. Lowinsky, "The Concept of Physical and Musical Space in the Renaissance," *Papers of the American Musicological Society,* 1946, pp. 57 ff.

97. Grove's *Dictionary of Music and Musicians* (Philadelphia: Presser, 1926), III, 786a, "Polyphonia."

98. On Platonism in music, see I. Horsley's review of the facsimile edition of G. Zarlino's *Le Institutioni Harmoniche* (1558) in *Music Libr. Assoc. Notes,* series II, 23 (1966–67):515–19; G. Zarlino, *The Art of Counterpoint,* trans. G. Marco and C. Palisca (New Haven: Yale Univ. Press, 1968); P. O. Kristeller, "Music and Learning in the Early Italian Renaissance" in his *Renaissance Thought II: Papers on Humanism and the Arts* (New York: Harper Torchbook, 1965), II, 156–59.

99. Montaigne, "Of the Inconstancy of Our Actions," *Essays,* II, 1 (Charles Cotton transl., 4 vols. [London: Reeves & Turner, 1902], vol. II, p. 142).

99a. For a different view see Ch. Perelman and L. Obrechts-Tyteca *The New Rheto-*

ric, A Treatise on Argumentation, trans. J. Wilkinson & P. Weaver (Notre Dame: Notre Dame Press, 1969).

100. Cf. Pedro Laín Entralgo, *The Therapy of the Word in Classical Antiquity,* trans. L. Rather & J. Sharp (New Haven: Yale Univ. Press, 1970).

101. For an introduction to thinking about the connection between depth psychology and rhetoric, see Kenneth Burke, *A Rhetoric of Motives* (Berkeley, Calif.: Univ. of California Press, 1969), pp. 19–46, 49–90; for basic rhetorical texts, T. W. Benson and M. H. Prosser, *Readings in Classical Rhetoric* (Bloomington, Ind.: Indiana Univ. Press, 1972) and J. Schwartz and J. A. Rycenga, *The Province of Rhetoric* (New York: Roland Press, 1965); the Terry Lectures and other writings of W. J. Ong, and again Frances Yates, *The Art of Memory,* which art belonged originally to rhetoric. A useful article reviewing recent works on Renaissance rhetoric is D. Weinstein, "In Whose Image and Likeness? Interpretations of Renaissance Humanism," *J. Hist. Ideas* 33 (1972):165–76. Q. Breen, "Giovanni Pico della Mirandola on the Conflict of Philosophy and Rhetoric," *J. Hist. Ideas* 13 (1952):384–426, takes up the essential question, then and now, of the relation between empty words ("pure rhetoric") and significant thought, i.e., the nominalist-realist controversy in another dress. Cf. N. S. Struever, *The Language of History in the Renaissance* (Princeton, N.J.: Princeton Univ. Press, 1970), pp. 5–39.

102. Cf. Seigel, "Petrarch and Valla," pp. 9–11.

103. Kristeller, "Renaissance Platonism," in Werkmeister, ed., *Facets,* p. 104.

104. V. L. Johnson, "The Humanism of Plutarch," *Classical Journal* 66 (1970).

105. T. R. Glover, *Conflict of Religions in the Early Roman Empire* (Boston: Beacon, 1960), chap. 3.

106. A. M. Patterson, *Hermogenes and the Renaissance: Seven Ideas of Style* (Princeton, N.J.: Princeton Univ. Press, 1970).

107. *Phaedrus* 273e.

108. Adolf Portmann, "Der Weg zum Wort," *Eranos-39 1970.*

109. A. N. Whitehead, *Modes of Thought,* p. 44.

110. Hegel, *Philosophy of Mind* (Zusatz 411), p. 150.

111. Cf. E. S. Casey, "Toward an Archetypal Imagination," *Spring 1974* (New York/Zürich, Spring Publ.), pp. 1–32 on the basic importance of naming the figures of imagination, and that they come already named.

112. To add one or two more northern figures important for depth psychology: Mesmer and magnetism; von Hartmann and Schopenhauer for the idea of the unconscious; Gall and Spurzheim for brain research; Adolph Meyer for American style in psychiatric classification; Münsterberg—but as we get into experimental psychology this paragraph makes the point: "It will have been noticed that our account has shown that in the nineteenth century experimental psychology was almost entirely a German and American science. As regards the origins of the experimental method, the initiative was overwhelmingly German; in fact, the only exception of any real importance was the work of Galton, and in England there was a complete failure to continue what Galton had begun—until experimentation was re-introduced from Germany by McDougall, Spearman and others early in the twentieth century." J. C. Flugel, *A Hundred Years of Psychology,* 2d ed. (London: Duckworth, 1951), p. 214. In a list of 538 individuals important to the field of psychology (between 1600 and 1967) one-third were workers in the German language, one-third Americans, and one-third British and French together. Only 11 Italians figured in this list. Robert I. Watson and Marilyn Merrifield, "Characteristics of Individuals Eminent in Psychology in Temporal Perspective: Part I," *J. Hist. Behav. Sci.* 9, no. 4 (1973):339–59.

113. Since this contrast between northern Reformation and southern Renaissance is archetypal, it is fraught with perils. Some of these archetypal considerations are noted by U. R. Ehrenfels, "Nord-Süd als Spannungspaar," *Antaios* 7, no. 2 (1965):101–25. The north-south pair brings with it the psychological symbolism of the upper-lower

polarity, so that the opposition of Reformation and Renaissance immediately takes on more than historical significance. One of the root metaphors of the field of Renaissance studies is just this polarity (cf. Ferguson, *Renaissance in Historical Thought*, pp. 255–56, 363–68, *et passim*). "The Renaissance" easily becomes an instrument for attacking "the North": Reformation, pietism, modernity, rationality, practicality, superego, and so on. Again Nietzsche provides the overstated maxim for this idea of the Renaissance: "Does anybody at last understand, *will* anybody understand what the Renaissance was? *The transvaluation of Christian values*, the attempt undertaken with all means, all instincts and all genius to make the *opposite* values, the *noble* values triumph . . . there has never yet been a more decisive question than the Renaissance." (FN, *The Anti-Christ* §61; cf. *Human, All-Too-Human* §237 and *Will to Power*, p. 75.

114. *MDR*, p. 269.

115. Cf. "Freud's Disturbance on the Acropolis" (articles by several hands) *American Imago* 26, no. 4 (1969):303–78. Further: Freud also had a "mysterious inhibition that had prevented him from visiting Rome" (until 1901); H. F. Ellenberger *The Discovery of the Unconscious* (New York / London: Basic Books / Allen Lane, 1970), p. 447.

116. North and South recapitulate two styles of psychology: one based on the Melanchthon of this chapter, the other on the Rogue Errant of Chapter 3. For, in the same years that psychology as a *subject* was introduced from on high into the German schools of the North, psychologizing as an *art* appeared below the Alps (the stairs and the belt, too) in the new picaresque novel: *La lozana andaluza* (1528), and especially, *Vida de Lazarillo de Tormes* (1554) (above, p. 165). The Northern approach is overtly called "psychology"; it is systematic and written in an objective voice, and has its well-known and high-standing author (Melanchthon). Southern psychologizing is not called such; it is episodic and written subjectively, and its author is anonymous *(Lazarillo)*. Both are moral tales mainly for or about the psyche of youth, and they are intimately bound with religion: the Northern attempts to align official psychology with religion and its morality, using psychology to support collective canons; the Southern attempts to see through official religion and its morality so as to subvert collective canons through psychologizing.

117. FN, *The Dawn of Day* §460: "At the present day we all live, relatively speaking, in a security which is much too great to make us true psychologists: some survey their fellow-men as a hobby, others out of ennui, and others again merely from habit; but never to the extent they would do if they were told 'Discern or perish!'"

Indexes

SUBJECTS